HIDDEN STRUCTURE

THE COMPUTER MUSIC AND DIGITAL AUDIO SERIES

John Strawn, Founding Editor
James Zychowicz, Series Editor

Digital Audio Signal Processing
Edited by John Strawn

Composers and the Computer
Edited by Curtis Roads

Digital Audio Engineering
Edited by John Strawn

Computer Applications in Music:
A Bibliography
Deta S. Davis

The Compact Disc Handbook
Ken C. Pohlman

Computers and Musical Style
David Cope

MIDI: A Comprehensive Introduction
Joseph Rothstein
William Eldridge, *Volume Editor*

Synthesizer Performance and
Real-Time Techniques
Jeff Pressing
Chris Meyer, *Volume Editor*

Music Processing
Edited by Goffredo Haus

Computer Applications in Music:
A Bibliography, Supplement I
Deta S. Davis
Garrett Bowles, *Volume Editor*

General MIDI
Stanley Jungleib

Experiments in Musical Intelligence
David Cope

Knowledge-Based Programming for
Music Research
John W. Schaffer and Deron McGee

Fundamentals of Digital Audio
Alan P. Kefauver

The Digital Audio Music List: A Critical
Guide to Listening
Howard W. Ferstler

The Algorithmic Composer
David Cope

The Audio Recording Handbook
Alan P. Kefauver

Cooking with Csound
Part I: Woodwind and Brass Recipes
Andrew Horner and Lydia Ayers

Hyperimprovisation: Computer-
Interactive Sound Improvisation
Roger T. Dean

Introduction to Audio
Peter Utz

New Digital Musical Instruments:
Control and Interaction Beyond
the Keyboard
Eduardo R. Miranda and
  Marcelo M. Wanderley, with a
  Foreword by Ross Kirk

Fundamentals of Digital Audio
New Edition
Alan P. Kefauver and David Patschke

Hidden Structure: Music Analysis
Using Computers
David Cope

Volume 23 • THE COMPUTER MUSIC AND DIGITAL AUDIO SERIES

HIDDEN STRUCTURE

Music Analysis Using Computers

David Cope

■

A-R Editions, Inc.

Middleton, Wisconsin

Library of Congress Cataloging-in-Publication Data

Cope, David, 1941–
　　Hidden structure : music analysis using computers / David Cope.
　　　　p. cm. — (Computer music and digital audio series : v. 23)
　　Includes bibliographical references and index.
　　ISBN 978-0-89579-640-0
　1. Music—Data processing. 2. Musical analysis—Data processing.
I. Title.

　ML74.C69 2008
　781.0285—dc22
　　　　　　　　　　　　　　　　　　　　　　　　2008019352

Pulchritudo est Splendor Ordinis.
Beauty is the splendor of order.
Saint Augustine (345–430)

Contents

List of Figures — xi

Preface — xxi

Description of CD-ROM — xxvii

Chapter One Background 1

    Principles and Definitions   1
    A Brief History of Algorithmic Analysis   7
    A Brief Survey of Computational Music Analysis   22
    Musical Examples   39
    Program Description   41
    Conclusions   43

**Chapter Two Lisp, Algorithmic Information Theory, 45
and Music**

    Lisp   45
    Definitions   50
    Musical Algorithmic Information Theory   62
    Musical Examples   74
    Program Description   90
    Conclusions   97

Chapter Three   Register and Range in Set Analysis   99

Basics of Set Theory   99
Register   112
Ranges and Vectors   118
Comparisons   120
Musical Examples   127
Program Description   139
Conclusions   144

Chapter Four   Computer Analysis of Scales in   145
Post-Tonal Music

Mathematical Sequences   145
Scales   148
Vector Classes and Metaclasses   153
Varèse's *Density 21.5*   160
Schoenberg's Six Little Piano Pieces, op. 19, no. 1 (1911)   169
Other Musical Examples   172
Program Description   182
Conclusions   188

Chapter Five   Function and Structure in Post-Tonal   189
Music

Object-Oriented Programming   189
Definitions   197
The Acoustic Theory of Chord Roots   201
Musical Tension   205
Context and SPEAC   210
Function   215
Form and Structure   217
Musical Examples   225
Program Description   225
Conclusions   228

Chapter Six	**Generative Models of Music**	**231**

Modeling   231
Recombinancy   234
Probabilities   249
Rules and Markov Chains   252
Musical Examples   269
Program Description   269
Conclusions   274

Chapter Seven	**A Look to the Future**	**275**

Principles   275
Mathematics   277
Artificial Intelligence   290
Muse   295
Musical Examples   305
The Future   310
Conclusions   316

Bibliography	**321**
Glossary	**331**
Index	**337**

List of Figures

Chapter 1

Figure 1.1 From Aristoxenus, *The Harmonics of Aristoxenus*, trans.. Henry S. Macran (New York: Oxford University Press, 1902), 249.

Figure 1.2 A woodcut of Boethius with an instrument designed for methodologically deriving tunings (an algorithm).

Figure 1.3 An example of Gregorian chant, Parce Domine, notated in neumes; the second staff is a continuation of the first.

Figure 1.4 An example of medieval organum.

Figure 1.5 The Guidonian hand, in which a specific note is assigned to each part of the hand. By pointing to a part of the hand, the conductor can indicate to a group of singers which note to sing.

Figure 1.6 An example of three-voice counterpoint around the time of Tinctoris.

Figure 1.7 The division of the octave according to Zarlino.

Figure 1.8 An exercise by Beethoven for his student Archduke Rudolph based on Fux's *Gradus ad Parnassum*.

Figure 1.9 Two diagrams from Rameau's *Treatise on Harmony* describing (a) the major (perfect) triad and its inversions, and (b) the dominant (fundamental) seventh chord and its inversions.

Figure 1.10 First published after Mozart's death in 1793 by J. J. Hummel in Berlin, this *musikalisches Würfelspiel* instruction page shows the first two phrases of number selections (chosen by throws of the dice) that were keyed to measures of music. Also shown, an example page of music by Haydn for this own *musikalisches Würfelspiel*.

Figure 1.11 A sample Schenker analysis of Bach's organ prelude *Wenn wir in höchsten Noten sein*.

Figure 1.12 Charles Babbage's first Difference Machine (1833), a forerunner of the modern-day computer.

Figure 1.13 The author, *Horizons for Orchestra*, in graphic format. Time moves left to right.

Figure 1.14 From Experiment 2 from Hiller and Isaacson, *Illiac Suite*, using the Illiac computer at the University of Illinois, ca. 1956.

Figure 1.15 Flowcharts for MUSANA and its analysis module.

Figure 1.16 Ten commands found in Humdrum.

Figure 1.17 Bach Chorale 002 from the Music Theory Workbench, version 0.1 (http://pinhead.music.uiuc.edu/~hkt/mtw/pdf/), by Heinrich Taube (accessed 24 July 2007).

Figure 1.18 An example of the OpenMusic visual programming environment of music for composition and analysis.

Figure 1.19 The first few measures of Stravinsky, Three Pieces for String Quartet (1914), 3rd movement.

Figure 1.20 Two screens from the Sets and Vectors program on the CD-ROM that accompanies this book.

Chapter 2

Figure 2.1 The first 2000 digits of π.

Figure 2.2 Morse's code for English letters and numbers.

Figure 2.3 An example of the kind of three-dimensional modeling of musical style by Böker-Heil.

Figure 2.4 Cellular automata output generated by the code in the text.

Figure 2.5 Examples of retrograde (b), inversion (c), and retrograde inversion (d) of a motive (a).

Figure 2.6 Two matrixes of the four-note motive of Figure 2.5. The first matrix provides the motive and its eleven transpositions (down from right to left) along with its retrograde and its eleven transpositions (read right to left). The second matrix provides the inversion and its eleven transpositions along with its retrograde inversion and its eleven transpositions.

Figure 2.7 A simple downward scale beginning on different pitches, thus producing different arrangements of whole and half steps.

Figure 2.8 Brief monophonic samplings of music by (a) J. S. Bach, Suite no. 1 in G Major for Violoncello Solo (1720), Minuet, mm. 1–8; (b) W. A. Mozart, Symphony no. 40 in G Minor, K. 550 (1788), 1st movement, mm. 1–5; (c) Ludwig van Beethoven, Symphony no. 5, op. 67 (1808), 1st movement, mm. 1–5; (d), Johannes Brahms, Symphony no. 1, op. 68 (1876), 4th movement, mm. 30–38; (e) Anton Webern, Variations for Piano, op. 27 (1936), 2nd movement, mm. 1–4; (f) Ernst Krenek, Suite for Violoncello, op. 84 (1939), 1st movement, mm. 1–4; (g) The author, Three Pieces for Solo Clarinet(1965), 1st movement, mm. 1–3.

Figure 2.9 Bartók, *Mikrokosmos*, no. 81.

LIST OF FIGURES   xiii

Figure 2.10   AIT structural analysis of the music presented in Figure 2.9.
Figure 2.11   A simple graph showing four parameters of a melody by Brahms (presented at the top of the figure).
Figure 2.12   Pitches reduced to intervals for pattern matching.
Figure 2.13   Bartók, *Mikrokosmos*, no. 81, from Figure 2.9, in a Dynamic Musical AIT graph.
Figure 2.14   Multigraph output for the beginning of Stravinsky, Three Pieces for String Quartet (1914), shown in Figure 1.19.
Figure 2.15   Two mazurkas in the style of Chopin for analytical comparison.
Figure 2.16   Two DMAIT graphs representing the Chopin mazurkas shown in Figure 2.15.
Figure 2.17   A prelude by Chopin comparable in length to the pieces in Figure 2.15.
Figure 2.18   A Dynamic Musical Algorithmic Information Theory graph of the Chopin prelude shown in Figure 2.17.
Figure 2.19   Sample Multigraph output.

Chapter 3

Figure 3.1   Symbols representing several ways in which sets can be more formally compared.
Figure 3.2   A Venn graphic of set theory logical deductions.
Figure 3.3   Root positions of triads have a smaller range between their outer notes.
Figure 3.4   A clock face arranged to allow clearer visualization of pitch-class relationships.
Figure 3.5   The [1,6,t] pitch-class set does not resolve to the pitch-class set [0,5,9] (9 distance when rotated to 0) because of the smaller range of [6,t,1] (7 distance and equating to [0,4,7] when rotated to 0).
Figure 3.6   A straightforward example of the use of set theory to find similarities in post-tonal music.
Figure 3.7   (a) [e,0,2,5,7,8] is [0,1,3,6,8,9] when rotated one number clockwise; (b) [6,7,9,0,2,3] is [0,1,3,6,8,9] when rotated six numbers clockwise; (c) [7,6,4,1,e,t] is [0,1,3,6,8,9] when rotated seven numbers counterclockwise; (d) [0,e,9,6,4,3] is [0,1,3,6,8,9] when rotated twelve numbers counterclockwise.
Figure 3.8   The opening 4 measures of Schoenberg, Six Little Piano Pieces, Op. 19, no. 6.
Figure 3.9   The opening measures of Claude Debussy, *La cathédrale engloutie* (The Sunken Cathedral), 1909.
Figure 3.10   A conversion chart relating decimal to duodecimal notation.

Figure 3.11   A more understandable and musical way to think in terms of duodecimal notation.

Figure 3.12   Conversion methods used for decimal to duodecimal numbers and vice versa.

Figure 3.13   Subtraction, addition, multiplication, and division using arbitrary numbers in duodecimal notation.

Figure 3.14   Two two-set progressions showing pitch classes (first), t-normal form (second), and prime (third).

Figure 3.15   Same reduction as Figure 3.14 but with registers intact in the form of duodecimal notation.

Figure 3.16   Range notation shown to the lower right.

Figure 3.17   Arnold Schoenberg, Suite for Piano, op. 25 (1923), Gavotte, mm. 1–6, with groupings circled and numbered.

Figure 3.18   Computer analysis of Schoenberg's Gavotte by tetrachords and trichords as shown circled and numbered in figure 3.17.

Figure 3.19   Webern, *Variations* (1936), mm. 1–7.

Figure 3.20   Webern analysis by dyads (a) and trichords by hand (b) as shown circled—dyads by solid line and trichords by dotted line—in Figure 3.19.

Figure 3.21   Nine measures from Boulez, *Structures* (1952).

Figure 3.22   Boulez analysis by tetrachords by hand as shown circled in Figure 3.21.

Figure 3.23   Webern, Concerto for 9 Instruments, op. 24, 1st movement, mm. 1–7.

Figure 3.24   (a) Calculations of registral information in Webern, Concerto for 9 Instruments, op. 24, 1st movement, mm. 1–3.

Figure 3.25   Webern, Concerto for 9 Instruments, op. 24, 1st movement, last 7 measures.

Figure 3.26   Calculations of registral information from Figure 3.25.

Figure 3.27   Boulez, Second Sonata for Piano (1948), 2nd movement, beginning.

Figure 3.28   Calculations of registral information in mm. 1–6 in Boulez, Second Sonata for Piano (1948), 2nd movement.

Figure 3.29   The author, *Triplum* for flute and piano (1975), beginning.

Figure 3.30   Calculations of registral information in the author's *Triplum* for flute and piano (1975), mm. 1–7.

Figure 3.31   The author, *Triplum* for flute and piano (1975), mm. 98–104.

Figure 3.32   Another passage from the author's *Triplum* for flute and piano (1975), m. 43.

Figure 3.33   The 97 possible origin sets for [0,2,6].

LIST OF FIGURES xv

Chapter 4

Figure 4.1   Beethoven, Piano Sonata in C Major, op. 53, beginning.

Figure 4.2   The numbers of iterations per pitch of the 298 pitches present in Beethoven, Piano Sonata in C Major, op. 53, beginning (C, 48; C-sharp, 1; D, 26; E-flat, 11; E, 17; F, 57; F-sharp, 2; G, 52; A-flat, 16; A 13; B-flat, 31; B, 24).

Figure 4.3   A list of all 77 linear interval vector classes.

Figure 4.4   Four sets of scales related by symmetry (a, b, and c) and repeating pattern (d).

Figure 4.5   Beethoven, Piano Sonata op. 7, mm. 97–105.

Figure 4.6   A series of possible scales, with each successive scale possibility lacking one of the previous scale's notes, the one with the shortest overall duration. Each line here represents the scale's transposed pitch-class set beginning on 0, its linear interval vector, and the original pitch-class set in ascending order.

Figure 4.7   Varèse, *Density 21.5* for solo flute.

Figure 4.8   Computer scale analysis of the phrases of the three sections of Varèse, *Density 21.5* (see Figure 4.7), with author's determination of best scale possibility in boldface.

Figure 4.9   Computer analysis of Varèse, *Density 21.5*, by complete section with author's determination of best scale possibility in boldface and secondary possibilities marked by "*" and "†."

Figure 4.10 Unordered but nontransposed scale pitch classes for each section in Figure 4.7.

Figure 4.11 The first section of Varèse, *Density 21.5*, with non-scale tones circled.

Figure 4.12 Schoenberg, Six Little Piano Pieces, op. 19, no. 1 (1911).

Figure 4.13 Computer readouts from a three-phrase analysis of Schoenberg, Six Little Piano Pieces op. 19, no. 1.

Figure 4.14 Computer analysis of the entirety of Schoenberg, op. 19, no. 1.

Figure 4.15 From the author's Concerto for Cello and Orchestra (1994).

Figure 4.16 The author, Concerto for Cello and Orchestra (1994), computer analysis by phrase.

Figure 4.17 Computer analysis of the excerpt from the author's concerto in Figure 4.15, by section.

Figure 4.18 Computer analysis of the entirety of the excerpt from the author's concerto shown in Figure 4.15.

Figure 4.19 Selected measures of the solo cello part of the author's concerto. The scale used in the third movement has a related complement used much as the dominant key might be used in a tonal concerto.

Figure 4.20   A scale analysis of Stravinsky, Three Pieces for String Quartet (1914), 3rd movement (opening), as shown in Figure 1.19.

Figure 4.21   A pitch field that covers a span of two-plus octaves and contains two exclusionary hexachord pitch-class sets.

Figure 4.22   A scale with a range of two-plus octaves for the example shown in Figure 4.21.

Figure 4.23   An example where the notes C-sharp, G, and B appear only in the upper register and the notes E-flat, F, and A appear only in the lower register (Arnold Schoenberg, *Das Buch der hängenden Gärten*, II).

Figure 4.24   The scale differences between a one-octave representation and a two-octave representation of the music in Figure 4.23.

Chapter 5

Figure 5.1   One possible overview of the structure of a work of music that is at one and the same time a visual/musical representation and an OOP representation.

Figure 5.2   Examples where (a) roots remain the same but tensions change and (b) tensions remain fairly equal but roots change, demonstrating how neither process alone can determine function in post-tonal music.

Figure 5.3   The overtone series from the fundamental C.

Figure 5.4   (a) Interval derivations from the overtone series along with their root designations, and (b) interval root strengths shown in order of strength.

Figure 5.5   Six groupings to serve as examples of the root-identification process.

Figure 5.6   A list of intervals weighted according to their tension levels.

Figure 5.7   Figuring interval weights from the bass note by using the chart in Figure 5.6 produces 0.3 (M3 at 0.2 + P5 at 0.1), .5 (m3 at 0.225 + m6 at 0.275), and 0.8 (P4 at 0.55 + M6 at 0.25), respectively. The minor triad and its inversions produce 0.325 (m3 at 0.225 + P5 at 0.1), .45 (M3 at 0.2 + M6 at 0.25), and 0.825 (P4 at 0.55 + m6 at 0.275).

Figure 5.8   The augmented triad at 0.475 (M3 at 0.2 + m6 at 0.275), the diminished triad at 0..775 (m3 at 0.225 + A4 at 0.55), the dominant seventh chord at 1.0 (M3 at 0.2 + P5 at 0.1 + m7 at 0.7), and the diminished seventh chord at 1.125 (m3 at 0.225 + A4 at 0.65 + M6 at 0.25).

Figure 5.9   Four chords producing tensions of 1.2 (M3 at 0.2 + P5 at 0.1 + M7 at 0.9), 1.25 (m3 at 0.225 + P5 at 0.1 + m7 at 0.7), 0.55 (M3 at 0.2 + P5 at 0.1 + M6 at 0.25), and 2.0 (M3 at 0.2 + P5 at 0.1 + M7 at 0.9 + M2 at 0.8).

Figure 5.10 Chord tensions adding to 1.0 (M2 at 0.8 + M3 at 0..2), 1.225 (m2 at 1.0 + m3 at 0.225), 1.8 (m2 at 1.0 + M2 at 0.8), and 1.475 (P4 at 0.55 + m7 at 0.7 + m3 at 0.225).

Figure 5.11	A simple lookup table of metric tensions for principal beats in twelve different meters.
Figure 5.12	(a) J. S. Bach, Chorale no. 42, demonstrating the same chord in differing contexts; (b) Schoenberg, Six Pieces for Piano, op. 19, no. 6, opening measures, demonstrating the same types of contextual differences.
Figure 5.13	SPEAC analysis of the music in Figure 5.12a and b.
Figure 5.14	An example of a unification as derived from Schoenberg, Three Piano Pieces, op. 11, no. 1: (a) the unification, and (b) the first 8 measures of the work from which the unification was drawn. Note the other unifications present here as well.
Figure 5.15	Two patterns, a target pattern and a potential matching pattern. If the `*intervals-off*` controller were set to 2, the two patterns would not match. However, if the `*intervals-off*` controller were set to 3, the two patterns would match.
Figure 5.16	A phrase of music by Mozart (a); a machine-composed replication (b); the meta-pattern that binds them together (c).
Figure 5.17	Various levels (gradient map) of music revealed by applying filters.
Figure 5.18	The opening few beats of a graphical analysis of Stravinsky, Three Pieces for String Quartet (1914), 3rd movement.
Figure 5.19	A root analysis of Stravinsky, Three Pieces for String Quartet (1914), 3rd movement.
Figure 5.20	SPEAC analysis (by chord change) of Stravinsky, Three Pieces for String Quartet (1914), 3rd movement.
Figure 5.21	A structural graph of a section from the author's *Triplum* for flute and piano.

Chapter 6

Figure 6.1	(a) Mozart, Piano Sonata K. 279, 1st movement, mm. 1–3; (b) results of the Melodic Predictor; (c) Mozart, Piano Sonata K. 533, 1st movement, mm. 1–4; (d) results of the Melodic Predictor.
Figure 6.2	Recombination process leading to the completion of a new Bach-like chorale phrase.
Figure 6.3	An example of differing types of internal patterns causing problems in recombination: (a) and (b) originals, (c) a recombination without regard to texture sensitivity.
Figure 6.4	An example of Experiments in Musical Intelligence output: the beginning of the Rondo Capriccio for cello and orchestra arguably in the style of Mozart.

xviii HIDDEN STRUCTURE

Figure 6.5   An example of allusion in (a) an Experiments in Musical Intelligence replication; and (b) a Beethoven bagatelle Op. 119, no. 1 (1820), upon which it is partially based.

Figure 6.6   A Bach chorale as example of a jigsaw puzzle.

Figure 6.7   The Bayes rule.

Figure 6.8   A state-transition matrix for a first-order Markov chain involving all twelve notes of the chromatic scale.

Figure 6.9   The upper left-hand corner of a second-order Markov chain state transition matrix.

Figure 6.10   (a) Original, Bartók, *Mikrokosmos*, no. 71, transposed to begin on G; (b–f) five computer extensions beginning five notes from the end of the passage.

Figure 6.11   (a) Original, Bartók, *Mikrokosmos*, no. 77, transposed to begin on D; (b–d) three computer extensions beginning five notes from the end of the passage.

Figure 6.12   A simple two-voice counterpoint in which each voice moves stepwise in various directions.

Figure 6.13   A post-tonal example, where the various two-note groupings do not have clear functionalism.

Figure 6.14   Two possible nonidentical computer extensions (b and c) to the original by Bartók (*Mikrokosmos*, no. 80) presented in (a).

Figure 6.15   Three different forms of analysis provided by Alice.

Figure 6.16   The rule (((3 3) 2 1) ((5 1) -2 2) ((0 0) 2 3) ((8 5) -1 4)) in music notation.

Figure 6.17   Extending voice-leading rules.

Figure 6.18   Several student-created extensions (b–d) based on Bartók (a), *Mikrokosmos*, no. 81.

Figure 6.19   The rule (((19 16) -3)) in music notation.

Chapter 7

Figure 7.1   The top ten levels of Pascal's triangle.

Figure 7.2   Pascal's triangle shown stacked to the left and modulo 2 with the zeros identifying the Sierpinski gasket (a), and zeros removed (b) to make the graphic more readable.

Figure 7.3   A simple 5 × 5 magic square in which all horizontal ranks and vertical columns sum to 65.

Figure 7.4	A magic square containing intervals that equate (when added together) to 5 in top-to-bottom and left-to-right directions, along with musical examples.
Figure 7.5	The author, Concerto for Cello and Orchestra, 2nd movement (excerpt).
Figure 7.6	A magic cube with both incremental numbers and music intervals (with directions).
Figure 7.7	A formal analysis of the first 89 measures of Bartók, Music for Strings, Percussion and Celeste (Lendvai 1983, p. 74), based on the golden mean and the Fibonacci series.
Figure 7.8	The first 14 measures of Varèse, *Density 21.5*, with much the same pitch classes as the silver variation.
Figure 7.9	A simple model of a neural network.
Figure 7.10	A simple example of an association network.
Figure 7.11	An example of Muse's grouping process.
Figure 7.12	All of the possible permutations of a six-note list of nonrepeating numbers not including the original arrangement ([0,2,7] [1,5,8]) and its retrograde ([1,5,8] [0,2,7]).
Figure 7.13	A view of the listener window after the completion of one analysis by Muse.
Figure 7.14	Muse's program includes a function called `sleep`.
Figure 7.15	The *Eine Kleine Stück* arguably in the style of Arnold Schoenberg by Experiments in Musical Intelligence.
Figure 7.16	Schoenberg, Three Piano Pieces, op. 11, no. 1 (opening).
Figure 7.17	The first page of the score to Beethoven, Symphony no. 5, revision.
Figure 7.18	*Dies irae*, a medieval Latin sequence and the first words of the Requiem Mass.
Figure 7.19	(a) A passage from the Mystic Circle of the Young Girls in Stravinsky, *The Rite of Spring*; (b) a passage from Stravinsky, Three Pieces for String Quartet.
Figure 7.20	(a) A passage from the 3rd movement of Stravinsky, Three Pieces for String Quartet; (b) a similar passage in the Symphonies of Wind Instruments.
Figure 7.21	A post-tonal work by the author resembling Stravinsky's style.

Preface

Today's computers provide music theorists with unprecedented opportunities to analyze music more quickly and accurately than ever before. Whereas analysis once required several weeks or even months to complete and was often replete with human errors, computers now provide the means to accomplish these same analyses in a fraction of the time and with far more accuracy. However, although such computer music analyses represent significant improvements in the field, computational analyses using traditional approaches do not in themselves constitute the true innovations in music theory that computers offer. In this book, I introduce a series of analytical processes that—by virtue of their concept and design—can better, and in some cases *only*, be accomplished by computer programs, presenting unique opportunities for music theorists to better understand the music they study.

As an example, when comparing computational and human analysis, we need to distinguish between time differences of minutes or hours and of months or years. Analyses that may take a human minutes, hours, or days may still be undertaken by hand. Analyses that require a human months or even years may not even be considered feasible. Without these latter analyses, however, our range of choices of analytical processes becomes arbitrarily limited. With computers able to reduce our months or years to fractions of seconds and accuracy to near perfect, music analysts must rethink many theories that they may have previously dismissed as impossible due to the magnitude of the undertaking. Computers can not only reduce our fatigue and increase our accuracy, but they can open whole new worlds previously considered unachievable—if considered at all.

Many readers of a book like this might value an annotated bibliography of currently available software for tonal and post-tonal music analysis, but most would find this kind of listing woefully out of date the very day it became available; the field simply changes too rapidly to make this kind of offering practical. Instead, this book—with the exception of the broad introductory first chapter—focuses on several unique approaches to music analysis offered by computer programs. Although these approaches do not represent an all-encompassing and integrated global theory of music analysis, they do represent significantly more than a compilation of loosely related computer program descriptions. Chapter 5, on function in post-tonal music, for example, firmly depends on the scalar foundations presented in

Chapter 4. Likewise, the logic of Chapter 7's presentation of a multi-tiered approach to musical analysis depends on the material of all of the preceding chapters. In short, this book represents an integrated view of computer music analysis.

Hidden Structure also centers on post-tonal rather than tonal music for several reasons. First, as we shall see in this chapter, tonal music analysis has a long and distinguished history that details approaches to melody, harmony, counterpoint, form, and structure. Although the advent of computer technology can certainly add tools and allow the discovery of new concepts, the range of potential for truly new approaches is, I feel, somewhat limited compared to the potential for analytical possibilities in post-tonal music. Second, many diverse and useful programs for tonal music analysis already exist. In fact, most early computer computational experiments with music analysis involved tonal music. On the other hand, although many computer pitch-class set programs exist, little beyond this easily created software is currently available. Third, and possibly most important, post-tonal music represents the *lingua franca* of today's concert music, the music in which I am most interested and to which I wish to devote my research time.

The ideas described in this book are ordered from simple to complex, and from more traditional to possibly more innovative. Chapter 2's focus on information theory mirrors the work done by early music theorists using computers, while Chapter 6's concentration on computer modeling parallels more recent work in computer composition using rule acquisition. Most of these ideas also share common perspectives. For example, they have the same post-tonal focus, use similar artificial-intelligence approaches, and share the same computational foci. Thus, this book represents an integrated view of music analysis rather than a potpourri of interesting but unrelated analytical perspectives.

Although this book is meant for a general audience, with the only prerequisite being the ability to read music, it is particularly intended for both musicians interested in the application of computers to the understanding of music and computer scientists—both professionals and those amateurs who enjoy the sport of benign hacking—wishing to use their expertise to better understand music. Given my suspicion that many of these individuals do not share a great deal of common ground, I have attempted to educate each group in the territory of the other. I therefore define the terms and concepts used very carefully. For example, music theorists will require an understanding of information theory, programming, and so on. Likewise, non–music theorists will require an understanding of musical set theory, chord roots, and so on. By doing this, however, I fear that both will consider many of the chapters here uneven, at least in the sense that computer scientists, for example, understand set theory, just not musical set theory, and vice versa for musicians. Thus, readers may find themselves in shallow water for one section of a chapter and then suddenly in deep water. I apologize for the lack of uniformity that may result. Hopefully, the chapter subheadings will allow those already familiar with one or more of the concepts described to skip to the next section relevant to their interests if they so desire. I believe that those who stick with this book, despite its bumpy ride, will gain a new appreciation for the views of music offered here.

Chapter 1 begins with principles and definitions, followed by a survey of historical algorithmic analysis processes and a broad overview of the computer music programs in use today. This overview does not just list the many different implementations of particular analytical processes, but describes representative examples of them. For example, pitch-class set analysis programs in Java can be found at dozens of Internet sites at present, the variations between them limited primarily to differences in graphical user interfaces. Therefore, the coverage here is relatively limited. Other programs, such as the Humdrum Toolkit, that provide more universal algorithms are discussed in more detail. Chapter 2, on music and algorithmic information theory, describes how a form of compression (replacing redundant material with signifiers to conserve space) can reveal important statistics about post-tonal music. It also proposes an analytical technique that incorporates a dynamic integrative approach to aspects of pitch, rhythm, texture, and dynamics in an attempt to understand the constantly changing foci of musical works.

Chapter 3, on set analysis of register and range, introduces a duodecimal notation for representing pitch-class sets, a notation that, by virtue of its having a base (radix) of twelve, allows both register and pitch class to share one relatively simple notation. Integrating these two interrelated aspects of musical pitch in a pitch-class abstraction enables the comparison of equivalent prime-form sets with significant registral differences, revealing contrasts as significant as those between prime-form sets that share very similar registral arrangements. Chapter 4 presents a computer analysis of musical scales and describes a method for generating all possible equal-tempered scales and an approach to efficiently discovering and cataloging these scales, particularly in post-tonal music. Because scales have scale degrees that in tonal music signify musical functions, the concept of post-tonal scale analysis has far-reaching implications. This is the subject of Chapter 5, which more fully explores the implications of discovering function in post-tonal music, defining and analyzing potential musical progressions, cadences, chromatic harmonies, hierarchies, and so on.

Chapter 6 focuses on generating rules from music itself, rather than imposing user-prescribed rules. I end in Chapter 7 with a possibly brazen (but hopefully useful) look to the future at some of the areas of musical analysis I feel will develop over the next few decades thanks to the availability of new computational tools.

I have chosen commonly analyzed musical examples for this book so that readers will be able to better compare the results of the analytical processes I describe here with the results of other, more standard analytical techniques. I have also interpolated examples of my own music here and there in order that readers may more directly ascertain how the techniques described further prove valuable in the creative process. I explicitly used the analytical processes described in these compositions, and these works represent the best cases I can *prove* of such usage.

I have limited the scope of study for this book to classical post-tonal music. Other genres of music might serve equally well. However, classical post-tonal music provides a comprehensive range of music over a significant historical period. As well, my own background consists almost exclusively of classical tonal and post-tonal music, and hence I lack the expertise to intelligently discuss other genres of music. Readers may offset this shortcoming by applying the techniques defined and described here to whatever style of music they know best.

The various computer programs discussed in this book, along with MP3 versions of all of the book's musical examples, are available on the CD-ROM that accompanies this book. The programs are written in Common Lisp, of which two versions are available: (1) Macintosh platform, or (2) any platform that supports Common Lisp. To ensure that these latter programs will perform in different environments requires the omission of platform-dependent code such as all Musical Instrument Digital Interface (MIDI) and graphical user interface (GUI) functions. Full documentation and operating instructions are included with each program.

As time permits, I will provide code updates for new versions of the Macintosh operating system on my Web site (arts.ucsc.edu/faculty/cope). However, if history proves accurate, as soon as I write new platform-dependent programs, system hardware or software changes will once again render the code almost immediately obsolete. Furthermore, the software for the programs in this book, although very helpful in demonstrating the principles of each chapter and in clarifying the analytical principles proposed, is not critical to the understanding of the material presented.

Whenever possible in this book, I have included the thoughts of music theorists, musicologists, mathematicians, computer scientists, and cognitive scientists whose work complements or poses the greatest challenges to the ideas presented here. My apologies to those whose work may seem relevant, but to which I have not referred here due to space limitations.

Many individuals have advised me in this study of computer music analysis, particularly graduate students and colleagues at the University of California at Santa Cruz (notably Paul Nauert, Ben Carson, and Daniel Brown). I also owe immense gratitude to Nico Schüler for forwarding a copy of his dissertation (2000), without which I would have floundered more than I already have in the first chapter's history of computer music analysis. Keith Muscutt, Eric Nichols, and Irene Natow provided much-needed advice (editorial and otherwise). Many of the ideas in this book originated from my teaching over the years, and I thank the many classes of students who acted as guinea pigs for my theoretical explorations. Without support from colleagues and students such as these, this book could not have been completed.

Hidden Structure describes a few of the ways in which I believe computer programs can contribute significantly to the analysis of music, particularly to the often difficult-to-understand post-tonal music of our time. Although computer programs—

through their incredible speed and accuracy—certainly aid our ability to analyze this music in more or less traditional ways, creating programs that analyze music using more indigenous computational approaches offers greater challenges and potential rewards. I hope that my descriptions of several such programs here will encourage others to continue to seek newer and more revealing analytical processes in the future.

Acknowledgements

The author and publisher are grateful for the use of the following material:

Figure 1.14 Theodore Presser Company
Figure 1.15 Permission granted by Nico Schuller.
Figure 1.17 Bach Chorale 002 from the Music Theory Workbench version 0.1 (http://pinhead.music.uiuc.edu/~hkt/mtw/pdf/), Heinrich Taube, author.
Figure 1.18 Permission granted by IRCAM.
Figure 1.19 © Copyright 1923 by Hawkes & Son (London) Ltd
    Reproduced by kind permission of Boosey & Hawkes Music Publisher Ltd
Figure 2.9 © Copyright 1940 by Hawkes & Son (London) Ltd
Figure 2.15 Reproduced by permission of Spectrum Press (spectrumpress.com)
Figure 3.8 © 1913, 1940 by Universal Edition A.G. Wien/UE 5069
Figure 3.17 Used by permission of Belmont Music Publishers, Los Angeles
Figure 3.19 © 1937 by Universal Edition A.G. Wien/UE 10881
Figure 3.21 © 1955 by Universal Edition (London) Ltd. London/UE 12267
Figure 3.23 © 1948 by Universal Edition A.G. Wien/UE 11830
Figure 3.25 © 1948 by Universal Edition A.G. Wien/UE 11830
Figure 3.27 Heugel and Co. 1950
Figure 3.29 1975 Carl Fischer Music Publishers
Figure 3.31 1975 Carl Fischer Music Publishers
Figure 3.32 1975 Carl Fischer Music Publishers
Figure 4.7 G. Ricordi and Co.
Figure 4.11 G. Ricordi and Co.
Figure 4.12 © 1913, 1940 by Universal Edition A.G. Wien/UE 5069
Figure 4.23 Dover Publications 1995
Figure 5.12b © 1913, 1940 by Universal Edition A.G. Wien/UE 5069
Figure 5.13b © 1913, 1940 by Universal Edition A.G. Wien/UE 5069
Figure 5.14b Belmont Music Publishers, Los Angeles 1910
Figure 5.19 © Copyright 1923 by Hawkes & Son (London) Ltd
    Reproduced by kind permission of Boosey & Hawkes Music Publisher Ltd
Figure 6.5 Reproduced by permission of Spectrum Press (spectrumpress.com)
Figure 6.10a © Copyright 1940 by Hawkes & Son (London) Ltd
Figure 6.11a © Copyright 1940 by Hawkes & Son (London) Ltd

Figure 6.14a © Copyright 1940 by Hawkes & Son (London) Ltd
Figure 6.18a © Copyright 1940 by Hawkes & Son (London) Ltd
Figure 7.7 Lendvai, Ernö. 1983. *The Workshop of Bartók and Kodály*. Budapest: Editio Musica.
Figure 7.8 G. Ricordi and Co.
Figure 7.15 Reproduced by permission of Spectrum Press (spectrumpress.com)
Figure 7.16 Belmont Music Publishers, Los Angeles 1910
Figure 7.19 © Copyright 1923 by Hawkes & Son (London) Ltd
    Reproduced by kind permission of Boosey & Hawkes Music Publisher Ltd
Figure 7.20 © Copyright 1923 by Hawkes & Son (London) Ltd
    Reproduced by kind permission of Boosey & Hawkes Music Publisher Ltd

Description of the CD-ROM

The CD-ROM that accompanies this book contains materials that augment the text of *Hidden Structure*.

MP3S ON THE CD-ROM

The CD-ROM contains MP3s of all of the musical examples presented in this book, labeled according to figure number. These MP3s are machine performed using MIDI (Musical Instrument Digital Interface) files and Macintosh Quicktime Musical Instruments. The results are thus mechanistic in performance and relatively shallow in timbral quality and are not intended as masterful performances. They simply provide simple aural replications of the figures in the book for those unable to play or otherwise hear them.

SOFTWARE ON THE CD-ROM

The software found on the CD-ROM includes all of the programs described in this book. Details on how to operate this software are found below, in the chapters of this book, and in the files containing the software. Triangulation of these three sources should provide readers who lack a background in computer programming with the ability to run the code.

The software found on the CD-ROM is written in Common Lisp in source code form (readable as opposed to object code; unreadable compiled binary code). The source code requires Common Lisp in order to function. For programs labeled (CL), any form of Common Lisp (of which there are many free available forms for use on any computer platform) may be used. For such programs, simply download any Common Lisp, load the program into the CL program by any of several methods (see the CL program itself for a description of these processes), and then follow the instructions provided at the top of each source code file, which is readable in any text program. For programs labeled MCL (Macintosh Common Lisp), you must download a form of MCL that works with your particular computer (see the digitool.com Web site for more information) and follow the instructions provided.

The source code consists of a series of variable declarations (preceded by "defvar") and function definitions (preceded by "defun") enclosed in various parentheses that help connect variables and processes. Objects (denoted by "defclass") define windows, menus, and so on. No knowledge other than this general prescription is required to run the code provided here.

I created the software here primarily for demonstrating the principles expressed in the associated chapter of this book. All of the program runs in the figures, for example, result from using this software. However, the code is not bulletproof. In other words, loading some music (e.g., performed music) may create problems for some of the functions and thus cause programs themselves to fail. Ensuring that code can endure any input not only would take hundreds of hours of testing and even then be incomplete, it would also require several times the amount of code provided here, making the result unreadable except by experts. Problems encountered with these programs should be reported to the author at howell@ucsc.edu.

SOFTWARE ON THE CD-ROM BY CHAPTER

Chapter 1
Sets (CL/MCL)
Visualize (MCL)

Chapter 2
Comparison (CL)
Multigraph (MCL)

Chapter 3
SetMath (CL)
Set Multiples (CL)
Set Database Analysis (CL)
Register (CL)

Chapter 4
Scale Analysis (CL)

Chapter 5
Root (CL)
Structure Map (CL)
Structure Graph (MCL)

Chapter 6
Markov (CL)
Extend (CL/MCL)

Chapter 7
    Neural Net (CL)
    SPEAC (MCL)
    Muse (CL)

ONE
Background

> Throughout the centuries, the arts have undergone transformations that paralleled two essential creations of human thought: the hierarchical principle and the principle of numbers. In fact, these principles have dominated music, particularly since the Renaissance, down to present-day procedures of composition.
>
> Iannis Xenakis, *Formalized Music* (1971), 204

This chapter begins with definitions of the principles and terms that act as foundations for the ideas, processes, and programs to follow. It continues with a survey of historical algorithmic music analyses (often called paper algorithms) and a brief look at the computer music programs in use today and some representative examples of particular analytical processes. It concludes with a description of two simple programs, one for visualizing music of all types and the other for delineating pitch-class sets, particularly in post-tonal music.

PRINCIPLES AND DEFINITIONS

As I mentioned in the preface, *Hidden Structure* does not build a single theory of post-tonal music, but rather describes several diverse methodologies for computer analysis. However, this book does focus on four central principles:

1. all music consists of patterns;
2. all pitch patterns can be reduced to scales;
3. all elements of scales have different functions; and
4. all patterns, scales, and functions in music are best understood by modeling their processes.

The first three principles listed here seem plain enough. The last, however, deserves elaboration. The term "modeling" as used here refers to the building of accurate replicas of objects or phenomena in order to better understand them. The concept of modeling as an alternative to reverse engineering, though not new, has—with the advent of computational technology—gained a significant following in recent years. For example, Stephen Wolfram (2002) has argued that traditional scientific methodology is like a salmon losing ground against a strong current, waging a futile battle in its attempts to answer the important scientific questions of our day. He further argues that the only true revelations of the universe will come from computationally modeling it. Without either agreeing or disagreeing with Wolfram's point of view on science, I argue vigorously for the usefulness of modeling as an approach to musical analysis, as later chapters in this book will testify.

Each of the chapters in this book relates to all of the above principles to some extent. However, Chapters 1, 2, 3, 6, and 7 concentrate particularly on Principle 1, Chapters 4 and 7 on Principle 2, Chapters 5 and 7 on Principle 3, and Chapters 6 and 7 on Principle 4. These principles then provide a framework on which a more general theory might be developed. As the processes described in this book unfold, I will remind readers of how the material under consideration exemplifies these four principles.

Because the word *atonal* is somewhat vague and its invocation often has derogatory inferences (see Straus 1990, v), I use the term *post-tonal* here instead. There are several current definitions of this word, ranging from "not explicitly tonal" to "twelve-tone" or "serial." In this book, I will use a more liberal definition. This means that terms such as *polytonal, octatonal,* and *serial* all fall under the umbrella term *post-tonal*. This broad definition will make it unnecessary to differentiate between terms for music by, for example, Igor Stravinsky, Béla Bartók, Edgard Varèse, Arnold Schoenberg, and Anton von Webern.

The terms *music theory* and *music analysis* seem interchangeable to some. In this book, however, I define music theory as a more or less descriptive account of the principles of musical structure, and music analysis as the more or less factual account of what literally occurs in music itself. Anthony Pople has it right: "There is a broad historical distinction between music theory—which studies musical works in order to deduce 'more general principles of musical structure'—and music analysis, in which the interest is focused on individual pieces of music" (Pople 2004, 127). Therefore, whenever I refer to music theory, I am speaking of basic tenets that govern all music. When I refer to music analysis, I am speaking of specific instances of those principles in a more or less restricted body of music. For the most part, if not stated otherwise, this book deals with music *analysis* rather than music *theory*.

To some extent, then, music analysis as referred to here resembles cryptography, or code breaking. As Nicholas Cook puts it:

> Music is a code in which the deepest secrets of humanity are written: this heady thought assured musical studies their central place in ancient, medieval and renaissance thought. And though the study [analysis] of music no longer occupies quite so elevated a role in intellectual circles, some of today's most important trends in the human sciences still owe it a debt. (Cook 1987, 1)

We have already partially broken many such musical codes; after all, the discovery of function in tonal music, along with its ancillary, harmonic syntax, represents hundreds of years of cryptographic investigations. Yet, in the view of some analysts, more code breaking remains. For example, no convincing corollary has yet been found for function in post-tonal music, nor has a clear process for defining musical structure been revealed in post-tonal music, nor has a defined syntax been presented for most of the post-tonal music of the twentieth and twenty-first centuries. Even tonal music holds many mysteries yet undiscovered. Hopefully, the code breaking that remains can be enhanced with the aid of computers.

The term algorithm will be used often in this book and requires a clear definition. An *algorithm* (see Cope 2000, 1ff., for a more complete definition) is a recipe for achieving a goal in a finite number of clearly defined steps. For example, the instructions "extract the dysfunctional bulb by turning it counterclockwise, insert new bulb, turn new bulb clockwise several times until tight, and turn on the light" constitutes a simple algorithm for replacing a burned-out light bulb. Deoxyribonucleic acid (DNA) replication, blinking, breathing, and so on also represent algorithms. Note that algorithmic analysis does not depend on computer hardware or software.

The most interesting example of the notion of an algorithm is Alan Turing's 1952 experiment with computer chess. Turing—the oft-credited father of artificial intelligence—had so tired of waiting to challenge the first computer chess-playing program that he invited a friend to play a game of computer chess, with Turing assuming the role of computer. Turing spent days creating a paper algorithm, a list of rules required to respond to whatever imaginable move his opponent might make. Turing and his opponent's subsequent game lasted three or so hours, during which Turing rigorously followed the rules he had compiled. Turing eventually lost the game. He argued, however, that he lost because his program, called Turochamp, had not been complete or accurate enough. Thus, his point was made—by following his algorithm exactly he had fulfilled his role as computer. If a human computer could play chess algorithmically, then certainly a hardware computer following human-programmed rules could do so as well (see Standage 2002, 226–229, for more information).

Obviously, however, a computer can play such games only as well as its human-provided rules allow it to play. My point here is simple: computers simply obey the dictates of their programmers; they are limited only by the programmer's skill in developing the right algorithm. Computers are tools, nothing more and nothing less. Thus, although computers process data faster and more accurately than humans, algorithms for analyzing music have existed for centuries.

In tonal music, using dominant-tonic cadences, avoiding parallel fifths, resolving dissonances, creating formalistic canons and fugues, and other creative processes result from algorithms that composers invoke—whether they realize it or not—in order to plan their compositions and participate in the musical style of their day.

One could also argue the algorithmic foundation of much post-tonal music on the basis of the revelations of set theory alone. Serial music requires less substantiation. Even Cage's indeterminate music often relies on rigorously applied algorithms. In short, algorithms play significant roles in all music.

Interestingly, the traditional processes of tonal analysis that pervades music academia today represent an algorithm. The rules by which students reduce Bach chorales to registerless triads, reveal their inversions, and ultimately use roman and arabic numerals for describing functions and their inversions within keys clearly denote a set of instructions to achieve a particular goal—the standard definition of an algorithm.

Because computers offer the fastest, most accurate, and most efficient manner of applying algorithms to data, using computers for music analysis is a natural consequence of these ideas. Indeed, computers can process information exponentially faster than humans. For the most part, computers offer users the ability to extend themselves in ways that no other means can match. Given the right algorithm, then, computers present the best opportunity for music analysts to understand the music of the future and to better understand the music of the present and the past.

Before beginning a brief history of related music research and analysis, and because *Hidden Structure* conjures up very different meanings to different people, I would like to preface my historical survey with what I hope is a clear definition of what the title means for this book. Before stating this definition, however, I feel obliged to articulate what the title does *not* mean, along with my reasons for excluding such definitions.

Many readers, composers in particular, may take the title *Hidden Structure: Music Analysis Using Computers* to mean analysis of musical timbre. After all, most journals dealing with computer music composition (*Computer Music Journal*, *Perspectives of New Music*, *Journal of New Music Research*, etc.) routinely publish articles devoted to constructing and deconstructing musical sound, called synthesis. I suspect that were one to take a survey, the great majority of books and articles covering computer music analysis do so from the perspective of the analysis of timbre, rather than from the perspective of the analysis of compositional technique. Analysis of musical timbre, however, will not appear in this book, because the analysis to which I refer in its title covers the relationships between sounds and not the sounds themselves.

The title of this book may indicate to some the computer analysis of musical performance. Creating software to perform in the style of human performers has long been a focus of computer music research. Indeed, the performer's nuances of rhythm, meter, dynamics, articulation, and other parameters are a critical component of human appreciation of music, and their analysis would seem vitally important. Because this book can only cover so much territory, however, I have opted to not include computer music analysis of performance. In fact, including performance analysis would most likely obscure many of the points I wish to make.

Computers have also proven valuable in the translation of notated music (either in autograph or printed form) into digital data for computer performance, engraved-quality scores and part printing, storage, and other forms of digital coding. Such digitizing, however, though extremely important, does not in itself provide any true analysis of music and therefore does not represent a logical subject for this book.

Music perception is an absolutely critical component to understanding music, and, as such, one might expect to find music cognition an actual cornerstone of a book titled *Hidden Structure: Music Analysis Using Computers*. My reasons for excluding it here are many, but two are salient. First, studies of music cognition have only recently begun, and many of the initial results conflict with one another to the point of seriously confusing the current state of research. Second, this book is based, at least in part, on the assumption that the analytical process discussed can be programmed. Research in music cognition often results from studies relating to statistics of how human subjects react to musical input, rather than objective—and thus programmable—principles and data.

Readers interested in the analysis of electronic music (see Simoni 2006), improvised music, music of oral traditions, and other such topics will also be disappointed, because this book will not shed much light on these important topics. At the same time, most of the principles described here can be applied to these connected areas of research. I leave such application, however, to other, more qualified individuals.

What, then, does the title *Hidden Structure: Music Analysis Using Computers* actually mean? In brief, this book focuses on the analytical study of Western classical-music notated scores that can be represented digitally. Although a number of individuals have attempted to quantify important aspects of music such as performance practice (Lawson and Stowell 1999; Rink 1995) and other nonnotatable information that composers may have intended beyond the actual score, printed music remains the most reliable resource available for pitch, rhythm, dynamics, and other of its parameters. Thus, I have limited the investigations presented here to notated scores only.

Given my exclusion of several very important aspects of music, my actual definition of computer music analysis for this book may seem to many readers quite limited. This is intentional. The programs that accompany the chapters on this book's associated CD-ROM require such limitations. My work here is intended not to conjecture, but to prove. In order to provide these proofs, I must divide and conquer—a mantra I repeat ad nauseam to my students. *Hidden Structure* thus will, I hope, provide useful grist for others interested in understanding music, particularly music of the twentieth and twenty-first centuries.

This book's original title, "Algorithmic Music Theory," better describes the history that follows this definition of the subject. At least half of this history covers theories of music prior to the advent of computers, theories that nonetheless share a single important process—the algorithm. Thus, despite the revised title, I ask all readers to consider much of this chapter's contents in particular and the historical sections' contents in general as guided by my original title, focusing on algorithms rather than on the computer's ability to process data more quickly and more accurately than humans.

Before progressing to subsequent sections of this chapter, I should mention a few other caveats. Throughout the book, the processes described focus almost exclusively on pitch. I include rhythm (Chapters 2 and 5, for example), timbre, dynamics, articulations, and so on, but only occasionally. I do not intend this pitch bias to suggest that pitch represents the nadir of musical parameters, but rather to allow development of one aspect of music more thoroughly. I would rather not discuss, say, rhythm at all than discuss it shallowly just to ensure balance.

I also do not consider composer intent a factor in the music analysis discussed here. Although music analysts should not ignore intent, especially when the composer has made this intent public, composers are often unaware of many of the processes they use while composing. To ignore these other processes while focusing on the processes the composer has claimed as central to a composition would render analysis practically impotent. In short, at least for this book, composer intent will not take precedence over any other logical process that may be equally or more revealing.

Finally, although listening should inform analysis, the reverse should also be true. In fact, because I cannot predict what readers will hear in any of the examples in this book, I take the viewpoint that the analyses presented here inform listening and not vice versa. Listeners are biased by the music that they have heard, by their own unique biological and chemical constitutions, by cultural and other learned musical habits, and, of course, by personal musical sensibilities and aesthetics.

For millennia, astronomers and other celestial observers assumed that the sun and stars revolved around the earth. However, in the Renaissance, three noted astronomers, Nicolaus Copernicus (1473–1543), Johannes Kepler (1571–1630), and Galileo Galilei (1564–1642), independently formulated, developed, and defended a very different concept of the heavens: heliocentrism, the idea that the earth and other planets revolved around the sun. So objectionable was this new idea to most of the Western world that Galileo suffered severe scientific, social, and, in particular, religious persecution. Today, of course, we know that Copernicus, Kepler, and Galileo were correct, and their theories have subsequently been applied to star clusters, galaxies, and even clusters of galaxies called superclusters. In this instance, our original analytical approach—observing the sun and stars move across our sky—was actually an impediment to understanding the real physics involved. Although the original theories seem almost silly today, they can provide a very important lesson for music analysts: analytical methods for better understanding music, no matter their apparent worth in the short run, may in fact actually prevent our ability to really understand the music we study. Although I do not pretend to know the truth of this possibility, or, if true, a better way to proceed, I profoundly believe that alternate ways to analyze music should not be ignored, no matter how improbable they may seem. I hope that readers will bear these thoughts in mind as the book unfolds.

A BRIEF HISTORY OF ALGORITHMIC ANALYSIS

Almost all music analysis is algorithmic in the sense that it compares musical processes in a work under study to a corpus of known rules. I use two strategies to focus the following survey on particular algorithms: choosing only those algorithmic processes that have made significant and quantifiable changes in the manner in which music analysts analyze music, and wherever possible pointing readers interested in pursuing more information on those processes I do mention—or even processes that I do not explicitly mention but to which I implicitly refer—toward important general and specific sources. My use of the word *algorithm* in precomputational analysis also relates to analyses that are clearly programmable in some meaningful way. It is in this spirit, then, that I begin the history of computer music analysis long before the advent of actual computational hardware.

Furthermore, the following narrative in no way fully covers the subject of algorithmic music theory, which itself could fill a very large book. Indeed, if my premise is true—that most music analysis is algorithmic—then most volumes on the general subject of the history of music analysis written in the last millennium themselves cover this subject. Therefore, particularly because history is not my primary subject here, I include this brief outline in order to provide a broad context for the discussion that follows and, hopefully, direct readers toward many sources that they themselves can and should research further.

Note how, as the following historical outline proceeds, the reference to three of the four principles described at the outset of this chapter follow in incremental order, with early analytical approaches involving issues of pattern (shape, repetition, cadence, etc.), medieval studies interested in scale (modes, etc.), and eighteenth- and nineteenth-century analysis concerned with function (chord roots, etc.). The section that follows that will then deal with a similar incremental ordering, but, with the advent of computer analysis, include Principle 4—modeling in addition to reverse engineering.

Although Pythagoras (582–500 BCE; see Cazden 1958), Plato (427–347 BCE, especially *The Republic*), and Aristotle (384–322 BCE, especially *The Politics*) postulated many new ideas about the theory and analysis of music, most of these ideas were philosophical or mathematical in regard to tuning (the ratios of Pythagoras principally) and thus suggest algorithmic frequency determination not particularly related to the purpose of this history (Winnington-Ingram 1929). Aristoxenus (b. 354 BCE), in his two major books *Harmonics* and *Rhythmics*, attempted to define intervals (Principle 1), scales (Principle 2), keys, melody, and consonance, as well as various related ideas (Winnington-Ingram 1932). Although Aristoxenus avoided whenever possible defining his subjects in terms of tuning ratios—a very popular approach during this period—he was also an astronomer, and he found it advantageous to use numerical measurements when describing musical phenomena such as intervals, scales, and consonance. Figure 1.1 presents Aristoxenus's division of the tetrachord into thirty-two equal parts, each part being a twelfth of a tone. An early twentieth-century translation by Macran (1902) presents a series of enharmonic graphs representing the types and subtypes of the intervals and scales described more fully in the book itself.

Without the groundwork established by Aristoxenus, Claudius Ptolemy (second century CE, especially his *Harmonics*) could not have described the full complement of the Greek modes (Book III) and detailed them in ways that today could easily be programmed for analysis and composition (Shirlaw 1955). Ptolemy's limiting of the overall range of modes to two octaves (*systema teleion* or "perfect system") forced the modes in transposition to lose members at the upper limits of their range and regain them at the lower limit of their range, a particularly computable process. He also accepted the notion of seven modes (Principle 2), because that number produced the central octave of the male vocal range.

Ptolemy's studies, among others, prompted Aristides Quintilianus in the third century CE to divide the study of music into three principal categories: theoretical, practical, and numerical. Quintilianus's *Perí mousikēs* (On Music) further separates the purely theoretical study of music into four distinct groupings (scientific, technical, critical, and historical). Although these categories do not strictly apply to music theory, analytical processes are attached to aspects of each. Quintilianus's treatment of music as a numerical art connected it directly to mathematics and involved patterns (Principle 1) such as triads, which he considered an important concept allied with beauty.

Anicius Boethius (480–524), notably in his *De institutione musica*, inherited much of Ptolemy's modal concepts while continuing to advocate traditional Greek analytical processes: "Greatly influenced by Greek writers such as Nicomachus, Ptolemy, Euclid, Plato, and Aristotle, the young Boethius set out to write works treating arithmetic, music, geometry, and astronomy as disciplines that lead the soul to its first encounter with incorporeal knowledge" (Bower 2002, 141). Boethius's *De institutione musica* (c. 500) follows the ideal of the Greek quadrivium, and its conservatism deeply influenced the music theory of Western Europe for nearly the next millennium (Patch 1935). The five books of *De institutione musica* cover harmonics, proportions (Principle 1), semitones, and scales (Principle 2), and ends with a review of harmonics as seen particularly through Ptolemy's eyes. Boethius's seminal work provides a foundation for the compositional rules of his time (Boethius 1967). His prescriptive formulae allow for many computational translations (see Figure 1.2).

Centuries passed before Hucbald (840–930), in his *De harmonica institutione*, described the nomenclature necessary to realize many of Boethius's theories. Whereas Boethius's treatise is primarily theoretical, Hucbald's concentrates on the

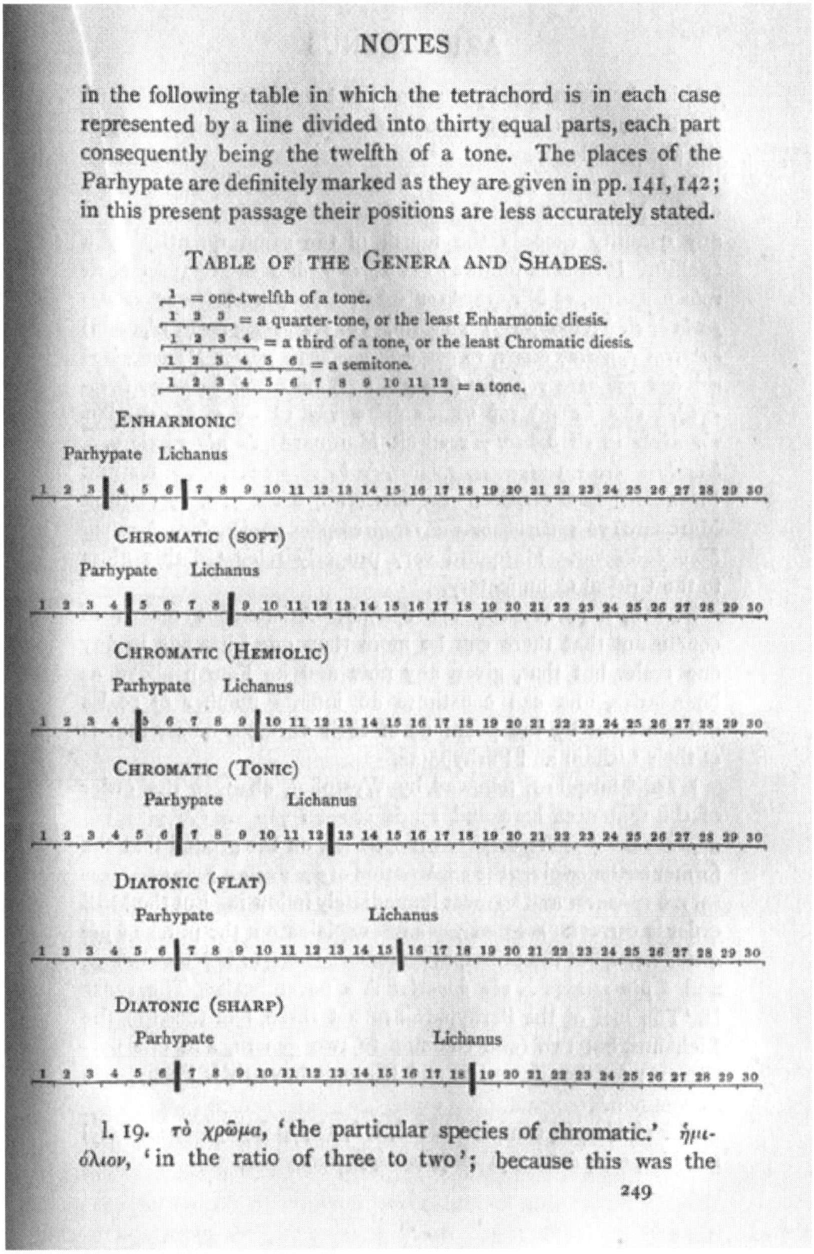

NOTES

in the following table in which the tetrachord is in each case represented by a line divided into thirty equal parts, each part consequently being the twelfth of a tone. The places of the Parhypate are definitely marked as they are given in pp. 141, 142; in this present passage their positions are less accurately stated.

TABLE OF THE GENERA AND SHADES.

1 = one-twelfth of a tone.
1 2 3 = a quarter-tone, or the least Enharmonic diesis.
1 2 3 4 = a third of a tone, or the least Chromatic diesis.
1 2 3 4 5 6 = a semitone.
1 2 3 4 5 6 7 8 9 10 11 12 = a tone.
ENHARMONIC
Parhypate Lichanus
1 2 3 4 5 6 7 8 9 10 11 12 13 14 15 16 17 18 19 20 21 22 23 24 25 26 27 28 29 30
CHROMATIC (SOFT)
Parhypate Lichanus
1 2 3 4 5 6 7 8 9 10 11 12 13 14 15 16 17 18 19 20 21 22 23 24 25 26 27 28 29 30
CHROMATIC (HEMIOLIC)
Parhypate Lichanus
1 2 3 4 5 6 7 8 9 10 11 12 13 14 15 16 17 18 19 20 21 22 23 24 25 26 27 28 29 30
CHROMATIC (TONIC)
Parhypate Lichanus
1 2 3 4 5 6 7 8 9 10 11 12 13 14 15 16 17 18 19 20 21 22 23 24 25 26 27 28 29 30
DIATONIC (FLAT)
Parhypate Lichanus
1 2 3 4 5 6 7 8 9 10 11 12 13 14 15 16 17 18 19 20 21 22 23 24 25 26 27 28 29 30
DIATONIC (SHARP)
Parhypate Lichanus
1 2 3 4 5 6 7 8 9 10 11 12 13 14 15 16 17 18 19 20 21 22 23 24 25 26 27 28 29 30

l. 19. τὸ χρῶμα, 'the particular species of chromatic.' ἡμιόλιον, 'in the ratio of three to two'; because this was the

249

FIGURE 1.1 From Aristoxenus, *The Harmonics of Aristoxenus*, trans. Henry S. Macran (New York: Oxford University Press, 1902), 249.

FIGURE 1.2 A woodcut of Boethius with an instrument designed for methodologically deriving tunings (an algorithm).

practical. *De harmonica institutione* assumes its readers' knowledge of Gregorian chant—see the example in Figure 1.3—and thus is directed to musicians and not to laymen (Weakland 1956).

The *Musica enchiriadis*, originally attributed to Hucbald but now considered anonymous, appeared concomitantly with *De harmonica institutione* and provided the first known instruction in organum (two-voice parallel-motion music, an example of which appears in Figure 1.4; Principle 1 and Principle 2) and thus demarcated a major turning point from monophony into an early type of polyphony. Like Hucbald's *De harmonica institutione*, the *Musica enchiriadis* had a completely practical intent as well as an algorithmic perspective in the sense of providing clear rules for composition and analysis:

> For example, he [Hucbald] (like *Musica enchiriadis*) uses no numerical interval ratios or monochord division. Instead, the scale, and the intervals that structure it, are taught empirically by means of concrete examples drawn from the plainchant melodies and intonation formulas of the *cantus* tradition, demonstrating by direct experience the connection between the two. This characteristically Carolingian pragmatic approach is evident throughout in Hucbald's continual citation of specific chant melodies to exemplify theoretical concepts. The concepts themselves, however, are adapted from late Roman writings on the ancient *ars musica*, especially Boethius's *De institutione musica*. (Cohen 2002, 318)

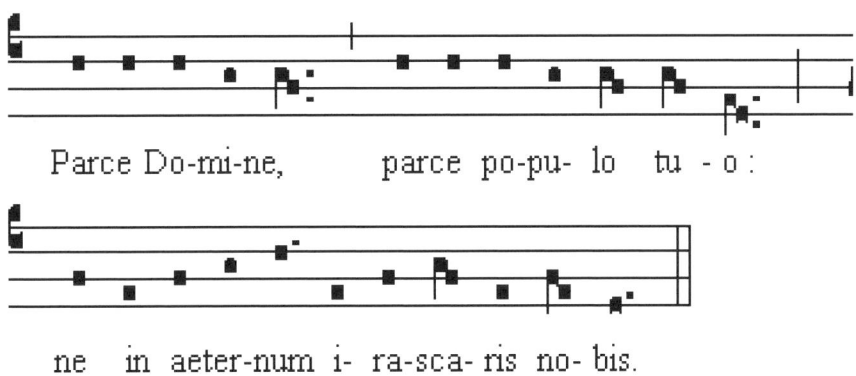

FIGURE 1.3 An example of Gregorian chant, Parce Domine, notated in neumes; the second staff is a continuation of the first.

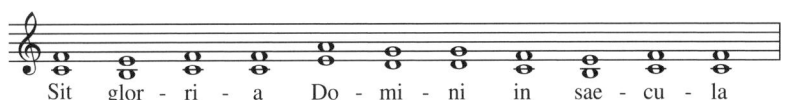

From the booklet edited by Gerald Abraham
accompanying *The History of Music in Sound*
(booklet published by Oxford University press);
examples reprinted with permission of the publisher

FIGURE 1.4 An example of medieval organum.

About this same time, Guido of Arezzo (995–1050) completed his *Micrologus* (1026), a work influenced by both Boethius and Hucbald as well as many of the theorists that came before them. The *Micrologus* was one of the most significant treatises on medieval music. Written in order to train the choir of the Arezzo Cathedral, *Micrologus* covers intervals (Principle 1), scales (Principle 2), species consonance, and the proper division of the monochord, all in great detail. The book is rich in insight, but limited by its focus—training vocalists. Guido developed clear descriptions of phrase structure and rhythmic meanings of neumes, among other things:

> Three brilliant pedagogical ideas have traditionally been attributed to Guido, earning him his honored place in the history of music pedagogy: staff notation, the system of hexachords, and his "classroom visual aid" for sight-singing

> performance, the "Guidonian Hand" ... these three innovations are so towering, that it is less often noted that the "Micrologus," besides being in effect an early sight-singing manual, is also one of the very first in another long line of music-pedagogical genres: the treatise on composition. (Wason 2002, 48–49)

The Guidonian hand, a visual aid for locating the semitones in the central part of the gamut (see Figure 1.5), serves as a kind of algorithm in itself, a simple organization of rules for memorization. Each portion of the Guidonian hand represents a specific pitch (in solfège, of which this is one of the first known instances) within the hexachord. The hand here spans nearly three octaves. Conductors or instructors would point to parts of their hands to indicate a sequence of pitches that the choir or students would then sing in proper order. More than any of the treatises discussed so far, Guido's *Micrologus* represents a perfect historical model for how theories and algorithms from any period can transfer to computation (Crocker 1958).

Guido's important contributions influenced the work of Johannes de Garlandia (1195–1272). Garlandia's *De mensurabili musica* proposed a new theory of consonances (Principle 1), dividing them into perfect (unisons and octaves) and imperfect (major and minor thirds) types, with fourths and fifths relegated to intermediate status. Garlandia classified dissonances into similar categories: perfect (minor seconds, tritones, and major sevenths), imperfect (major sixths and minor sevenths), and intermediate (major seconds and minor sixths). Garlandia also defined classes of organum, pitches, ligatures, and many other aspects of thirteenth-century music, making *De mensurabili musica* one of the most comprehensive and enumerative texts of its time (Crocker 1962). *De mensurabili musica*, though often overly exhaustive and confining in its limitations, provides clear algorithms for the practical use of rules in analyzing the music of its day.

Jacques de Liège's (1270–1340) *Speculum musice* (1340), an encyclopedic description of the music theory of the early fourteenth century, followed and built upon the work of Guido and Garlandia. Liège classified music theory into five categories: heavenly (*celestis*), cosmic (*mundana*), human (*humana*), instrumental (*sonorus*), and analysis (*practica*). However, most of his treatise concerns *sonorus* and *practica*, which involved modes—Principle 1—and measured (metered) music. Philippe de Vitry (1291–1361), especially in his *Ars nova* (1320), developed a series of signs that represented the division of notes into various short durations:

> Several of the texts which describe these new mensurations refer to the composer Philippe de Vitry as the inventor of the new system. Whether this is true or not, de Vitry was certainly a well-known advocate of the "new art" of musical composition in the fourteenth century, of which mensural innovations play such a prominent role. Indeed it is from the title of one of his treatises that the term *ars nova* was taken to describe this new style.... (Berger 2002, 635)

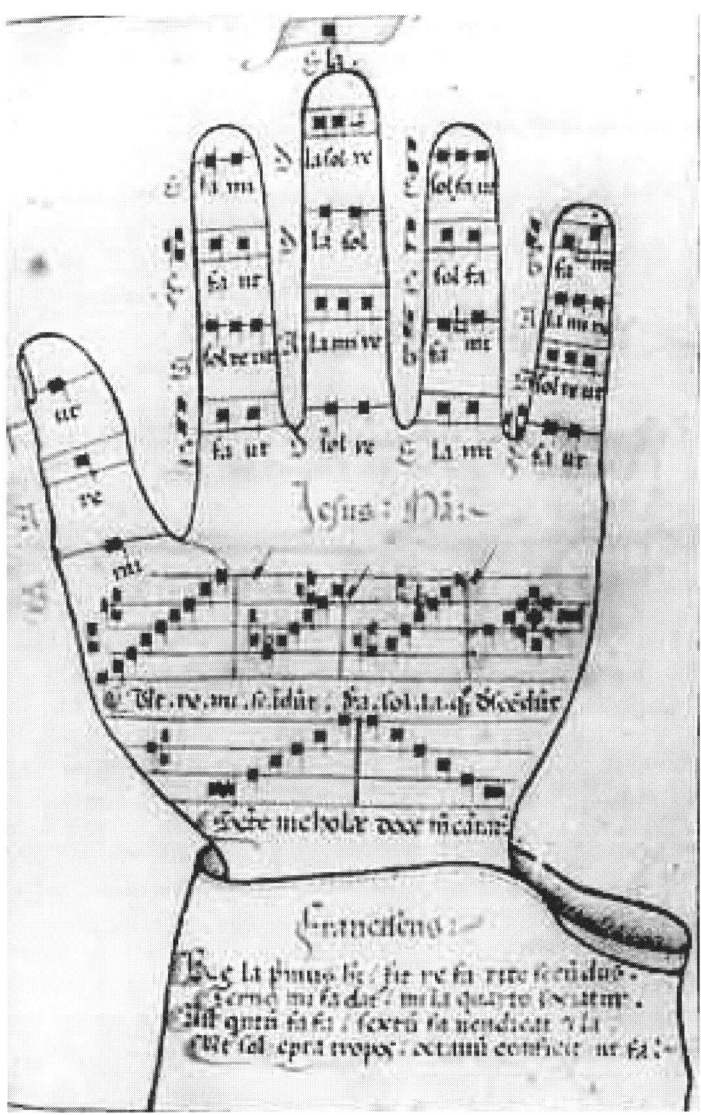

FIGURE 1.5 The Guidonian hand, in which a specific note is assigned to each part of the hand. By pointing to a part of the hand, the conductor can indicate to a group of singers which note to sing.

Both Liège's and de Vitry's writings have clear mathematical (programmable) aspects, even though, like many medieval theorists, these authors often navigate through religious and philosophical realms as well (Werner 1956).

Johannes Tinctoris (1436–1511) honed the work of Liège and de Vitry (especially in his *Liber de arte contrapuncti* of 1477). Tinctoris convincingly demonstrated that his theories of the uses and construction of dissonant suspensions (Principle 1) could help reveal the intricacies of the counterpoint of his time. His *Proportionale musices* (1473–1474) comprehensively describes temporal relationships based on proportions. Although Tinctoris was not a particularly original thinker, his prolific output and careful description of the rules that apply to the various forms of fifteenth-century music make his work vital to the history of theory and provide a clear model for rule-based algorithmic analysis. Figure 1.6 presents an example of florid counterpoint—free rhythmic values in all voices—from Tinctoris's era.

As sixteenth-century polyphony developed and flourished, the work of Gioseffo Zarlino (1517–1590), particularly his *Le istitutioni harmoniche* (1558) and *Dimonstrationi harmoniche* (1571); Henricus Glarean (1488–1563), notably his *Dodecachordon* (1547); and Nicola Vicentino (1511–1572), especially his *L'antica musica ridotta alla moderna prattica* (1555), helped to decipher the developing complex counterpoint and introduced chromatics into the diatonic modes (Principle 2). Zarlino was particularly influential in describing just intonation (see Figure 1.7) and the proper use of chromaticism. Many of the principles these music theorists espoused translate well to algorithms, particularly the rules of modal counterpoint (see Cope 2004).

Building on the work of Zarlino, Glarean, and Vicentino, several late sixteenth- and early seventeenth-century theorists (e.g., Thomas Morley in *A Plaine and Easie Introduction to Praticall Musicke* [1597]; Thomas Campion in *A New Way of Making Fowre Parts in Counter-point* [1618]; and Michael Praetorius in *Syntagma musicum* [1618]) developed algorithms for both composition and performance. Christoph Bernhard in his *Musica autoschediastika* (1601) and *Musica poetica* (1606) actually developed a system of classifying musical style. His descriptions and naming of several embellishments (Principle 1) and expressions in music were the first of their kind (Boorman 1980):

> Bernhard, working in North Germany in the decades just after the publication of Kircher's *Musurgia universalis* in 1650, made style the very foundation of his classificatory system. He retained, perhaps unconsciously, an underlying link to the Burmeister tradition, in that he saw musical figures as ornamenting a plain, diatonic musical style. But now, that plain style is explicitly identified as an actual style in the real musical world. (McCreless 2002, 862)

In the early eighteenth century, Joseph Johann Fux (1660–1741) completed his seminal *Gradus ad Parnassum* (1725), a book that survives to this day as a guide for writing species counterpoint. Fux had studied the writings of Zarlino and others, and his dialogue between master and pupil in *Gradus* lays out both the didactic and the aesthetic rules for sixteenth-century counterpoint (Principles 1 and 2) in ways

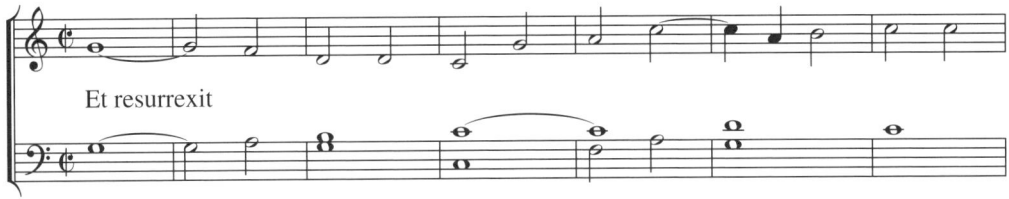

FIGURE 1.6 An example of three-voice counterpoint around the time of Tinctoris.

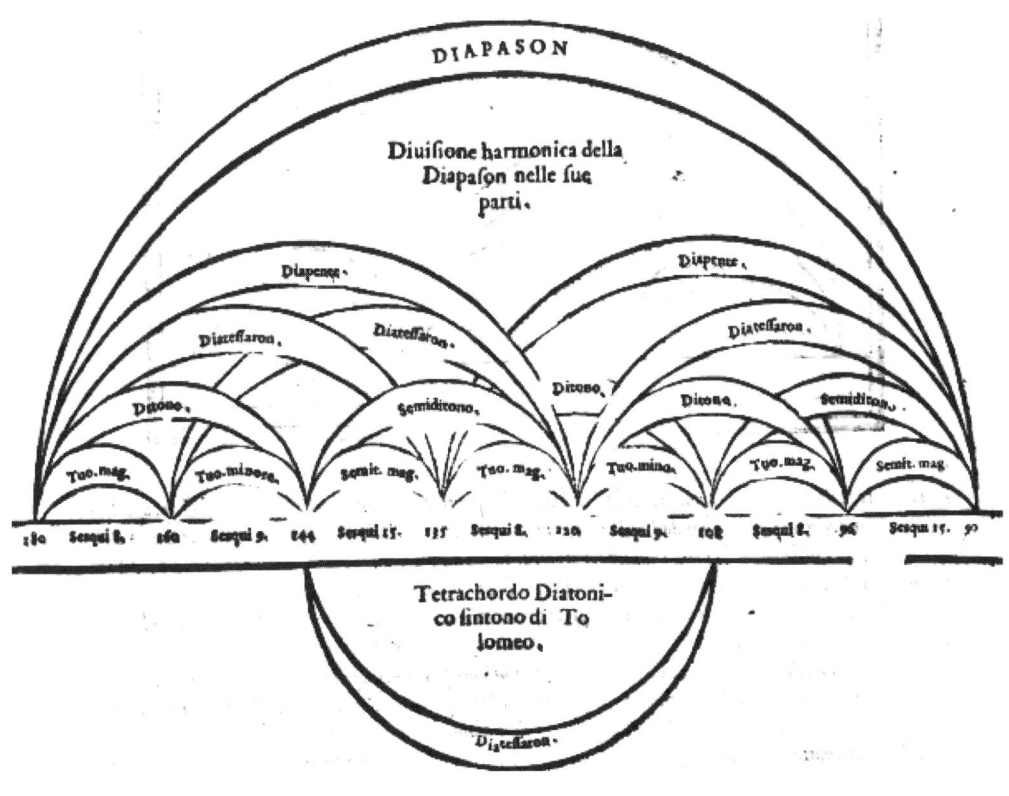

FIGURE 1.7 The division of the octave according to Zarlino.

that make computational implementation not only possible but also practical (see my description of the Gradus program in Cope 2004):

> Whereas the rules of Cochlaeus, Zarlino, and Aaron deal with surface situations, Fux's four rules operate abstractly, at a high level of generality. True, these rules do not cover all of the situations addressed by earlier theorists. For example, beginning and end, proximate location, and so on, are left to later discussion in specific contexts. In effect, the rules cover an infinitely wider range of situations. Taking two classes of consonance and mapping them on to three types of movement result in a regulation of great power and memorability. (Bent 2002, 560–561)

The four rules mentioned here refer to the four ways that perfect and imperfect consonances can precede and follow one another. Documented evidence exists that many composers of note (e.g., Beethoven, Brahms, and others) used Fux's *Gradus* for studying counterpoint. Figure 1.8 presents a manuscript page based on this text, attributed by some to Beethoven, who, these scholars believe, transcribed and embellished it for his student Archduke Rudolph.

Around this same time, Jean-Philippe Rameau (1683–1764), building on the theoretical studies of many of the theorists discussed thus far, described chords as emanating from a single source pitch (root).

> Rameau acknowledged that the inspiration for this breakthrough came from Descartes' method, which was to build a system of natural law on a self-evident principle. In his *Traité de l'harmonie réduite à ses principes naturels* (1722) Rameau identified this first principle as the first six divisions of the string; these could be shown to generate all of the consonant and dissonant intervals and chords as well as the rules for their interconnection. But it was first necessary to recognise as an *a priori* fact that a note and its octave-replicates were identical. From this ensued the principle of inversion. (Boorman 1980, 756)

Thus, Rameau laid the foundation for the now traditional functional analysis (Principle 3) of tonal music, the fundamental bass—a foundation that has proven eminently computational, as demonstrated in the next section.

Figure 1.9 presents two diagrams from Rameau's treatise on harmony (see Rameau 1971) describing (a) the major (perfect) triad and its inversions, and (b) the dominant (fundamental) seventh chord and its inversions (Principle 3). Rameau comments that "the largest triangle will contain the perfect chord, the source and the root of the other chords; these others will be contained in the two smaller triangles" (Rameau 1971, 41). The pitch names here refer to solfège scale degrees, and the numbers refer to partials of the overtone series projected from the bass pitch (root) of the chord. Thus, Do in Figure 1.9a is partial 4 of the C overtone series, two octaves above the fundamental C, and La in Figure 1.9b is partial 20 of the F overtone series. Although Figures 1.5 and 1.9 are separated by more than six hundred years, the algorithmic notation for both suggest at least one common perspective: methods of automatic generation and analysis of music.

FIGURE 1.8 An exercise by Beethoven for his student Archduke Rudolph based on Fux's *Gradus ad Parnassum*.

Johann Philip Kirnberger (1721–1783) continued to develop many of Rameau's ideas, especially the triad and its inversions, and extended these ideas into a notion of melodic function. He also divided dissonance into two categories: essential (such as the dominant seventh, Principle 3) and incidental (such as the suspension). His many books on theory (especially *Die Kunst des reinen Satzes in der Musick* of 1774–1779) could almost be used in classrooms to this day, so closely do they approximate current approaches to tonal analysis.

Kirnberger also invented the *musikalisches Würfelspiele*, or musical dice games, algorithmic combinatoria that also interested C. P. E. Bach, Haydn, and Mozart (Cope 1996). Figure 1.10 presents the first two pages of a published version of a *musikalisches Würfelspiel* attributed to Mozart, with the two matrices representing phrases of music and each column giving numerical choices of measures of music (not shown).

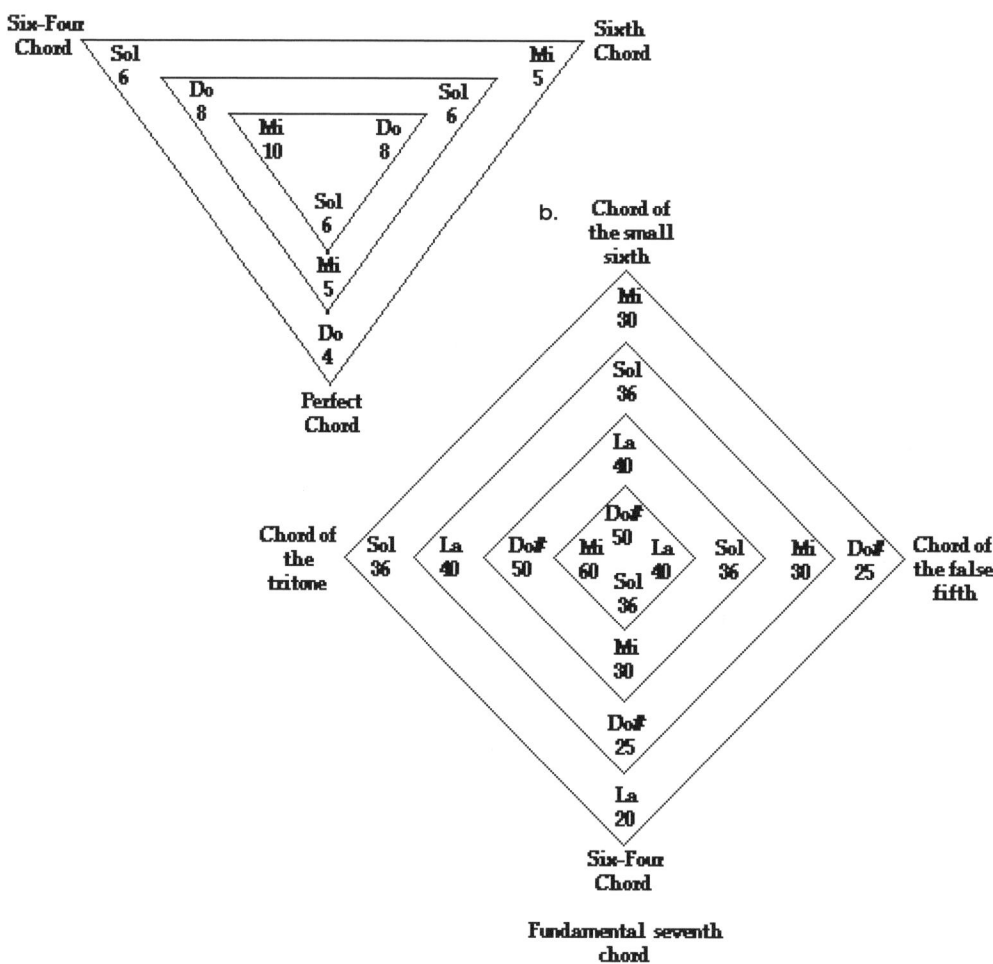

FIGURE 1.9 Two diagrams from Rameau's *Treatise on Harmony* describing (a) the major (perfect) triad and its inversions, and (b) the dominant (fundamental) seventh chord and its inversions.

Like Kirnberger, Joseph Riepel developed *musikalisches Würfelspiele*, often including such algorithmic exercises in his treatises (see *Grundregeln zur Tonordnung insgemein* [1755] and *Gründkliche Erklärung der Tonordnung insbesondere* [1757]):

> Especially noteworthy is the wide variety of ways in which he [Riepel] characterizes the organization and content of phrases. He thus distinguishes them on the

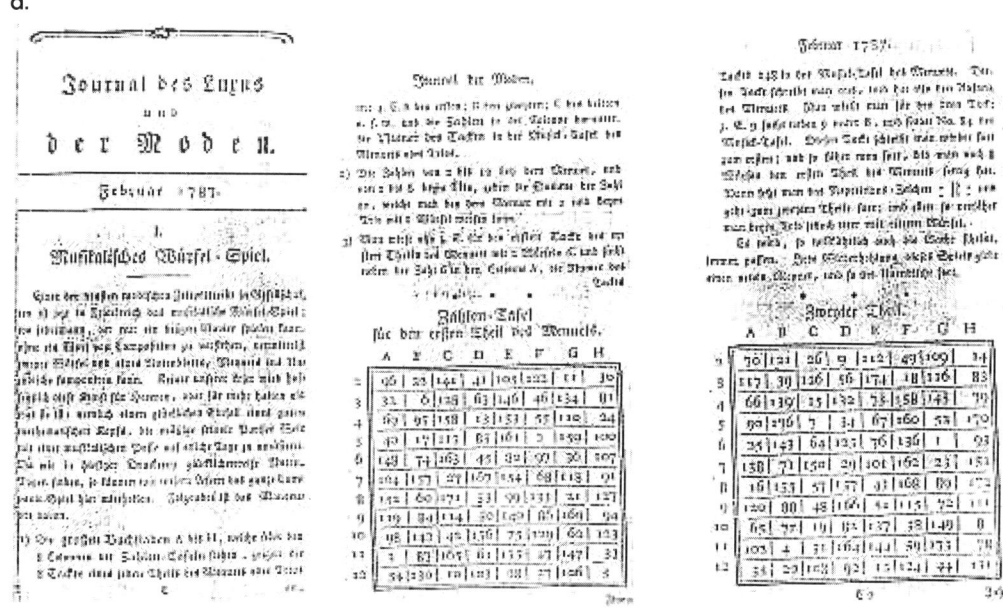

FIGURE 1.10 (a) First published after Mozart's death in 1793 by J. J. Hummel in Berlin, this *musikalisches Würfelspiel* instruction page shows the first two phrases of number selections (chosen by throws of the dice) that were keyed to measures of music. (b) Also shown, an example page of music by Haydn for this own *musikalisches Würfelspiel*.

basis of their rhythmic activity (a concern rarely addressed by eighteenth-century theorists), their overall melodic contour, their underlying harmonic support, their degree of melodic closure, and their length in terms of measure numbers. (Caplin 2002, 671)

Riepel further proposed the creation of major works using combinatorial procedures. Ratner comments that "Riepel proceeds along these lines as he works out melodic combinations in the construction of minuets, concertos, and symphonies. Within a given model he seeks to achieve optimum effects by substituting figures, phrases, and cadences" (Ratner 1970, 351).

Influenced primarily by Rameau, Moritz Hauptmann (1792–1868) in his *Die Natur der Harmonik und Metrik* of 1853 outlines a system of harmony based on logic. Although adopting Rameau's system of roots and inversion, Hauptmann developed harmonic successions based on common tones rather than exclusively on root progression (Principle 3). He avoided relating his theories to the overtone series, primarily due to its inclusion of both consonant and dissonant intervals, and also

b.

Menuet

Haydn

FIGURE 1.10 continued

because the series is infinite: "In Hauptmann's dualistic model, there are three 'functions' assigned to pitches that constitute major and minor triads (or as we will call the, following Hauptmann, 'klangs'): unity (*Einheit*); duality or opposition (*Zweiheit*); union (*Verbindung*)" (Klumpenhouwer 2002, 460). Hauptmann also approached rhythm and meter in innovative ways for his time. His overall analytical system represents one of the more highly computable and algorithmic approaches to musical analysis of the nineteenth century.

Hugo Riemann (1849–1919) developed many ideas of previous theorists but honed them in ways that allowed for different uses. For example, Riemann's refinement of antecedent-consequent phrase sets (see his *System der musikalishchen Rhythmik und Metrik* [1903]) led to their adoption by the theorists of his time. Riemann also provided broader definitions of tonic (T), dominant (D), and subdominant (S) functions (TDS) such that their applications in late romantic music made clearer sense to those dedicated to continuing to analyze tonal function where others had attempted to abandon it (Harrison 1994). Henry Klumpenhouwer notes that

> the function labels S, T, and D representing subdominant, tonic, and dominant, respectively . . . in Riemann's conception of them . . . have both a dynamic (that is, transformational) and topographical modality. The latter modality on its own is not Riemann's: he himself explicitly traces the origins of this concept of chord function to the work of Fétis. In Riemann's view functions also have a syntactic aspect, since complete harmonic phrases must have the structure TSTDT. Moreover, the syntactical functions may be served not only by the primary klangs in a tonality but also by the secondary klangs . . . that relate to the primary klangs. (Klumpenhouwer 2002, 468)

Interestingly, the TDS approach has achieved a revival of sorts in recent years, with many theorists applying it to analyzing functions in music hitherto considered nonfunctional (Principle 3).

Heinrich Schenker's (1868–1935) extraordinary contributions to music theory and analysis (notably his *Neue musikalisches Theorien und Phantasien*, created between 1906 and 1935) proposed major new perspectives on tonal music (see Schenker 1979). Relying on the work of many of the theorists previously discussed here, Schenker created a reductive process that presents foreground (*Vordergrund*), middleground (*Mittlegrund*), and background (*Hintergrund*) layers, each with successively more musical detail removed in order to reveal the music's fundamental structure (Salzer 1962). Schenker further defined a fundamental framework (*Ursatz*) and melody (*Urlinie*—descending diatonic scales from the mediant, dominant, and tonic at the octave). Many of Schenker's ideas appear in the Experiments in Musical Intelligence (Principle 4) computer program (see Cope 1991 and 1996). Figure 1.11 presents a sample Schenker analysis of a chorale prelude by J. S. Bach showing the $\hat{3}$–$\hat{2}$–$\hat{1}$ upper line and the basic I–V–I harmonic structure.

Paul Hindemith, in *The Craft of Musical Composition* (1942), details an overtone-series approach to defining chord roots, key centers, and as models for composing and analyzing harmonic tension (Principle 3). Although many of the theorists discussed up till now developed similar ideas, Hindemith's approach is nonetheless distinctive, if for no other reason than that he composed using his ideas as well as theorized about them. (See the analyses of parts of his symphony *Mathis der Maler* [1934] in Hindemith 1942.) Hindemith fought, with some success, for the universal application of his acoustically based ideas to the works of other composers. His principles form the basis of many of the computational ideas in Chapter 5.

The Schillinger System of Musical Composition (1946) by Joseph Schillinger represents a kind of benchmark for algorithmic music theory, analysis, and composition, containing as it does descriptions of many arithmetic formulae and other easily computable processes. Unfortunately, many of his ideas lack clarity, and his system has been severely criticized, fairly or not, for its misuse of certain mathematical terminology, axioms, and theorems. Nonetheless, Schillinger's system holds many interesting surprises, not the least of which is his approach to composite rhythm (the rhythm of all moving lines simultaneously) as a source for timbre.

Twentieth-century theorists other than Schenker and Schillinger—notably Rudolph Réti, Nicholas Ruwet, Jean-Jacques Nattiez, Leonard Meyer, Milton Babbitt, Allen Forte, Fred Lerdahl, and others—will be discussed in the next section of this chapter as well as in later chapters. Suffice it to say that most contemporary analysis techniques, especially as they relate to twentieth- and twenty-first-century music, include algorithmic processes that make them computationally inviting. Indeed, many current theories of post-tonal music have current computer implementations.

A BRIEF SURVEY OF COMPUTATIONAL MUSIC ANALYSIS

A brief word concerning the evolution of computers here may help provide perspective and context for the program descriptions to follow. Charles Babbage (1792–1871), often credited with creating the first computing machinery, recalled his first thoughts on this subject:

> One evening I was sitting in the rooms of the Analytical Society, at Cambridge, my head leaning forward on the table in a kind of dreamy mood, with the table of logarithms lying open before me. Another member, coming into the room, and seeing me half asleep, called out, "Well, Babbage, what are you dreaming about?" to which I replied, "I am thinking that all these tables (pointing to the logarithms) might be calculated by machinery." (Babbage 1864, 42)

Babbage's first Difference Machine is shown in Figure 1.12 (1833). Babbage described its purpose: "I considered that a machine to execute the mere isolated operations of arithmetic, would be comparatively of little value, unless it were very easily set to do its work, and unless it executed not only accurately but with great

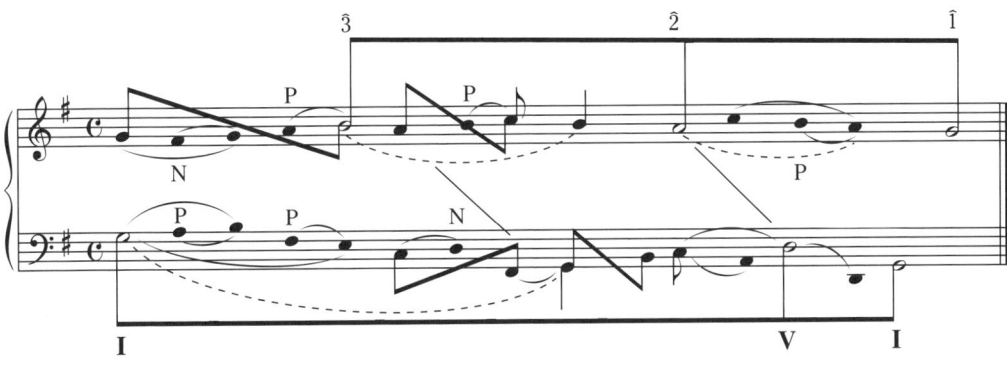

FIGURE 1.11 A sample Schenker analysis of Bach's organ prelude *Wenn wir in höchsten Noten sein*.

rapidity, whatever it was required to do." The engine relies on notched wheels whose teeth interlock in successive orders of ten. As cumbersome as this prototype is, certainly by today's standards, it operated quite effectively in its time. The central processors of contemporary computers, although exponentially smaller and faster than Babbage's original device, still use many of its same basic principles.

Ada Lovelace (1815–1852), a devoted associate of Babbage and the machine's first programmer, wrote in her notes:

> Again, [the Analytical Engine] might act upon other things besides number, were objects found whose mutual fundamental relations could be expressed by those of the abstract science of operations, and which should be also susceptible of adaptations to the action of the operating notation and mechanism of the engine. ... Supposing, for instance, that the fundamental relations of pitched sounds in the science of harmony and of musical composition were susceptible of such expression and adaptations, the engine might compose elaborate and scientific pieces of music of any degree of complexity or extent. (Lovelace 1843, 694)

Lovelace's notes were published in 1843 in volume 3 of Richard Taylor's *Scientific Memoirs*, with the author's name given as AAL. This passage may well be one of the first, if not *the* first, to mention music and computers (analytical engines) in the same breath.

Even with analytical engines and other such machines, Allen McHose, for over thirty years the chairman of the theory department of the Eastman School of Music, developed a statistical method for creating Bach chorales without such assistance (see McHose 1947 and 1951). His method would now be easily adaptable to computer software. McHose hand-counted the functions, inversions, and so on

FIGURE 1.12 Charles Babbage's first Difference Machine (1833), a forerunner of the modern-day computer.

in Bach chorales and ensured that students used these functions in proper proportions when writing exercises in four-part harmony. Over the years McHose's reputation by way of his books spread through American academia, and for a brief time his approach became the de facto standard for analytic instruction at the college level.

Speed and accuracy continue to be the most significant attributes of today's computers, which still, at their most fundamental level, only add, subtract, and store numbers. However, the sophistication of the layer upon layer of complexity added to this core has made computers nearly indispensable in today's world.

Born almost exactly one hundred years after Babbage's first dreams of computing technology, Alan Turing (1912–1953) had similar prophetic visions. In 1937 he published his first important paper describing his theory of the Turing machine. He subsequently played a significant role in the development of computers in Britain and became a strong supporter of artificial intelligence. Together with his friend David Champernowne, who, interestingly, later developed computer composing programs (Herik 2000; Hofstadter 1979), Turing invented one of the first chess-playing programs discussed earlier in this chapter.

Computer music analysis programs have existed in various forms for decades. Most of these programs follow more or less standard processes for analyzing tonal and post-tonal music; many are simple tools for making analytical tasks faster and more accurate. A relative few of these programs have full-fledged analysis packages capable of a variety of musical representations and—at least to some extent—are able to evaluate many different musical parameters (melody, harmony, rhythm, form, etc.).

As with the preceding brief history of algorithmic analysis, the following overview of computational music analysis is incomplete and could easily expand to several times its current size. I apologize to those whose programs I have omitted due to space limitations as well as to those whose programs I have mentioned but the descriptions of which are overly brief. With the availability of programs on the Internet, software-accompanying books on CD-ROMs, and to some degree programs available commercially, clearly one could devote an entire book to a proper discussion of this topic. My coverage here represents at least a fair sampling of the history of and general types of programs available at this time.

I begin with computer music visualizations. Many current computer music programs have such ancillary visualizations that allow users to see some sort of image usually generated in synchronicity with the sound produced. The resultant kaleidoscopic images reveal the dynamics and occasionally the pitches of their sources but provide little of use for serious analysis. In fact, most of these visualizations are artificially enhanced to make the images more visually attractive and thus lack authenticity. However, serious music visualizing began to develop around the same time as computer graphics (the 1950s). Visualization can be a very useful technique for comparing or otherwise generalizing the form of musical works. Images based on tessitura, texture, register, dynamics, rhythm, or other musical parameters can provide interesting and useful insights for music analysts. The most important aspect of such visualizations is that images can be captured and reproduced in spaces small enough for the eye to grasp the entirety of a work or movement, where more detailed representations require far more space and thus cannot be so easily seen at once. Issues of balance, shape, direction, points of arrival, and so on can often be easily seen in such visualizations, where they might otherwise be hidden.

Straightforward temporal diagrams of (usually) a single parameter of music can provide interesting and even valuable insights into music that other techniques may not so easily reveal. Such revelations are particularly important when viewing several such diagrams simultaneously, as shown, vertically aligned, in Figure 1.13. Here, the highest pitch (top) is followed in succession by texture, duration, dynamic, and relation to beat. The contrapuntal image thus produced reveals complementary points and points of disagreement that can provide useful information for analysts. However, one should not confuse such diagrams with actual analysis. Visual diagrams are useful tools for music analysts in that they provide information in ways that make possible comparisons that may otherwise defy analysis. Nevertheless, these diagrams in no way actually analyze music—such analysis remains for human users of computer programs to accomplish. Several visualization programs accompany this book on its CD-ROM and appear in many figures in later chapters.

Although computer composition programs can generate music by way of mathematics and many other processes (see Xenakis 1971), music analysis programs require that music be coded in some way that gives these programs access to its various parameters. Thus, the earliest programs of real interest to music analysts were those that presented logical music encoding methods. The MUSIC I–V series of programs (1957–1969; see Mathews et al. 1969) made significant strides with music encoding, and MUSIC V continues to act as a model for many music notation programs that, owing to their numerical abstractions, offer possibilities for computational analysis. Other programs, such as MUSTRAN, developed by Jerome Wenker beginning in 1962 (see Byrd 1970), include most of the common symbols for music notation.

The Digital Alternative Representation of Music Scores (DARMS), developed in 1963 by Stefan Bauer-Mengelberg (see Bauer-Mengelberg 1970), continues today as an important computer representation program based on the physical placement of information on a page of music. DARMS code is extremely accurate and currently appears in several dialects (Schüler 2000; Selfridge-Field 1997a). The Plaine and Easy Code (Brook 1965), devised by Murray Gould around 1964, and ALMA (Gould and Logemann 1970), created by Gould and George Logemann in the mid-1960s, are also excellent early examples of music digital representation. Michael Kassler developed IML (Intermediary Musical Language; see Robison 1967) and MIR (Musical Information Retrieval; ibid.) in the 1960s as well. The introduction of MIDI (Musical Instrument Digital Interface) code in the mid-1980s helped create a common interface between various electronic music instruments as well as links between electronic performance and digital storage (Schüler 2000; Selfridge-Field 1997a).

Although many of the above-named programs are idiosyncratic in that they served particular needs of the time, they have all contributed to the more universal availability of digital representations of music. ISMIR (the International Society for Music Information Retrieval) currently offers enormous potential for the establishment of a common protocol for music storage and retrieval for future computer

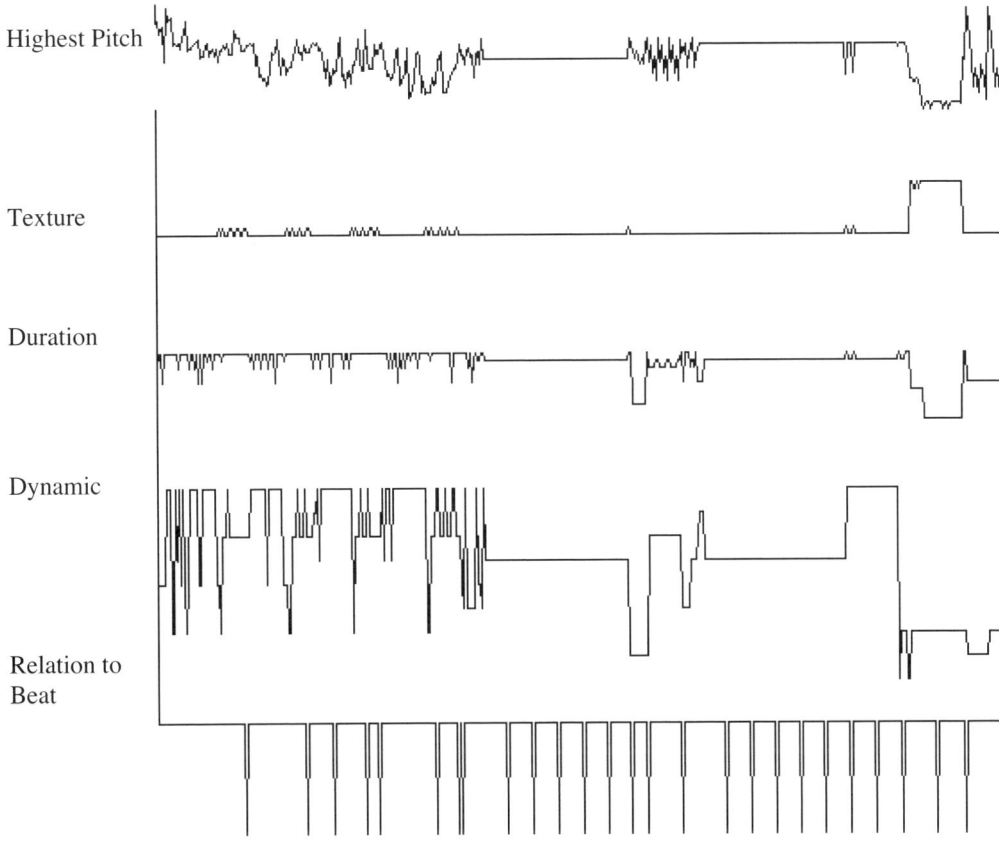

FIGURE 1.13 The author, *Horizons for Orchestra*, in graphic format. Time moves left to right.

music analysis. Combining hitherto large but differently configured databases with a unified interface will furnish a vast storehouse of available music for analysis by any of the processes described in this book. Indeed, a common data structure and robust software residing atop such a structure can provide the perfect domain for all types of analytical programs to study any style of music.

The mathematician Frederick Brooks used the Computation Laboratory at Harvard University in 1957 to analyze thirty-seven hymn tunes using first- through eighth-order Markov chains (see Chapter 6 for more information on Markov chains), thus becoming one of the first researchers to use computers to analyze music (Brooks et al., 1957). Brooks then used these analyses to create new hymn tunes. By many accounts, the resulting melodies were quite successful in emulating the basic style of the original tunes, thus becoming one of the first attempts to model as well as reverse-engineer music as a method for analysis (Principle 4).

Joseph Youngblood's work (1958) also stands out among those who attempted to use computational means prior to the wider acceptance and availability of computers for studying music. Youngblood used first-order Markov chains (Principle 1) in attempting to differentiate musical styles, particularly melodies by Schubert, Schumann, and Mendelssohn. He then based style identification on redundancies in terms of chromaticism and probabilities of scale-degree usage. Although Youngblood's results were not particularly persuasive, owing to his use of a small set of musical works, his research bears noting for its early date and utilization of characteristically computational analytical techniques.

Lejaren Hiller and Leonard Isaacson (Hiller and Isaacson 1959), in their landmark 1959 book *Experimental Music*, lay out several potential goals for computational music analysis: (1) the use of the Monte Carlo method (a process using laws of chance controlled by statistical norms) to experiment with and compare musical forms; (2) the analysis of musical styles based on entropy; (3) the generating and cataloguing of tone rows as cantus firmi for counterpoint (Principle 1); and (4) the analysis of musical timbres (see especially Hiller and Isaacson 1959, 165–170). Although *Experimental Music* focuses primarily on music composition rather than music analysis, much of their program descriptions, particularly those aimed at information theory and statistics, can easily be translated to analysis. Reverse-engineering the processes used to create the *Illiac Suite* (1956, named after the Illiac computer at the University of Illinois), for example, can prove enlightening when analyzing this work (which appears complete in an appendix to *Experimental Music*). Figure 1.14 presents Experiment 2 from the *Illiac Suite*.

Hiller and Isaacson also focus on modeling (Principle 4; see also Chapter 6 and 7 in *Hidden Structure*), where musical principles are tested for their veracity. Hiller and Isaacson comment that

> as a consequence of coding aspects of the problem as numerical information and generating experimental results by means of a computer, a computer is made to behave as a specialized, but unbiased composing apparatus existing in a completely isolated environment, subject only to the controls and information the music analyst might wish to supply. In this application, a computer is an ideal instrument by means of which analytical ideas can be tested. (Hiller and Isaacson 1959, 166)

Many of the other early attempts at the computer analysis of music (see Schüler 2000 for a complete discussion and detailed listing) have to do with information theory—the mathematical and physical study of information flow in a system. As applied to music, information theory involves the probabilities of repetition of musical patterns (Principle 1). If a musical pattern repeats many times, its probability increases, with its "information" (see Chapter 2 and the Glossary for definition) decreasing by inverse proportion (also see Shannon and Weaver 1949 and Pierce 1980

FIGURE 1.14 From Experiment 2 from Hiller and Isaacson, *Illiac Suite*, using the Illiac computer at the University of Illinois, ca. 1956.

for more details). As an example, during the 1960s Hiller collaborated with several of his students (including Calvert Bean, Robert Baker, and Ramon Fuller) in the computer analyses of sonata expositions by Mozart, Beethoven, Hindemith, and Berg (Schüler 2000) using information theory. Hiller and his students calculated their findings based on tempo and note densities. Another of the analyses undertaken by Hiller (see Hiller 1964) revealed redundancies in Webern's Symphony Op. 21 using higher-order Markov chains to track and predict intervals (Principle 1).

Milton Babbitt's work with musical set theory (see Babbitt 1955, 1960, 1961, and 1965), although not in itself actual computer music analysis, set the stage for an extraordinary number of later programs based on his computational approach to analyzing post-tonal music. Allen Forte's many articles and particularly his book *The Structure of Atonal Music* (1973) have continued to popularize this important approach to post-tonal music analysis. A number of chapters in *Hidden Structure* also involve set theory because of its value in comparing harmonic, melodic, and harmonic/melodic pitch patterns (Principle 1) in search of understanding post-tonal music (see also Forte 1993).

The 1960s continued with a series of notable experiments in computer music analysis. Eric Regener's design for his System for Analysis of Music (SAM; see

Regener 1967) includes an elaborate assembly-language program for a state-of-the-art (at the time) IBM 7090 computer. Though SAM seems to have been centered more on computational routines to define data types than on incorporating actual musical analysis, the software clearly demonstrates a serious programming attempt to stabilize what hitherto had been idiosyncratic efforts. The following year, Raymond Erickson's article on computer music analysis (Erickson 1968) summed up this problem: "There are as yet no standards for the encoding of music, no generally available musical analysis programs (as there are, for example, statistical program 'packages'), and no comprehensive theoretical systems for computer-aided analysis" (242). Although this and Erickson's later (1969) article paint a more positive future for the field, they do little to deter his pessimism about the then-current state of disarray in computer music analysis approaches.

Also in 1969, Stephan Kostka (1969, 1971) coded a series of programs to analyze the style of Paul Hindemith's string quartets. Kostka's programs defined the roots and classes of chords, definitions based to a degree on Hindemith's own principles as described in *The Craft of Musical Composition* (1942), discussed earlier in this chapter and in more depth in Chapter 5. Despite only partial success in his harmonic analysis, Kostka extended his research to include Hindemith's melodic style. Kostka's results were mixed, depending as they do on pattern matching for frequency of both literal and varied appearances (Principle 1). Ultimately, his attempts were limited by the sheer numbers of punch cards—required at the time for computer input—to represent even minimal musical data relating to musical style.

Harry Lincoln's 1970 book *The Computer and Music* contains many important articles on the computer analysis of music, including Youngblood (1970) on root progressions (Principle 3), Gerald Lefkoff (1970) on twelve-tone rows, and John Lofstedt and Ian Morton (1970) on the frequency of chord roots (Principle 3). *The Computer and Music* also contained one of the first articles on computer analysis of non-Western (Javanese) music by Fredric Lieberman (1970; see also Steinbeck 1976; Suchoff 1968). Owing possibly to the complexity of analyzing music of oral traditions as well as its origination as an academic field at roughly the same time computers became available, ethnomusicological research has often depended on computer processes for analyzing its musical data.

Nico Schüler quotes a particularly apt passage from Jan LaRue's article:

> May I recommend the computer to you as an instrument without human prejudices. It has its own prejudices, numerical and procedural. But these often act as stimulants and correctives, as healthy balances and supplements to human attitudes. With this new aid, the coming generation of musicologists should develop a style analysis that is comprehensive rather than selective, broad rather than personal, and rich in musical insight. (LaRue 1970, 197)

Given the few articles and books on the subject of computer music analysis in the 1960s and early 1970s, these remarks provided an incentive for others to follow in future decades.

Even given these many historical computer programs and theoretical descriptions of computer programs, computer music analysis research has remained secondary to more traditional paper analyses. As Nicholas Cook points out,

> computational approaches to the study of music arose just as the idea of comparing large bodies of musical data—the kind of work to which computers are ideally suited—became intellectually unfashionable. As a result, computational methods have up to now played a more or less marginal role in the development of the discipline. (Cook 2004, 103)

The 1970s, however, produced some very interesting ideas and computer programs for music analysis. Dorothy Gross (1975, 1980, and 1984) contributed significantly to the development of computer analysis, particularly in the 1980s, defining her projects rigorously and dividing them into logical categories such as grouping, analysis, and interval counting programs (Principle 1). Gross then combined the results of these analyses in comprehensive ways so that her results had both theoretical and applied value. Unfortunately, she used her computer programs to analyze small samplings of musical data typically involving just one piece each by composers such as Bach, Haydn, Chopin, and Dallapiccola. Fred Hofstetter (1973 and 1979) also made great strides in computer music analysis in the 1970s by describing procedures for identifying stylistic influences. His research, primarily using compiled interval counts, proved especially valuable in revealing cultural musical influences across various European political boundaries.

Otto Laske, better-known for his recent research in music cognition but nonetheless important for his publications in the 1970s, made inroads (see particularly 1972, 1973, and 1974) with what he calls a "generative theory of music" (1993). This generative theory follows the relationships between the syntactic structure of music (Principle 3) and its semantic representation—an early example of music cognition. Laske's KEITH, for example, is a rule-based system that initiates analytical discoveries by dividing music into three categories—what is said (linguistic), what is heard (sonological), and what is understood (analysis). Laske has also postulated several principles for cognitive musicology (1992) as well as generative grammars and music (1993; see also Lerdahl and Jackendoff 1983).

The 1980s produced activity in the computational analysis of both tonal and post-tonal music. For example, Bo Alphonce (1980) created programs that computed the transformations of prime forms of all possible pitch-class sets, produced software for the analysis of invariant sets and their subsets, and so on (Principle 1). Interestingly, Alphonce's research into computational grouping possibilities for post-tonal and serial music produced much the same kind of prodigious output as my own (see Cope 2005), including incredible numbers of both irrelevant and relevant possibilities. Without question, however, the work of Alphonce, like that of Gross, has had an immeasurable influence on those who followed.

Ann Blombach developed a computer program in 1982 that analyzed fifty major-key Bach chorales to determine whether harmony or counterpoint is more essential in their composition (Principle 1). Blombach used several parameters, such as statistical frequencies of pitch, duration, patterns, and rhythm, among others, in her analyses. Blombach's results demonstrate a subtle balance between the contrapuntal and harmonic aspects of the selected chorales. The Bach chorales—staples of most collegiate music theory curriculums—have subsequently been used for a wide variety of computational research, having proved their worth as a kind of benchmark for tonal voice-leading (Blombach 1981).

Dean Simonton (1980) analyzed transitions within the first six notes of 5,046 classical music themes by ten composers in order to discover the musical characteristics that tended to make them well-known (Principle 1). Simonton defined "well-known" as those works that had the most recordings, most performances, and/or most citations in the literature. He limited his studies to pitch alone (excluding rhythm and other parameters). Although Simonton attempted to correlate creativity and originality in these works as well, his research reached its limits and ultimately has not stood the test of time well. Nonetheless, the mere fact that he directly attempted to use computer analysis for such subjects as creativity and originality make his research historically important.

One of the first programs to use Allen Forte's approach to set theory (1973), the Computer-Assisted Set Analysis Program (CASAP), was developed by Charles Ruggiero and James Colman (1984). This program calculates prime forms, discovers similarities, and returns complex relations of sets identified by users. The Contemporary Music Analysis Package (CMAP) created by Craig Harris and Alexander Brinkman (Harris and Brinkman 1989) extends the CASAP program by Ruggiero and Colman by including invariance, ordered and unordered interval-class vectors, subsets, complements, adjacent interval vectors, and so on in its output. CMAP has subsequently been expanded and adapted to several platforms by Peter Castine (see Castine, Brinkman, and Harris 1990) and others (Principle 1).

Stephen Smoliar (1980), one of the first theorists to describe the transfer of Heinrich Schenker's structural analysis techniques for tonal music to a computer program, developed computational processes for the identification of the three structural levels (foreground, middleground, and background) and even computational definitions of the *Ursatz* (fundamental structure) in tonal music (Principle 3). Although some of Smoliar's work remains descriptive and has not yet been implemented, his detailed outlines of a full-scale program provide an excellent basis for an algorithmic representation of Schenker's ideas.

The MUSANA program developed by Nico Schüler and Dirk Uhrlandt (see Schüler and Uhrlandt 1994) analyzes pitch, duration, and meter statistically for mean, standard deviation, frequency correlation, autocorrelation, entropy, and so on (Principle 1). The program makes comparative analyses of musical styles based on personal, genre, and/or period. MUSANA, though somewhat limited in its scope both musically (to classical music) and computationally (to statistics), furthers many important analytical possibilities for research into musical style. Figure 1.15 shows two flowcharts, one of MUSANA as a whole (a), and the other the analysis

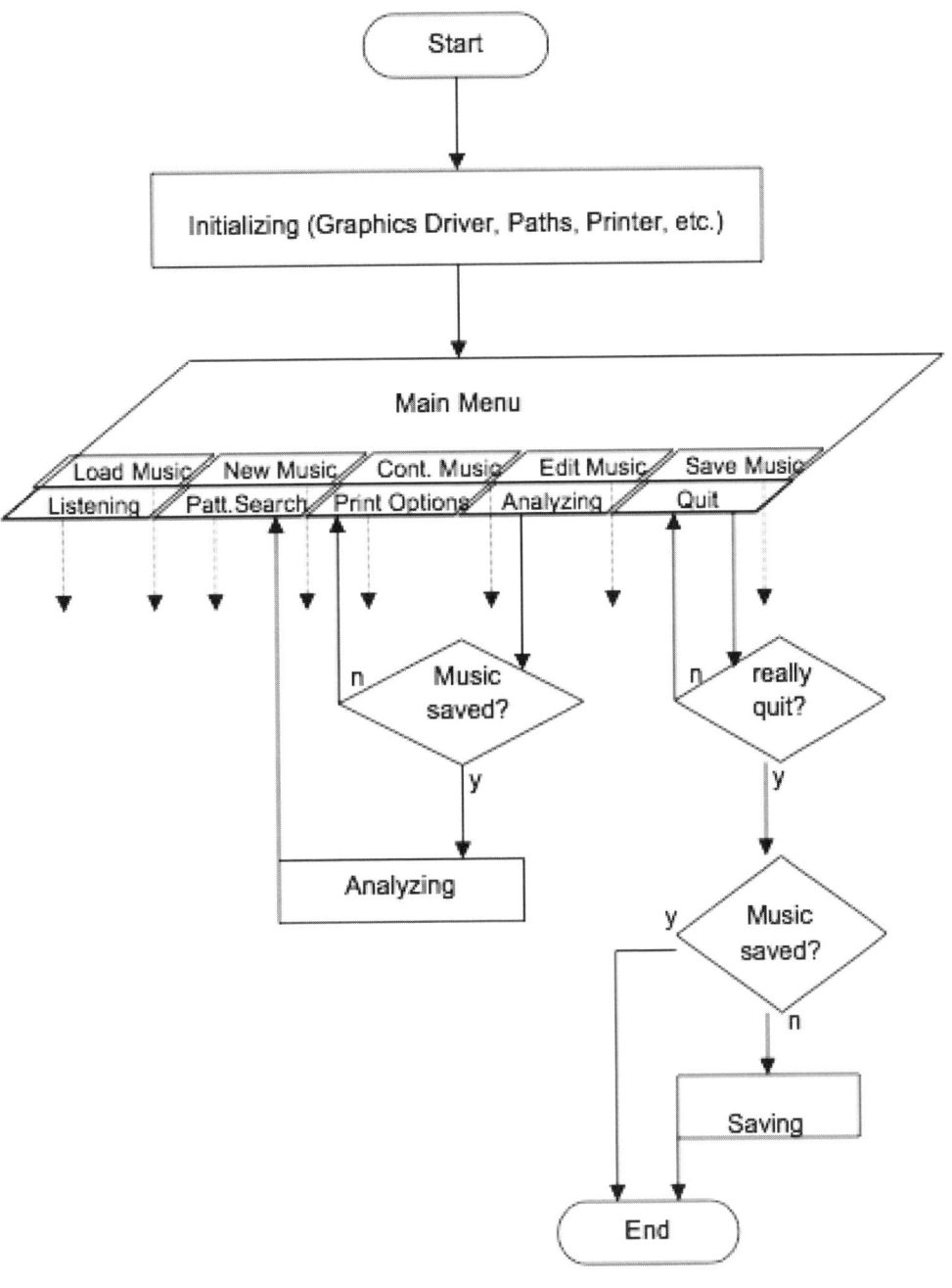

FIGURE 1.15 Flowcharts for MUSANA and its analysis module.

34 HIDDEN STRUCTURE

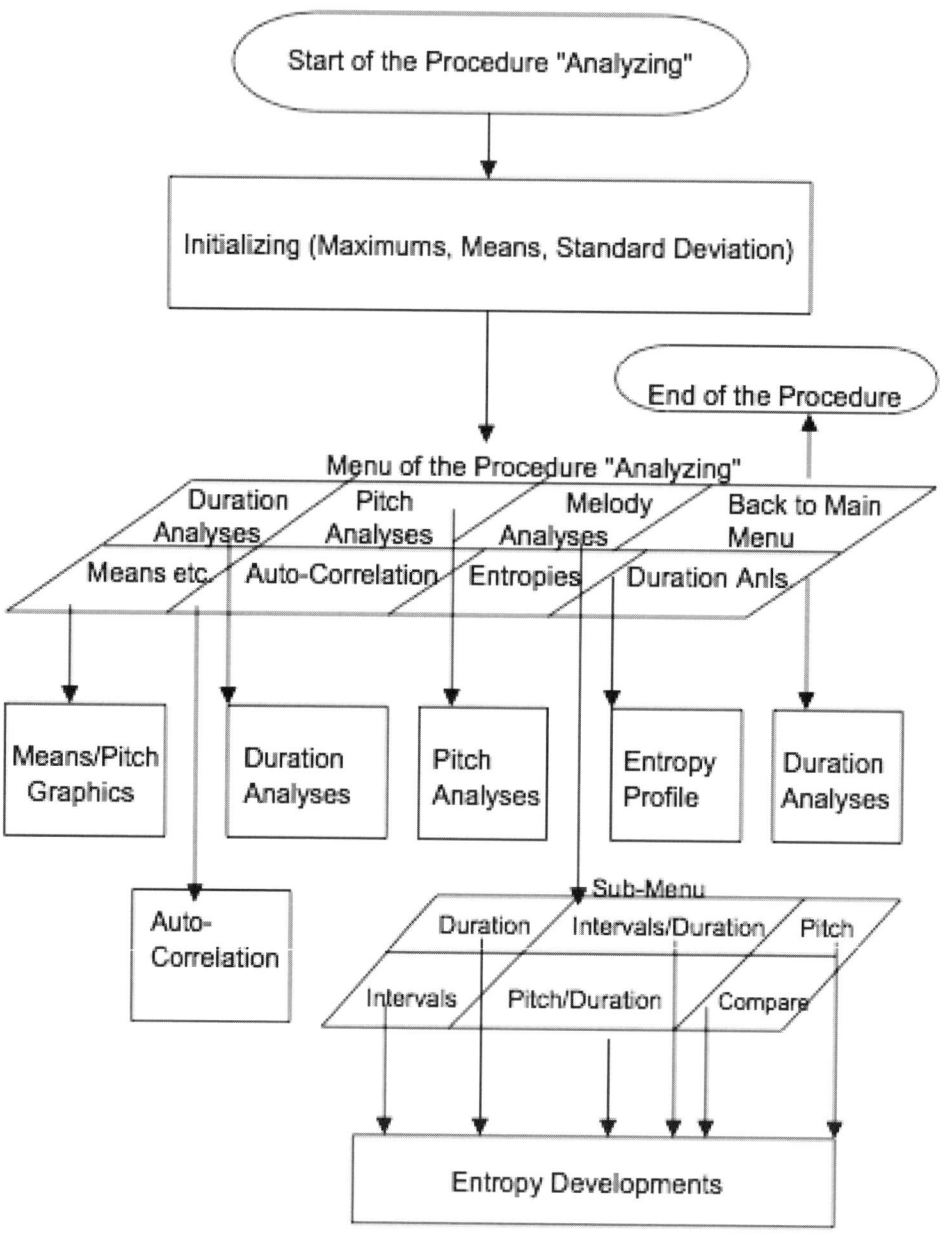

FIGURE 1.15 continued

portion of the MUSANA program (b). Flowcharts such as these represent algorithms and demonstrate points of decision, data input, beginning and end points, and computational activity.

John Schaffer (1994) created a program that allows users to define criteria during the analytical process. The program consists of a relational database and allows user interaction during analysis. Schaffer also incorporates a form of fuzzy logic in his system so that matches of nonequal but related patterns are not overlooked (Principle 1). Schaffer developed his program primarily for the pitch-class set analysis of post-tonal music.

Mira Balaban has described a number of programs based on computational processes designed to analyze music for its hierarchical structure (see especially Balaban 1992). Balaban's approach involves explicit and implicit descriptions of music based on variable grouping sizes. Peter Desain and Henkjan Honing developed a program in the POCO software package primarily for analyzing and generating expression in music (Honing 1990). Their extensive papers on this subject belong to a larger broad-based project named "Music, Mind, Machine." Most interesting about this research is its reliance on digital sound as data, rather digital representations of music notation. Kemal Ebcioglu worked for several years developing his CHORAL (1992) system for harmonizing Bach chorales (Principle 3). His work is particularly important because it uses a form of predicate calculus (symbolic logic) to indicate the fundamental rules generating the music. Jamshed Bharucha has used neural nets (see Chapter 7) to analyze harmony. One of his programs, MUSACT (Bharucha 1993), incorporates standard connectionist architecture for modeling harmonic structures and then properly identifying them (Principle 3).

In the 1990s several very different research projects developed that had an important influence on the field of computer music analysis. For example, the Humdrum Toolkit, developed by David Huron (1995 and 1999), a powerful Unix-based music information-retrieval computer program, searches for particular motives, compares voice-leadings in various repertoires, counts suspensions, defines and catalogues harmonic progressions, analyzes dissonance in relation to metric position, and performs other such operations (Principles 1, 2, and 3). Conceived as a set of utilities rather than a single large program, Humdrum offers a command-line approach to extracting particular data and statistics. The program requires music in Humdrum format; currently available databases include traditional and folk music, a limited number of popular songs, and a somewhat small—given the amount available—number of more or less complete standard classical repertories (e.g., Bach's Brandenburg concerti, all of the Beethoven symphonies, Bartók's complete *Mikrokosmos*, the Corelli trio sonatas, the Debussy piano preludes, Mozart's complete string quartets, etc.). Written in cross-platform Unix, Humdrum Toolkit is available as freeware for a wide variety of computer platforms.

In some ways, the Humdrum Toolkit is more suited to locating, identifying, counting, and classifying provided instances of musical or textual (lyrics) data than to actually analyzing these data. This is not to say the program does not provide information that can prove invaluable for analysis. However, most of the analysis must take place elsewhere (e.g., with users or another computer program). Humdrum Toolkit serves as an important resource for both musicologists and music theorists requiring reliable statistical data for their research, and as such it represents a valuable tool for computer music analysis. Figure 1.16 presents ten commands from the many possibilities to give readers a sense of the breadth of the program.

In 2001 David Temperley and Daniel Sleator created the Melisma Music Analyzer, which derives meter, voicings, phrases, key, and chord function from tonal music. Melisma (for Modular Event-List-Input System for Music Analysis) consists of separate modules that can be detached or added as needed during analysis. The program runs in a Unix environment with source code available from the authors (Temperley and Sleator 1999). In 2002 Guerino Mazzola and Oliver Zahorka developed a program called RUBATO that is likewise modular. RUBATO analyzes, composes, and/or performs music, and the modular architecture of the program allows for third-party developers to create modules for specialized tasks. The creators of RUBATO pride themselves on its scientific basis, though many of the processes they use have traditional musical roots. RUBATO's graphics are quite elegant and helpful during the analytical process, and the weighting system produces interesting results. However, the output typically requires a further analysis that Mazzola calls an "analysis of analysis" (Mazzola 2002, 855).

The Tonalities program, created by Anthony Pople at the University of Nottingham, was designed for analysis of Western tonal music of the late nineteenth and early twentieth centuries. Tonalities allows users to analyze passages of music in terms of differing keys that may be detailed from a range of supplied options. Interestingly, Tonalities is an add-on to Microsoft Excel spreadsheet software. Excel has the advantage of being a professional, well-supported business program and the disadvantage of requiring that all data have a specialized format. Tonalities therefore requires that users be conversant both with Excel and with certain types of rhythmic notation such as those explained in *The Rhythmic Structure of Music*, by Cooper and Meyer (1960), and *A Generative Theory of Tonal Music*, by Lerdahl and Jackendoff (1983).

The Music Theory Workbench (MTW), developed by Heinrich Taube at the University of Illinois, is a powerful program for analyzing tonal music, particularly the 371 Bach chorales as collected by Riemenschneider (1941). MTW takes a short musical work and outputs an analysis in the form of an annotated graphic score like the one shown in Figure 1.17. The analysis includes chord and inversion classification (Principle 1), nonharmonic tone determination, primary and secondary tonal center identification (Principle 2), and a functional harmonic analysis (Principle 3). The encoded database of Bach chorales consists of automatically translated MIDI files downloaded from the Web.

The analysis process for the MTW program follows a straightforward series of steps. First, information is parsed from an ASCII (American Standard Code for Infor-

cents	translate selected Humdrum pitch-related representations to cents
diss	calculate the degree of sensory dissonance for successive spectra (**
fin2hum	translate Finale files to Humdrum
hint	determine harmonic intervals between concurrent pitches for Humdr
key	estimate the key for a Humdrum passage
mint	determine melodic intervals between successive pitches for Humdru
nf	determine normal form for successive vertical sonorities in Humdrur
pattern	exhaustively locate and count user-defined patterns in a Humdrum ir
record	record live MIDI input in Humdrum **MIDI** data format
solfg	translate selected Humdrum pitch-related representations to French s

FIGURE 1.16 Ten commands found in Humdrum.

mation Interchange) score into a time line of vertical sonorities that can be identified as triads or seventh chords. These sonorities are then classified as to type (major, minor, diminished, augmented, seventh chord, etc.) and inversion. Sonorities that are not classifiable as chords are subjected to nonharmonic tone analysis, with the resulting nonharmonic tone or tones identified as to their type (passing, neighbor, suspension, etc.). MTW uses harmonic rhythm to determine points to assign harmonic function to two or more sonorities with—possibly—different roots. Given a tonal center confirmation, the analysis proceeds with key identification and produces a functional harmonic analysis of all the sonorities in the time line. Pivot chords between two keys are identified when a single sonority serves two or more functions in its harmonic context.

Many current algorithmic music composition programs (also called computer-assisted composition programs) offer valuable analysis tools. For example, OpenMusic (OM) from IRCAM (Institut de Recherche et Coordination Acoustique/Musique) in Paris, Elody from Grame in Lyon, France, Symbolic Composer, Alice (ALgorithmic Interactive Composing Environment), Common Music from CCRMA (Center for Research in Music and Acoustics) at Stanford, and many more have analysis components. Some (particularly OM and Alice) offer users the ability to alter the program to increase its analytical capabilities. Figure 1.18 presents an overview of OM's graphic interface and various forms of music notation.

Many other computer analysis programs exist than the ones I have mentioned here, including those available on the Internet, through university research centers, and, in some cases, commercially.

HIDDEN STRUCTURE

FIGURE 1.17 Bach Chorale 002 from the Music Theory Workbench, version 0.1 (http://pinhead.music.uiuc.edu/~hkt/mtw/pdf/), by Heinrich Taube (accessed 24 July 2007).

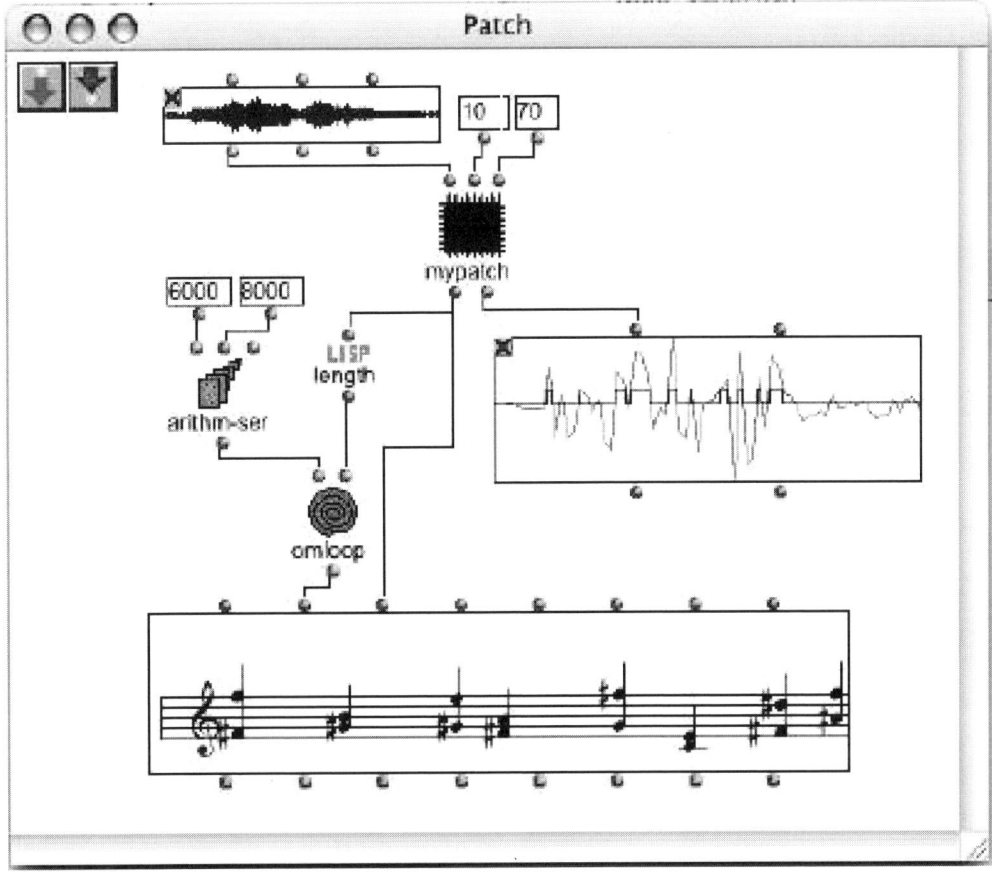

FIGURE 1.18 An example of the OpenMusic visual programming environment of music for composition and analysis.

MUSICAL EXAMPLES

In each chapter of this book I will present its analytical process as applied to the third piece of Stravinsky's Three Pieces for String Quartet (1914) in order to provide readers with a sense of continuity and to involve them in a somewhat more complete analysis of one work. The beginning of this music appears in Figure 1.19.

The Three Pieces for String Quartet (1914) were completed during the period in which Stravinsky was occupied with composing his larger work *Les noces* (1914–1916). Stravinsky later twice returned to these pieces to form the first three of his

FIGURE 1.19 The first few measures of Stravinsky, Three Pieces for String Quartet (1914), 3rd movement.

Four Studies (1928 and 1952, the fourth being *Madrid*) for orchestra. Because this chapter does not focus on a single analytical approach but rather presents a brief history of algorithmic and computer analysis, I here present this music with several historical methods of analysis that will not otherwise be covered in this book. These methods include tonal, polytonal, and formal techniques.

Tonally analyzing the music in Figure 1.19 requires a liberal definition of tonal harmony, for often chords apparently built in thirds require imaginary or altered members. The first chord, for example, could be classified as an E-flat seventh chord in third inversion with a missing third. The second chord could then translate to a D seventh chord, also in third inversion (D–F–A–C-sharp, respelled). The third chord then poses problems, requiring a creative solution—possibly a C major altered ninth chord (C–E–B-flat–D-sharp). As the phrase continues, such chordal analysis becomes less and less clear, particularly when one attempts to discern the key as well as the resulting functions.

Polytonality would seem to offer more opportunity for logical analysis of this piece. The opening phrase in Figure 1.19 contains all pitches but A-flat. The only two keys that make sense for a polytonal analysis of this opening passage that omit A-flat are B-flat major and D major, the initiating notes that represent the alto and bass voices beginning in Figure 1.19. Unfortunately, although the upper two voices and many notes from the viola and cello fit nicely into B-flat major, D major does not appear likely in any of the music here. The more likely analysis suggests C major and B-flat major with the lone G-flat (F-sharp) acting as a chromatic nonharmonic tone.

Formally, the third of Stravinsky's Three Pieces for String Quartet resembles a rondo with three returning fragments, of which Figure 1.19 presents two. The music throughout this piece repeats with different rhythms, meters, accents, and so on characteristic of his style in this and other periods of his compositional life. The enigmatic solo viola ending the piece (not shown here) suggests that Stravinsky intended a less-than-convincing set of key relationships. Yet through his use of dynamics, phrase lengths, and other musical parameters, Stravinsky achieves a quite convincing movement. As we shall see in later chapters, this work provides many surprises beyond this simple narrative analysis.

PROGRAM DESCRIPTION

The computer code accompanying this book on CD-ROM exemplifies a number of the analytical processes described in this chapter. For example, the Visualize code presents a kind of seismic graph display of several parameters of the music in its database. The graphs this software creates (the Macintosh Common Lisp version only) produces images like that shown in Figure 1.13, with severe fluctuations indicating highly variable information content and stable horizontal lines representing unchanging content. Although these graphs are very useful for visually accessing and overviewing large segments of music, they do not represent actual musical analysis. In other words, although not nearly as precise as more traditional musical scores, the graphs represent a useful alternative by presenting the same music in far less space.

42   HIDDEN STRUCTURE

The Sets Analysis code on the CD-ROM accompanying this book represents a simple example of the kind of program available from many different sources on the Internet in various forms (Java, etc.). The Macintosh version of this program on the CD-ROM presents a straightforward "Identify Set" window when choosing Lookup from the menu at startup (see Figure 1.20). The program then provides the

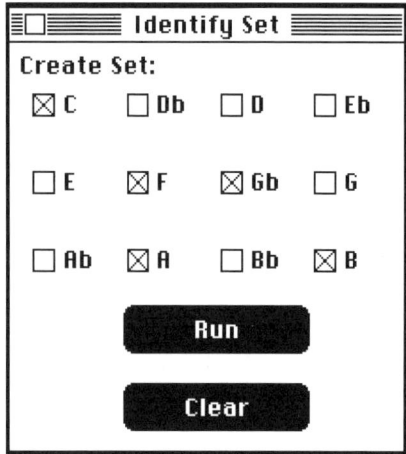

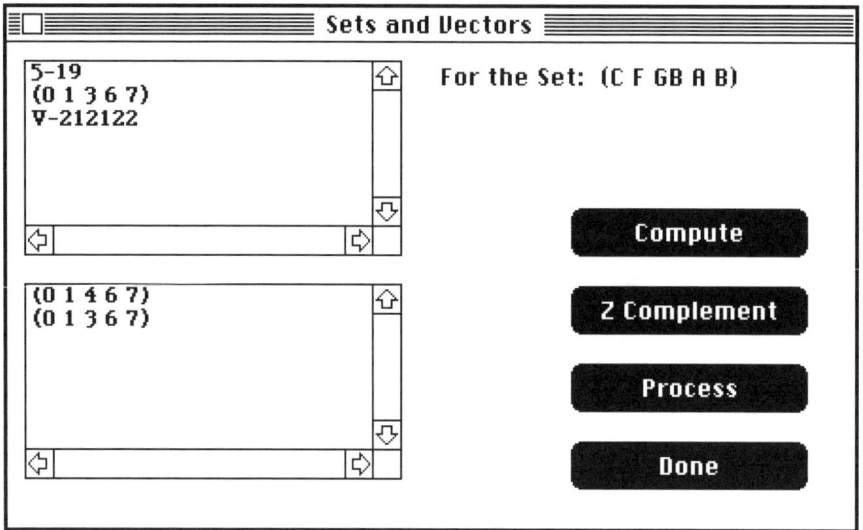

FIGURE 1.20 Two screens from the Sets and Vectors program on the CD-ROM that accompanies this book.

pitch-class set name, vector, lookup process, and any Z-related pairs for input sets from three to nine pitches, as described in Forte (1973) and in the introduction to set theory at the beginning of Chapter 3 of this book. The Common Lisp version of this program works in the same way, but without menu or window shortcuts. Information about how to access the various forms of sets appears in the header documentation in the code file.

CONCLUSIONS

This chapter has briefly covered an enormous time span—from Pythagoras to the current day, almost 2,500 years of music theory and analysis. Although it obviously provides a brief overview rather than a detailed history, this background does establish the context for the more experimental processes described in the chapters to come. For example, Chapter 2 will explore the potentials of information theory and one of its subfields, algorithmic information theory. These fields, both subsumed under the general umbrella of discrete mathematics, have enormous potential for revealing important information about all disciplines, not the least of which is music.

TWO
Lisp, Algorithmic Information Theory, and Music

> Estimates of the relative degrees of order and disorder of different samples of music or different sections of given musical structures could be attempted. This is suggested since entropy seems to be a more useful variable than less well-defined concepts such as "harmonic tension."
>
> Lejaren Hiller and Leonard Isaacson, *Experimental Music* (1959), 167

In the epigraph at the beginning of this book I quote Saint Augustine's statement that "Beauty is the splendor of order." This notion of order—also mentioned by Hiller and Isaacson in the epigraph to this chapter—represents a particularly important perspective in computer-assisted analysis, for all of the techniques I describe in this book depend, in one way or another, on the order present in music. For example, this chapter explores the very essence of order and its contradiction, chaos, by describing a means—computer programming—and one of the fundamental types of computational analysis of order and chaos: *information theory*. Creating computer programs for analysis typically requires a computer programming language. I begin this chapter by describing a computer language called Lisp. All of the software accompanying this book on CD-ROM is written in Lisp, and much of this software references information theory in one form or another. Understanding a few of the basics of Lisp will help readers to negotiate their way through the source code and to run the software presented here. I continue this chapter by introducing algorithmic information theory (AIT), a subset of information theory, that analyzes data for the amount of information (non-redundant data) it possesses. Musical algorithmic information theory (MAIT) applies AIT to musical works to determine their inherent information content for comparison to other works and as a revelation of the dynamic music information content (DMAIT). As such, this chapter concerns Principle 1 (music as pattern), as discussed in Chapter 1.

LISP

Lisp (a malformed acronym for List Processing) is one of many programming languages designed to create computer programs. Conceived and first implemented in the late 1950s by John McCarthy and his associates at MIT, Lisp has had many devotees, especially in the field of artificial intelligence. Originally available in many flavors, the most often used form of Lisp today is Common Lisp, available on every standard computer platform and uniform in use through a standard reference manual (Steele 1990). Some commercial versions of Common Lisp come with ancillary code to aid users in creating their own applications. These versions of Common Lisp require a second, platform-dependent manual.

Booting—initializing—Common Lisp typically produces a Listener window ready for command-line input. This input in the Listener window is evaluated—interpreted—by Lisp whenever users follow input with the return key. Code may also be typed into a text window. However, code typed into a text window will not be interpreted until users explicitly invoke it. Invoking interpretation usually results from typing some combination of implementation-dependent keyboard and/or mouse commands.

Although many important types of information exist in Common Lisp, the two most important types are *functions* and *data*. Functions are operatives that create or alter data in useful ways. Data represents information upon which functions operate. In Lisp, functions are typically used individually or combined with other functions to produce more complex processes and output. User-defined functions can be included alongside built-in functions; the results are—as the axiom goes—often greater than the sum of their parts.

In order to keep complicated processes in Common Lisp clear, the language requires parentheses, in part to distinguish between data and functions, as well as to clarify different functionally initiated actions. In other words, when entering functions or data into a Listener window, users must partition their boundaries and firing order with parentheses. Furthermore, information entered into the Listener window will be evaluated by Lisp unless preceded by a single quote ('). The following code provides a simple example of these concepts, where the "?" represents a typical prompt provided by the form of Common Lisp used:

```
? (first '(1 2 3))
```

Note that the data here—a simple list of numbers—is surrounded by parentheses to indicate its inclusiveness, with the single quote identifying the data as a list not to be evaluated (although Lisp can evaluate numbers, it cannot evaluate *lists* of numbers) until the function `first` has had an opportunity to act on that list of data. The data that functions act upon is also called that function's *arguments*. The Lisp function `first` in the above code returns the first element of its argument, which must be a list. Therefore, when users hit the return key after the entry of the above code, Lisp produces the number 1. Although these procedures may at first seem arcane, they make more sense with practice.

In effect, Common Lisp evaluates the function `first`, with which it is familiar, and then applies that function to the data with which it is not familiar. Functions always appear to the left in a parenthetical representation, with data to the right. Thus, a simple mathematical expression such as

```
? (* 1 2)
```

equates to "1 times 2," the result of which will be 2 when, again, users hit the return key. Neither the number 1 nor the number 2 requires single quotes here because Lisp recognizes individual numbers.

Lisp operations can also be nested to produce more interesting results. The code, for example,

```
? (first (rest '(1 2 3)))
```

produces the number 2, because Lisp first evaluates the function `rest` (meaning all but the first), which returns the rest of its argument '(2 3), and then evaluates the function `first`, which returns the first element of the result of the `rest` operation. This nesting of parentheses can produce some very complicated-looking code. However, one can always unwrap the parentheses to see how the functions operate on the output of other functions by separating the sublists, beginning with the most deeply nested one. Typically, this means that the functional operations are read from right to left rather than vice versa. Fortunately, Lisp provides another primitive—a built-in function that accomplishes very simple things—in this case called `second`, that produces the same result but using just one function call, as in

```
? (second '(1 2 3))
```

Data can also be nested in sublists according to whatever plan the programmer feels will reveal the information best. For example, I often use sublisted data for musical notes in lists such as

```
((0 60 1000 1 127)(1000 62 1000 1 127)(2000 64 1000 1 127)
 (3000 65 1000 1 127) . . .
```

for the first four notes of a C-major scale played one after the other. Here, the entries in each sublist pertain to ontime (in thousandths of a second), pitch (where middle C is 60 and increments in both directions refer to half steps up or down), duration (in thousandths of a second), channel (1–16), and loudness (0–127, with 0 representing silence). Because very large works contain very long lists of note-events (i.e., thousands of separate notes), these note-event lists can often become quite difficult to read. Lisp therefore provides a method of assigning symbols to represent data. By using the Common Lisp function `setf`, for example, all the notes of a musical work can be placed in a kind of container (variable), the name of which users can then call without having to write out or read all of the separate events and their contents. For example, the code

```
? (setf musical-work '((0 60 1000 1 127)(0 62 1000 1 127)
                       (0 64 1000 1 127)(0 65 1000 1 127)
                       . . . .
```

places all of the data that follows its name into the `musical-work` container. Typing

```
? (first musical-work)
```

and pressing the return key then produces the note-event (0 60 1000 1 127). Note that one need not use the single quote here because musical-work has already been defined, and thus Common Lisp recognizes and can interpret its meaning.

Another Common Lisp primitive, cons, creates lists from—typically—an atom (number or letter) and a list, as in

```
? (cons 1 '(2 3))
```

which returns the list (1 2 3) following the return key. Like the function setf, described previously, cons requires two arguments, "constructing" (the word from which cons derives) a new list combined from its two arguments. Unlike setf, cons does not place the data or results in a container (variable).

Some functions in Common Lisp—called conditionals—test data for certain attributes. For example, the function if tests its first argument and returns its second argument if it proves true, or its third argument if the first argument proves false. The following code provides a simple example:

```
? (if (numberp 1) t nil)
```

where the first argument to the function if acts as the test here (*if* 1 is a number), the second argument t indicates that true should be returned if the first argument is true, and the third argument indicates that nil (or false) should be returned if the first argument is not true. This combination is often termed an *if-then-else* clause. In this case, hitting the return key will produce t because 1 is a number. The function numberp is called a *predicate* (a function that typically returns true or false as applied to a single argument).

Lisp is widely known for its use of *recursion*, functions that call themselves during execution with lesser and lesser elements of their arbitrary-length list arguments. Using recursion therefore means that users need not know the actual length of list arguments in order to access them, a great advantage when manipulating vast amounts of information. The following code describes a user-defined recursive function called add-one that adds 1 to each of the elements in its list argument. Note that the function defun defines functions in Common Lisp.

```
(defun add-one (list-of-numbers)
  (if (null list-of-numbers) ()
      (cons (+ 1 (first list-of-numbers))
            (add-one (rest list-of-numbers)))))
```

The interpretation of this function can be described in the following way:

> (line 1) the first line of code names the function and declares the variables that will represent its argument(s) in a list (in this case only one named argument exists). Function and argument variables should be named according to what they do or represent in order to render the code as readable as possible;

(line 2) the function if in this case tests the argument list-of-numbers to ascertain if it contains data, and if empty it *then* returns an empty list (second line of code);

(line 3) if (*else*) the list still contains entries, the code constructs a list consisting of 1 added to the first of add-one's list argument and (line 4) the result of add-one's continued application to the remainder of the list.

The terminating code (or second line) in the definition of add-one must occur first, because if the function add-one were to attempt to add 1 to an empty list, it would fail (because (), read also as nil, does not contain a number in its final recursive call).

Lisp novices often find the recursion in functions such as add-one difficult to comprehend. There are several ways to explain recursion beyond the code itself. Possibly the clearest explanation involves nesting the application of actions that take place on a sample argument. Using '(1 2 3) as a simple example, add-one first tests its argument to ensure that it contains numbers. Our argument at this point consists of '(1 2 3), and so it defaults to lines 3 and 4 of the add-one definition. The cons function interprets its first argument as 1 plus the first number of '(1 2 3), computes this as 2, and proceeds as in

```
(cons (+ 1 1) (cons (+ 1 2) (cons (+ 1 3) ()))) 
```

which when read from right to left produces the following reduction

```
(cons 2 (cons 3 (cons 4 ()))) 
```

When computed, add-one produces the list (2 3 4), exactly the outcome desired. The first call to cons (on the right here) returns the list (4), the second call to cons returns the list (3 4), and the final call to cons produces the list (2 3 4). At this point, novices usually ask why not use the above code rather than creating a complicated recursive function called add-one to perform it. The answer, of course, is that recursive functions in Lisp can operate on arbitrary-length lists, making add-one capable of adding 1 to all of the elements of lists of any length—lists that would otherwise require the typing of immense numbers of numbers and subsequent calls to cons.

Although this brief description of Common Lisp fails to describe many of the thousands of built-in functions and most of what programmers can really accomplish with the language, readers should be able to load, use, and at least partially understand the code that accompanies this book if they carefully read the descriptions that appear near the top of each file. I will also occasionally place Lisp code in the text of this book to clarify points made and reinforce the processes described here. For a more detailed description of Lisp, see Cope 1991, chapter 3; Graham 1995; Steele 1990; Touretzky 1990; and Wilensky 1986.

DEFINITIONS

Because this chapter covers many subjects dependent on the concept of *information*, I begin with a clear definition of that word in the context used here. "Information," when it pertains to *information theory*, means the non-redundant portion of any string of numbers. As example, the floating point representation of the fraction $1/3$, or 0.333333333333..., holds very little information, because the redundant repetition of 3s extends infinitely and can be expressed more succinctly as a fraction. In contrast, the number π, or 3.141592653589793..., with its apparently endless non-patterned and non-repeating sequence of numbers, contains a very high level of information. Of course, being an infinite sequence of the arrangements of the numbers 0 through 9 means that, when exploded to individual digits, π does contain patterns and number repetitions (as seen here in Figure 2.1, the first two thou-

3.14159265358979323846264338327950288419716939937510582097494459230781640628620899862803482534211706798214808651328230664709384460955058223172535940812848111745028410270193852110555964462294895493038196442881097566593344612847564823378678316527120190914564856692346034861045432664821339360726024914127372458700660631558817488152092096282925409171536436789259036001133053054882046652138414695194151160943305727036575959195309218611738193261179310511854807446237996274956735188575272489122793818301194912983367336244065664308602139494639522473719070217986094370277053921717629317675238467481846766940513200056812714526356082778577134275778960917363717872146844090122495343014654958537105079227968925892354201995611212902196086403441815981362977477130996051870721134999999837297804995105973173281609631859502445945534690830264252230825334468503526193118817101000313783875288658753320838142061717766914730359825349042875546873115956286388235378759375195778185778053217122680661300192787661119590921642019893809525720106548586327886593615338182796823030195203530185296899577362259941389124972177528347913151557485724245415069595082953311686172785588907509838175463746493931925506040092770167113900984882401285836160356370766010471018194295559619894676783744944825537977472684710404753464620804668425906949129331367702898915210475216205696602405803815019351125533824300355876402474964732639141992726042699227967823547816360093417216412199245863150302861829745557067498385054945885869269956909272107975093029553211653449872027559602364806654991198818347977535663698074265425278625518184175746728909777727938000816470600161452491921732172147723501414419735685481613611573525521334757418494684385233239073941433345477624168625189835694855620992192221842725502542568876717904946016534668049886272327917860857843838279679766814541009538837863609506800642251252051173929848960841284886269456042419652850222106611863067442786220391949450471237137869609563643719172874677646575739624138908658326459958133904780275
9

FIGURE 2.1 The first 2000 digits of π.

sand digits of π). However, these patterns and repetitions appear in small groups of numbers, at least when π is represented—as it is here (and elsewhere)—short of its assumed infinite size.

In order to make sure that all readers understand the difference between compression (reducing out redundant information and replacing it with place holders) and simple representation, note here that the symbol π does not indicate a useful form of compression, even though anyone who knows its meaning could resurrect some particular part of π if it were discovered in data. Representations for data compression must contain code that generates the original numeric forms of what they represent, not just other convenient symbols. Otherwise, we would require special symbols for every conceivable number sequence and would need to reference a large lexicon each time such symbols appeared in compressed data. Although I will soon discuss a possible case for such a compression model in relation to music, as a general rule, this kind of compression would require more symbols—more likely partial symbols—and lookup time than any possible usable system could manage.

The terms *information* and *entropy* are often used interchangeably. Although these two may seem somewhat unrelated, they do share one critical dimension. Information measures the amount of non-redundant information in data, while entropy measures the amount of improbability or unpredictability in data. A high degree of information therefore signifies a high level of improbability, unpredictability, or non-redundancy. A high level of entropy in data indicates the same thing. For the purposes of this book, however, I will use the term *information* rather than *entropy* to avoid any possible confusion with entropy's meaning in physics—more related, among other things, to heat or energy exchanges between hot and cold bodies.

This definition of information does not indicate preference or aesthetic value. One string of numbers is no better or worse than another string of numbers based on its higher or lower level of information content. One might especially assume preference or value when the string of numbers represents music—that in a musical work somehow high information content is preferable to low, or vice versa. In actuality, calculating the information content of a string of numbers—musical or not—simply indicates its level of redundancy versus what some refer to as randomness (I prefer the term *unpredictability*).

The notion of redundancy or non-redundancy plays very important roles in defining information as used here. In effect, redundancy, although the complement or opposite of information, can provide immensely important clues that allow understanding of a message even when that message is garbled. For example,

> Every sentence in any language is highly redundant. A sentence of English—or of any other language—always has more information than you need to decipher it. This redundancy is easy to see. J-st tr- t- r—d th-s s-nt-nc-. The previous sentence was extremely garbled, all of the vowels in the message were removed. However, it was still easy to decipher it and extract its meaning, The meaning of a message can remain unchanged even though parts of it are removed. This is the essence of redundancy. (Seife 2006, 11)

Of course, omitting vowels is just one method of garbling messages. For example, Hebrew and Arabic lack explicit vowels, and thus speakers of these languages would not find Seife's example at all disconcerting.

Information theory is a branch of communications theory that deals with the amount and accuracy of information when transmitted from a source through a medium to a destination. The information referred to in information theory can be discrete, such as alphanumeric information (letter-and-number combinations), or continuous, such as speech and music. Information theory has many practical uses, including cryptography, data compression, error correction, and the like.

> Suppose we have a message source which produces messages of a given type such as English text. Suppose we have a noisy communications channel of specified characteristics. How can we represent or encode messages from the message source by means of electrical signals so as to attain the fastest possible transmission over the noisy channel? Indeed, how fast can we transmit a given type of message over a given channel without error? (Pierce 1980, 44)

Founded by Claude Shannon (Shannon and Weaver 1949), information theory depends heavily on statistics and probabilities. Shannon developed a theory that actually produces relatively believable text from even a pseudo-random group of letters and/or spaces—a mock example of a message received from a very noisy medium. Shannon began with a series of six processes (the "orders" here indicate the levels of probabilities taken into consideration):

1. Zero-order *symbol* approximation as in ZZFYNN PQZF LQN, where errors and correct symbols exist side by side
2. First-order *symbol* approximation (including letter frequency), as in ID AHE RENI MEAT, where letter frequency is taken into consideration as well as which letter likely follows which letter
3. Second-order *symbol* approximation, as in RENE ID AHA MIET, where letter ordering two steps back is taken into consideration
4. Third-order *symbol* approximation, as in HE ARE ID TI NEAM, where letter ordering three steps back is taken into consideration
5. First-order *word* approximation, as in I DARE HE IN TAME, where letters and now words are taken into consideration
6. Second-order *word* approximation, as in I DARE HE NAME IT, where letters, words, and probable word order are taken into consideration (Pierce 1980)

Using simple letter and word probabilities such as these enables communication systems to reconstruct information from noisy or corrupted messages.

The importance of information theory has become more apparent with time:

> The theory of information did not seem all that important at first. True, it changed the way cryptographers and engineers thought about their work; true, it set the

groundwork for building the computers that would soon become part of everyday life. But even the founder of information theory, Claude Shannon, had no idea just how far-reaching his idea would become. (Seife 2006, 56)

Morse code can provide a more concrete example of how information theory works, particularly how information theory works with unknown languages. Samuel Morse invented Morse code in 1837. This code, which survived for many decades as the most popular type of telegraph, Teletype, or other form of communication, consists of combinations of short and long signals (dots and dashes) representing letters of the alphabet. Letters that occur frequently are represented with single dots or dashes or, at most, combinations of two dots and/or dashes. Conversely, rarely used letters typically consist of longer combinations of dots and dashes. This coding system makes it easier for telegraphers to quickly type and decode messages. In fact, Morse's code gained some 15 percent in speed over other methods of communication in its heyday, the pre-telephone period, and concomitantly enabled telegraph communications that connected most of the civilized world. Dots, dashes, and spaces are also much easier to use computationally because they can be expressed in binary using just three representations (00, 01, 10, for space, dot, and dash, respectively), whereas the English-language alphabet requires at least twenty-six separate binary representations, not including spaces, numbers, or special characters.

Morse code offers a good example for demonstrating one use of information theory. For instance, not knowing the language used (Morse code), how much noise is present in the medium, or where this noise occurs in the output, among other problems, makes the task of interpreting information very difficult. One encounters these same difficulties in, for example, attempting to understand messages from past civilizations or decipher radio messages in the search for extraterrestrial intelligence (SETI). Music, when represented in numbers, actually poses similar problems, as we shall see. The process of interpreting noisy transmitted messages is the very essence of communications theory and the origins of information theory—the study of information loss and recovery.

Using Morse code instead of letters and spaces allows us to more easily imagine the code as a language about which we have no prior knowledge (most readers will likely find themselves in exactly that position here). According to Shannon, our ability to translate a message—even with attendant noise—lies in direct proportion to our understanding of the probabilities involved. For example, Shannon's previously discussed six-step process can be applied with the assumed notion that all languages have inherent similarities, with much the same basic letter and word probabilities. No doubt not precisely true in all cases, this assumption enables a logical—if not accurate—translation, even without knowing which dots, dashes, and spaces appear as a result of noise in the medium. The following code interpretation follows these same six steps:

(1) —•• —•• ••—• —•— —• —• •—• —•— —•• ••—•   •—•• —•— —•

(2) •• —•• •— •••• • •—• • —• •• — • •— —

(3) •—• • —• •   •• —••   •— •••• •—   — •• • —

(4) •••• •   •— •—• •   •• —••   —   ••   —• • •—   —

(5) ••   —•• •— •—• •   •••• •   •• —•   — •— — •

(6) ••   —•• •— •—• •   •••• •   —• •— — • •• —

Each line of Morse code here represents exactly the same letters in the examples included in the letters-and-words presentation of Shannon's six steps. The concept of using probabilities to create order from chaos will also prove quite valuable in Chapter 6 of this book, which presents programs using Markov chains to model post-tonal music in varying styles.

Figure 2.2 shows the basic Morse code symbols for each letter of the alphabet, selected special characters, and the numbers 1 through 10. Interestingly, I produced the above code translation of English into Morse using the following simple recursive Lisp function..

```
(defun translate-into-morse-code (letters)
  (if (null letters)()
      (cons (second (assoc (first letters) morse-code))
            (translate-into-morse-code (rest letters)))))
```

The Lisp primitive `assoc` in the third line of code here associates letters with their Morse code equivalents stored in the variable `morse-code`.

Information theory can also prove useful in exposing what is *not* present in a message. For example, in 1939 Ernest Wright authored a book titled *Gadsby*, some 239 pages long, in which there is not a single instance of the letter "e"—the most commonly used letter of the English alphabet. Of course, this omission wreaks havoc on the probabilities inherent in overcoming noise in message transmission using Shannon's theory. The following first paragraph from Wright's book provides a good example of his narrative:

> If youth, throughout all history, had had a champion to stand up for it; to show a doubting world that a child can think; and, possibly, do it practically; you wouldn't constantly run across folks today who claim that "a child don't know anything." A child's brain starts functioning at birth; and has, amongst its many

Letters										
•-	-•••	-•-•	-••	•	••-•	--•	••••	••	•---	-•-
a	b	c	d	e	f	g	h	i	j	k
•-••	--	-•	---	•--•	--•-	•-•	•••	-	••-	•••-
l	m	n	o	p	q	r	s	t	u	v
•--	-••-	-•--	--••	•-•-	•--•-	----	••-••	--•--	---•	••--
w	x	y	z	ä	á	ch	é	ñ	ö	ü

Punctuation

•-•-•-	--••--	••--••	•----•	-•-•--	-••-•
period	comma	question mark	apostrohe	explanation mark	slash
-••••-	-••-•	-•--•-	•-••-•		
hyphen	fraction sign	parentheses	quotation mark		

Numbers

•----	••---	•••--	••••-	•••••	-••••	--•••	---••	----•	-----
1	2	3	4	5	6	7	8	9	0

FIGURE 2.2 Morse's code for English letters and numbers.

infant convolutions, thousands of dormant atoms, into which God has put a mystic possibility for noticing an adult's act, and figuring out its purport. (Wright 1939, 1)

Because the frequency of no other letter of the alphabet can replace the frequency of the letter "e," Shannon's six-step process will reveal its absence without much difficulty. Few composers, for example, have refused to use the pitch C, or sixteenth notes, or a *piano* dynamic marking. However, the fact that many composers did omit certain pitches from a composition, did not use certain duration combinations, or made other such choices can be as useful to musical analysis as determining what these same composers included in these same compositions. Obviously, any analytical approach that did not make such omissions clear would be far less useful than one that did. After all, although *Gadsby* certainly has many other attributes as a novel, any analysis not recognizing its missing "e"s would certainly be incomplete.

Although most of the examples of information theory presented thus far have involved language and not music, and although these examples display clear relevance to messages and the meaning derived from such messages, the term *information* as used from now on in this book will not imply message *or* meaning, but only the non-redundant information present in data. I have relied primarily on language constructs thus far because they more easily convey the points being made.

I have also described information theory here primarily to set the stage for a definition of *algorithmic* information theory (a subset of information theory that will be described shortly). However, one can imagine many uses for information theory itself in music. For example, as mentioned in Chapter 1, most early attempts at

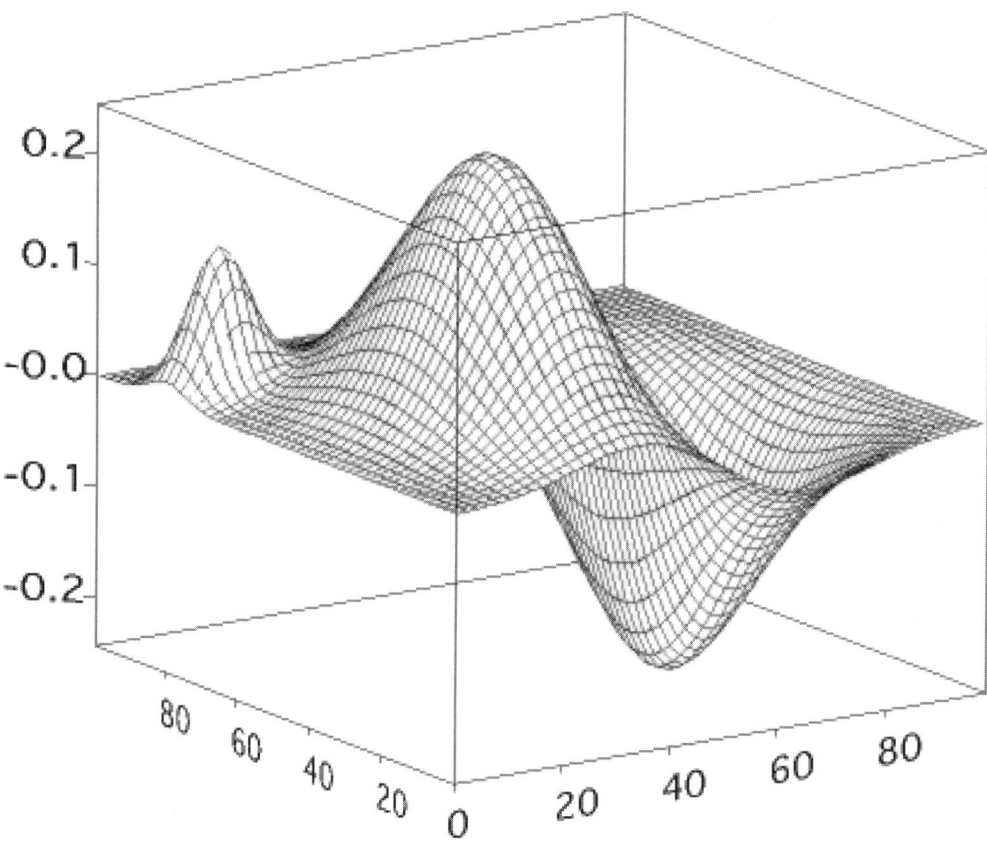

FIGURE 2.3 An example of the kind of three-dimensional modeling of musical style by Böker-Heil.

computer music analysis involved information theory. Norbert Böker-Heil's research with information theory and musical style analysis (see Böker-Heil 1972), for example, produced interesting three-dimensional modeling of the type shown in Figure 2.3. His plots of the information content of Palestrina, Rore, and Marenzio particularly demonstrates their similarities and differences. Although the mathematics are too complex to present here, suffice it to say that the large amount of data that information theory analyzes and characterizes can be usefully represented and compared in such graphic outputs.

Furthermore, by better understanding how composers convey their intentions through information in the form of music notation to performers who present this information to audiences using voices and instruments, and how audiences interpret this performed information, analysts can more thoroughly clarify their various relationships. Each of these areas (intention, performance, and cognition) represents a significant potential for noise—mistakes—to enter into the process of communication, prompting questions about information flow—the basic principle of information theory. Therefore, information theory can lead us to a better understanding of how we perceive music, one of the foci of music cognition.

Algorithmic information theory (AIT), a branch of information theory, concentrates less on the communication accuracy of information and more on the precise amount of non-compressible information contained in a message. In fact, algorithmic information theory assumes that the information content in the data it analyzes is completely accurate. Compressing a photograph, for example, typically involves replacing the many thousands of bits representing the various colors with symbols, thus identifying—so far as possible—the redundancy present. Because photographs often have several areas consisting of one color, using symbols to represent these colors and their general locations can reduce the bit size of a photographic file significantly. Analyzing such compressed files can reveal a great deal about their constitution—principal colors, balance of colors, and so on. Although compression alone cannot usually determine the subject of a photograph, the abstract analyses that result from compression provide information not immediately available from viewing the photograph in its original state. As we shall see, whatever compression coding AIT uses must be able to restore, or decompress, the photograph to its precise original state from the compressed data. Such compression/decompression algorithms are referred to as *codecs*. AIT is the basis of many other operations, including such processes as cryptography, information entropy, and data compression.

The more compact we make data in AIT, the better the compression model. The reason for this is not so much to save storage space, but to produce the best algorithm for reducing the data. In effect, we have matched the data to the most efficient algorithm. Of course, the algorithm used must remain consistent when applied to different data of the same type, or comparisons between data will be uneven. Also, uncompressed data file sizes reflect very little about their makeup, while the use of appropriate and consistent algorithms to compress these same data files reveals a great deal—their relative information content.

Gregory Chaitin (the originator of algorithmic information theory) commented on how AIT defines

> the complexity of something to be the size of the simplest theory for it, in other words, the size of the smallest program for calculating it. This is the central idea of algorithmic information theory (AIT), a field of theoretical computer science. Using the mathematical concept of program-size complexity, we exhibit irreducible mathematical facts, mathematical facts that cannot be demonstrated using any mathematical theory simpler than they are. (Chaitin 2005, 175)

As example, earlier in this chapter we discovered that the fraction $1/3$ represents information more succinctly than 0.3333333 .... Of course, our second example, π, is just a symbol. We have not actually reduced the level of redundancy, but simply replaced the infinite sequence with a convenient symbolic representation. However, we can compress such numbers effectively using mathematics, as in

$$\pi = A/R^2$$

where A represents the area of a circle and R represents the radius of that same circle. Even the formula just described can be slightly more compressed to

$$\pi = C/D$$

where C represents the circumference of a circle and D represents the diameter of that same circle. AIT searches for the most economical way of expressing data. In Lisp, π exists as a constant (an unalterable variable), but both formulae above can still be expressed as

(/ A (* R R))

and

(/ C D)

where the terms A, R, C, and D refer to the previously described characteristics of a given circle. The latter formula much more concisely expresses 3.141592653589793 . . . , and thus even the numerical representation of π can be compressed to a fraction of its size.

Number sequences such as 2, 4, 8, 16, 32, 64 . . . can often reduce easily as well, because these continuing powers of 2 can be expressed as

$$f_n = 2^n$$

meaning that the sequence results from incrementally increasing powers of the number 2, with n beginning at 1. Thus, how we compress information greatly influences how much information a series of numbers actually possesses. Although it may seem highly unlikely that musical data will easily reduce to mathematical formulas, no method should be overlooked as a possible compression technique. What may seem improbable as a tool for reducing an entire composition often turns out to be exactly the right approach to compressing smaller sections of the same composition, sections that might otherwise not be reducible by any other means.

Another method of reducing number strings involves rules, a subject I discuss in more detail in Chapter 6. Rules that can regenerate their source material exactly can be extracted from musical data in many ways. For example, the rules of two-dimensional cellular automata (algorithms that produce simple graphic output that follow constraints) can prove very useful. As I will explain in Chapter 6, rules can relate to musical attributes and can actually generate missing material as easily as they regenerate compressed material.

A rule in a two-dimensional graphic automata takes the form of eight constraints that govern whether or not a position in a given row will remain empty or be filled, based on the state of positions in a preceding row (Wolfram 2002). For example, the following rule coded in Lisp

```
(defvar *rules*
  '(((* * *) *)
    ((* * o) o)
    ((* o *) o)
    ((* o o) *)
    ((o * *) o)
    ((o * o) *)
    ((o o *) *)
    ((o o o) o)))
```

dictates (line 2 above) that if a currently open position ("o") is preceded by three filled ("*") positions (i.e., each of the three contiguous positions directly above it), the new position will be filled, and so on. There are 256 (2^8) possible rules such as the one presented above. Each of these rules leads to a predictable outcome. Further variations arise, however, with different initial rule settings of the automata. For example, Figures 2.4a and 2.4b use a single filled position in the initiating line. Quite different immediate results occur with different rule settings, although many of these eventually settle down into patterns similar or identical to those provided by a single entry in the initiating line.

The recursive Lisp code presented below produces graphs similar to those shown in Figure 2.4 using the rule appearing above.

```
(defun produce-automata (number start rules)
  (if (zerop number) ()
      (cons start
            (produce-automata
              (1- number)
              (cons 'o (butlast (create-new-row start rules)))
              rules))))

(defun create-new-row (old-row rules)
  (if (null old-row) ()
      (cons (apply-rule (firstn 3 old-row) rules)
            (create-new-row (rest old-row) rules))))

(defun apply-rule (group rules)
  (let ((test (second (assoc group rules :test #'equal))))
    (cond (test)
          (t 'o))))

(defun firstn (n list)
  (if (or (zerop n)(null list))()
      (cons (first list)
            (firstn (- n 1)(rest list)))))
```

In Figure 2.4a, the output appears much as it will in any Common Lisp Listener window when running the above code, although I have enhanced the image here by removing all of the empty spaces and parentheses to make the graph more readable. In Figure 2.4b, I have turned this output on its side so that time is represented left to right (rather than top to bottom) to better resemble musical data.

The asterisks here could translate to pitches on a vertical twelve-pitch grid with the circles representing rests, or vice versa. Although I suspect that no complete work will reveal cellular automata origins, I have often found that small sections of many works reduce quite effectively following such processes.

Many types of compression techniques other than those I have described here have been and are currently in use. Large pattern lexicons, for example, offer the ability to place markers wherever certain patterns occur, requiring a lookup sequence in that same lexicon during regeneration. Musically such pattern lexicons make sense, because it would be quite possible to store, say, 10,000 three- to ten-pitch patterns in a lexicon, each pattern having its own designation that then represents that same pattern every time it occurs in a piece of music.

Such formulae, sequences, lexiconic lookups, and so on prove surprisingly robust in reducing small segments of musical data. Any process, no matter what its likelihood of success, that eliminates the need to prosaically list data verbatim will aid in compressing data and thus produce more accurate levels of information content. Even using several methods simultaneously can be effective, the only drawback being the obvious need for a more complicated process to resurrect the data precisely to its original form.

Interestingly, only highly random number strings not reducible by pattern redundancy, mathematical formulae, sequences, or lexicons approach 100 percent information content. Some mathematicians conjecture that completely irreducible numbers exist; they call them Ω (omega). These Ω numbers would consist of infinite sequences of bit combinations in which no repetitions, patterns, or correlations exist (see Chaitin 2005, 76). Chaitin believes that Ω numbers exist even though no one to date, including him, has discovered one. Indeed, no one has actually presented a single such number or revealed the mathematics that would produce it. (Ω provokes numerous important scientific debates, such as the existence of fundamental [quantum] randomness; see Cope 2005, chapter 4; Chaitin 2005, 201–203).

In summation, then, AIT seeks to compress strings of numerical information to their smallest possible size by using symbols to represent repeating numbers or patterns of numbers. Thus, a sequence such as 2, 4, 5, 7, 8, 2, 4, 5, 7, 8 could reduce to 24578r, where "r" represents the repeating sequence of numbers. The information content of this simple string of ten numbers would thus equate to 0.6 or 60 percent, because 24578r is six symbols, rather than the ten symbols used in the original sequence.

Note that using symbols in the manner just described, though suited for discovering musical information content, does not follow precisely AIT binary compression processes. For example, symbols can often contain nearly as much physical

a.
```
oooooooooooooooo*oooooooooooooooo
oooooooooooooooo***ooooooooooooooo
ooooooooooooooo*o*o*ooooooooooooo
oooooooooooooo**o*o**oooooooooooo
ooooooooooooo*ooo*ooo*ooooooooooo
oooooooooooo***o***o***oooooooooo
ooooooooooo*o*ooo*ooo*o*ooooooooo
oooooooooo**o**o***o**o**oooooooo
ooooooooo*ooooooo*ooooooo*ooooooo
oooooooo***ooooo***ooooo***oooooo
ooooooo*o*o*ooo*o*o*ooo*o*o*oooooo
oooooo**o*o**o**o*o**o**o*o**ooooo
ooooo*ooo*ooooooo*ooooooo*ooo*oooo
oooo***o***ooooo***ooooo***o***ooo
ooo*o*ooo*o*ooo*o*o*ooo*o*ooo*o*oo
oo**o**o**o**o*o*o**o**o**o**o**o
oooooooooooooooo*oooooooooooooooo
oooooooooooooooo***ooooooooooooooo
ooooooooooooooo*o*o*ooooooooooooo
oooooooooooooo**o*o**oooooooooooo
ooooooooooooo*ooo*ooo*ooooooooooo
oooooooooooo***o***o***oooooooooo
ooooooooooo*o*ooo*ooo*o*ooooooooo
oooooooooo**o**o***o**o**oooooooo
ooooooooo*ooooooo*ooooooo*ooooooo
oooooooo***ooooo***ooooo***oooooo
ooooooo*o*o*ooo*o*o*ooo*o*o*oooooo
oooooo**o*o**o**o*o**o**o*o**ooooo
ooooo*ooo*ooooooo*ooooooo*ooo*oooo
oooo***o***ooooo***ooooo***o***ooo
```

b.

FIGURE 2.4 Cellular automata output generated by the code in the text.

data as the data they represent, causing little actual compression (e.g., five-character symbols replacing five-digit patterns hardly reduce number strings in terms of actual size). Therefore, the process described above is not so much intended to reduce size significantly, but to direct us toward information content.

An important component of AIT is that the files compressed must be "lossless," that is, they must be restorable (by reverse processing) to their precise original form. This principle—the recovery of exactly the data compressed—is essential to the AIT process described in this chapter. Were it not for this reverse engineerability, compression would not require such rigorous techniques, and our resultant information-content percentages would be suspect. The function called `compression` described later in this chapter makes restoration possible by having the symbols that represent musical repetitions and patterns contain instructions that allow restoration. This regenerative ability is a key element of AIT processes, and although only the Comparison program has that capability, the Multigraph program—both described later in this chapter—lacks it simply so that the information can be read into physical graphs for visual presentation. As one might imagine, the more complex the music, the more difficult full regeneration—pitch, duration, dynamics, articulation, metrical positioning, and so on—becomes. Unlike text, or pixels in a digital photograph, each parameter of music alters the other related parameters in ways that make compression very difficult. As we shall soon see, separating these musical elements from one another allows for more flexibility in the AIT process.

MUSICAL ALGORITHMIC INFORMATION THEORY

Algorithmic information theory did not reach a level of interest or success comparable to that achieved in the early years of computer music analysis by information theory. However, there have been several somewhat inadvertent uses of musical algorithmic information theory. For example, MIDI presents an interesting example of compression. Compared to complex notation program files, MIDI produces accurate results with a fraction of the storage space required. However, MIDI also loses a significant amount of information owing to its score representation approach (see Selfridge-Field 1997b).

Musical algorithmic information theory involves specialized processes. What appear to the eye and ear of a musician as obviously related motives will not easily submit to standard AIT compression. Thus, musical AIT as I define it here incorporates several forms of musical variation that help reduce strings of numbers to much smaller amounts of information than traditional mathematical compression could. For example, in music, the number string "2 4 5 7 3 5 6 8" can be reduced to "2 4 5 7 t1," where "t" means "transpose" and "1" signifies that adding 1 to each of the first set of four numbers creates the second set of four numbers. This process effectively reduces otherwise apparently non-reducible strings. Retrogrades, inversions, inversion retrogrades, and all their possible transpositions represent yet further information algorithms that, though not typically used to reduce strings in AIT, have appeared in music for centuries. The terms *inversion*, *retrograde*, and *inversion retrograde* mean precisely what the words signify. Inversion indicates that the pattern appears inverted (upside down). Figure 2.5b presents an example of inversion in musical notation, the inversion of Figure 2.5a. Figure 2.5c shows an example of retrograde (backward), and Figure 2.5d shows retrograde inversion (backward and upside down). These variation types have been used for centuries in Western classical music. However, the manner in which they are presented here results from Arnold Schoenberg's groundbreaking work with serial music in the early twentieth century.

In order to reveal all of the possible transpositions of the inversion, retrograde, and inversion retrograde, Figure 2.6 presents two matrixes of these types of musical variations and their transpositions of the four-note motive of Figure 2.5. Figure 2.6a lists the original motive and all of its eleven transpositions from left to right, along with their retrogrades from right to left. Figure 2.6b lists the inversion of the original motive and all of its eleven transpositions from left to right, along with their retrogrades from right to left. Typically, motives and variations such as these are referenced by "P" for prime (the original motive), "I" for inversion, "R" for retrograde, and "RI" for retrograde inversion.

Figure 2.6 requires slightly more explanation, for the entries appear in what are called their pitch-class form. Pitch classes—as discussed in more detail in Chapters 3 and 4—are pitches devoid of their register, or 0 through 11 (in this case 10 and 11 are represented by "t" and "e" respectively). In effect, pitch class states that all Cs (0) belong to the same pitch class regardless of the register (octave) in which they appear in music. Using pitch classes instead of pitches or numbers that include octaves makes a matrix like that in Figure 2.6 much easier to read.

Another important kind of musical variation occurs often in tonal music, where, for example, a simple downward scale can appear beginning on different pitches, thus producing different arrangements of whole and half steps. Such tonal variations of simple motives require that a pattern matcher recognize similarities between like-designed motives that vary not only by transposition but by locations of internal half steps. Figure 2.7 provides a simple example of such relationships. In this figure, the downward scale appears three times in sequence, with the location of the half step sliding to the left by one interval on each recurrence. Clearly such a

FIGURE 2.5 Examples of retrograde (b), inversion (c), and retrograde inversion (d) of a motive (a).

64   HIDDEN STRUCTURE

a.

0	5	3	2
1	6	4	3
2	7	5	4
3	8	6	5
4	9	7	6
5	t	8	7
6	e	9	8
7	0	t	9
8	1	e	t
9	2	0	e
t	3	1	0
e	4	2	1

b.

0	7	9	t
1	8	t	e
2	9	e	0
3	t	0	1
4	e	1	2
5	0	2	3
6	1	3	4
7	2	4	5
8	3	5	6
9	4	6	7
t	5	7	8
e	6	8	9

FIGURE 2.6 Two matrixes of the four-note motive of Figure 2.5. The first matrix provides the motive and its eleven transpositions (down from right to left) along with its retrograde and its eleven transpositions (read right to left). The second matrix provides the inversion and its eleven transpositions along with its retrograde inversion and its eleven transpositions.

FIGURE 2.7 A simple downward scale beginning on different pitches, thus producing different arrangements of whole and half steps.

presentation to the ear would sound like a statement and two tonally transposed repetitions. To a computer program unaware of such tonal musical forms, however, the sequence would appear as twelve incompressible notes. Therefore, the code provided with this book on CD-ROM contains a series of functions that take into account such tonal variations.

There are many other ways in which musical motives can be varied and yet retain a representable connection to the original (or "prime") upon which it is modeled. For example, interpolated pitches, excised pitches, and raised or lowered pitches can all give further opportunities for algorithmic compression. Although such variations may be more difficult to represent and regenerate than simple inversion, retrograde, and so on, they nonetheless provide compression possibilities that most nonmusical approaches do not offer. This is the essence and value of what I term MAIT.

The information content of a musical work—the part that cannot be further reduced—consists of material that does not repeat sufficiently, exactly, or in recognizable variation, such that a symbol can replace it to compress that passage. In effect, the higher the information content of music, the more it tends toward the random (chaotic); conversely, the lower the information content, the more the music tends toward organized repetition and variation (order). Such observations might tend to suggest that lower-information-content music is more developed and well formed, while higher-information-content music is more erratic and disorganized. These comments, of course, further suggest that better music has lower information content and vice versa. However, making such distinctions implies aesthetic rather than objective values. What information content in music identifies for analysts is how that music relates to other music by the same composer, the music of other composers, the style of the time, the form of the music, and many other features soon to be discussed. Information content in music does not imply aesthetic value, although, arguably, it might contribute to personal aesthetic evaluations.

My use of Musical AIT began in 2003, when I first utilized an algorithm to discover the information content of works by such diverse composers as Bach (eighteenth century) and Webern (twentieth century) in order to see if outwardly contrasting styles might be comparable in terms of their algorithmic information content. This research revealed that several composers of different centuries, whose styles differ significantly, have more-similar information contents than many composers of similar styles of the same century. Making such comparisons may indicate that like-information-content works have more in common than one might initially imagine. What that in-commonness is, of course, remains to be seen.

For example, the information contents of various segments of works by J. S. Bach (0.51), Mozart (0.45), Beethoven (0.50), Brahms (0.64), Webern (0.88), Ernst Krenek (0.87), and David Cope (0.63), determined using a very simple compression scheme, demonstrate interesting apparent contradictions, with Brahms closer to Cope than to Beethoven, and Bach closer to Beethoven than to Mozart. Of course, most of the information figures here are expected. The Bach, Beethoven, and Mozart examples have relatively low information content, and Brahms, Cope, Krenek, and Webern have relatively high information content, covering a range of 0.45 to 0.88 overall. These numbers result from analyzing brief monophonic samplings of the music only (i.e., a short melodic phrase typical of the composer's work; see Figure 2.8), chosen in order that all of the music appear here rather than

FIGURE 2.8 Brief monophonic samplings of music by (a) J. S. Bach, Suite no. 1 in G Major for Violoncello Solo (1720), Minuet, mm. 1–8; (b) W. A. Mozart, Symphony no. 40 in G Minor, K. 550 (1788), 1st movement, mm. 1–5; (c) Ludwig van Beethoven, Symphony no. 5, op. 67 (1808), 1st movement, mm. 1–5.

just referencing larger works which, interestingly, remain relatively faithful to these information-content results.

Musical segments and works also retain individuality. For example, it is noteworthy that each musical work has its own information signature. That is, no two works contain precisely the same amount of information. Thus, one could, for example, identify entire works by their MAIT information content. Determining the information content of a musical work can also identify many other of its important aspects. For example, comparing levels of information between two works can help determine the general style of the music. Minimalism, for example, often produces

FIGURE 2.8 continued
(d) Johannes Brahms, Symphony no. 1, op. 68 (1876), 4th movement, mm. 30–38; (e) Anton Webern, Variations for Piano, op. 27 (1936), 2nd movement, mm. 1–4; (f) Ernst Krenek, Suite for Violoncello, op. 84 (1939), 1st movement, mm. 1–4; (g) The author, Three Pieces for Solo Clarinet(1965), 1st movement, mm. 1–3.

a low level of information, while indeterminism generally contains a high level of information. Most music, of course, falls between these two extremes; music with subtle variations is lower in information, and music containing surprising contrasts is higher in information.

Interestingly, information in MAIT consists of two general types. The first contains data that occurs repeatedly in various forms throughout the remainder of the work being analyzed, as previously discussed. The second contains data unique to its single appearance in a work. To differentiate these two types of information requires a program that can mark the two types in some way. Here, I use a very simple number that precedes the actual patterns that vary (type 1) and thus serves two purposes: marking the repeating patterns and informing analysts of the number of occurrences found in one form or another. Unique information (type 2) poses some very interesting questions. First, what overall role does unique information play in a work of music? Second, is unique information locationally sensitive, and if so, does it serve particular musical purposes (e.g., cadences, phrase initiations, etc.)? Third, what percentage does each type of information occupy? Even broader questions such as "Why does such information even exist in a work?" seem appropriate. My initial studies of these two types of information have produced quite interesting results: Webern and Bach, for example, have virtually no unique information, while Beethoven and Brahms have significant amounts. Unfortunately, these results are preliminary and incomplete, and I shall leave it to others to discover whether such interesting relationships exist.

Furthermore, and what is possibly more important, examining the information and redundancy portions of data more closely can prove quite rewarding. Analyzing music for its inherent structure typically means stripping away music that is structurally less important in order to reveal the more significant structural material. Because it would seem natural for variations to develop from source material rather than vice versa, removing redundancy to reveal musical sources seems a logical analytical process for music. MAIT accomplishes exactly this because it uses the most effective algorithm possible for compression of music. For example, Figure 2.10 presents a simple example of Figure 2.9's music with all of the redundant information removed from the score. Although clearly this smattering of music does not equate to, say, the kind of structural analysis described by Heinrich Schenker (Schenker 1979), the pitches here do offer quite interesting and revealing views of the non-redundant data present in the work they represent. Note that most of the music remaining in Figure 2.10 appears near the beginning of the work. This is typical for such representations because motive originals occur before their variations. Only motives that originate late in a work or non-varied note-events unrelated to motive originals appear later in these reduced representations.

Traditional music analysis—including post-tonal analysis—does not require restoration, as does MAIT. In fact, if music analysis required the same lossless regenerative abilities as MAIT, music analysis—even tonal music analysis—would look very different than it does today. It is worth keeping this in mind when evaluating

FIGURE 2.9 Bartók, *Mikrokosmos*, no. 81.

FIGURE 2.10 AIT structural analysis of the music presented in Figure 2.9.

the results of music compression. Without reverse-engineering capability, music analysis could take a wide variety of speculative forms that would stand only the scrutiny of logic, not the absolute value of accurate accountability to the original form from which it derives.

Thus far in this chapter, we have concentrated our analytical methods on MAIT, which provides us the ability to compare music of radically different styles in possibly useful ways. Although this comparison can prove useful for some analytical processes, most analysts will likely consider it superficial rather than central to serious musical analysis. I will not contest this perception because, though interesting, the process has yet to prove valuable in realistic ways for my own research. In contrast to this interesting but somewhat tangential analytical approach, I therefore now present a more meaningful use of MAIT called Dynamic Musical AIT (DMAIT).

When I listen to music, my mind's ear shifts from one musical parameter to another. Melody, harmony, dynamics, timbre, rhythm, and other parameters all jostle for my attention, with each prevailing at one time or another. When analyzing a work, however, I find myself concentrating on just harmony, just form, and so on, rather than allowing my analysis to shift in focus as my listening does. There are probably many reasons I isolate one aspect of the music in this way. Primarily this single-mindedness is due to my not having an easy method of analytically deciding when, where, and how to represent my shift of focus.

Algorithmic information theory often yields quite convincing reasons why my focus shifts when I simply listen to the work I am also analyzing. By indicating the parameter—pitch, rhythm, meter, and so on—that offers the most information at any given point in a work, MAIT can provide distinct points where the priority of information shifts from one musical parameter to another. This ability of DMAIT to clearly indicate the points where one might move one's attention from listening to one aspect of the music to another could therefore have significant value.

I know of no empirical data to verify my contention, however. Rather than develop this subject—more rightfully belonging to the field of music cognition—I will restrict my comments here to the analytical implications of this process. I will concentrate on the interplay of information and redundancy between several, but not all, musical parameters that suggests an analysis of any one parameter alone cannot sufficiently address the true implications of the music.

The following DMAIT approach to analysis therefore incorporates and integrates running commentaries on aspects of pitch, rhythm, meter, timbre, dynamics, and other related parameters in an attempt to understand the full import of a musical work. Breaking information into parameters in this way can reveal a great deal about a work as it develops over time. Such analyses can often agree with more traditional analyses and at times disagree with them, providing interesting new insights into the music.

DMAIT systematically refigures MAIT for several musical parameters simultaneously. For instance, information content for pitch and rhythm computed anew from the beginning of a composition for each added beat provides a continuous map of both their individual information levels and their interplay over time. Using such processes reveals which parameter might produce the most useful analytical results at any particular point in time. As well, dynamically plotting the information content of several parameters of music at once can yield many insights into form, structure, and other aspects of a musical work or passage. Figure 2.11 provides a simple graph showing the pitch (register), rhythm (meter), dynamics (articulation), and texture (timbre) of a work by Brahms, presented in standard notation at the top of the figure. The parenthetical comments after each parameter above represent associated but not incorporated parameters that figure to one degree or another into the analytical process.

The graph in Figure 2.11 also represents a kind of DMAIT fingerprint possibly identifying the work and, to some extent, indicating the composer of that work (if not already known). Although graphs of some works may appear similar, in fact every work produces a unique DMAIT fingerprint, especially when reading the floating-point numbers that produce the graph. Even two or three vertical slices of such graphs demonstrate their individuality in terms of information content (or redundancy, depending on your point of view).

Note that the graph in Figure 2.11 shows all four parameters initiating at the highest points of information content—consistent in all such graphs because redundancy cannot exist without preceding information. Interestingly, each musical parameter here tends to eventually flatline into either horizontal or slightly rising or falling lines. This flatlining results from the fact that so much data has been collected that new information is scarce and has little impact. To avoid this flatlining in longer works, I employ a moving DMAIT aperture of several beats preceding the already calculated information content, rather than recomputing information continually from the very beginning of the work. This produces more distinctive active lines that rarely settle into invariant configurations. Such apertures can lead to somewhat misleading graphs when attempting to use DMAIT for formal and structural analysis.

Choosing intervals over pitches or vice versa in DMAIT is not a trivial decision. Pitches provide important information about chromaticism in tonal music. DMAIT will spike at each secondary chromaticism and ascend with modulation. Post-tonal music typically rotates so quickly through the twelve pitches of the chromatic scale that information often remains high. Using intervals, on the other hand, provides more insight into post-tonal music, informing analysts more directly about the structure of the music. Figure 2.12 presents pitches reduced to intervals for pattern matching. Note that the information here appears quite different than its pitch counterpart.

A chromatic scale presents an excellent and simple example of the differences between using pitch and interval when calculating information content in music. From the perspective of pitches, a chromatic scale—with no repeating pitches—represents a consistently high level of information. From the perspective of intervals,

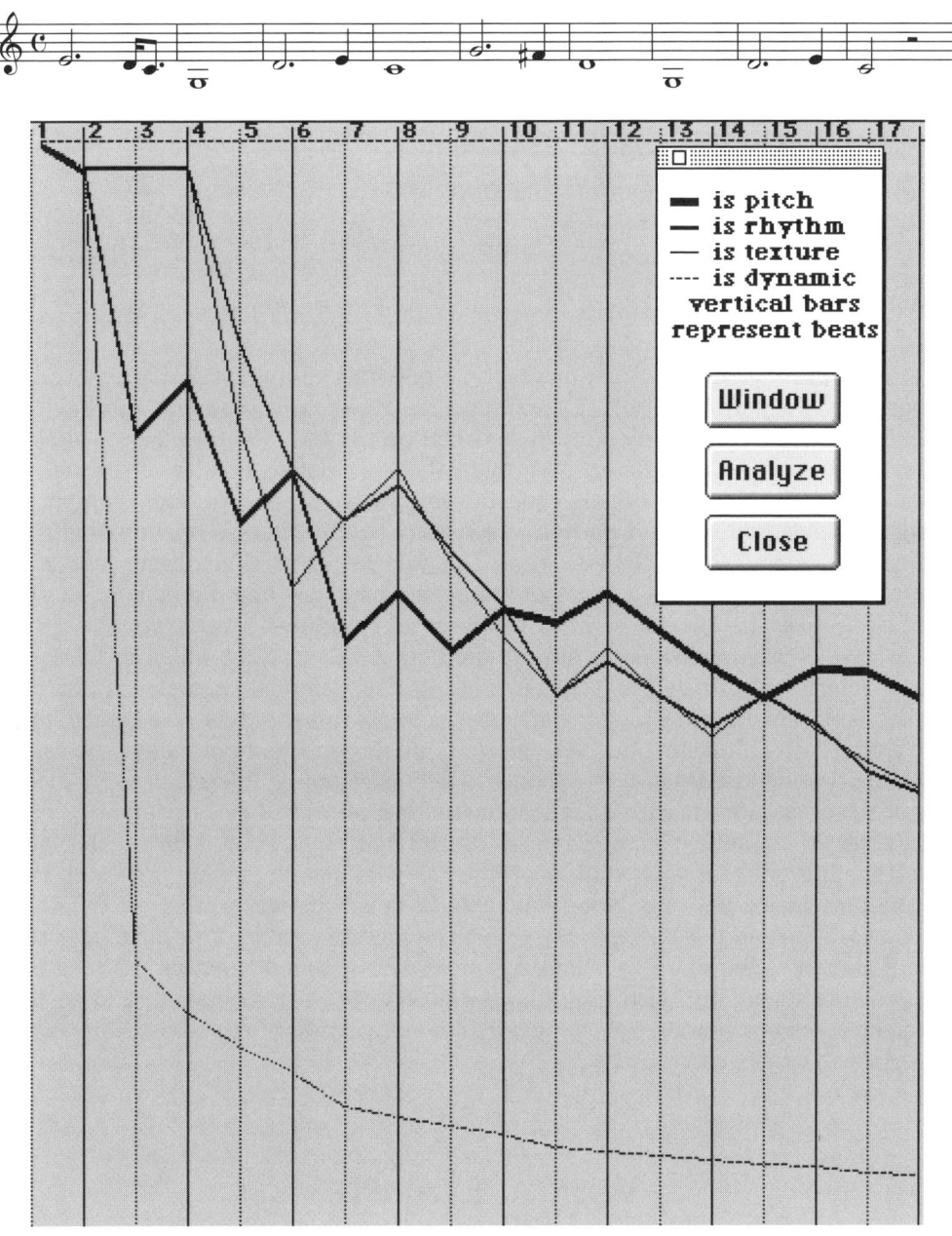

FIGURE 2.11 A simple graph showing four parameters of a melody by Brahms (presented at the top of the figure).

FIGURE 2.12 Pitches reduced to intervals for pattern matching.

however, a chromatic scale—containing only one interval type, the minor second—represents a very low level of information. Thus, data representation can have significant impact on the derivation of information content. Neither view—pitch or interval—is correct or incorrect. However, the contrasting results of the two approaches requires that one gauge the output within its appropriate context and choose the best approach for particular genres (e.g., tonal versus post-tonal music).

Figure 2.13 presents a DMAIT reduction of Bartók's *Mikrokosmos* no. 81 of Figure 2.9. The vertical lines represent larger-than-a-beat time increments to allow complete works to appear in full on a typical computer screen. As this graph shows, DMAIT accomplishes far more than just revealing which musical dimension is particularly emphasized at a given time; it also demonstrates aspects of form (spikes with slow diminishment, particularly in rhythm), points of arrival (spikes with little or no diminishment, particularly in pitch), and hints of many musical developments such as variation or changes in accompaniment figures.

For those keeping track of Lisp code to this point, I have included a single change to the variable `*horizontals*` in the code file "Piano Roll" in the folder called "multigraph" for this chapter on the CD-ROM accompanying this book to alter the time increment size. Note that I use the Lisp macro `defvar` to define initially a variable and the Lisp macro `setq` to change a variable. This is an important differentiation: attempting to change a previously defined variable with `defvar` will prove unsuccessful. Also note that data presented between a #| and a |# is considered documentation in Lisp, just like data following a semicolon. None of this material will be evaluated by Lisp.

MUSICAL EXAMPLES

The Multigraph program (described in more detail in the next section of this chapter) produces output like that shown in Figure 2.14 for the beginning of Stravinsky's Three Pieces for String Quartet (1914) and confirms what those who know this

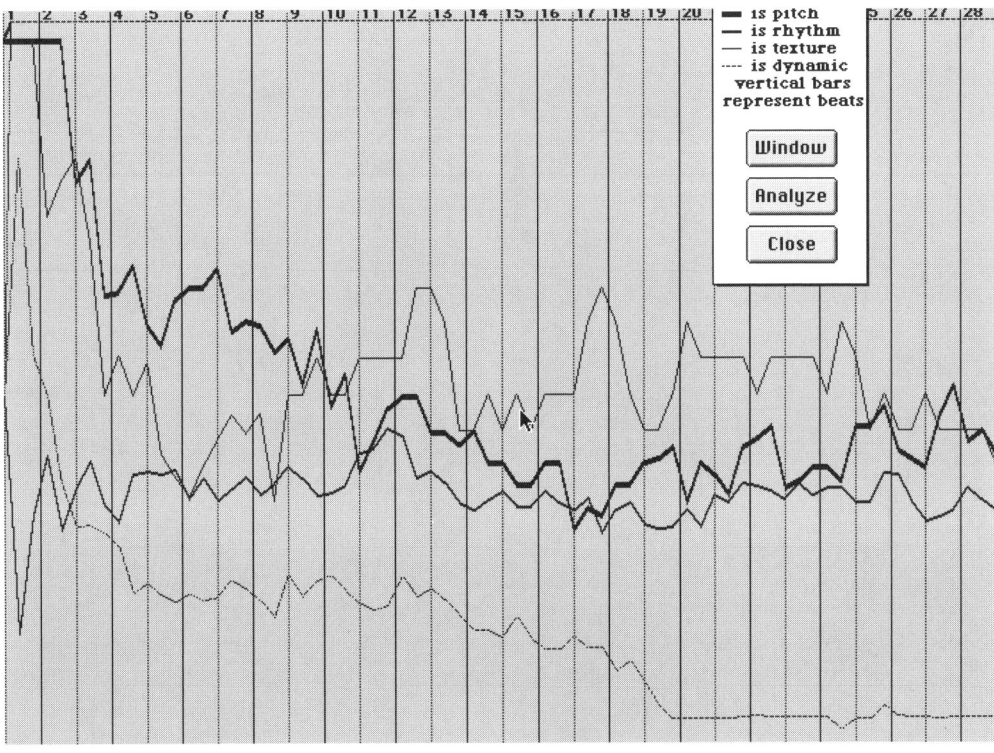

FIGURE 2.13 Bartók, *Mikrokosmos*, no. 81, from Figure 2.9, in a Dynamic Musical AIT graph.

work might well anticipate—information resides primarily in pitch, with texture, dynamics, and rhythm quickly leveling to nearly zero information content. Although these observations may be predictable, the spikes in the pitch information represent useful indications of the manner in which new material is introduced in this work when the surface of the music seems otherwise highly repetitious.

When I first began using AIT, it provided a useful though certainly not comprehensive tool for gauging the stylistic authenticity of works created by my program Experiments in Musical Intelligence. In other words, comparing the AIT analyses of a work produced by Experiments in Musical Intelligence with one from the music in a database by the composer being emulated offered an interesting way to evaluate style effectiveness. Such comparisons, although not explicitly involving the intervals, harmonies, rhythms, and so on of the two works, ascertain the overall consistency of the information flow.

As an example, the following two mazurkas in the style of Chopin represent the computational and the human-created works involved in one such comparison.

76　HIDDEN STRUCTURE

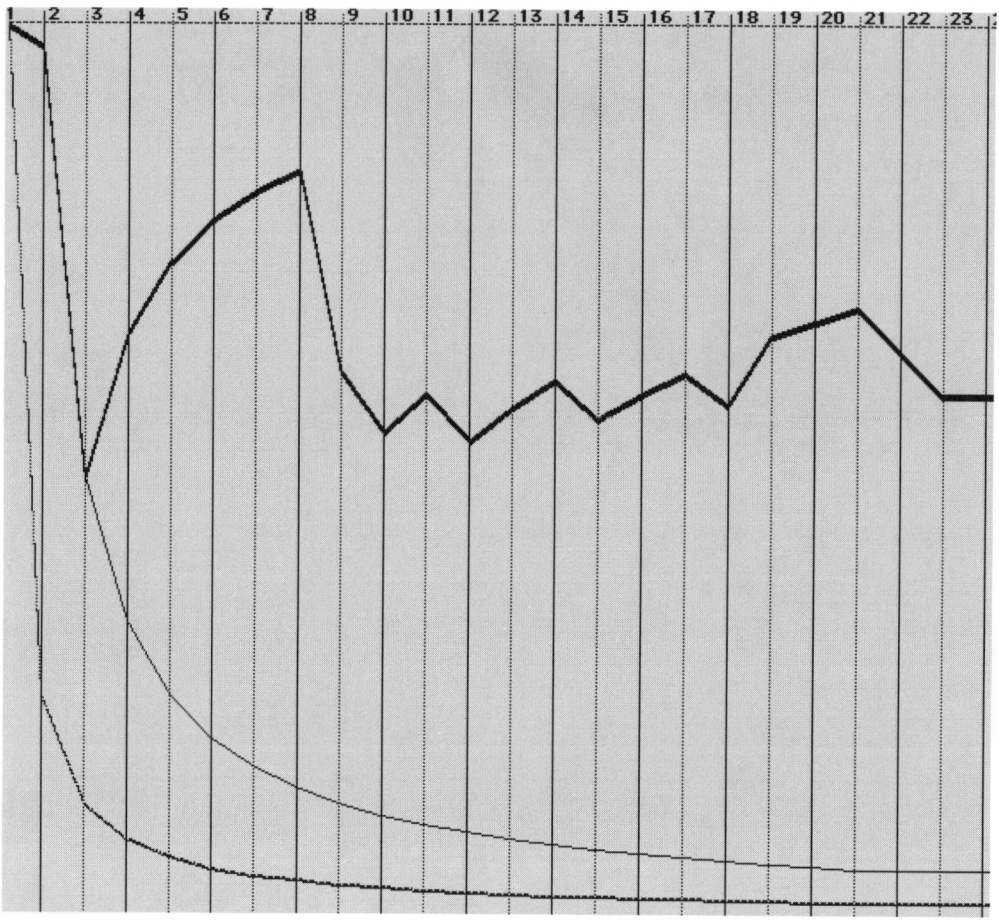

FIGURE 2.14 Multigraph output for the beginning of Stravinsky, Three Pieces for String Quartet (1914), shown in Figure 1.19.

Figure 2.15 presents these two mazurkas in full. Note that the latter Chopin mazurka was not present in the Experiments in Musical Intelligence database during the composition of its own mazurka. I make this clear at this point so that readers will understand that the similarity in information content of the two works did not result from their inclusion in the computer program's output of one of the models upon which it was based. Both works are presented here in like manner; that is, neither piece has dynamics or articulation, and neither was performed in the MIDI file that produced the data. However, in order to make the comparison more logical, both pieces are of roughly the same length.

FIGURE 2.15 Two mazurkas in the style of Chopin for analytical comparison.

FIGURE 2.15 continued

LISP, ALGORITHMIC INFORMATION THEORY, AND MUSIC 79

FIGURE 2.15 continued

FIGURE 2.15 continued

FIGURE 2.15 continued

FIGURE 2.15 continued

Figure 2.16 presents the two DMAIT graphs representing these two mazurkas, with each graph roughly matching the other. The two graphs certainly differ, as would be expected, because any two works will have somewhat differing information identities. However, the contours of both works' analyses—the important characteristic—resemble one another quite closely.

Because DMAIT measures only the flow of information resulting from repetition, variation, and contrast, the mazurka form (especially given the brevity of both of the works in Figure 2.15 and their lack of explicit repetition) is not responsible for the similar shapes of information content in the two graphs. Nor can one count too heavily on the similarity of the characteristic rhythms of the right hand, factors that result from the Experiments in Musical Intelligence recombinant mode of composition (see Cope 2001). Thus, the information in the graphs results from the flow of musical ideas and the rate at which these ideas develop as each piece progresses through time. Because information content does not constitute a part of the Experiments in Musical Intelligence's mode of operation, one can only surmise that the highly similar information-content contours occur as a direct by-product of the process of composition. The similarity of the two graphs validates the relative authenticity of the output of Experiments in Musical Intelligence.

Were such parallel comparisons rare between the human-composed works and replications produced by Experiments in Musical Intelligence, this similarity between the two mazurkas might be considered coincidental. However, I have made such analyses time and again with roughly comparable results. Such comparisons lead me to conclude that Emmy's process of composition does not differ significantly from that of human composers (see Cope 2005, particularly chapter 12). My conclusions do not derive from observation of the information content alone (see also Cope 2001). I understand the reluctance on the part of many readers to accept this conclusion, and to some degree I share this same skepticism of the belief that humans compose by hybridizing what they have previously heard. However, the information provided here seems to indicate that they do.

To give readers an idea of how works of non-comparable information contents compare, Figure 2.17 presents a prelude by Chopin of comparable length to the two mazurkas of Figure 2.15. The contour of the graph shown in Figure 2.18 varies significantly from both of the contours presented in Figure 2.16. Remembering that although the um-pah-pah of the left hand in the mazurka and the somewhat less repetitious left-hand configuration of the prelude do not in themselves contribute much to the overall information variability, the contrast between the prelude and both mazurka analyses proves quite substantial.

Standard non-musical algorithmic information theory typically compresses binary data to binary data for efficiency. Binary data uses only two numbers—0 and 1—appearing right to left in columns following successive powers of 2 but originating with 1. To read these numbers, begin from the rightmost number and count the columns as 1, 2, 4, 8, 16, 32, 64, 128, and so on, with 0 meaning to add 0 and 1 meaning to add that the column's number when computing the result. For example,

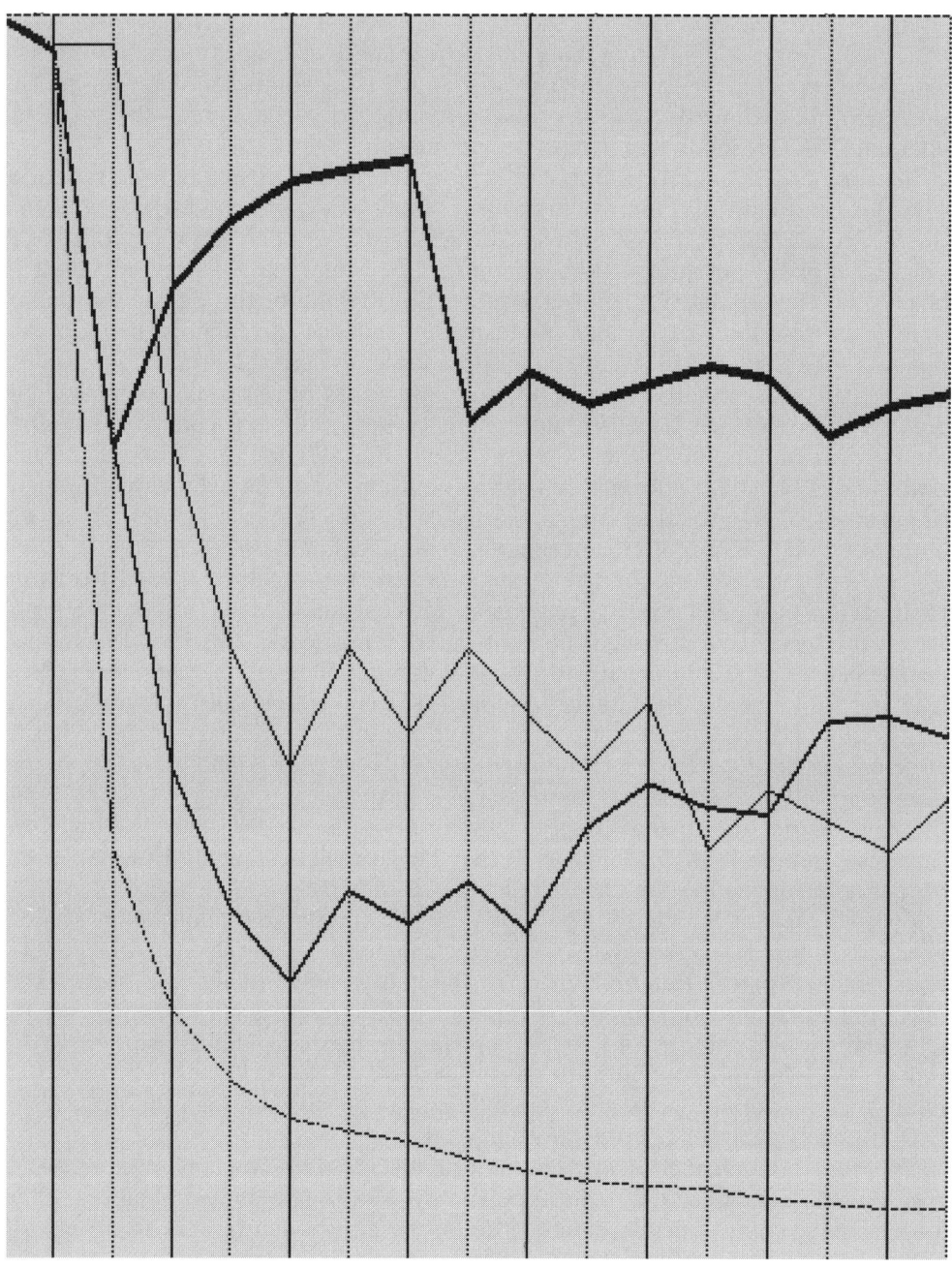

FIGURE 2.16 Two DMAIT graphs representing the Chopin mazurkas shown in Figure 2.15.

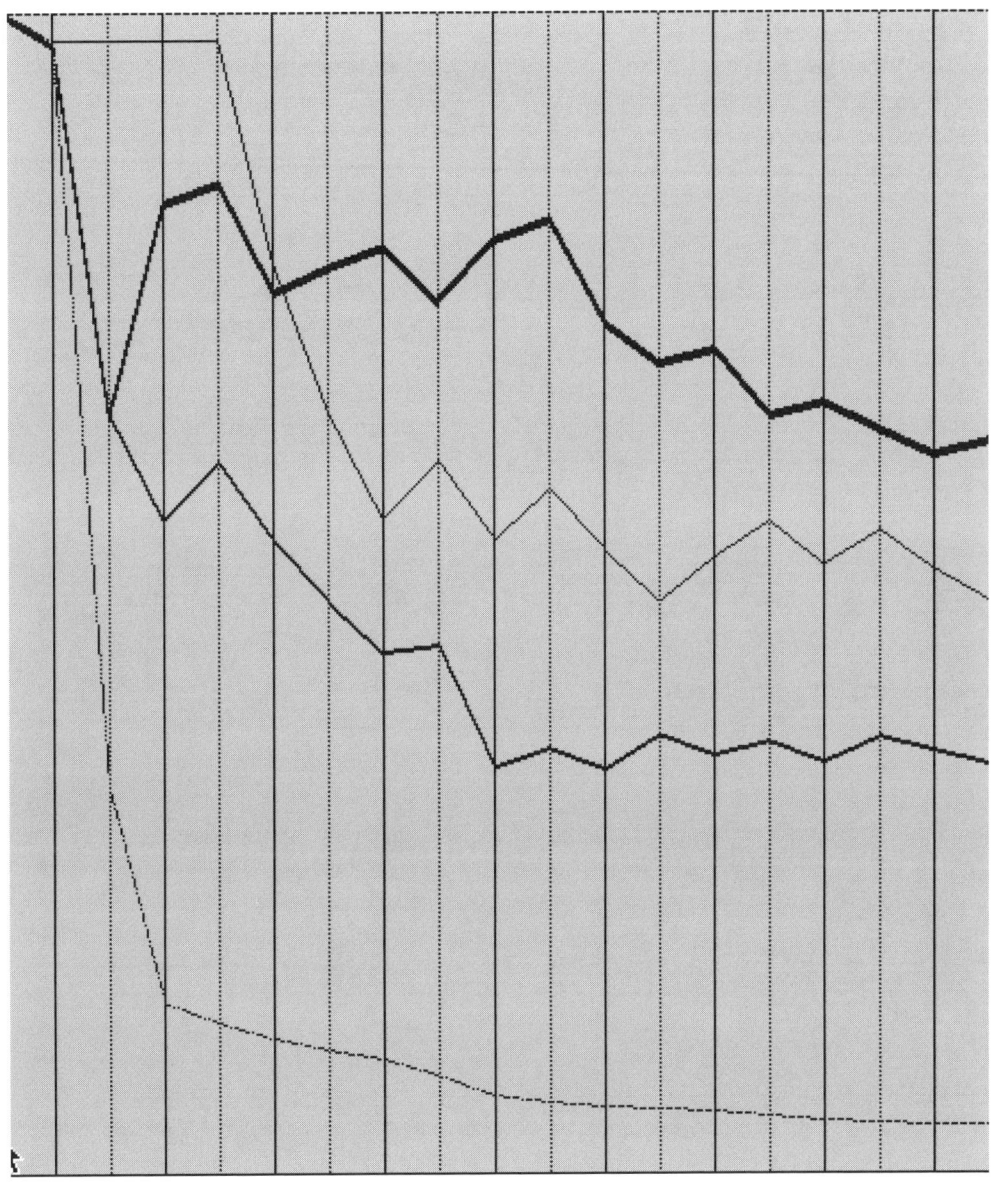

FIGURE 2.16 continued

FIGURE 2.17 A prelude by Chopin comparable in length to the pieces in Figure 2.15.

FIGURE 2.17 continued

FIGURE 2.17 continued

a byte of information—eight columns of binary data—creates the full range of decimal numbers between 0 and 128 with, for example, 0 equal to 00000000, 1 equal to 00000001, 2 equal to 00000010, 3 equal to 00000011, 128 equal to 10000000, and so on. Binary numbers can be added, subtracted, multiplied, and otherwise operated on, just as decimal numbers can.

I have avoided using binary data here for two reasons. First, binary data requires a fluency in reading that most readers do not possess. Second, and possibly more important, this ability to read binary data becomes particularly important when actually viewing the compressed data as described earlier in this chapter. In fact, when analyzing music using MAIT, I represent pitches as note-events rather than just pitch numbers. My reasons are simple: note-events incorporate location, duration, and other qualities that inform analysis more usefully than do either pitch or binary pitch information alone.

For example, the following data provides very useful details about the type and location of the compressed information in a work.

LISP, ALGORITHMIC INFORMATION THEORY, AND MUSIC   89

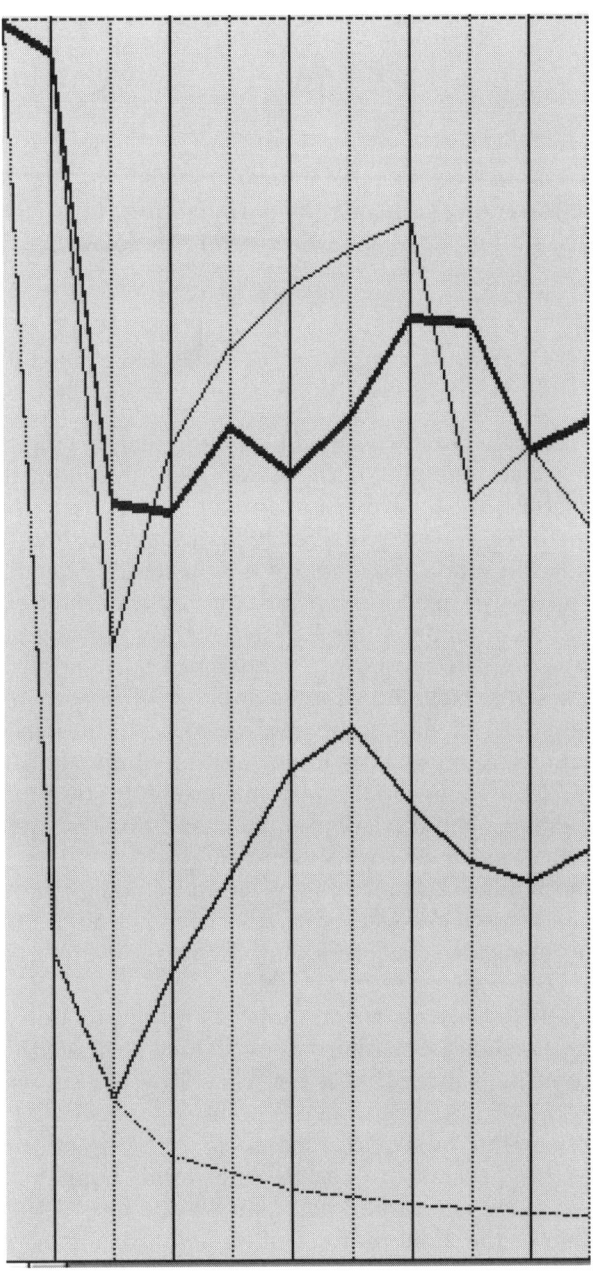

FIGURE 2.18   A Dynamic Musical Algorithmic Information Theory graph of the Chopin prelude shown in Figure 2.17.

```
((0 60 1000 1 127)(1000 72 1000 1 127)(2000 71 1000 1 127)
 (4000 72 1000 1 127)(5000 67 1000 1 127)(6000 76 1000 1
   127)
 (7000 74 1000 1 127) T6 T4 TI6 TR4 T0)
```

This forty-two-note passage poses its information only at the outset, with all remaining entries representing transpositions, transposed inversions, or retrogrades of the original pitch patterns. On the other hand, the following brief nineteen-note passage

```
((0 60 1000 1 127)(1000 72 1000 1 127)(2000 71 1000 1 127)
 T2 T3 R6 T4 (15000 72 1000 1 127)(16000 71 1000 1 127)
 (17000 67 1000 1 127)(18000 74 1000 1 127))
```

concludes with a completely new motivic idea after several simple variations of the initial one. Reading even complex compressed files presented in this manner for their information content can prove enlightening in matters of form, structure, melodic invention, and so on. Only note-events, or a similar notation standard such as MIDI, can provide this kind of readable and interpretable detail.

Interestingly, I have also used Multigraph, the program that created the preceding analyses, in my own compositional processes. By viewing graphs of an unfinished work I am able to gain important insights into how various parameters of my work-in-progress presents itself and as a result either change aspects of the composition thus far composed or alter my views as to how the music should proceed from that point onward. Analysis is as important for composers as it is for analysts, and it seems to me these tools should be considered from both points of view.

I have kept the examples in this chapter short and thin-textured in order to facilitate easier understanding of the processes described. Readers should be able to follow the code on the CD-ROM more easily without complex harmony and counterpoint confusing the issue. However, with several small alterations, this code will function using any musical parameters and can analyze quite complex post-tonal music with basic AIT processes.

Interestingly, John Pierce, one of the pioneers of information theory, asked and then answered the question Does information theory have anything concrete to offer concerning the arts? "I think that it has very little of serious value to offer except a point of view, but I believe that the point of view may be worth exploring" (Pierce 1980, 253). For the most part, Pierce was referring here to composing, not analysis. However, his pessimism seemed even more pointed later in this same source: "Perhaps in some age of bad art, man will be forced to [make] stochastic art as an alternative to the stale product of human artisans. So much for information theory and art" (Pierce 1980, 267). Although I understand Pierce's point of view, I must respectfully disagree with these comments. The amount of information that a work of art possesses seems quite important, for it relates to the amount of information contained in other works by the same composers, or in works by other composers in the same style. Dynamically gauging the information content of a time-based work of art such as music as it releases that information seems particularly important.

However, AIT also produces more questions than it answers. For example:

1. What role do rests (silences) play in music information (currently, note-events do not represent rests)?
2. How does DMAIT shed light on first, second, and subsequent hearings, where multiple listenings resist surprise?
3. How do note ontimes figure into algorithmic information theory, given that no two note-events in performed music can occur at precisely the same time when ontimes figure into the compression model?
4. Does DMAIT truly provide a formal or structural model of a piece of music? Would anyone suggest, for example, that removing redundant material from a printed musical score could rival a Schenkerian analysis in revealing fundamental structure?
5. Do certain compression profiles for music relate in some way to what we feel are masterworks?

Although certainly a valuable tool in analyzing music—particularly in its dynamic form of representation, as described in this chapter—algorithmic information theory falls short of providing the kind of deeply meaningful analysis that music analysts seek. The unbiased but also often unmusical approach that algorithmic information theory takes requires more musical detail in both its processes and its analyses than I have included here. The analytical approaches in the chapters to come will hopefully provide more of this kind of musical detail.

PROGRAM DESCRIPTION

Before describing the programs accompanying this book on CD-ROM, I think important to demonstrate how pattern matching—the core of information theory—works, and particularly how it can work in Lisp. As an example, the following Lisp code pattern matches two equal-length lists of pitches against one another according to prime, retrograde, inversion, and retrograde inversion forms, as well as all twelve transpositions for each form. Note how the process here divides into three separate functions (`get-intervals-from-pitches`, `compare-interval-lists`, and `reverse-sign`) that are then combined in ways that make the top-level function (`pattern-match`) quite powerful. Note that Common Lisp allows for document strings (in "") after the declaration of argument variables. These document strings can be retrieved and help someone reading the code for the first time to understand its purpose. The function `or` (in `compare-interval-lists`) represents a Boolean query that returns t if any one of its arguments (arbitrary number) is true.

```
(defun pattern-match (pitch-list-1 pitch-list-2)
  "Determines whether two pitch-lists are equal in one of 48
   ways."
  (compare-interval-lists (get-intervals-from-pitches
                             pitch-list-1)
                          (get-intervals-from-pitches
                             pitch-list-2)))
(defun get-intervals-from-pitches (pitch-list)
  "Returns intervals from its pitch-list argument."
  (if (null (rest pitch-list)) ()
    (cons (- (second pitch-list)(first pitch-list))
          (get-intervals-from-pitches (rest pitch-list)))))
(defun compare-interval-lists (list-1 list-2)
  "Compares by retrograde, inversion, and retrograde inversion."
  (if (or (equal list-1 list-2)
          (equal (reverse list-1) list-2)
          (equal (reverse-sign list-1) list-2)
          (equal (reverse (reverse-sign list-1)) list-2))
      t))
(defun reverse-sign (number-list)
  "Turns intervals upside down."
  (if (null number-list)()
    (cons (* (first number-list) -1)
          (reverse-sign (rest number-list)))))
```

Running the following argument lists with `pattern-matching` will return `t` for prime transposition

'(60 62 64 62) '(62 64 66 64) ;

for retrograde

'(60 62 64 62) '(64 66 64 62) ;

for inversion

'(60 62 64 62) '(62 60 62 64) ;

for retrograde inversion

'(60 62 64 62) '(64 62 60 62) .

The function `get-intervals-from-pitches` first tests its argument (second function in code here) to see if the *rest* of its list argument is empty or not, rather than the usual test for whether the argument itself is empty. This variation on a theme results from the fact that the last pitch in the argument cannot be compared to a nonexistent following element for its interval. Another way to view this involves the use of `second` in the third line of actual code for `get-intervals-from-pitches`, where, with but one number remaining in the list, the call to `second` would return `nil`. Code variations such as this are often required for specialized cases.

Note that the function `pattern-match` is not very elegant in that it simply returns `t` or `nil` in comparing two equal-length arguments. A more complete search of a musical work for patterns will require further higher-level functions to collect patterns of varying lengths and compare them with the patterns of an entire work (a recursive function). Programmers must also decide whether to search note lists incrementally or contiguously. Incremental pattern matching requires that patterns begin on each new note of a work, while contiguous pattern matching requires that patterns follow one after the other with no overlapping pitches. In essence, incremental pattern matching moves the aperture one pitch at a time, whereas contiguous pattern matching moves the aperture to the note following the current pattern. Incremental pattern matching is far more thorough, but it requires more computing time than does contiguous pattern matching.

Note that Common Lisp contains a number of simple pattern matchers as default primitive functions. The function `equal`, for example, determines whether two patterns are equal or not. Functions such as `>`, `<`, and so on compare numbers to determine whether one is greater or less than the other. These functions, however, offer little more than absolute matching. In other words, they contain no forgiveness. Forgiving pattern matchers that detect inexact matches and, for example, measure pattern relations as mostly equal, partly equal, or in some other relation can be extremely useful but require more intricate code than that presented here (see Cope 1996 for examples). Such forgiving pattern matchers also must clearly designate what the variations consist of; otherwise the matching will be of relatively little value for MAIT analysis.

In order to ensure that every possible pattern is considered, the program called Compression on the CD-ROM accompanying this book collects and labels pitch patterns of length equal to, or less than, half the length of its argument incrementally down to three pitches in length. Groups of two pitches—an interval—do not constitute musical patterns worth matching. Larger patterns are matched first to avoid the necessity of separately labeling the many smaller patterns that would match within these larger patterns if they themselves match. Patterns are tested for equalness, transposition, retrograde, inversion, and inversion retrograde and for all possible transpositions of these three variations. To accomplish these matches, pitches are reduced to intervals and those intervals then matched (see Figure 2.12). Searching by intervals rather than pitches allows the matching process to capture relationships that would otherwise require several intermediate stages. Finally, in a separate stage, the program checks for repeated pitches.

Each discovered pattern match is labeled according to (1) its transposition; (2) its variation type, as in "I" for inversion, and so on; (3) the length of the pattern;

(4) and—following a slash—the position of the pattern of which it is a variation. Thus, the label

-2T4/1

represents a major second (-2) downward transposition (T) of a four-pitch pattern (4) beginning on pitch 1 (1) of the list of pitches provided as argument to the compression function. Although one might argue that this multi-component symbol itself contains so many aspects of the pattern that it does not represent a true reduction of information, I remind readers that the programs I describe here should not be measured by their capacity to compress data so much as by their ability to identify the true information content present in that data. In fact, a large sequence of numbers would reduce to a single number if the spaces were removed. Of course, this number would also be unreadable without a guide of some sort to extract each individual number. The point, however, remains that each individual member of a symbol used to represent data should be counted separately and compared to the original list in order to truly discover the compression involved. Labels such as -2T4/1 will therefore count as six rather than one member of a sequence. Of course, when dealing with very large repeating or repeating-with-variation patterns, such representations can also significantly compress data.

The compression function does not analyze for rhythm, dynamics, channel, or other parameters, in order to keep the process simple for demonstration. All symbol-designated patterns are assumed to have the same durations, with ontimes figured as immediately following the preceding pattern. Thus, the pitch pattern 60, 62, 64 (2, 2 in intervals) followed by a 4T3/1 indicates that the pitch pattern 64, 66, 68 (2, 2) follows it in order. I switch back and forth from pitches to intervals here because the actual program uses pitches as input but processes the information as intervals.

The compression function operates by command line using the format

(compression '(64 64 64 65 66 67 67 67 67))

where the term *compression* represents the compressing function and the list of numbers represents the list of pitches to be compressed. The return from such a function call, as in

(64rep3/1 65 2irt4/1 67)

indicates that the original list of nine pitches reduces to a list of four indicators—two symbols and two non-involved intervening pitches. Note that the repeating (rep) symbol begins with the repeating pitch 64. Note as well that because the repeating pitches begin in place, the place indicator reads as 1.

The compression-ratio function produces a percentage ratio of the number of pitches used as argument and the number of pitches and symbols returned. Thus, the call

(compression-ratio '(64 64 64 65 66 67 67 67 67))

returns

0.44,

that is, the ratio of returned symbols and pitches to pitches alone.

This simple AIT compressing program functions on lists of pitches of arbitrary length, typically representing solo melodic lines. Nonetheless, the program can also compress sublists of, say, pitch and channel (timbre choice), pitch and duration, and grouped pitches for harmony. Even in its pitch-alone matching state, however, the program reveals interesting aspects of information relativity between various works by composers spanning several centuries, as mentioned earlier in this chapter. For example, the music shown in Figure 2.8 provides the following output:

```
(compression-ratio (get-pitches bach))
0.5128205128205128

(compression-ratio (get-pitches beethoven))
0.5

(compression-ratio (get-pitches brahms))
0.6428571428571429

(compression-ratio (get-pitches cope))
0.625

(compression-ratio (get-pitches krenek))
0.8666666666666667

(compression-ratio (get-pitches mozart))
0.45

(compression-ratio (get-pitches webern))
0.875
```

where the Beethoven and Mozart examples have relatively low information content, Bach has moderate information content, and Brahms, Cope, Krenek, and Webern have relatively high information content, covering a range of 0.4 to 0.88 overall.

The function `get-pitches` shown above follows the same recursive process that `add-one` and `translate-into-morse-code` used:

```
(defun get-pitches (note-events)
     (if (null note-events) ()
         (cons (second (first note-events))
               (get-pitches (rest note-events)))))
```

As previously described, each note-event contains five elements: ontime, pitch, duration, channel, and loudness. Therefore, the above function could retrieve any of these elements by replacing the use of `second` in line 3 with `first`, `third`, `fourth`, or `fifth`, depending on the element desired, with the name of the function in lines 1 and 4 also changed to reflect the retrieved element (as in `get-on-times`, etc.).

The DMAIT code called Multigraph on the CD-ROM accompanying this book compresses pitch, rhythm, texture, and dynamics and presents a chart of these parameters, as shown in many figures of this Chapter and in Figure 2.19. The vertical lines in this graph indicate new entrance points for pitches in this music and not equal time increments (though horizontal distance still represents linear time). The counterpoint of the four lines here demonstrates its varying—based on all previous material presented—information content.

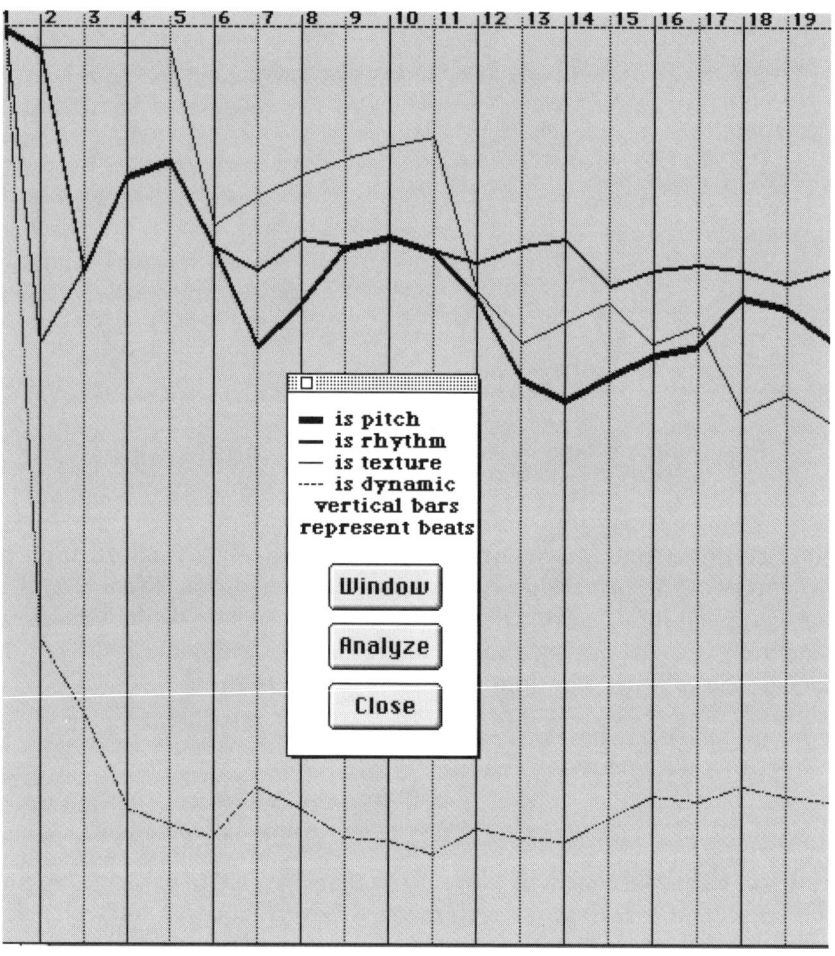

FIGURE 2.19 Sample Multigraph output.

Multigraph uses a variable that represents the largest segment of music used for determining the information content. Typically set to twenty onset points, this variable can be increased to any number desired. Because the variable determines the largest segment and the program then uses segments of successively smaller sizes down to three, the larger this variable, the longer the information determination will take. With a window of twenty the program can still take several minutes to complete its calculations, even on very fast machines. When the window is set higher, the program may require several hours to compute and graph its findings, depending on the speed of the computer's processor.

CONCLUSIONS

This chapter has concentrated on information theory—an important field in communications theory and artificial intelligence, among others—and on how, in particular, algorithmic information theory proves useful for analyzing music. In contrast, the following two chapters focus on musical set theory, a hybrid of mathematics and music. The examples given and the code shown will be more specific than those in this chapter and likely strain most non-musician's abilities to maintain their levels of understanding. I hope that the introductory material to each of these two chapters will enable those less skilled in reading and understanding music to follow the arguments with a minimum of confusion.

THREE
Register and Range in Set Analysis

> I also want to say that I did not invent the unordered pitch-class set. That was the creation of a far higher power—and I don't mean Milton Babbitt.
>
> Allen Forte, "Banquet Address: SMT, Rochester 1987" (1989), 97

This chapter begins with a brief outline of mathematical and musical set theory. Both of these representations/processes involve pattern matching, a principal focus of algorithmic information theory, discussed in Chapter 2. This chapter continues by exploring many of the important elements of music that pitch-class notation—integral to musical set theory—ignores as analysts attempt to discover their most effective reductions. The duodecimal process presented here resolves such discrepancies, and I use several works from the standard post-tonal repertory to demonstrate how it does so. Each of these processes—set theory and duodecimal notation for register inclusion—fall under Principle 1, as described at the outset of Chapter 1. The modest goals of the current chapter allow both those familiar with mathematics but unfamiliar with music, and those familiar with music but unfamiliar with mathematics, to find common ground before the book takes more adventuresome directions in Chapter 4 and beyond.

BASICS OF SET THEORY

Set theory belongs to a branch of mathematics known as *discrete* mathematics. Discrete mathematics focuses on fixed, discontinuous numbers in contrast to, for example, algebra and calculus, which cover the continuous domain of all real numbers. The study of prime numbers represents a good example of discrete mathematics in that only numbers that are divisible by themselves and 1 qualify as prime. Discrete mathematics has many branches, such as number theory, game theory, and group theory, as well as set theory.

Mathematical set theory—along with logic and predicate calculus—represents one of the axiomatic foundations of mathematics. A mathematical set is denoted by numbers enclosed in braces (curly brackets) and separated by commas, as in

{0,1,2}. Set theory relates sets in many ways. For example, the set {0,1,2} is a subset of the set {0,1,2,3,4}, in that all three members of the first set belong to the second set (common membership). The set {5,6,7} is not a subset of the set {0,1,2,3,4}, because none of the members of the first set belong to the second set. Such simple comparisons represent one of the manifold ways in which set theory relates sets according to membership.

Figure 3.1 presents several methods in which sets can be more formally compared. The notation 12 ∈ {8,10,12}, for example, indicates that 12 is a member of the set {8,10,12}. Conversely, the notation 11 ∉ {8,10,12} states that 11 does not belong to the set {8,10,12}. The notations ⊂ and ⊆ indicate two forms of subsets—sets whose members all belong to another set. A *proper* subset (⊂) refers to a range of possible subsets belonging to another set that do not include exactly and only that set itself. In contrast, the second notation for a subset here (⊆, referred to as *improper*) means that the range of possible subsets of one set *does* exactly and only include another set. The symbol ⊄, in contrast, indicates that a set is not a subset of another set. The special symbol ∅ defines the empty set {}. Two of the many operative mathematical set-theory notations, presented last in Figure 3.1, represent important relationships between two sets: ∪ indicates a *union* of two sets, creating a third set that contains all the elements of both original sets, while ∩ indicates an *intersection* between two sets, creating a third set containing only the elements that both the original sets have in common. The following five examples present logical applications of these symbols:

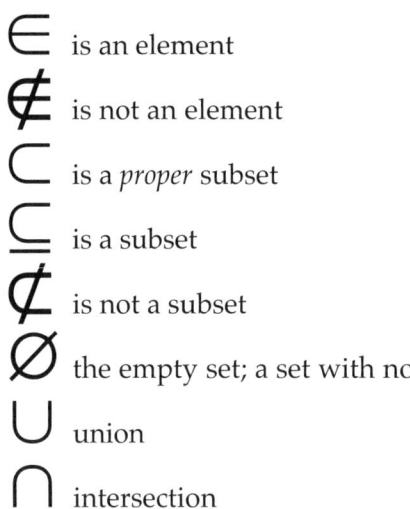

∈ is an element
∉ is not an element
⊂ is a *proper* subset
⊆ is a subset
⊄ is not a subset
∅ the empty set; a set with no
∪ union
∩ intersection

FIGURE 3.1 Symbols representing several ways in which sets can be more formally compared.

$\{1,4,5\} \subset \{0,1,2,3,4,5\}$
$\{1,4,5\} \subseteq \{1,4,5\}$
$\{1,4,5\} \not\subset \{0,2,5\}$
$\{1,4,5\} \cup \{0,4,5\} = \{0,1,4,5\}$
$\{1,4,5\} \cap \{0,4,5\} = \{4,5\}$

Combinations of these and other relationships in mathematical set theory produce extremely valuable results and principles that impact all of the various forms of mathematics. The following example provides a simple demonstration, with sets here given variable letter names so that the examples extend beyond particular sets to sets in general:

<if
$A \subseteq B \cap C$
then
$A \subseteq B$
and
$A \subseteq C$

In order to facilitate understanding of such set-theory operations, in 1880 John Venn (1834–1923) invented a visual process that demonstrated set containments and overlaps. Figure 3.2 presents a Venn diagram of the logical deductions presented above. Because A is a subset of the intersection of B and C ($A \subseteq B \cap C$), then A is also a subset of B ($A \subseteq B$) and a subset of C ($A \subseteq C$).

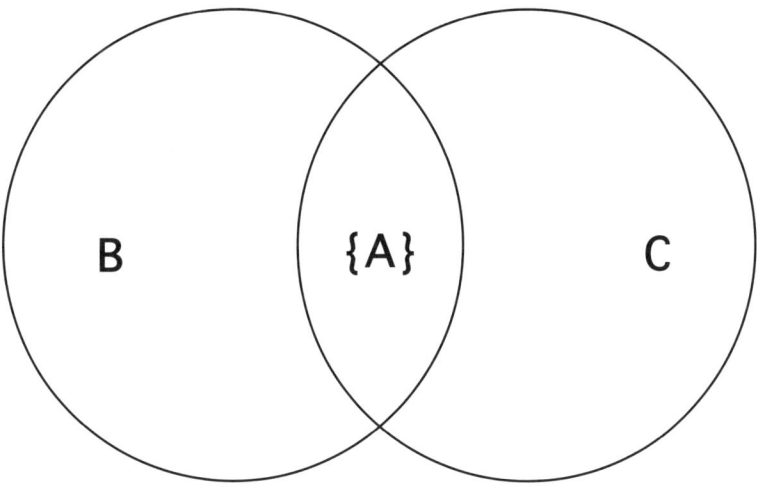

FIGURE 3.2 A Venn graphic of set theory logical deductions.

This brief introduction to mathematical set theory does not do justice to this extraordinary field of study. I have limited my discussion of it simply because musical set theory does not typically use these symbols or operations. However, musical set theory not only invokes the principles of mathematical set theory, but also includes many of its own unique comparison techniques, as we shall soon see. For those musicians interested in pursuing the mathematical side of set theory in more detail, several dozens of good books await your study, a number of which I include in the bibliography (Devlin 1993; Ferreirós 1999; Halmos 1974; Lawvere and Rosebrugh 2002; Levy 1979).

Musical set theory was initially introduced by Milton Babbitt (1960 and 1961), embellished by Allen Forte (1973), and further developed by John Rahn (1980) and George Perle (1991). Babbitt was

> concerned primarily with those set properties—pitch class and intervallic, order-preserving and merely combinational—and those relationships between and among forms of the set which are preserved under the operations of the system, and which—in general—are independent of the singular structure of a specific set. Here, to the end of discovering certain compositional consequences of set structure, the concern will be with those attributes of set structure which maintain under the systematic operations only by virtue of the particular nature of a set, or of the class of sets of which it is an instance, together with a particular choice of operations. (Babbitt 1961, 129)

Musical set theory follows many of the same tenets of mathematical set theory. However, several special conditions apply in musical set theory that do not apply in mathematical set theory. For example, musical set theory invokes the notion of *pitch class* (presented briefly in Chapter 2), where register (octave) no longer applies and where the pitch C-natural equals 0, C-sharp equals 1, and so on to B-natural, which equals 11. The process of reducing out the register of a pitch (i.e., all C-naturals belonging to the pitch class 0) is often termed *modulo 12*, modulo being a mathematical process that returns only the remainder when dividing one number by another number. All doublings as well as registration disappear when reducing pitches to pitch-class sets. Representing pitch in this way initiates a process that attempts to reveal similarities between sets of pitches that otherwise may appear quite different in number form and/or musical notation. No pitch class should appear twice in a pitch-class set.

To help differentiate musical set theory from mathematical set theory, musical set theory typically uses brackets rather than curly braces for set notation, as in [0,4,7], the set for a C major triad in root position. Other easily recognizable sets include the C minor triad [0,3,7] and the C dominant seventh chord [0,4,7,t] where "t" represents the number 10 ("e" represents the number 11), which allows a single digit/letter symbol to be used for each of the eleven pitch classes.

In mathematical set theory, the order of the elements within a set is irrelevant. However, the notion of ordered and unordered sets *is* important in musical set theory. *Ordered* sets follow the order of pitches and pitch classes found in the music under analysis. On the other hand, *unordered* sets follow ascending order, ignoring the order of pitches and pitch classes found in the music being analyzed. A simple example may be useful here. As noted in Chapter 2, pitches are typically represented as 60 for middle C, 61 for middle C-sharp, and so on. Thus, an ordered pitch set could appear as [66,69,62], given that this represents the order of these pitches in the grouping selected from the music for this set. The ordered pitch-class version of the [66,69,62] set would then be [6,9,2]. The unordered pitch-class version of the [66,69,62] set would then be [2,6,9].

In traditional music theory, triads are typically analyzed from their root pitches upward. Root positions of triads generally share a common feature: they have a smaller range between their outer pitches than do triads in inversion. Figure 3.3 provides an example of this. Here we see a D major triad in its three incarnations: root position, first inversion, and second inversion. Note that the perfect fifth between the outer pitches of the root-position triad spans a smaller interval than the minor sixth and major sixth that form the outer boundaries of the two inversions. The same is true in differentiating what is called the "normal" form of pitch-class sets, with the exception that smaller intervals between inner pitch classes can also count (described shortly), though the outer pitches of the set take precedence.

As an example, the ordered set [6,9,2] has a distance of eight between its outer pitch classes, 6 and 2. This is figured by incrementally counting upward from pitch class 6 to pitch class 2, beginning again at 0 after 11 (or "e"): 7, 8, 9, t, e, 0, 1, 2, or eight steps. This counting upward is important, because counting downward from 6 to 2 does not include pitch class 9, necessary because we want to include all members of the set in our computations.

Reviewing Figure 3.3 while reading the following description may help readers understand these machinations more clearly. Unordering the set [6,9,2] creates a total of three sets with the farthest-separated numbers inclusive of the remaining pitch class: the original [6,9,2], [9,2,6], and [2,6,9], counting upward from the lowest pitch class in each case. The pitch-class set [6,9,2] has a distance of eight between its outer pitch classes, 6 and 2, as previously shown. The pitch-class set [9,2,6] has a distance of nine between its outer pitch classes, 9 and 6, proved by counting upward from pitch class 9 to pitch class 6. However, the pitch-class set [2,6,9] has a distance of only seven between its outer pitch classes, 2 and 9. Thus, the pitch-class set [2,6,9] represents the normal (unordered) form of the ordered

FIGURE 3.3 Root positions of triads have a smaller range between their outer notes.

set [6,9,2]. A glance back at Figure 3.3 proves this yet further, because the root-position D major triad represents pitch classes 2, 6, and 9, in that order, from the lowest pitch upward.

Using a traditional twelve-hour analog clock face provides a much easier way to visualize numerical pitch-class relationships (see Figure 3.4) and to compute the normal form of sets. The internal x's here denote the pitch-class set [6,9,2], called "unordered" at this point because once placed on the clock face, the original order of the pitches in the music can no longer be ascertained. The set [2,6,9] clearly represents the normal form because beginning and counting clockwise from pitch class 6 produces an distance of eight between outer pitches, and beginning and counting clockwise from pitch class 9 creates a distance of nine between outer pitches, both of which are larger than the clockwise distance of seven between the outer pitches of [2,6,9].

Figure 3.5 presents another set for normal form pitch-class analysis. The [1,6,t] pitch-class set shown here does not produce the smallest outer range, because the outer pitch classes produce a distance of 9, larger than the smaller range of 7 produced by [6,t,1]. Using clock faces to discover the various forms of a set is analogous to using Venn diagrams in mathematical set theory. Although they are mainly graphic devices, both Venn diagrams in mathematics and clock faces in music make analysis by human beings far easier and often even inviting.

Up to this point we have been reading pitch-class sets clockwise. Reading sets counterclockwise adds a powerful comparative tool for discovering more similarities between apparently diverse pitch-class sets, particularly post-tonal pitch-class sets. This process, called mirror inversion, means that all intervals appear pre-

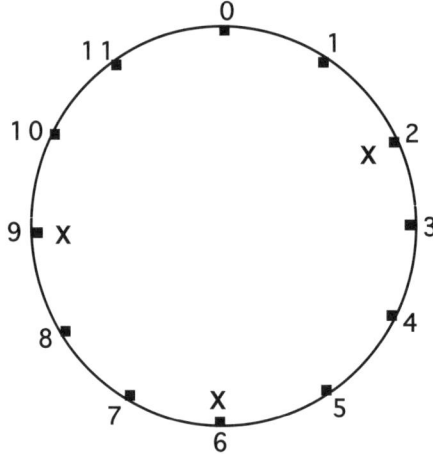

FIGURE 3.4 A clock face arranged to allow clearer visualization of pitch-class relationships.

cisely inverted in musical notation. In Figure 3.5, two sets have the same distance between outer pitches: [6,t,1] figured clockwise, and [1,t,6] figured counterclockwise. In situations such as this, the pitch-class set with the smallest internal intervals packed toward the pitch of origin wins, Thus, pitch-class set [1,t,6] (read counterclockwise from 1) succeeds because it has an internal interval of 3 (1 to t read counterclockwise equals 3) rather than 4 (6 to t read clockwise). At this point, we transpose this smallest form ([1,t,6]) to 0 by reading the intervals counterclockwise and beginning with "0" replacing "1," creating what we call its "prime form," the set [0,3,7].

In like form, the pitch-class set [2,6,9] when figured as above on a clock face and transposed becomes [0,3,7] in prime form. This procedure, while it might seem somewhat artificial, closely resembles the process we use when analyzing for musical function in tonal music, where a pitch set in one register reduces to a V^7 in C major (e.g., [G,B,D,F]), and a pitch set in another register reduces to a V^7 in D major (e.g., [A,C#,E,G]). Because major and minor keys do not typically exist in post-tonal music as they do in tonal music, [0,3,7] represents all major *and* minor triads and their inversions. This apparent contradiction should not be particularly bothersome because the reductive process is intended to reveal similarities, not equivalencies.

Figure 3.6 presents a straightforward example of using set theory to discover similarities in post-tonal music. The four chords in this example appear very different both in pitch content and in register. To a discerning ear, however, they sound similar in many ways. Each of these sets reduces to the same prime form

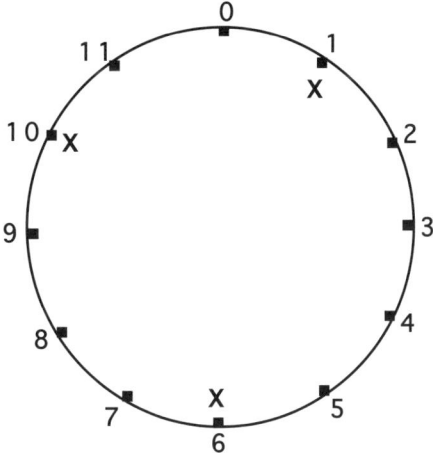

FIGURE 3.5 The [1,6,t] pitch-class set does not resolve to the pitch-class set [0,5,9] (9 distance when rotated to 0) because of the smaller range of [6,t,1] (7 distance and equating to [0,4,7] when rotated to 0).

106 HIDDEN STRUCTURE

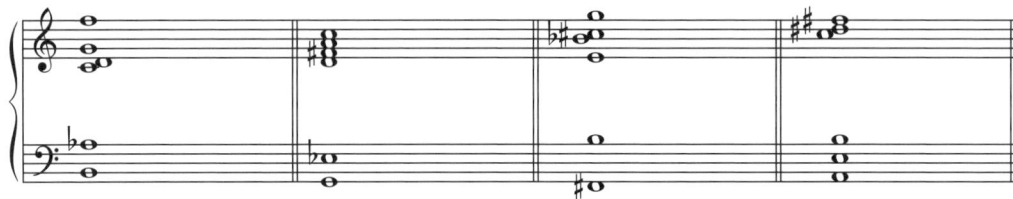

FIGURE 3.6 A straightforward example of the use of set theory to find similarities in post-tonal music.

[0,1,3,6,8,9] following the processes just described. Figure 3.7 shows each chord in Figure 3.6 represented on a clock face by the process used to discover the prime form provided in the figure caption.

There are, then, typically three forms of pitch-class sets: *ordered*, *normal*, and *prime*. The *ordered* form indicates that the order of pitches in the set matters (thus, [0,1,3] and [1,3,0] represent different sets even though they contain the same pitch classes). The *normal* form (unordered because it no longer reflects the order in the music) accounts for the normal inversions of, for example, triads, and places sets so that they cover the smallest overall range. The *prime* form then accounts for mirror inversions of sets, finding the smallest outer range, packing pitch classes toward the pitch class of origin, and transposing the result to begin on 0. These definitions generally follow those of Babbitt (1961) and Forte (1973, see esp. 4–5). In summary, then, the following presents one instance of these three forms of the same pitch-class set:

[6,9,2]   ordered form
[2,6,9]   normal form
[0,3,7]   prime form

The above set, initially a major triad in first inversion (ordered form), appears as a root-position normal form, and then as a minor triad in inverted and transposed-to-zero form.

Unfortunately, the fact that all major and minor triads ultimately reduce to a minor triad in prime form means that an unambiguous major triad expressed in post-tonal music will be lost during analysis. It is not that the prime-form minor triad is objectionable, but that the normal-form major triad cannot be clearly discerned from the minor triad in the prime form. Many analysts have reverted to a two-form version called a *representative* form: T_n, read as normal form transposed, and T_nI, read as normal form transposed with inversion taken into account (see Rahn 1980, 75–76). Rahn also uses the term *type*, while still others use the terms *pitch-structure* (Howe 1965) and *chords* (Regener 1974). Morris (1987, see esp. 79) offers these and other classification systems of pitch-class sets. These extra forms are used to

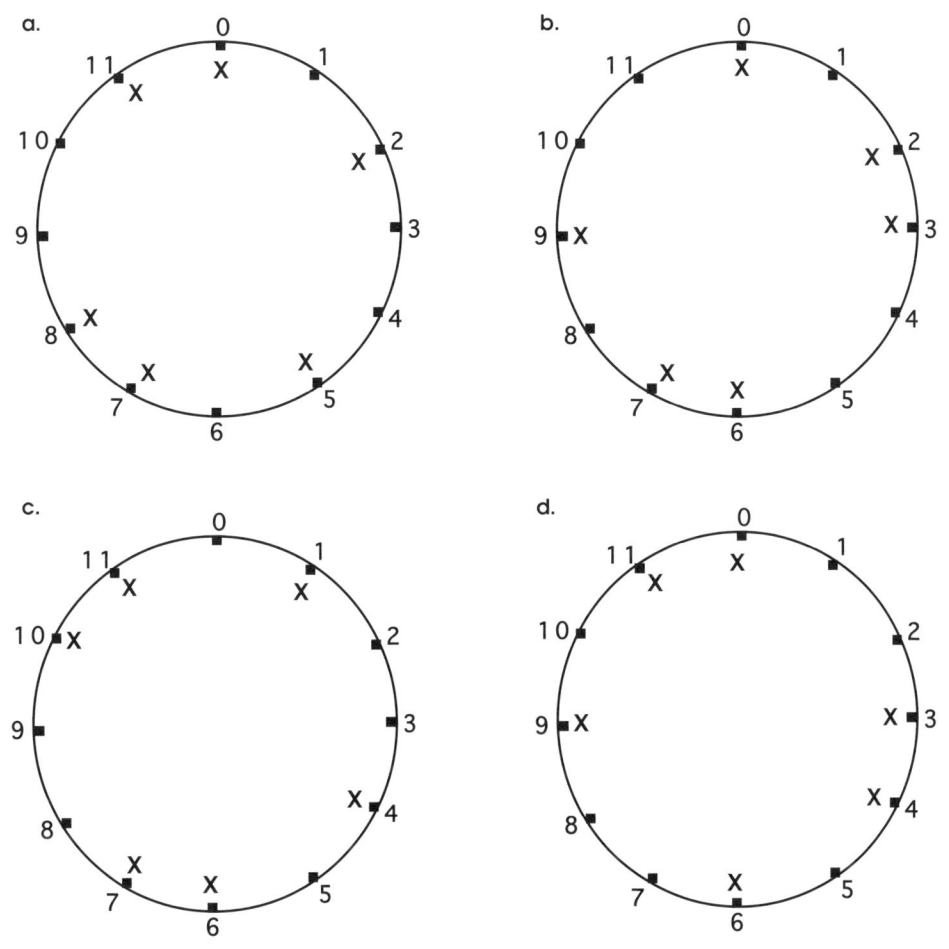

FIGURE 3.7 (a) [e,0,2,5,7,8] is [0,1,3,6,8,9] when rotated one number clockwise; (b) [6,7,9,0,2,3] is [0,1,3,6,8,9] when rotated six numbers clockwise; (c) [7,6,4,1,e,t] is [0,1,3,6,8,9] when rotated seven numbers counterclockwise; (d) [0,e,9,6,4,3] is [0,1,3,6,8,9] when rotated twelve numbers counterclockwise.

account for works in which the two forms of many sets, such as the major triad—original and inversion—appear in important places in the music being analyzed and thus should be reflected in the analysis of that music. Also, valuable characteristics of same-prime-form sets can be revealed when comparing only normal forms (e.g., numbers of common tones, etc. [see Straus 2005, 71–72]).

One simple solution that many of my theory colleagues and I have adopted—that of simply transposing the currently accepted normal form to zero—is called the t-normal form (for transposed normal form). Thus, the ordered pitch-class set [6,9,2] would translate to the following forms:

[2,6,9]   normal form
[0,4,7]   t-normal form
[0,3,7]   prime form

Keeping track, then, of the manners in which ordered, normal, t-normal, and prime forms interact with one another in music becomes much easier and more obvious. The interplay of t-normal and prime forms expressed in this way becomes immediately apparent in works where composers juxtapose pitch-class sets of the same prime form but different t-normal forms in their music.

From here on I will be using both this zero-based t-normal form and the more traditional normal form. This will become increasingly important in the following discussions in this chapter when the mathematical creation of sets helps us to understand how logical new sets—otherwise considered unrelated—result from pairings of sets that appeared previously. Extending "normal order" to t-normal order has no direct effect on computer applications of music analysis. However, as will be seen in this and later chapters, the manner in which the programs accompanying this book on CD-ROM use this "t-normal order" has a substantial effect on the ability to clearly describe a program's operation and the principles that enable that program to work effectively.

Translating pitch sets into t-normal pitch class sets can be accomplished in Lisp quite easily, as the following code demonstrates:

```
(defun translate-to-t-normal-pitch-class-set (set)
  (translate-to-pcs (sort-and-clean set)))

(defun sort-and-clean (set)
  (my-sort #'< (remove-duplicates (modulo12 set))))

(defun modulo12 (set)
  (if (null set)()
      (cons (mod (first set) 12)
            (modulo12 (rest set)))))

(defun translate-to-pcs (mod-set
  &optional (first-set (first mod-set)))
  (if (null mod-set)()
      (cons (abs (- first-set (first mod-set)))
            (translate-to-pcs (rest mod-set) first-set))))
```

The function `translate-to-t-normal-pitch-class-set` here acts as a top-level operator of the two functions `sort-and-clean` and `translate-to-pcs`. The function `sort-and-clean` simply maps `modulo12` (a simple recursive function that uses the Lisp primitive mod to reduce all elements of its set argument to within the range 0–11) onto its argument, removes all duplicates, and then sorts the result into ascending order. The function my-sort (available in many of the code files on the CD-ROM accompanying this book) bypasses the side effects of Lisp's somewhat unpredictable standard sort function. The function translate-to-pcs then transposes the set to begin on 0 by subtracting the first element of the set from each of its members. The use of Lisp's &optional keyword in the first line of translate-to-pcs allows for optional arguments that users do not have to use when calling the function and that here enable the variable first-set to continue to represent the first element of mod-set even though mod-set is slowly diminishing in size, owing to recursion. The arguments to &optional come in lists in which the first element is the name of a variable and the second element the default data contained in that variable. Running this code with varying arguments produces:

```
? (translate-to-t-normal-pitch-class-set '(60 64 67))
(0 4 7)
? (translate-to-t-normal-pitch-class-set '(60 63 67))
(0 3 7)
? (translate-to-t-normal-pitch-class-set '(60 63 67 70))
(0 3 7 10)
? (translate-to-t-normal-pitch-class-set '(64 67 79 84))
(0 4 7)
```

Note that the last data converted here contains octave doubling and an inversion that nonetheless convert to the same result as the first test.

Set-theory analysis provides many other tools for understanding post-tonal music. For example, interval vectors (counts of all the intervals present in a set) provide interesting ways for analysts to relate prime forms of sets that may otherwise seem unrelated. Vectors are represented by six-digit counts of the intervals of a minor second, major second, minor third, major third, perfect fourth, and augmented fourth; the remaining intervals in the octave are considered mirror inversions of these intervals. Thus, the set [0,1,3] has the vector 111000, because 0,1 is a minor second, 0,3 is a minor third, and 1,3 is a major second (all of the possible intervals contained in the set). As an example of vector relationship, consider the two sets [0,1,3,7] and [0,1,4,6], both of which have the same vector, 111111. Other pitch-class-set comparison techniques include similar but not equivalent prime forms of pitch-class sets indicating variation techniques in use. Analyzing interval-class sets as well as pitch-class sets can also help analysts discover interesting contrasts and similarities in post-tonal music. Processes such as these represent but a few of the ways that musical set theory can aid in our fundamental understanding of post-tonal music.

Although musical set theory does not reveal function in the way that tonal analysis does in tonal music, using musical set theory to decipher similarities between complex and otherwise apparently unrelated groupings of pitches often provides insights into music otherwise considered impenetrable. The manner in which composers limit their compositions to just a few of the 208 possible prime forms of chords between trichords (three-pitch groupings) and nonachords (nine-pitch groupings) indicates that set theory provides a valuable tool for analyzing post-tonal music. (The other chord forms are tetrachords, pentachords, hexachords, septachords, and octachords, respectively.)

One of the biggest problems analysts face when using set theory to analyze post-tonal music is how to group music into appropriate collections for revealing the optimum number of logical set relationships. Computer programs can aid significantly in this process by using extraordinary accuracy and speed to remove the drudgery from what can otherwise be an enormously time-consuming process of trial and error. Even brute-force computer programs that simply compare sets of ever-decreasing sizes to find the sets that appear most often can minimize the effort of what would otherwise take an analyst weeks or even months to do by hand. Of course, such computer programs cannot make intuitive leaps or musical decisions. They do, however, offer analysts a palette of possibilities from which they can then choose the most promising alternative.

Before describing more innovative programs for analyzing post-tonal music, I will first demonstrate a function (define-and-lexicon-all-patterns in the file called *database* in the folder called *sets database*) that groups and analyzes music for sets and—what is possibly more important—set variances, returning its best guess for one or more sets as the basis of the music under study. This program uses a straightforward previously discussed technique known as pattern matching and includes several processes that are important for understanding this and subsequent chapters. The primary focus of these processes involves separating grouping and pitch-class-matching programs into discrete tasks and comparing only groupings that match. This focus will eliminate the need to match all possible groupings, thus reducing the time necessary for analysis and increasing the potential for varying the parameters for subsequent analyses. Furthermore, we can collect similar—in whatever ways we wish to define—pitch-class patterns and include them as well by selecting other, related lexicons. Thus, by collecting patterns before comparing them and carefully distributing them into appropriately named lexicons, we not only speed the process of pitch-class matching, but we also make a wide range of pitch-class matching possible without having to redo the grouping process. Pattern matching in this way reveals a wide variety of possibilities not otherwise evident in pattern-matching systems that require grouping and matching simultaneously.

As mentioned previously, equivalent but transposed pitch-class sets can be represented by T_n, where "T" represents the word transposition and the subscript "n" indicates the distance between two fundamentally equivalent pitch-class sets. For example, the normal-form sets [2,4,5,7] and [5,7,8,t] have three half steps separating them, the second set therefore having a T_3 relationship to the first set. In this book, we simply transpose both sets to the same *t-normal* form ([0,2,3,5]). In either case, the process involves addition and/or subtraction of two pitch-class sets that are assumed to be equivalent. The notion of adding and subtracting the elements of two *non-equivalent* sets to achieve a third set, however, is less intuitive. For example, consider the same pitch-class set ([2,4,5,7]) added to the pitch-class set [2,5,9,t]. The result ([4, 9, 14, 17]), when reduced modulo 12 and transformed to t-normal form, produces a new pitch-class set of [0,2,3,7], similar in many ways, but not equivalent to, the two sets that produced it. Although this creation of new pitch-class sets from the addition or subtraction of two dissimilar pitch-class sets may seem far-fetched for analysis, when three different pitch-class sets appear as the primary sets of a work under analysis and two of these may be added or subtracted to produce the third, the process seems more purposeful.

Multiplying and dividing pitch-class sets by each other may seem an even more remote process than adding and subtracting such sets. However, these processes become immediately less remote when we encounter them in music. As an example, Figure 3.8 presents the pickup and opening four bars of Schoenberg's op. 19, no. 6 from *Sechs kleine Klavierstücke*.

The t-normal forms of the first two trichords here, [0,3,5] and [0,5,7], show little relation to the third trichord's t-normal form, [0,1,8] ([0,1,4] in prime form). However, when the [0,3,5] and [0,5,7] t-normal forms are multiplied together (i.e., when multiplying the aligned pitch classes of each set modulo 12), the new set results in the t-normal form [0,3,e], or [0,1,4] in the prime form. Thus, the three sets share a common multiple. I have included a small program called SetMath on the CD-ROM accompanying this book that accepts either normal forms or unordered pitch-class sets and provides a series of results in the following form:

```
(run-sets '(0 3 5) '(0 5 7))
Added sets: (0 8)
Subtracted sets 2 from 1: (0 10) Subtracted sets 1 from 2: (0)
Multiply sets: (0 3 11)
```

FIGURE 3.8 The opening 4 measures of Schoenberg, Six Little Piano Pieces, op. 19, no. 6.

Note that the t-normal forms of the two input sets use parentheses instead of brackets and lack commas, the results of using Lisp. Note also that multiplying and otherwise mathematically combining sets can cause duplications, resulting in an output of fewer pitch classes.

Before proceeding further, I remind readers here of my earlier comments about composer intent. What composers do or do not intend to include in their music, though of interest, should not deter analysts from revealing discovered relations, no matter how unlikely these relations may seem to the perceived concept of the work as we know it. I further remind readers that analysis informs listening as well as vice versa. Whether a process that exists in music can be heard or not should not deter us from appreciating its presence.

To this point, sets in this book have primarily been comprised of pitch classes. Readers should be reminded, however, that sets may consist of representations of any parameter of music. For example, rhythmic information such as sets of durations in thousandths of a second [1000,4000,2000,8000], channel settings [1,4,2,3], dynamics [55,60,75,45], and so on can all produce useful relationships when permuted and compared. I have even found interesting results when creating formal sets as in [a,a,b,b,c,a,b] for the purpose of comparing the forms of entire works. Such formal collections remind us that sets may consist of many different kinds of symbols other than numerical information, as in this case, where the alphabetical letters represent phrases of a particular type of musical thematic or harmonic data.

Musical set theory involves far more than I have described here. In fact, the principles expressed thus far in this chapter barely cover the fundamentals of what can be a very complex and often personal approach to understanding post-tonal music. However, given that this book attempts to cover a wide variety of approaches, I leave it to individual readers to explore musical set theory further, using books of their own choosing or those in the bibliography (particularly Forte 1973; Lewin 1987; Straus 2005).

REGISTER

Many post-tonal composers use register in important ways in their music. Unfortunately, register often gets lost when analyzing this music using pitch-class sets. For example, register does not accompany pitch-class sets when they are reduced to their normal and prime forms. This is unfortunate, because equivalent prime-form sets with significant registral differences can often sound as contrasting as different prime-form sets that share registral arrangements (Bruner 1984; Gibson 1986 and 1988; Isaacson 1996). At the least, when viewed in their registral contexts, some equivalent prime forms seem more equal than other equivalent prime forms (Kuusi 2003). I have found in both my analysis and my composition that retaining register information during grouping and reduction allows me to compare pitch-class sets more meaningfully.

In the following section, I present a duodecimal notation for representing pitch-class sets, a notation that—by virtue of its radix of 12—allows both register and pitch class to share one simple notation. After demonstrating this notation, explaining its mathematical manipulations, and presenting a series of simple musical excerpts by which I hope to convince readers of the usefulness of this notation, I then provide musical examples of my own and other composers' music from both analytical and compositional perspectives. I also discuss several register-related analytical parameters, including range, interval mapping, interval summations, and linear interval vectors, each of which provides further insight into the music under analysis.

Tonal music offers many examples of the importance of register. For instance, the beginning of Claude Debussy's *La cathédrale engloutie* (1909), shown in Figure 3.9, presents two related but varied musical ideas that are distinguished in part by their registral separation. One idea appears in both hands at the onsets of mm. 1, 3, and 5, with its wide separation of register, resultant open fourths and fifths, and slow rhythmic progression. The second idea appears in the center register of the keyboard with close-knit planing in both hands. Interestingly, the first chord of this prelude is echoed in the second chord, which follows immediately after the first, with no difference in their pitch-class content, only in their lowest pitches—the

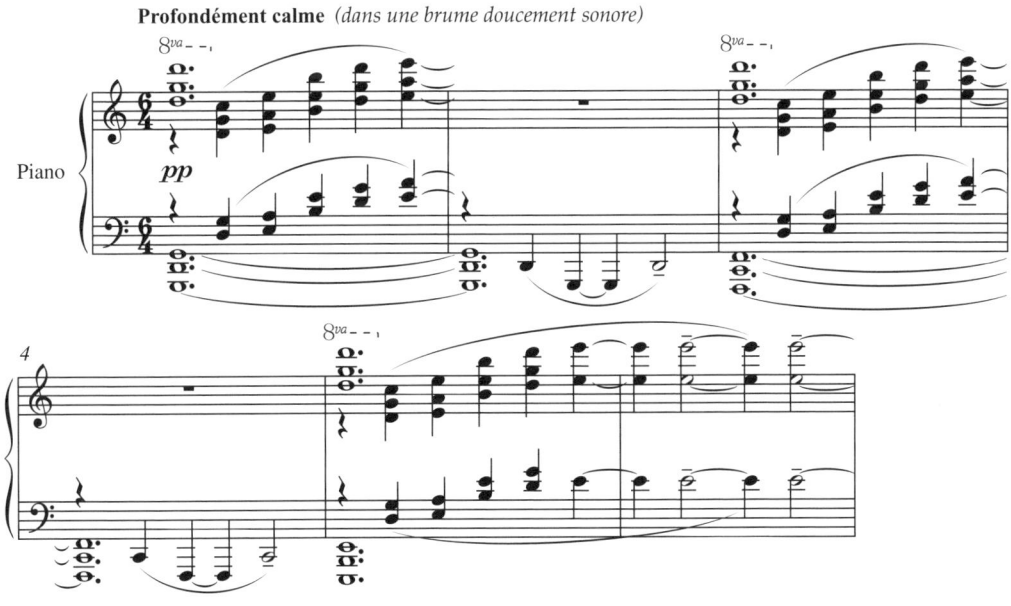

FIGURE 3.9 The opening measures of Claude Debussy, *La cathédrale engloutie* (The Sunken Cathedral), 1909.

second chord being a closed-position inversion of the initial dyad. Clearly these two basically equivalent chords play extremely different roles, as is highlighted by their registral variance.

Register matters in this work, as it does in most music. Even in Bach chorales, register can determine the inversion, position (open or closed), voice-leading, and certainly the resonance of a harmony or passage. Most tonal and post-tonal analytical techniques, however, exclude register from their reductive notations. I have long sought a way to retain register in these analytical notations, especially in post-tonal music, where register often plays such an important role. Although one could make the same kind of case for rhythm, timbre, and other important elements in post-tonal music, register seems so closely tied to the kinds of pitch analysis involved in post-tonal pitch-class processes that it has always seemed to me paradoxical not to include it—if indeed a logical way to do so can be found.

Duodecimal numbering offers a more inherently musical way to notate equal-tempered pitch classes than does decimal numbering. The duodecimal system contains twelve different numerals, rather than the ten numerals of the decimal system, making duodecimal equivalent to the twelve pitch classes of the chromatic scale. (Note here that the terms dodecimal and duodecimal mean roughly the same thing. I have chosen to use the word duodecimal because mathematicians clearly prefer duodecimal, and because I wish to clearly differentiate this term I describe from the term *dodecaphonic*, occasionally used to describe twelve-tone or serial music.)

Duodecimal counting resembles decimal counting in many ways. The primary difference between the two systems occurs at the point in which the numbers extend beyond the limit indicated by the name of the numbering system. For example, the ten decimal numerals range from 0 to 9 inclusive, for a total of ten, before transcending to its "tens," such as 10, 11, and so on. In contrast, the twelve numerals of the duodecimal system count from 0 through 9 and then on to "t" and "e" inclusive, for a total of twelve (again, "t" and "e" represent ten and eleven, respectively) before transcending to its "tens," as in 10 and 11, with these latter numbers equating to 12 and 13 in the decimal system. For non-musicians, counting in duodecimal can be tedious and confusing. However, for musicians the match of duodecimal numbers to the twelve-pitch equal-tempered scale makes a nice fit. For every duodecimal number, the leftmost digit represents the octave, and the rightmost digit indicates the pitch class within that octave (with the single-digit numbers 0–e having an implied 0 register).

Figure 3.10 provides a straightforward conversion chart that relates decimal to duodecimal notation. The left-hand number in each pair in a column represents decimal notation, and the parallel right-hand number its duodecimal equivalent. Figure 3.11 presents a possibly more musically meaningful way to think in terms of duodecimal numbers, with each horizontal row representing a complete octave. The duodecimal number 60 equates to middle C, with 70, 80, 90, and so on representing successive octaves above middle C. Interestingly, the term "octave" derives from the diatonic scale, as do major and minor seconds, steps and half steps, and

0	0	21	19	42	36	63	53	84	70		
1	1	22	1t	43	37	64	54	85	71		
2	2	23	1e	44	38	65	55	86	72		
3	3	24	20	45	39	66	56	87	73		
4	4	25	21	46	3t	67	57	88	74		
5	5	26	22	47	3e	68	58	89	75		
6	6	27	23	48	40	69	59	90	76		
7	7	28	24	49	41	70	5t	91	77		
8	8	29	25	50	42	71	5e	92	78		
9	9	30	26	51	43	72	60	93	79		
10	t	31	27	52	44	73	61	94	7t		
11	e	32	28	53	45	74	62	95	7e		
12	10	33	29	54	46	75	63	96	80		
13	11	34	2t	55	47	76	64	97	81		
14	12	35	2e	56	48	77	65	98	82		
15	13	36	30	57	49	78	66	99	83		
16	14	37	31	58	4t	79	67	100	84		
17	15	38	32	59	4e	80	68	101	85		
18	16	39	33	60	50	81	69	102	86		
19	17	40	34	61	51	82	6t	103	87		
20	18	41	35	62	52	83	6e	104	88		

FIGURE 3.10 A conversion chart relating decimal to duodecimal notation.

60, 61, 62, 63, 64, 65, 66, 67, 68, 69, 6t, 6e
70, 71, 72, 73, 74, 75, 76, 77, 78, 79, 7t, 7e
80, 81, 82, 83, 84, 85, 86, 87, 88, 89, 8t, 8e
90, 91, 92, 93, 94, 95, 96, 97, 98, 99, 9t, 9e
. . . . and so on

FIGURE 3.11 A more understandable and musical way to think in terms of duodecimal notation.

so on. Although I certainly do not recommend here that we develop new terms to more accurately represent these intervals, I do suggest—particularly in the case of post-tonal analysis—that we adopt duodecimal notation to represent the twelve pitch classes and their registers.

Figure 3.12 demonstrates how to convert decimal to duodecimal numbers and vice versa. To convert decimal to duodecimal numbers, first divide the decimal number by 12 to obtain the register digit, and then use the remainder as the pitch-class digit. To convert duodecimal to decimal numbers, multiply the left-hand digit (register) of the duodecimal notation by 12, and then add the right-hand digit (pitch class) to the result.

Figure 3.13 shows duodecimal addition, subtraction, multiplication, and division using arbitrary numbers. As one can see, these processes do not quickly reveal their underlying principles, especially for those more familiar with calculating in decimal numbers. Musicians, however, typically add and subtract using relatively small numbers that do not pose particularly difficult problems. Indeed, octave transposition—the most common calculation in music—is even easier in duodecimal notation than in decimal notation; simply add or subtract the number of octaves of the transposition from the left-hand number, leaving the right-hand number intact.

For those readers familiar with MIDI pitch numbering, duodecimal numbers may cause some initial confusion. For example, in duodecimal notation the number 75—which in MIDI terms equates to the E-flat an octave and a minor third above middle C—represents pitch class 5 (or F) in the seventh octave. However, distinguishing these two approaches to numbering will become easier after one studies the analyses presented in this chapter. The benefits of using duodecimal notation when analyzing examples of post-tonal music using wide register separations far outweigh any initial difficulties encountered.

For those interested in how to pronounce duodecimal numbers with letters, the t ("Tee") and e ("Eee") sound just as one might imagine, with combinations figured

58 decimal	4t duodecimal
divide by 12 for left digit	multiply left digit by 12
right digit is remainder of above	add right digit
= 4t duodecimal	= 58 decimal

FIGURE 3.12 Conversion methods used for decimal to duodecimal numbers and vice versa.

```
    2E      2E      E      18
   +11     -20    * 2     /4
   ----    ----   ----    ----
    40      E      1T      5
```

FIGURE 3.13 Subtraction, addition, multiplication, and division using arbitrary numbers in duodecimal notation.

as composites of these, as in "TenTee," "TenEee," "TwentyTee," "TwentyEee," "ThirtyTee," "ThirtyEee," and so on. Knowing these pronunciations is invaluable when discussing analyses using duodecimal numbers.

Clearly, reducing ordered pitches to ordered pitch classes causes registral information to disappear. As previously described, this does not occur when using duodecimal notation, where the left digit retains this information. Figuring the normal and prime forms of pitch-class sets in duodecimal notation follows the same processes as those used in decimal notation, with the exception that the left-hand digit of each number does not change during reduction. The left-hand digit remains paired with the possibly changing numbers of the right-hand digit pitch classes, as often required when figuring normal and prime forms of pitch-class sets. The arrangements of these duodecimal numbers may also shift during reduction. Thus, the ordered duodecimal set [52,60,73] ([2,0,3] in decimal notation) becomes [60,52,73] ([0,2,3] in decimal notation) in unordered normal form, and [70,51,63] ([0,1,3] in decimal notation) in prime form. Although possibly confusing at first, these processes become quite natural with continued use.

Figure 3.14 presents examples of decimal reductions. The analysis of the 2 two-chord progressions in Figures 3.14a and 3.14b follow the standard musical set-theory practice of first creating a t-normal form, and then a prime form of the sets. Figures 3.15a and 3.15b then show these same reductions with registers intact as duodecimal numbers. Again, the left-hand register digits remain with their right-hand counterparts during this process. Other than that single rule, reducing pitch sets to their normal and prime forms is as straightforward with registral indications as it is without.

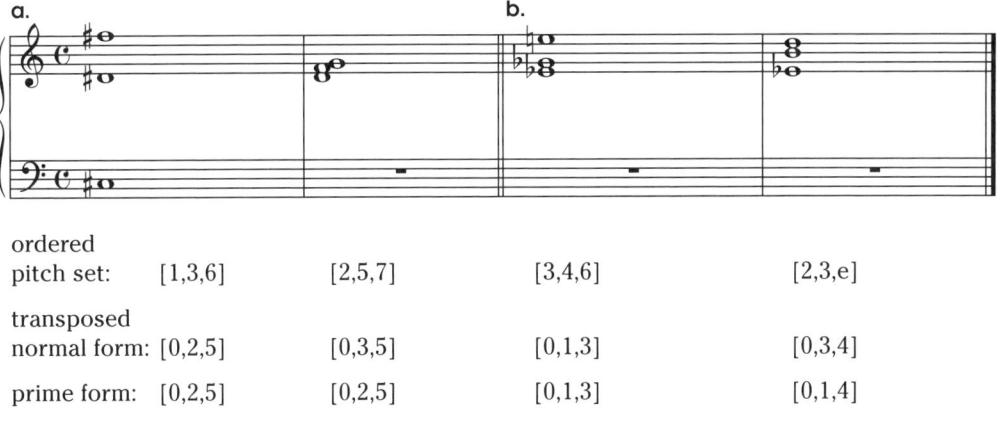

FIGURE 3.14 Two two-set progressions showing pitch classes (first), t-normal form (second), and prime (third).

118   HIDDEN STRUCTURE

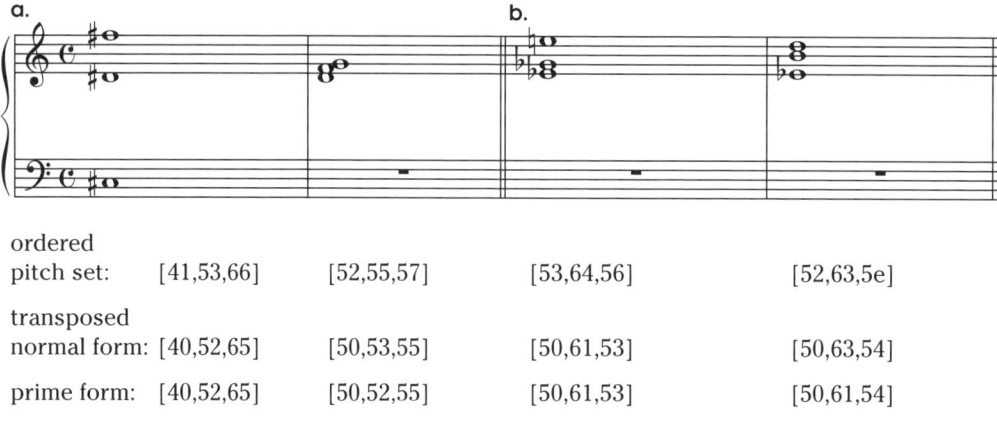

ordered pitch set:	[41,53,66]	[52,55,57]	[53,64,56]	[52,63,5e]
transposed normal form:	[40,52,65]	[50,53,55]	[50,61,53]	[50,63,54]
prime form:	[40,52,65]	[50,52,55]	[50,61,53]	[50,61,54]

FIGURE 3.15   Same reduction as Figure 3.14 but with registers intact in the form of duodecimal notation.

Duodecimal notation can reveal differences between equivalent pitch-class sets as well as similarities between different pitch-class sets. For example, in Figure 3.14a, the two sets have identical prime forms. However, these first two sets differ significantly in register, as shown by the 4, 5, 6 and 5, 5, 5 registral indications in Figure 3.15a, a duodecimal registration analysis of the same chord set as in Figure 3.14a. The second pair of chords, shown in Figures 3.12b and 3.15b, differs slightly ([0,1,3,] and [0,1,4]) in their prime forms, but they share identical ordered registration (5, 6, 5), demonstrating how differing sets can relate to one another by similar registration.

RANGES AND VECTORS

Registral notation has drawbacks in that with C (or 0) as an arbitrary register shift point, some sets appear registrally quite different when they are actually very similar or equivalent. For example, setting C to 0 forces a set such as [5e,60,5t] to look more registrally diverse than it actually is. This set spans but two semitones, even though the register shifts twice. On the other hand, the set [63,6e,61] covers a range of ten semitones, even though the register remains the same for each member of the set. To counteract this disparity, I use a range index R as in R_{10}, where R stands for range and the subscript 10 represents the interval distance between the highest and lowest pitches of the set. Hence, the pitch class–register set [5e,60,5t] has a range of R_2 and the pitch class–register set [63,6E,61] has a range of R_{10}, thus distinguishing their differences in range even when their registers may suggest the

[63,6e,61]$_{r_{10}}$

FIGURE 3.16 Range notation shown to the lower right.

opposite. This range notation then appears to the lower right of the duodecimal pitch-class sets, as shown in Figure 3.16.

The stage of pitch-class set analysis prior to reduction to normal, t-normal, and prime forms offers analysts an opportunity to compare interval contents of groupings under study. The duodecimal-numbered ordered set [50,64,56], for example, has a decimal interval content of (16, -10). This interval content matches exactly the (16, -10) decimal-numbered intervals of the [28,40,32] duodecimal-numbered ordered set. These observations would not be possible if one simply compared these same sets in decimal t-normal form ([0,2,6]) or in unordered decimal prime form ([0,2,6]), or even in their duodecimal t-normal ([60,52,56], [40,32,28]) and prime ([50,62,56], [40,42,26]) forms, where set manipulations have altered the original pitch-class orders.

To ensure that interval mapping follows principles consistent with the logic in the music being analyzed, pitches must be sorted by time and—for simultaneously sounding pitches—from lowest to highest. Although this latter process may seem arbitrary or biased by tonal concepts, figuring chords from their lowest pitches upward guarantees that the range covered and the order of the pitches for mapping will remain consistent from one grouping to the next.

Pitch-class set reduction prior to determining normal, t-normal, and prime forms also offers opportunities to calculate and compare interval summations of pitch-class sets. These summations indicate the direction-sensitive intervallic differences between the first and last pitches of groupings. Summations can prove quite valuable for comparing groups whose intervallic content is quite different, but whose overall interval directions are consistent. For example, equality or inequality in the values of these numbers, especially in non-vertical groupings, can indicate interesting aspects of either the composer's composition techniques and/or analysts' grouping processes. Equalities often reveal interesting and possibly important details about a work's motivic structure. Summations appear in decimal form, with minus signs indicating downward motion.

Direction-insensitive linear (ordered) interval vectors provide further useful information for comparing the basic interval content of set motions. I use *linear* interval vectors—each interval figured only in respect to each pitch's immediately following pitch—because although these linear vectors still fold intervals into the compacted range of an augmented fourth or less, they nonetheless do not count intervals from each pitch class to every other pitch class as do traditional vectors. For example, a standard interval vector of the set [0,1,3] would be 111000, but the linear interval vector would be 110000, the intervals between the neighboring elements of the set. Linear interval vectors often reveal interesting and important relationships between sets that would not be accessible from standard vector analysis. For example, the ordered duodecimal sets [60,64,66,59] and [50,46,52,45] both produce the standard interval vector of 110121. However, these same sets produce linear interval vectors of 010110 and 000111, respectively. Sets with similar shapes have the same or similar interval vectors, while sets with different shapes that reduce to the same prime forms need not have the same or similar linear interval vectors. Comparing linear interval vectors has proven quite valuable in my analysis processes, as I will soon describe.

The program Register on the accompanying CD-ROM groups music examples algorithmically. The program then extracts pitch classes from these groupings, simultaneously figures and retains register, and produces appropriate sets of duodecimal numbers. Following this, the program then calculates the total range covered, as well as the resultant prime-form set (ensuring that the register numbers neither change nor separate from their pitch classes), along with an interval map of the ordered pitch set, an interval summation of the ordered pitch set, and the set's linear interval vector. Finally, the program rearranges and presents this information as a single list of sublists, as in:

(((60 71 74) r13) ((7e 6t 72) (-13 4) -9) 100100))

The first sublist here—(60 71 74)—represents the prime form of the grouping in duodecimal numbers. The r13 paired with this first sublist indicates the original ordered range of the grouping in numbers of half steps in absolute-value decimal numbers. The sublist of (7e 6t 72) contains the original ordered pitch-class set in duodecimal numbers. The (-13 4) sublist describes the interval map of the ordered set in decimal numbers. The -9 that follows the interval map represents the summation in decimal numbers, with negative numbers reflecting downward direction. The last entry in this list—100100—defines the linear interval vector of the grouping.

The groupings of music in the figures of this chapter represent my own or my program's choices and are not intended in any way to indicate optimum or even preferable approaches. Obviously, changing the sizes or locations of the groupings of this music can and often does produce different analytical results from those shown. I welcome such alternate perspectives and the potential they offer for even more insights into the music being analyzed.

COMPARISONS

Register's lists of duodecimal pitch classes in their prime and ordered forms, ranges, contour maps, summations, and ordered interval vectors present information that analysts can then compare for similarity and developmental structure. Figures 3.17 and 3.18 show a typical example of both a work in which register plays an important role, and a computer analysis that provides useful information as to the nature of that role. Many of the melodic intervals in Schoenberg's Suite for Piano op. 25, Gavotte (1923) in Figure 3.17 approach or exceed octaves, with some (e.g., the last measure in the figure) expanding to two octaves or more. Even a cursory reading of this music gives the impression that the composer has definite ideas for the deployment of register and range. The contrapuntal nature of the two register- and hand-separated melodic lines, combined with held notes, helps group the music here into naturally forming trichordal and tetrachordal collections for analysis.

The registral analysis of Schoenberg's Gavotte, shown in Figure 3.18, reveals very interesting similarities and relationships between particular groupings of this music. I have placed markings (*, †, ‡, and °) after associated linear interval vectors to point out equivalencies. Additionally, duplicate ranges and interval summations appear in boldface. Interestingly, the first four entries in Figure 3.18 match the second four entries in terms of their prime forms (not including the registers) and their linear interval vectors—both are paired ABCD (*, †, ‡, and °) statements. In other words, the first four prime-form sets match the second four prime-form sets, substantiating and reinforcing their relationships. The ranges have many duplicates

FIGURE 3.17 Arnold Schoenberg, Suite for Piano, op. 25 (1923), Gavotte, mm. 1–6, with groupings circled and numbered.

1. (((70 72 83 76) **r15**) ((84 75 77 71) (-11 2 -6) **-15**) 110001)*
2. (((60 41 62 53) r23) ((4e 60 59 6t) (13 -3 13) 23) 201000)†
3. (((60 71 74 86) r30) ((76 73 88 62) (-3 17 -30) -16) 001011)‡
4. (((60 41 53) r13) ((59 60 4e) (3 -13) -10) 101000)°
5. (((60 62 53 76) **r15**) ((5t 69 67 71) (11 0 0 -2 6) **15**) 110001)*
6. (((50 61 42 53) r25) ((43 52 55 64) (11 0 3 11) 25) 201000)†
7. (((60 51 54 66) **r10**) ((58 5e 66 60) (3 0 7 0 0 -6) 4) 001011)‡
8. (((50 41 53) **r14**) ((55 52 43) (-3 0 -11) **-14**) 101000)°
9. (((70 72 77) **r10**) ((70 75 7t) (5 5) 10) 000020)
10. (((60 52 65) **r14**) ((59 66 6e) (9 5) **14**) 001010)
11. (((60 61 72) r11) ((62 63 71) (1 10) 11) 110000)

FIGURE 3.18 Computer analysis of Schoenberg's Gavotte by tetrachords and trichords as shown circled and numbered in figure 3.17

and similarities as well (shown in boldface), which in some cases (see lines 1 and 5, for example) coincide with similarities in the music and at other times relate very different sets to one another (see lines 7 and 9, for example). Interestingly, many of the different-ranged groupings here closely approximate one another (see, e.g., ranges in lines 2 and 6, lines 4 and 8, lines 4 and 5, etc.).

This often-analyzed work (see, e.g., Straus 2005, 205–12) represents one of Schoenberg's first attempts at serialism. The row used here has only four distinct forms—P_4, P_t, I_4, and I_t—integrating the pitch content of this music, which otherwise relies on dynamics, articulation, and, of course, register and range for variety. However, as the analysis in Figure 3.18 points out, even register and range conform to somewhat regular patterns of equivalence and similarity that provide further cohesion.

Set grouping usually follows harmonies, rhythms, articulations, or similar guides in music. However, register and range can also provide excellent boundaries for selecting or supporting pitch grouping for pitch-class set analysis. Webern's Variations, op. 27 (1936), for piano, the first seven measures of which appear in Figure 3.19, offers a good example of register and range support for alternate grouping possibilities. The op. 27 Variations is a highly serialized work in which unison A-naturals (here shown in m. 2, but also appearing elsewhere in this work and notable for their striking contrast to the otherwise registrally diverse sets) act as a kind of portal through which contrapuntally sounding versions of a twelve-tone row switch hands

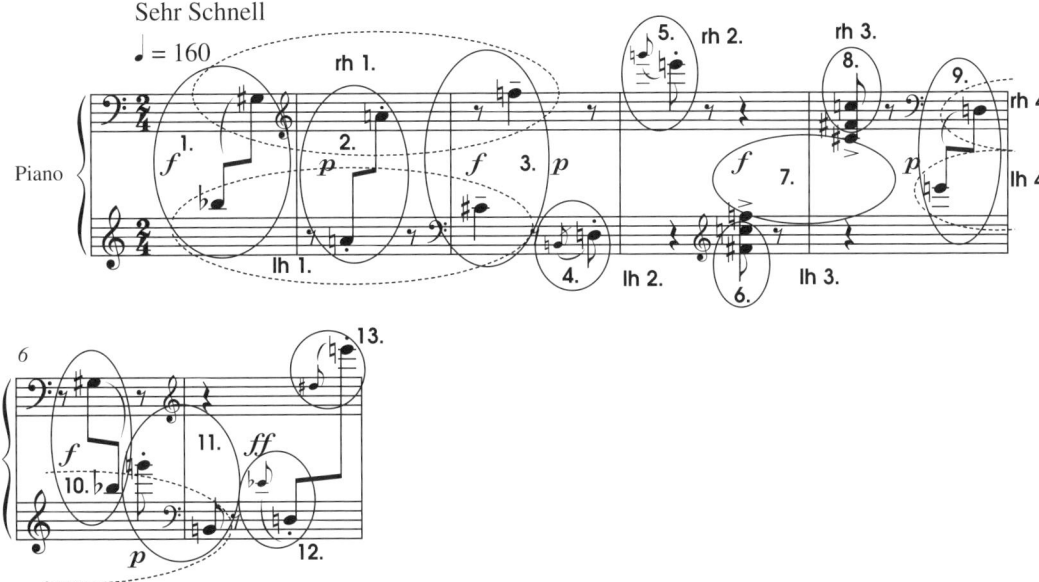

FIGURE 3.19 Webern, *Variations* (1936), mm. 1–7.

and registers. The dyad analysis in Figure 3.20a of the first few measures of this work indicates a natural grouping based on the beamed duplets. I have again placed correlated signs (*, †, ‡, ^, and °) after certain lines to show linear interval vector equivalencies. All but three of the ranges also have correlates, as shown by the boldfaced "r" numbers here. The "nil" initiating each list in this analysis indicate the dyad is an interval rather than a set.

From the dyad analysis in Figure 3.20, Webern's Variations clearly demonstrates consistency in terms of register and range. Also, only the unison in m. 2 resists vectoral similarity to other sets. However, grouping trichords by voice in this work—as shown in the analysis in Figure 3.20b—provides further insight into Webern's intricate formalisms. Even the unison A-natural dyad contributes to the coherent structure of the Variations in this trichordal analysis. The parallel-numbered right-hand/left-hand tetrachords here often occur in different registers but share equivalent linear interval vectors. The symbols following each line of this analysis (#, @, +, and ~) again indicate the connections between sets with identical vectors. Boldface ranges relate equivalencies. Clearly, this trichordal analysis reveals as much of the integration in this work as does the dyad analysis.

Comparing non-equivalent pitch-class sets often proves as useful as comparing equivalent sets. For example, the ranges and registers of differing pitch-class sets can reveal important information. The first nine measures from Boulez's *Structures* (1952), shown in Figure 3.21, serve as a good example. The tetrachordal analysis in

(a)
1.   ((nil **r26**) ((7t 58) (-26) **-26**) 010000)*
2.   ((nil r0) ((69) (0) 0) 000000)
3.   ((nil **r16**) ((61 75) (16) **16**) 000100)‡
4.   ((nil **r3**) ((4e 52) (3) **3**) 001000)^
5.   ((nil **r3**) ((87 84) (-3) **-3**) 001000)^
6.   ((nil **r6**) ((66 70) (6) **6**) 000001)°
7.   ((nil **r16**) ((75 61) (-16) **-16**) 000100)‡
8.   ((nil **r6**) ((66 70) (6) **6**) 000001)°
9.   ((nil r38) ((84 52) (-38) -38) 010000)*
10. ((nil **r26**) ((58 7t) (26) **26**) 010000)*
11. ((nil r44) ((87 4e) (-44) -44) 000100)‡
12. ((nil **r13**) ((63 52) (-13) **-13**) 100000)†
13. ((nil **r13**) ((73 84) (13) **13**) 100000)†

(b)
right hand
1.   (((60 71 64) r21) ((7t 69 61) (-13 -8) -21) 100100)#
2.   ((nil **r3**) ((87 84) (-3) -3) 001000)@
3.   (((70 61 66) **r11**) ((61 66 70) (5 6) 11) 000011)+
4.   (((50 81 56) **r41**) ((52 58 87) (6 35) 41) 100001)~

left hand
1.   (((50 61 65) r13) ((58 69 61) (13 -8) 5) 100100)#
2.   ((nil **r3**) ((4e 52) (3) 3) 001000)@
3.   (((60 71 76) **r11**) ((66 70 75) (6 5) 11) 000011)+
4.   (((70 41 86) **r41**) ((84 7t 4e) (-6 -35) -41) 100001)~

FIGURE 3.20 Webern analysis by dyads (a) and trichords by hand (b) as shown circled—dyads by solid line and trichords by dotted line—in Figure 3.19.

REGISTER AND RANGE IN SET ANALYSIS 125

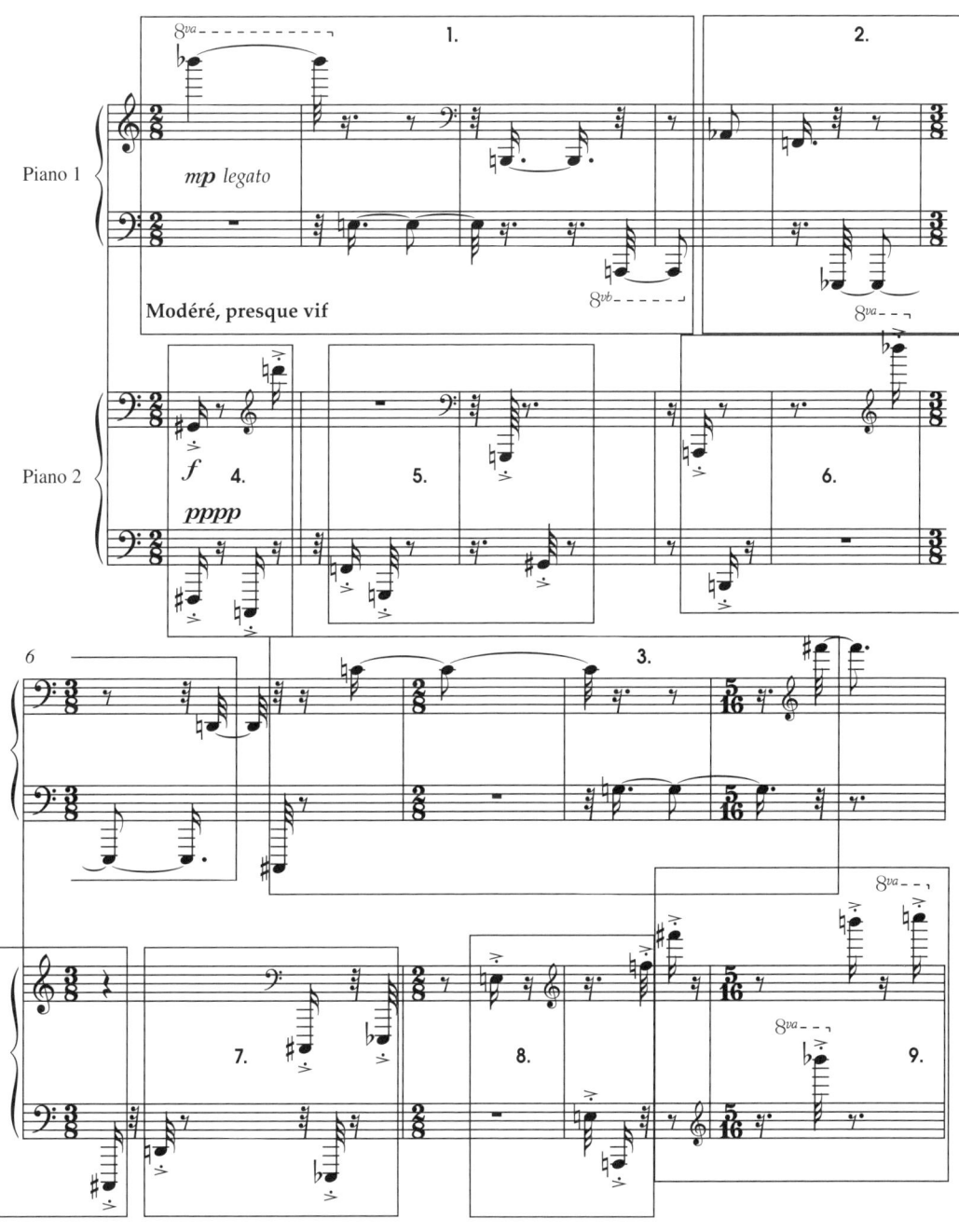

FIGURE 3.21 Nine measures from Boulez, *Structures* (1952).

126 HIDDEN STRUCTURE

Figure 3.22, in contrast to the Schoenberg and Webern analyses just presented, yields very few matches between any aspects of pitch-class sets, registers, ranges, interval mappings, summations, or linear interval vectors. The boldfaced selections here point out the two vector and range equivalencies and, conversely, the paucity of otherwise obvious relationships.

What appears as inconsistencies, or at least difficult-to-relate sets, however, can reveal interesting patterns. For example, the ranges of 85, 17, and 65 in the right hand and of 62, 13, 81, 13, 44, and 18 in the left hand demonstrate alternations of large and small intervals. Although these intervals—with the exception of the interval 13, which occurs twice in the left hand—vary in exact size, the dramatic contrasts of these alternating numbers present similar patterns. The summations in the right hand (-71, -3, and 65) move upward, while the summations in the left hand (-14, 3, -10, -11, 25, and 18) simultaneously move upward, downward, and then upward again. This directional pivoting provides a kind of precarious balance for this passage, which the numbers indicate by their differences rather than their similarities. The linear interval vectors—aside from the two that equate—have several similarities, indicated here in italics and underlining. Clearly, however, this analysis demonstrates more differences than similarities.

The registral and other types of analyses of each passage in Figures 3.17, 3.19, and 3.21 provide important information not otherwise available in strict pitch-class

right hand
1. (((30 91 22 57) r85) ((9t 29 54 3e) (-85 31 -17) -71) 100020)
2. <u>(((40 31 43 46) r17) ((48 33 42 45) (-17 11 3) -3) 101010)</u>
3. (((30 61 56 87) r65) ((31 57 60 86) (30 5 30) 65) 000012)

left hand
4. (((80 32 46 38) r62) ((48 82 30 36) (42 -62 6) -14) 010002)
5. **(((40 31 43) r13) ((45 37 48) (-10 13) 3) 110000)**
6. (((30 91 32 34) r81) ((3e 9t 39 31) (71 -73 -8) -10) 200100)
7. **(((30 41 32) r13) ((42 31 33) (-13 2 0) -11) 110000)**
8. (((50 71 35) r44) ((54 39 75) (0 -19 44) 25) 000110)
9. <u>(((100 81 92 86) r18) ((86 8e 9t t0 (5 11 2) 18) 110010)</u>

FIGURE 3.22 Boulez analysis by tetrachords by hand as shown circled in Figure 3.21.

set analyses. The often widely spaced intervals, though noticeable to the eye and ear, do not lend themselves to quick mental analysis. Thus, providing the computer-generated duodecimal registers, ranges, interval maps, summations, and linear interval vectors enhances analysts' abilities to access these important contributors to this music. Revealing this information during pitch-class set analysis helps with grouping, relating similar and dissimilar sets, and finding logic when comparing sets that otherwise seem disparate and possibly even illogical. Analyzing longer musical passages produces further benefits, as the following analyses will now attest.

MUSICAL EXAMPLES

Anton Webern's Concerto for Nine Instruments (op. 24) provides an excellent example of how register can play an important role in the analysis of a work. As many analysts have demonstrated (Bailey 1991; Straus 2005; Williams 1997), Webern's row for this highly formalized music consists of four trichords, each of which reduces to a [0,1,4] unregistered prime form, as clearly shown in mm. 1–3 of the first movement in Figure 3.23, a two-keyboard arrangement of this work. The equivalent prime-form pitch-class sets in these measures occur in various registers and sound different in many respects. However, the ranges of these trichords are precisely the same in each case—13. This equivalence remains true in the second statement of the row in mm. 4 and 5. In the third presentation of the row in m. 6 and the first half-beat of m. 7, however, the ranges for the trichords shift to 15, 13, 13, and 15, adding a subtle nuance to the otherwise static pitch-class sets. This range variation extends further in the fourth row statement—from beat 2 of m. 7 through m. 8—with each pitch-class set covering the interval of 11.

The full iteration of the row in Figure 3.23 appearing in mm. 9 and 10 (less the F-natural appearing in piano one on the last eighth note of m. 10) presents a striking contrast to the entirely single-sounding pitches thus far encountered in this work. However, in each case, these dyads and trichords all reiterate the opening range interval of 13. This consistency gives this passage a continuity that it might otherwise lack owing to its changes in texture. The line numbering in Figure 3.24 follows the numbering that identifies each of the groupings in Figure 3.23.

The ordered register sets of Webern's row demonstrate interesting permutations. Mm. 1–3, for example, use the ordered registers of (7, 6, 7), (8, 8, 7), (6, 6, 7), and (7, 8, 7) for its trichords. Mm. 4 and 5, however, have (7, 6, 7), (7, 8, 8), (7, 6, 6), and (7, 8, 7) as ordered registers; each of the trichord register collections are retrogrades of the associated originals. The third statement of the row in m. 6 through the first beat of m. 7 has registrations of (8, 7, 6), (6, 7, 7), (8, 7, 7), and (6, 7, 7) for its trichords, each a different arrangement of one or more of the original sets. This kind of register-motivic play continues throughout the work.

FIGURE 3.23 Webern, Concerto for 9 Instruments, op. 24, 1st movement, mm. 1–7.

FIGURE 3.23 continued

1. (((60 71 74) r13) ((7e 6t 72) (-13 4) -9) 100100)
2. (((80 71 84) r13) ((83 87 76) (4 -13) -9) 100100)
3. (((60 71 64) r13) ((68 64 75) (-4 13) 9) 100100)
4. (((80 71 74) r13) ((70 81 79) (13 -4) 9) 100100)
5. (((60 71 74) r13) ((72 6t 7e) (-4 13) 9) 100100)
6. (((80 71 84) r13) ((76 87 83) (13 -4) 9) 100100)
7. (((60 71 64) r13) ((75 64 68) (-13 4) -9) 100100)
8. (((80 71 74) r13) ((79 81 70) (4 -13) -9) 100100)
9. (((70 61 84) r15) ((81 79 6t) (-4 -11) -15) 100100)
10. (((70 61 74) r13) ((65 76 72) (13 -4) 9) 100100)
11. (((70 81 74) r13) ((84 73 77) (-13 4) -9) 100100)
12. (((70 71 64) r15) ((68 70 7e) (4 11) 15) 100100)
13. (((70 71 74) r11) ((70 7e 73) (11 -8) 3) 100100)
14. (((70 81 84) r11) ((84 78 87) (-8 11) 3) 100100)
15. (((80 71 74) r11) ((79 85 76) (8 -11) -3) 100100)
16. (((60 71 64) r11) ((71 62 6t) (-11 8) -3) 100100)
17. (((80 71 74) r13) ((70 79 81) (9 4) 13) 001100)
18. (((60 71 64) r13) ((64 68 75) (4 9) 13) 001100)
19. (((80 71 84) r13) ((76 83 87) (9 4) 13) 001100)
20. (((60 71 74) r13) ((6t 72 7e) (4 9) 13) 001100)

FIGURE 3.24 (a) Calculations of registral information in Webern, Concerto for 9 Instruments, op. 24, 1st movement, mm. 1–3.

Comparing interval maps and summations of ordered pitch-class sets also reveals a good deal about the formalistic nature of Webern's concerto. For instance, the first eight of the twenty trichordal analyses given in Figure 3.24—calculations of registral and other information from mm. 1–10 in Figure 3.23—show interval-mapping combinations of the positive and negative intervals of 13 and 4 only, and interval summations of the positive and negative interval of 9. The final four trichords in Figure 3.23 and resultant ordered interval-map analyses in Figure 3.24 contain only the intervals of positive 4 and 9, along with their summations of 13. The twenty trichords here contain but five different absolute intervals (4, 8, 9, 11, and 13) in their maps, with all but the interval 9 appearing in both positive and negative directions. The interval summations contain only four absolute intervals (3, 9, 13, and 15), with 9, 3, and 15 appearing in both positive and negative direction, and with 15 and -15 occurring but once each.

In the final measure of the first movement of this concerto (shown in Figure 3.25), the ranges and summations unify to 11 owing to the chordal nature of the trichords, which helps to produce a strong cadential resolution as well as a contrast to the somewhat more varied approach to range in the opening twenty trichords. Interestingly, the final chord of this movement of the concerto—the first time more than three pitches have sounded simultaneously—creates polytonal B major and E-flat minor triads, reminding us that throughout his work, Webern has alluded to similar triadic relationships, which seem slightly beyond reach due to intervening notes. Figure 3.26 presents a computer analysis of the excerpt in Figure 3.25, with the music grouped by trichord. Note the consistent ranges, the varied-in-direction but nonetheless equally consistent summations, and the different vectors used in the final four trichords. As with the opening passage of this work, shown in Figure 3.23, Webern demonstrates his tight control over all of the musical elements described in this chapter.

Range and register in Webern's concerto deserve as much attention as do its pitch, rhythm, articulation, timbre, and other components. By condensing, expanding, and varying the ranges and registers of his trichords, Webern produces a subtle tension that adds significantly to the effectiveness of this music. Seeing register, range, and other elements of this music represented in analysis notation reveals some of the important roles these parameters play in the deployment of pitch classes in this work.

The second movement of Boulez's Piano Sonata no. 2 (1950) presents another example of interesting uses of register and range in post-tonal music. The first six-plus measures of this movement appear in Figure 3.27. The initial four tetrachords of this music, distinctly separated into four measures, consist of two different alternating prime-form decimal sets ([0,1,2,3] and [0,1,2,7]). Boulez enhances the pairing of these sets by using similar ranges (in the case of decimal set [0,1,2,3], R_{38} and R_{37}, respectively) and identical ranges (in the case of decimal set [0,1,2,7], both with R_{13}), as shown in the analysis in Figure 3.28.

The ensuing four tetrachords in this movement pair as two differently duodecimal versions of the decimal set [0,1,2,3] followed by the decimal sets [0,2,6,8] and [0,2,5,8]. These latter four tetrachord groupings follow articulation and beaming rather than temporal order. The ranges of R_{33} and R_{35}, followed by the ranges of R_{44} and R_{27}, enhance these pairings. Although in Boulez's sonata range and register do not have the exactness as in Webern's concerto, they nonetheless contribute to the sonata's sense of logic in the tetrachordal groupings and their various interrelationships.

Comparisons of interval maps and interval summations of linear pitch-class sets also need not be as exact as in Webern's concerto to inform us of important aspects of musical structure. Boulez, for example, does not seem to formalize these

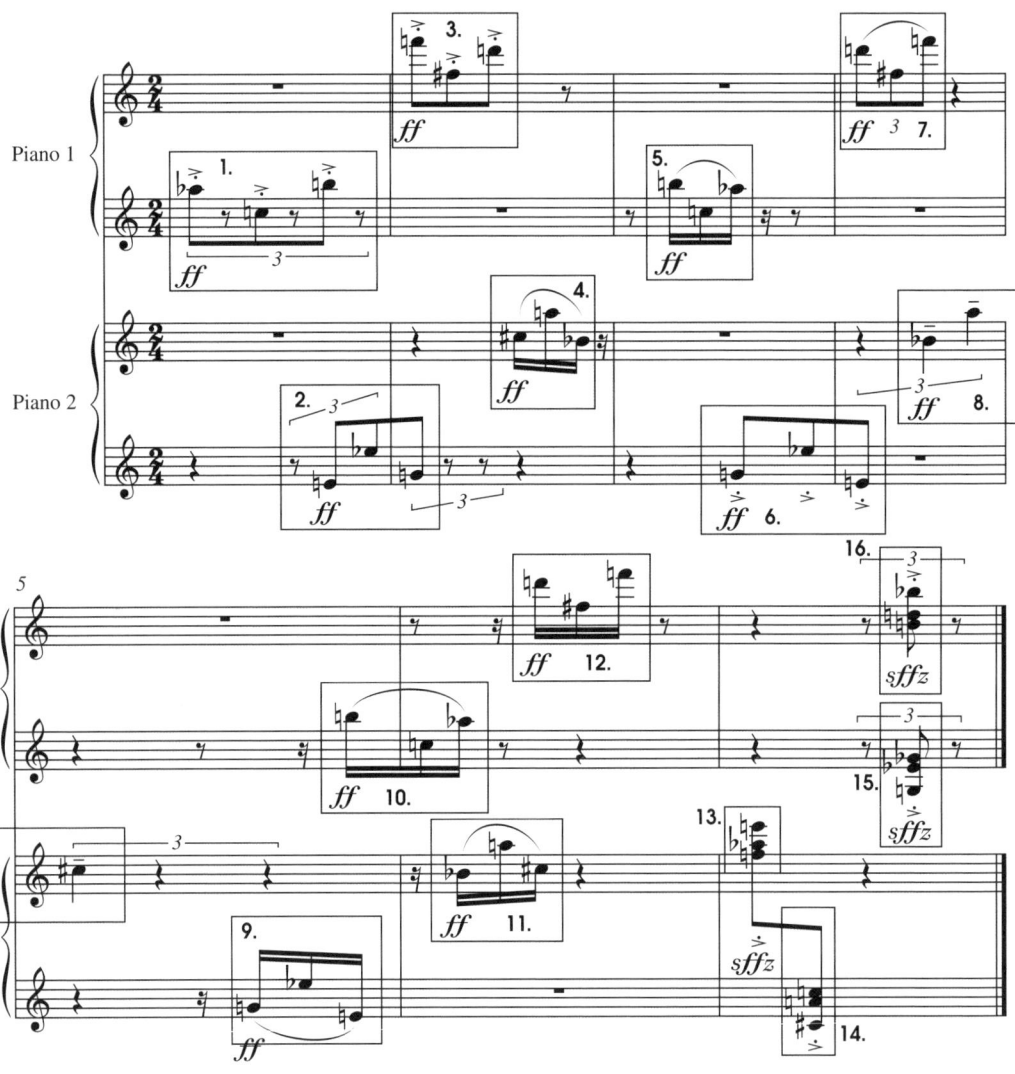

FIGURE 3.25 Webern, Concerto for 9 Instruments, op. 24, 1st movement, last 7 measures.

aspects of his sonata in the ways in which Webern does, as seen in Figures 3.23 and 3.25 and their associated analyses in Figures 3.24 and 3.26. However, the interval summations in Boulez's sonata nonetheless provide interesting information about the nature of the various sets. In the opening four tetrachords, for example, Boulez uses 23, -5, -27, and 7, alternating large and small interval summations, and in his

1. (((70 71 74) r11) ((78 70 7e) (-8 11) 3) 100100)
2. (((70 61 64) r11) ((64 73 67) (11 -8) 3) 100100)
3. (((70 81 84) r11) ((85 76 82) (-11 8) -3) 100100
4. (((70 61 74) r11) ((71 79 6t) (8 -11) -3) 100100)
5. (((70 71 74) r11) ((7e 70 78) (-11 8) -3) 100100)
6. (((70 61 64) r11) ((67 73 64) (8 -11) -3) 100100)
7. (((70 81 84) r11) ((82 76 85) (-8 11) 3) 100100)
8. (((70 61 74) r11) ((6t 79 71) (11 -8) 3) 100100)
9. (((70 61 64) r11) ((67 73 64) (8 -11) -3) 100100)
10. (((70 71 74) r11) ((7e 70 78) (-11 8) -3) 100100)
11. (((70 61 74) r11) ((6t 79 71) (11 -8) 3) 100100)
12. (((70 81 84) r11) ((82 76 85) (-8 11) 3) 100100)
13. (((80 71 74) r11) ((75 78 84) (3 8) 11) 001100)
14. (((60 71 64) r11) ((61 69 70) (8 3) 11) 001100)
15. (((50 61 64) r11) ((57 63 66) (8 3) 11) 001100)
16. (((70 61 74) r11) ((6e 72 7t) (3 8) 11) 001100)

FIGURE 3.26 Calculations of registral information from Figure 3.25.

second grouping of four tetrachords (following beams and legato marks) we find similar summations of -22, 10, -14, and 27, two relatively large and two relatively small variations of his original summations. With the exception of the final map here, each of his ordered interval maps contains either two positive and one negative interval, or two negative and one positive interval, also providing consistency for this passage.

I use register and range as an integral part of my composing processes. In the opening of my *Triplum* for flute and piano (1975), for example, pointillistic sets of various sizes act as an introduction to the piece. As shown in Figure 3.29, this introduction begins with an [80,71,62] prime form trichord that spans an interval range of 14 (see m. 1 of Figure 3.29), though the decimal prime form of the set ([0,1,2]) covers only a major second. This opening group precedes a similar chromatic duodecimal tetrachord ([60,71,62,63]) encompassing the same range of 14 (see m. 2 through the first two beats of m. 4). Like the first grouping, the prime form of the set again consists of consecutive minor seconds. This tetrachord then expands to a

134 HIDDEN STRUCTURE

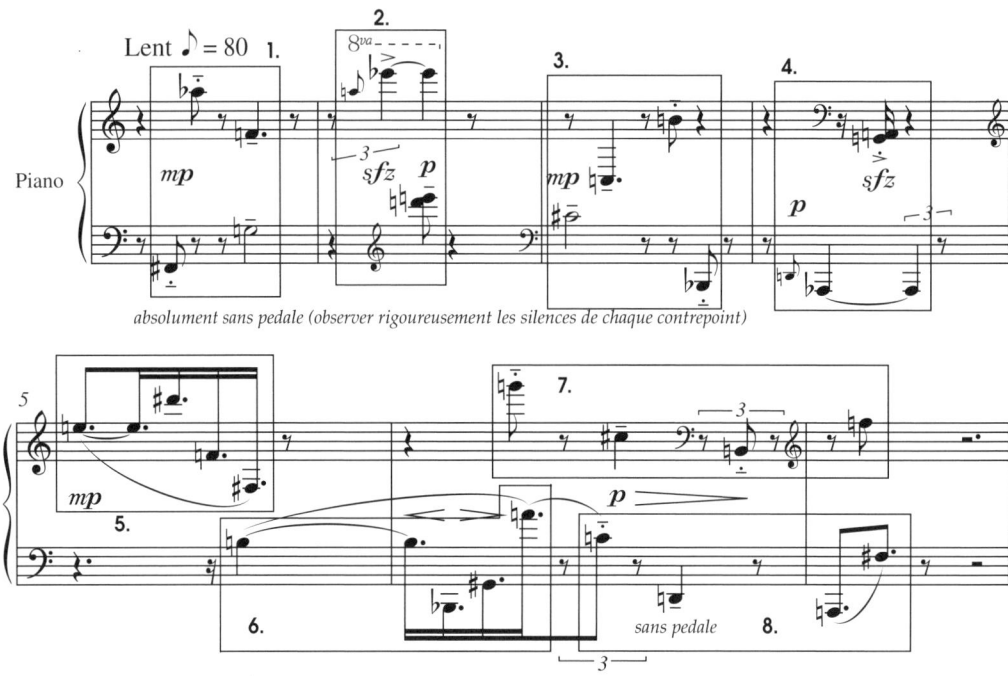

FIGURE 3.27 Boulez, Second Sonata for Piano (1948), 2nd movement, beginning.

1. (((70 51 42 63) r38) ((46 78 57 65) (38 -25 10) 23) 120000)
2. (((80 91 82 87) r13) ((89 93 82 84) (6 -13 2) -5) 110001)
3. (((60 51 62 33) r37) ((61 50 6e 3t) (-13 23 -37) -27) 300000)
4. (((40 31 42 47) r13) ((42 38 47 49) (-6 11 2) 7) 110001)

(as notes are beamed and by legato marks)
5. (((50 61 72 83) r33) ((74 83 65 56) (11 -22 -11) -22) 210000)
6. (((50 31 62 43) r35) ((5e 3t 48 69) (-25 10 25) 10) 210000)
7. (((80 72 76 48) r44) ((87 71 4e 75) (-18 -26 30) -14) 010002)
8. (((40 62 35 58) r27) ((39 42 56 60) (5 16 6) 27) 000111)

FIGURE 3.28 Calculations of registral information in mm. 1–6 in Boulez, Second Sonata for Piano (1948), 2nd movement.

pentachord grouping, which extends the range to 16, as shown in the second half of mm. 4–6. Measure 7 through the first half of m. 8 produces the [60,71,64] ([0,1,4] decimal) trichord, providing a significant break from the more compressed prime-form sets heard thus far in this work. However, the interval range 11 of this grouping continues the somewhat large registral separations of these pitch classes. This short grouping is then followed by a [50,61,72,64,75] set beginning in the second half of m. 8 and continuing through m. 9, and spanning the range of 22, the widest interval yet covered. Measure 10 and the first half of m. 11 then return to a range similar to that used in the work's beginning (13) and the same prime-form trichord ([0,1,2] decimal), but with the ordered registers shifted slightly—from [7,8,6] to [6,5,4].

In the second half of m. 11 and extending through m. 12, the initial prime-form trichord of this work implodes to the packed range of a major second, providing a dynamic contrast to the wide ranges thus far presented. Although other aspects of the music—rhythm, dynamics, and so on—have changed here, this sudden range compaction provides the primary impetus for a turn in the music's direction. This compact version of the [0,1,2] decimal prime-form set continues through another iteration in m. 13 and the first half of m. 14. A return to the wider range of m. 13 then follows in the remainder of mm. 14 and 15.

Register and range provide the principal driving force for the music in this opening section. The simplistic descending chromatic scale—the primary pitch source for this section of *Triplum*—produces a rather static melodic and harmonic base that otherwise creates little tension. Without the accordioning range here, this opening passage would doubtless have little forward momentum and leave *Triplum* with little motivation for its ensuing sections.

The computer analysis for this passage of *Triplum*, shown in Figure 3.30, reveals interesting interval maps and summations. Even though the sets here have varying numbers of pitch classes (from three to five), the interval maps contain many similar intervals and repeated motions indicative of the motivic imitations in the music. Only the trichords lack this feature. Although the summations repeat only one interval (-1, stated three times), all but the final summation show a series of downward or static motions (-1, -3, -14; 0, -8, -13; and -1, -1, 11), clearly the result of the descending chromatic-scale foundation of this music, though not its necessary consequence.

The seven measures of *Triplum* shown in Figure 3.31 provide another example in which range and register contribute to this music's momentum. The piano part of this passage consists of several groups, all but one of which cycles through six ascending major sevenths (the last group has seven). Because the number of pitches in these collections does not divide the chromatic scale evenly, and because I connect the end of each set with the beginning of the following set via the next pitch class of the ongoing descending chromatic scale, each grouping of ordered pitch classes is different. The rigid range of each contributing interval and this cycling through the downward chromatic scale while moving upward in register creates a static canvas on which the flute—playing a modal Navajo melody—tonicizes C.

FIGURE 3.29 The author, *Triplum* for flute and piano (1975), beginning.

REGISTER AND RANGE IN SET ANALYSIS   137

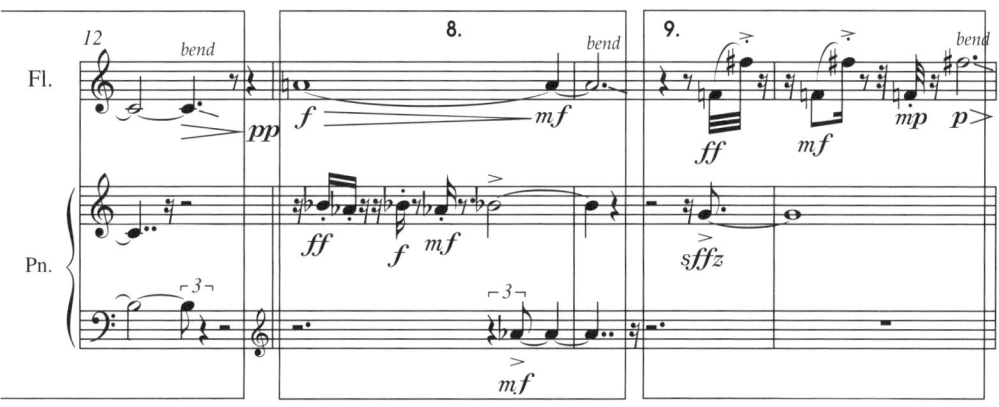

FIGURE 3.29 continued

1. (((80 71 62) r14) ((70 81 6e) (13 -14) -1) 110000)
2. (((60 71 62 63) r14) ((6t 79 68 67) (11 -13 -1 0) -3) 300000)
3. (((70 61 62 63 64) r16) ((76 65 63 62 64) (-13 -1 -1 -1 2 -1 -1 2) -14) 620000)
4. (((60 71 64) r11) ((69 70 61) (11 -3 3 -11) 0) 202000)
5. (((50 61 72 64 75) r22) ((67 76 79 6t 5e) (11 3 -11 -11 0 0) -8) 301000)
6. (((50 61 42) r13) ((60 51 4e) (-11 -2) -13) 110000)
7. (((60 61 52) r2) ((60 61 5e) (1 -2) -1) 110000)
8. (((60 61 62) r2) ((69 6t 68) (1 -2 2 -2 2 -2) -1) 150000)
9. (((60 71 62) r13) ((67 65 76) (-2 13 -13 13 -13 13) 11) 510000)

FIGURE 3.30 Calculations of registral information in the author's *Triplum* for flute and piano (1975), mm. 1–7.

In m. 46 of *Triplum*—an extended thirty-four-second proportionally notated section of music, shown in Figure 3.32—I use register to help establish a nine pitch-class set. In this section, pitch classes retain their initial registers, which are broadcast over a two-plus octave range. The vertical dotted lines in Figure 3.31 provide the timing in seconds, with pitches occurring proportionate to their horizontal visual locations with respect to these dotted lines. Were each pitch class here to appear in various registers rather than just one, the conglomerate—the normal ordered [60,81,72,63,74,66,78,69,7t] duodecimal nonachord set—would be much less

FIGURE 3.31 The author, *Triplum* for flute and piano (1975), mm. 98–104.

perceivable. The music would also lose its wind-chime effect, so important to this particular moment in the piece.

The register-static trichord that appears twice separately in the flute and piano ([65,67,6e] or F-natural, G-natural, and B-natural) gains prominence from its deployment of otherwise unused pitch classes and from its complementary relationship with the backdrop of the register-frozen wind-chime keyboard music, producing a complete twelve-pitch combination. Register thus plays an extremely important role in this passage, even though no actual register shifting takes place.

Obviously, grouping this excerpt into several smaller collections of pitch classes could produce fragments of the nonachord and thus create a false analysis of the stasis in this passage. Such an analysis would also mask the polarity of the nonachord-trichord relationship. Again, the register-frozen pitch classes enhance both the aural and visual impression that no actual change—apart from the twice-occurring complementary trichord—takes place. Clearly, this music depends on register as much as it depends on pitch class and other factors.

As just demonstrated, aspects of register and range can prove useful even in the analysis of large groupings such as phrases and sections. For example, I have found that with certain composers and works, range and register maps yield information about phrase length, location of entrances of new material, or positions of impending cadences not easily revealed by analysis of pitch class and other elements of the music alone. Of course, such maps can occasionally be deceiving, as when their extremes define merely the range limits of instruments rather than important characteristics of the music itself. Although studying rhythm, timbre, and other salient features can significantly impact our understanding of a work, analyzing for register, range, interval maps, summations, and linear interval vectors, as shown by the analyses presented here, can also provide valuable insights.

PROGRAM DESCRIPTION

The software called Register (Macintosh and PC compatible), available on the CD-ROM accompanying this book, takes a series of ordered note-events and returns the prime form in duodecimal numbers, its registration in decimal numbers, the ordered pitch-class set in duodecimal numbers, the ordered interval map in decimal numbers, the interval summation in decimal numbers, and the linear interval vector. As shown previously in the text and figures, these returned sets take the form (((80 71 62) r-14) ((70 81 6e) (13 -14) -1) 110000).

I have also placed the music of the figures in this chapter as note-events on the CD-ROM accompanying this book, both as examples for readers to use and for verifying the findings presented in the figures here. Shared linear interval vectors obviously play a significant role in my interpretation of these analyses. I encourage

FIGURE 3.32 Another passage from the author's *Triplum* for flute and piano (1975), m. 43.

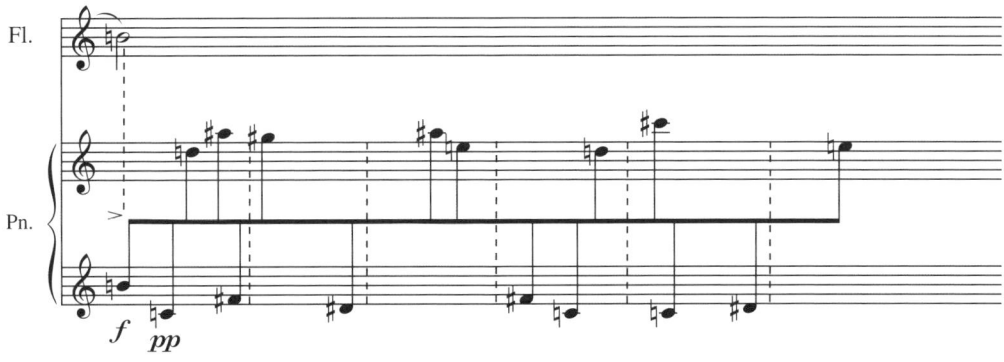

FIGURE 3.32 continued

readers to compare and cross-reference the other parameters to obtain further insights into the music represented by this data.

Maintaining registral information in duodecimal notation when reducing pitches to pitch-class t-normal and prime forms, and using this information to calculate range, contour maps, interval summations, and linear interval vectors, can significantly enhance the analysis of many post-tonal works. Although such information exists in the music itself, it can easily be lost amid the various machinations that ordinary pitch-class set analysis requires. Combining register with pitch class in a relatively simple duodecimal notation enables analysts to more fully account for the roles register and range play in many post-tonal works and hence contributes to a fuller understanding of that music.

I have also included a program called Set Multiples that produces all the possible combinations of prime-form sets that multiply to an individual prime form set—more or less a reverse process of that described in SetMath. The top-level function `find-all-source-multiples-of`, provided a single argument, produces a list of all possible combinations of sets that multiply to that set. Although this function and process may seem more of use to composers than to analysts, `find-all-source-multiples-of` can provide a long series of possible source sets for analysis when simple neighboring sets do not multiply to successive sets. For example, in Figure 3.32, m. 7, the new set [0,2,6] occurs (E–D–G♯). This set seems somewhat removed from the sets that appeared earlier in this work. However, running `find-all-source-multiples-of` on this new set produces many possible groups of sets, including [0,2,5] and [0,1,4], the sets appearing in the first few measures of the piece, another rationale for including these sets at this point in the piece.

Figure 3.33 presets the ninety-seven possible origin sets for the decimal set [0,2,6]. The parentheses here are organizational and relate to the programming language rather than to any preferred notation. The lack of commas results from the same source. I have left these in the output in this figure to make sure that readers who use the software provided with this book are prepared for the difference between most of this book's notation and the output they will experience. Also, the two sets to the left (aggregated by super parentheses) are the sources, and the final set—the same in each case—represents the result of the multiplication of the first two sets. Note further that as the list progresses, the multiplication of much larger sets than the trichord output appear as multiples. The smaller set output results from the duplications that reduce out from the mathematics involved.

I do not intend to suggest here that such additions, subtractions, and multiplications occur commonly in post-tonal music, just that simple mathematical processes such as those described here do occur and that analysts should be aware of this fact. Sets that seemingly arrive from nowhere in music often relate to earlier- or later-appearing sets by way of these processes, and including them in analysis can enhance one's understanding of how differing sets can relate to one another. Computer programs make such machinations more quickly and accurately acquirable, as a few paper computations should easily prove.

Mapping one multiplier across a single set can also produce interesting results (see Morris 1987, 42), particularly for composers. In fact, Morris's book and that of John Rahn (1980) contain many extraordinary machinations of pitch-class sets that, given the proper computer program, could make very interesting tools for post-tonal analysis. Rather than produce such programs here, I point readers to these and other fine sources (especially Lewin 1987) for further research.

Stravinsky's Three Pieces for String Quartet (1914) produces some interesting instances of set computations. For example, the first two tetrachordal sets occurring at the beginning of his quartet as beats 2 and 3 produce the decimal prime form [0,1,4,7] when multiplied together, the same set that concludes the passage in m. 7. This kind of interrelationship between sets helps to unify what could otherwise seem to be dislocated, even arbitrary, set progressions. The voice-leading, though certainly the connecting principle for the repeating sets, is therefore not the only glue that holds them together as a unified whole. Schoenberg's comment that "chords are formed merely as accidents of voice leading, and they have no structural significance since responsibility for the harmony is borne by the melodic line" (Schoenberg 1983, 312) notwithstanding, Stravinsky's chordal sets represent important correspondences in this music.

Because I will be using sets more abstractly for most of the remainder of this book, I will not compel readers to continue reading the duodecimal registral notation as presented in this chapter. I have omitted the registral information not because of difficulties that might be encountered with the notation, but from the lack of relevance this added information has to the topics being discussed. I will, however, return to duodecimal pitch-class sets in Chapter 7. The various processes described in this and upcoming chapters will coalesce into Muse, a computer program designed to analyze post-tonal music from the many different perspectives provided here.

((((0 1 2) (0 2 4)) (0 2 6))
(((0 1 4) (0 2 5)) (0 2 6))
(((0 2 4) (0 1 5)) (0 2 6))
(((0 1 5) (0 2 6)) (0 2 6))
(((0 2 5) (0 1 6)) (0 2 6))
(((0 2 5) (0 2 6)) (0 2 6))
(((0 1 2 3) (0 2 3 6)) (0 2 6))
(((0 1 2 3) (0 2 4 8)) (0 2 6))
(((0 1 2 4) (0 2 3 6)) (0 2 6))
(((0 1 2 4) (0 2 4 6)) (0 2 6))
(((0 1 2 4) (0 2 4 8)) (0 2 6))
(((0 1 2 4) (0 2 6 8)) (0 2 6))
(((0 1 2 5) (0 2 3 6)) (0 2 6))
(((0 1 4 5) (0 2 3 6)) (0 2 6))
(((0 2 3 5) (0 1 2 6)) (0 2 6))
(((0 2 3 5) (0 1 4 6)) (0 2 6))
(((0 2 3 5) (0 2 4 6)) (0 2 6))
(((0 1 2 6) (0 2 3 6)) (0 2 6))
(((0 1 2 6) (0 2 4 6)) (0 2 6))
(((0 1 2 6) (0 2 3 7)) (0 2 6))
(((0 1 2 6) (0 2 4 8)) (0 2 6))
(((0 1 5 6) (0 2 4 6)) (0 2 6))
(((0 2 4 6) (0 1 3 7)) (0 2 6))
(((0 2 4 6) (0 1 6 7)) (0 2 6))
(((0 2 4 6) (0 2 3 7)) (0 2 6))
(((0 2 4 6) (0 2 4 7)) (0 2 6))
(((0 2 4 6) (0 3 4 7)) (0 2 6))
(((0 2 4 6) (0 1 5 8)) (0 2 6))
(((0 1 5 7) (0 2 4 8)) (0 2 6))
(((0 1 6 7) (0 2 4 8)) (0 2 6))
(((0 1 6 7) (0 2 6 8)) (0 2 6))
(((0 2 3 7) (0 1 4 8)) (0 2 6))
(((0 2 4 7) (0 1 5 8)) (0 2 6))
(((0 2 4 7) (0 3 5 8)) (0 2 6))
(((0 2 5 7) (0 1 4 8)) (0 2 6))
(((0 3 4 7) (0 2 5 8)) (0 2 6))
(((0 3 4 7) (0 2 6 8)) (0 2 6))
(((0 2 5 8) (0 2 6 8)) (0 2 6))
(((0 2 6 8) (0 3 5 8)) (0 2 6))
(((0 1 2 3 4) (0 2 3 4 6)) (0 2 6))
(((0 1 2 3 5) (0 2 3 4 6)) (0 2 6))
(((0 1 2 3 6) (0 2 3 4 6)) (0 2 6))
(((0 1 2 3 6) (0 2 3 4 7)) (0 2 6))
(((0 1 2 3 6) (0 2 3 6 8)) (0 2 6))
(((0 1 2 4 6) (0 2 3 6 8)) (0 2 6))
(((0 1 2 4 6) (0 2 4 5 8)) (0 2 6))
(((0 1 2 4 6) (0 2 4 6 8)) (0 2 6))
(((0 1 2 5 6) (0 2 3 6 8)) (0 2 6))
(((0 2 3 4 6) (0 1 2 3 7)) (0 2 6))
(((0 2 3 4 6) (0 1 2 6 7)) (0 2 6))
(((0 2 3 4 6) (0 1 2 6 8)) (0 2 6))
(((0 2 3 4 6) (0 1 4 5 8)) (0 2 6))
(((0 1 2 6 7) (0 2 4 6 8)) (0 2 6))
(((0 1 3 4 7) (0 2 4 5 8)) (0 2 6))
(((0 1 3 4 7) (0 2 4 6 8)) (0 2 6))
(((0 1 3 6 7) (0 2 4 6 8)) (0 2 6))
(((0 2 3 4 7) (0 1 4 5 8)) (0 2 6))
(((0 2 3 4 7) (0 1 4 6 8)) (0 2 6))
(((0 2 3 4 7) (0 3 4 5 8)) (0 2 6))
(((0 1 2 4 8) (0 2 4 6 9)) (0 2 6))
(((0 1 2 6 8) (0 2 4 6 9)) (0 2 6))
(((0 1 3 5 8) (0 2 4 6 9)) (0 2 6))
(((0 1 3 7 8) (0 2 4 6 9)) (0 2 6))
(((0 2 3 5 8) (0 2 4 6 8)) (0 2 6))
(((0 2 3 5 8) (0 1 4 6 9)) (0 2 6))
(((0 2 3 5 8) (0 2 4 6 9)) (0 2 6))
(((0 2 3 6 8) (0 2 4 5 8)) (0 2 6))
(((0 2 4 5 8) (0 2 4 6 8)) (0 2 6))
(((0 2 4 5 8) (0 1 3 6 9)) (0 2 6))
(((0 2 4 5 8) (0 2 4 6 9)) (0 2 6))
(((0 2 4 5 8) (0 1 2 4 7)) (0 2 6))
(((0 2 4 6 8) (0 3 4 5 8)) (0 2 6))
(((0 3 4 5 8) (0 2 4 6 9)) (0 2 6))
(((0 1 2 3 4 6) (0 2 3 4 6 8)) (0 2 6))
(((0 1 2 3 4 6) (0 2 3 4 6 9)) (0 2 6))
(((0 1 2 3 5 6) (0 2 3 4 6 8)) (0 2 6))
(((0 1 2 3 5 6) (0 2 3 4 6 9)) (0 2 6))
(((0 1 2 6 7 8) (0 2 4 6 8 10)) (0 2 6))
(((0 1 2 6 7 8) (0 2 3 4 6 9)) (0 2 6))
(((0 2 3 4 5 7) (0 2 4 6 8 10)) (0 2 6))
(((0 1 2 4 7 8) (0 2 4 6 8 10)) (0 2 6))
(((0 1 3 4 7 8) (0 2 4 6 8 10)) (0 2 6))
(((0 1 4 5 8 9) (0 2 3 4 6 8)) (0 2 6))
(((0 2 3 4 6 8) (0 1 2 3 6 9)) (0 2 6))
(((0 1 2 4 6 8) (0 2 4 6 8 10)) (0 2 6))
(((0 1 3 4 6 8) (0 2 4 6 8 10)) (0 2 6))
(((0 1 3 4 6 9) (0 2 4 6 8 10)) (0 2 6))
(((0 1 3 5 6 9) (0 2 4 6 8 10)) (0 2 6))
(((0 2 4 6 8 10) (0 2 3 4 6 9)) (0 2 6))
(((0 1 2 3 4 8) (0 2 3 4 6 9)) (0 2 6))
(((0 1 2 3 7 8) (0 2 3 4 6 9)) (0 2 6))
(((0 2 3 4 5 8) (0 1 2 3 6 9)) (0 2 6))
(((0 1 2 3 5 8) (0 2 3 4 6 9)) (0 2 6))
(((0 1 2 3 6 8) (0 2 3 4 6 9)) (0 2 6))
(((0 2 3 4 5 6 8) (0 1 2 3 6 7 9)) (0 2 6))
(((0 1 2 3 4 6 8) (0 2 3 4 6 7 9)) (0 2 6))
(((0 2 3 4 6 7 9) (0 1 2 3 5 6 8)) (0 2 6))

FIGURE 3.33 The 97 possible origin sets for [0,2,6].

CONCLUSIONS

This chapter has explored a number of important roles that both range and register play in post-tonal music, and how analysis of these properties can lead to important revelations. The simple duodecimal notation proposed will certainly enhance set-theoretical analysis. At the outset of this chapter I noted that its modest goals would allow "both those familiar with mathematics but unfamiliar with music, and those familiar with music but unfamiliar with mathematics, to find common ground before the book takes more adventuresome directions in Chapter 4 and beyond." Chapter 4, then, takes the somewhat unusual view that because musical scales have served music analysts well for centuries, they should continue to serve as a tool for analyzing post-tonal music. Computers can in fact provide a perfect vehicle for extracting such scales from apparently non-scalar chromatic music. Thus, Chapter 4 lays a foundation for Chapter 5's provocative notion that scales can provide a foundation for revealing function in post-tonal music.

FOUR
Computer Analysis of Scales in Post-Tonal Music

> Discussing pitch centricity in post-tonal music is more complicated than identifying the tonic of a tonal piece. In post-tonal music, we can talk about an entire spectrum of centric effects. At one extreme, represented by much twelve-tone music, there is little or no sense of centricity. Even so, of course, the pitch classes are not treated identically, and it is important to be sensitive to any kind of special treatment accorded to pitch classes or pitch-class sets. At the other extreme, many post-tonal pieces are deeply preoccupied by questions of centricity.
>
> Joseph Straus, *Introduction to Post-Tonal Theory* (2005), 133

For over a millennium, musical scales have provided a fundamental palette upon which music analysts could build superstructures for determining modes and keys—primary ingredients in music theory. With the advent of highly chromatic and serial music in the early twentieth century, scales lost favor as a basis for describing such notions as key and function. In this chapter, I suggest that scales may yet have a place in the analysis of post-tonal music, and that computers offer an extraordinary opportunity for analysts to rediscover the importance of scales in all music. After all, scales define the most frequently occurring pitches in a work of music, and—after nearly a century of discussion and dissension—most analysts now agree that no work portrays its various pitch classes as truly equal. This chapter, then, centers on Principle 2 as described in Chapter 1 of this book.

MATHEMATICAL SEQUENCES

A mathematical sequence, of which a musical scale is an example, is an ordered list of objects (typically numbers) of finite or infinite length. The order of the elements of a sequence matters, unlike the order of mathematical sets, discussed in Chapter 3. For example, the same elements of sequences may return, and their position and order in that sequence is important. Notated sequences that extend indefinitely usually terminate in ellipses, such as 1, 2, 3, 4, 5 . . . , to indicate their infinite continuation. Sequences often result from the application of algorithms such as

[0, 1, 2, 3, 4, 5, 6, 7, 8, 9, 10, 11, 12 . . .],

expressible as $U_n = n + 1$, where, to each number n in a sequence $U_1, U_2, \ldots U_n$, there corresponds a number U_n. Known as an ascending incremental sequence of numbers in decimal notation, a duodecimal version of this sequence produces the chromatic scale in music. A sequence of odd integers such as

[1, 3, 5, 7, 9, 11, . . .]

could be notated as

$U_n = 2n - 1$

and

[1, 3, 6, 10, 15, 21, . . .]

as

$U_n = n(n + 1)/2$,

and so on.

More interesting and useful sequences include the famed Fibonacci sequence, created in the thirteenth century by Leonardo of Pisa (also known as Fibonacci). The Fibonacci sequence consists of numbers created by the addition of two previous numbers:

[0, 1, 1, 2, 3, 5, 8, 13, 21, 34, 55 . . .]

It is usually seeded with a given 0, 1. As will be further discussed in Chapter 7, this sequence produces what is often called the golden mean or golden section, resulting from the division of a given number in the sequence by its predecessor. In terms of the notation just used, the Fibonacci sequence could be expressed as $U_n = U_{n-1} + U_{n-2}$. Many other methods for figuring the golden mean exist mathematically as well.

There are virtually an infinite number of sequences, all of which—by using modulo 12—can be reduced to a particular musical scale. For example, the Fibonacci sequence produces the scale [0,1,2,3,4,5,7,8,9,t,e]—all members of the chromatic scale except its midpoint, 6—from the following code:

```
(defun create-sequence-scale (sequence)
  "Produces a scale out of the sequence in its arg."
  (my-sort #'< (remove-duplicates
                (loop for element in sequence
                      collect (mod element 12)))))

(defun fibonacci (limit n1 n2)
  "Creates a fibonacci sequence up to first arg."
  (if (> n2 limit)()
      (cons (+ n1 n2)
            (fibonacci limit n2 (+ n1 n2)))))
```

```
(defun my-sort (function lists)
  "Non-destructive sort."
  (loop for sorted-item in
        (sort (loop for item in lists
                    collect (list item)) function :key #'car)
        collect (first sorted-item)))
```

The use of the Lisp macro `loop`—in the function `create-sequence-scale`—requires some explanation here. The `loop` macro allows many of its arguments to appear without parentheses, thus making it both more readable and, unfortunately, less Lisp-like. In this function, `loop` states that the variable `element` will represent in turn each member of its sequence argument, thus applying `mod` 12 to each in turn and returning it in a list supplied by the use of `collect`.

Applying the function `create-sequence-scale` to a variety of number sequences provides quite interesting results. For example, the following results from using this function on all of the primes up to 100

[1,2,3,5,7,e]

and the

```
(defun additive-sequence
  (limit &optional (start 0)(increment 1))
  (if (> start limit)()
      (cons start
            (additive-sequence limit (+ start increment)(1+ increment)))))
```

function produces output in the form of

(0 1 3 6 10 15 21 28 36 45 55 66 78 91 105 120 136 153 171 190 210 231 253 276 300 325 351 378 406 435 465 496 528 561 595 630 666 703 741 780 820 861 903 946 990 1035 1081 1128 1176 1225 1275 1326 1378 1431 1485 1540 1596 1653 1711 1770 1830 1891 1953 2016 2080 2145 2211 2278 2346 2415 2485 2556 2628 2701 2775 2850 2926 3003 3081 3160 3240 3321 3403 3486 3570 3655 3741 3828 3916 4005 4095 4186 4278 4371 4465 4560 4656 4753 4851 4950)

producing the octatonic scale, when reduced with `create-sequence-scale`,

[0,1,3,4,6,7,9,t]

and so on. The number of sequences and resulting scales produced is dependent only on the imaginations of those inventing and using this kind of code.

The following polynomial formula creates a scale with quite interesting dimensions:

$f_n = (a * 3n) + (b * 2n) + (c * n) + d$

producing the pitch-class scale of

[0,2,3,5,6,9,e]

when A equals 5, and B, C, and D each equal 2. The Lisp function that creates the sequence for the above output appears below.

```
(defun polynomial-sequence
  "Creates a sequence within limit based on polynomial
  equation."
    (modulo limit &optional (start 0)(n 1)(a 5)(b 2)(c 2)
    (d 2))
  (if (> start limit)()
    (cons (mod start modulo )
          (polynomial-sequence modulo
                               limit
                               (+ (* a (* n n n))
                                  (* b (* n n))
                                  (* c n) d)
                               (+ n 1)))))
```

Obviously many other sequences possess interesting potentials for musical use. Whether such sequences originate from algorithmic or mathematical sources hardly matters, as long as the resulting scales prove useful for analyzing music. The following discussion assumes that scales are examples of both finite sequences *and* sets, though in the latter case differences appear as I will soon describe.

SCALES

Musical scales represent an important resource for composers and for the music analysts who analyze the music of these composers. Scale analysis has not, however, found as well recognized a place in the canon of analytical processes available for post-tonal music as it has for tonal music. This section of this chapter presents a computer approach for quickly and efficiently discovering scales in post-tonal music. After initially defining an algorithm that produces all possible one-to-twelve-pitch equal-tempered scales for reference, I describe a system of linear interval vector analysis that abstracts these scales into collections of similar scales based on shared traits. I then explain a series of analytical techniques for revealing scales in post-tonal music. These techniques are intended to enhance, not replace, other approaches to analysis such as pitch-class set theory (see Chapter 3). Finally, several examples of scales used in post-tonal composition demonstrate the effectiveness of using such an approach to better understand at least some post-tonal music.

For many hundreds of years, scales have played an important role in defining Western classical modal and tonal music (Hindemith 1942; Schoenberg 1983).

Scales provide important information for interpreting harmonic function, chromaticism, and modulation (Carey and Clampitt 1989; Gamer 1967). Even in twentieth- and twenty-first-century musical styles, scales—octatonic, whole tone, chromatic, and so on—have contributed to the interpretation and appreciation of many quasi-tonal works (Agmon 1989; Browne 1981). For reasons that are not fully clear, however, scale analysis has not played a leading role in the analysis of most post-tonal music, but has taken a back seat to grouping approaches such as pitch-class set theory, which reveal, I believe, incomplete (though significant) insights into musical structure (Clough 1980; Morris 1987; Perle 1996; Rahn 1980; Straus 1990). Defining and mapping scales in post-tonal music can provide important information, ultimately contributing to a more complete understanding of this music, regardless of its style or the formal compositional techniques used (Lindley and Turner-Smith 1993).

In order for readers to fully understand my arguments regarding non-tonal scales and their use, I review here a few of the fundamental ways in which traditional Western classical composers use tonal scales. I realize that for most readers, my comments here may seem painfully obvious. However, not making these points will seriously undermine my ability to persuade these same readers of my contention that scales participate significantly in post-tonal music.

The passage from the first movement of Beethoven's Piano Sonata op. 53 shown in Figure 4.1 begins and ends in C major, even though many pitches foreign to C major eventually appear. In fact, this passage could represent the chromatic scale, because all twelve pitches appear here in one form or another. Even musical amateurs can generally find this chromaticism by eye. However, actually counting the pitches produces a more accurate result. Figure 4.2 gives the exact number of each pitch class in the 298 pitches present in this example.

Not surprisingly, the C major scale pitches far outnumber the non–C major scale pitches in Figure 4.1—by 237 to 61. Interestingly, however, some individual non-scale pitches outnumber scale pitches. For example, B-flat outnumbers D-natural, A-natural, and E-natural, and A-flat outnumbers A-natural in these rankings. If one were not aware of the important roles keys play in tonal music, the scale here might be construed as C–D–E–F–G–A-flat–B-flat–C, rather than as C major. Including durations when figuring these weightings does little to counter this analysis. My first point, then—that simply counting pitches does not necessarily lead one to an accurate conclusion regarding the scale in use—suggests that other important factors must be considered. Clearly, nonharmonic tones, secondary harmonies, modulations to other keys or regions, and meter, among other elements, all play crucial roles in establishing a particular key or scale in tonal music. The lone C-sharp that begins in m. 4, for example, has but one iteration, indicating its lesser value. The two F-sharps at the end of m. 2, occurring one after another as the third of a repeated secondary dominant-of-the-dominant harmony, may actually further establish C major as the key in use, rather than the contrary. The B-flat, A-flat, and E-flat here occur in a B-flat major region beginning in m. 5 and not ending until the feint

FIGURE 4.1 Beethoven, Piano Sonata in C Major, op. 53, beginning.

C	48
C♯	1
D	26
E♭	11
E	17
F	57
F♯	2
G	52
A♭	16
A	13
B♭	31
B	24

FIGURE 4.2 The numbers of iterations per pitch of the 298 pitches present in Beethoven, Piano Sonata in C Major, op. 53, beginning (C, 48; C-sharp, 1; D, 26; E-flat, 11; E, 17; F, 57; F-sharp, 2; G, 52; A-flat, 16; A 13; B-flat, 31; B, 24).

to C minor that occurs in mm. 11 and 12. I will not describe the possible reasons Beethoven chose to allude to B-flat major here, because his rationale has little relevance to this discussion of scales. The important point I wish to make is that tonal music—and, one might therefore assume, post-tonal music—includes many pitches foreign to the scales it represents.

The two most notable uses of chromaticism in Figure 4.1 (secondary and modulatory or regional) must also be allowed—in principle, if not in exact form—in any scalar analysis of post-tonal music. Not allowing post-tonal composers the same kinds of access to temporary and transpositional chromaticism would subject the analysis of post-tonal music to the same misreading that deriving a twelve-pitch scale from the Beethoven excerpt would create for tonal music.

Traditional major and minor scales, as well as more recent alternatives such as octatonic and other nontraditional scales, have dominated traditional music analysis for decades. However, thousands of other scales exist that, for one reason or another, have not received similar attention. Examining the full panoply of these scales will help clarify the role they can play in post-tonal music (Lewin 1987; Slonimsky 1947). I shall limit my studies here to twelve-tone equal temperament to avoid the incredible combinatorial possibilities engendered by including other tuning systems.

To compute all possible arrangements of from one to twelve different pitch classes of equal temperament, I use twelve-digit binary (base 2) numbers that indicate the on-off states of each pitch class in the chromatic scale (e.g., 110110110110, with [1] equaling the presence and [0] equaling the non-presence of each pitch class). Because the scales in this collection of scale classes contain the pitch of origin—in this case, C, or pitch class 0—the number of possible scales computes to 2,048, or 2^{11}, where the number 2 represents the possible presence or non-presence of a pitch class in a scale and the exponent 11 indicates the number of available pitches above C or pitch class 0. A list of these scales appears on the CD-ROM accompanying this book. This list begins with the scale [0] and proceeds through scales of increasing numbers of pitch classes in ascending order. The list ends with the chromatic scale [0,1,2,3,4,5,6,7,8,9,t,e]. In binary notation, these scales range from 000000000001 to 111111111111, with only eleven of these twelve digits—the leftmost eleven—switching states from 0 to 1, and vice versa.

As expected, many of the scales on this list closely resemble one another. For example, the major scale [0,2,4,5,7,9,e] has much in common with the Dorian mode [0,2,3,5,7,9,t]. Both of these scales contain two half steps and five whole steps. In order to more easily discover these kinds of similarities, I use what I call *linear interval vectors*. Linear interval vectors (introduced in Chapter 3) result from figuring each interval of a scale in ascending order from scale degree to scale degree up to and including the interval produced by the penultimate scale member and the projected octave above pitch class 0 (12). In other words, for a scale consisting of eight ascending pitch classes including the octave above the first pitch class, there would be a total of seven intervals. These intervals are then collected and notated following the standard musical-vector practice of listing minor seconds first, major seconds to the right, and so on up through the augmented fourth, with intervals beyond the augmented fourth mirror-inverted to their smaller sizes (i.e., perfect fifths become perfect fourths, minor sixths become major thirds, and so on). Thus, a scale with two minor seconds and five major seconds produces a linear interval vector of 250000.

As mentioned earlier, the term *linear interval* here differentiates this type of vector from a standard musical vector, which contains every possible interval figured from all but the last pitch class of a grouping of pitch classes. Standard musical vectors used for scales with many pitches have such high numbers of certain intervals as to make these vectors less useful for scales. For example, the scale [0,1,2,3,4,6,8,t] would have a standard musical vector of 474643 and a linear interval vector of 440000, the latter revealing more immediately accessible scale information. Linear interval vectors also indicate similarities between scales that otherwise may not be clearly evident.

Linear interval vectors do not account for the internal order of the intervals they represent. For example, the major scale and all the related church modes have the same vector of 250000. The linear interval vector of 250000 allows for many other arrangements of these intervals as well. For example, the 250000 vector also includes the ascending melodic minor ([0,2,3,5,7,9,e]) scale. Several other interesting scales, such as [0,1,2,4,6,8,t] and [0,1,3,4,6,8,t], share this vector as well. Although these different arrangements that have the same vector may seem unrevealing when analyzing post-tonal music, they provide very helpful information regarding scale similarity.

The harmonic minor [0,2,3,5,7,8,e] scale resolves to the 340000 linear interval vector. Whole-tone ([0,2,4,6,8,t] 060000), octatonic ([0,1,3,4,6,7,9,t] or [0,2,3,5,6,8,9,e] both as 440000), pentatonic ([0,2,4,7,9] 032000), and chromatic ([0,1,2,3,4,5,6,7,8,9,t,e] w00000, with "w" representing the number 12) provide examples of other often used scales and their linear interval vectors.

Because standard pitch-class sets can contain up to twelve pitch classes and theoretically extend over any period of musical time, distinguishing scale sets from pitch-class sets can occasionally prove difficult. Therefore, I limit pitch-class sets in this book to those groups of pitches that appear in relatively close proximity to one another and that occur over a period of musical time of less than a phrase. Scale sets, on the other hand, typically result from analyzing one or more phrases of music. Scale sets may also have implied scale membership or, conversely, include pitch classes foreign to the scale set, representing other distinctions between scale sets and pitch-class sets. Although these distinctions may seem somewhat vague, they will become clearer when analyzing scales in specific musical examples later in this chapter.

VECTOR CLASSES AND METACLASSES

As previously discussed, scales with equivalent linear interval vectors bear strong resemblance to one another and thus belong to the same linear interval vector class. Collecting all possible scales into linear interval vector classes produces 77 distinct scale types, reduced from the 2,048 possible scales. Figure 4.3 lists all 77 linear interval vector classes from the smallest number of pitch classes (the single-interval or octave scale) to the largest number of pitch classes (the continuous half-step or chromatic scale). Every possible equal-tempered scale belongs to one of these 77 classes and shares one or more characteristics with other members of that same class. Six of these 77 vector classes have unique single members: those representing scales consisting of one mirrored interval, as in 002000, where the two minor thirds identify a minor third and its mirror, the major sixth. The other numbers of differing intervals in linear interval vector classes range from two different intervals (as in 210000) to four different intervals (as in 121100).

Viewing a list such as that shown in Figure 4.3 proves much more productive than consulting the entire list of 2,048 scales as presented on the CD-ROM accompanying this book. Each line in this figure contains two items, a version of the scale in pitch-class numbers and the linear interval vector of that same scale. Interestingly, even this more compact representation contains several rather straightforward scale classes that I find less useful when distinguishing between analyzing or composing music. Therefore, I use a special metaclass notation indicating only the number of half steps each linear interval vector class contains. This shorthand notates the number of half steps in the scale followed by "Ω" (Greek letter omega),

[0] 000000
[0,1] 200000
[0,2] 020000
[0,3] 002000
[0,4] 000200
[0,5] 000020
[0,6] 000002
[0,1,2] 210000
[0,1,3] 111000
[0,1,4] 101100
[0,1,5] 100110
[0,1,6] 100011
[0,2,4] 020100
[0,2,5] 011010
[0,2,6] 010101
[0,2,7] 010020
[0,3,6] 002001
[0,3,7] 001110
[0,4,8] 000300
[0,1,2,3] 301000
[0,1,2,4] 210100
[0,1,2,5] 201010
[0,1,2,6] 200101
[0,1,2,7] 200020
[0,1,3,5] 120010
[0,1,3,6] 111001
[0,1,3,7] 110110
[0,1,4,7] 102010
[0,1,4,8] 101200
[0,2,4,6] 030001
[0,2,4,7] 021010
[0,2,4,8] 020200
[0,2,5,8] 012100
[0,3,6,9] 004000
[0,1,2,3,4] 400100
[0,1,2,3,5] 310010
[0,1,2,3,6] 301001
[0,1,2,3,7] 300110
[0,1,2,4,6] 220001
[0,1,2,4,7] 211010
[0,1,2,4,8] 210200
[0,1,2,5,8] 202100
[0,1,3,5,7] 130010
[0,1,3,5,8] 121100
[0,1,3,6,9] 113000
[0,2,4,6,8] 040100
[0,2,4,6,9] 032000
[0,1,2,3,4,5] 500010
[0,1,2,3,4,6] 410001
[0,1,2,3,4,7] 401010
[0,1,2,3,4,8] 400200

[0,1,2,3,5,7] 320010
[0,1,2,3,5,8] 311100
[0,1,2,3,6,9] 303000
[0,1,2,4,6,8] 230100
[0,1,2,4,6,9] 222000
[0,1,3,5,7,9] 141000
[0,2,4,6,8,t] 060000
[0,1,2,3,4,5,6] 600001
[0,1,2,3,4,5,7] 510010
[0,1,2,3,4,5,8] 501100
[0,1,2,3,4,6,8] 420100
[0,1,2,3,4,6,9] 412000
[0,1,2,3,5,7,9] 331000
[0,1,2,4,6,8,t] 250000
[0,1,2,3,4,5,6,7] 700010
[0,1,2,3,4,5,6,8] 610100
[0,1,2,3,4,5,6,9] 602000
[0,1,2,3,4,5,7,9] 521000
[0,1,2,3,4,6,8,t] 440000
[0,1,2,3,4,5,6,7,8] 800100
[0,1,2,3,4,5,6,7,9] 711000
[0,1,2,3,4,5,6,8,t] 630000
[0,1,2,3,4,5,6,7,8,9] 901000
[0,1,2,3,4,5,6,7,8,t] 820000
[0,1,2,3,4,5,6,7,8,9,t] t10000
[0,1,2,3,4,5,6,7,8,9,t,e] w00000

FIGURE 4.3 A list of all 77 linear interval vector classes.

signifying "to the end of all of the possible numbers." Therefore, 0Ω represents all scales containing no half steps, 1Ω indicates all scales containing one half step, and so on. The representation 4+Ω signifies all scales containing four or more half steps. Thus, one can quickly scan a scale for the number of half steps it contains and then denote its metaclass with a number and a symbol. The whole-tone scale therefore belongs to the 0Ω metaclass, the major scale and the church modes are included in the 2Ω metaclass, the harmonic minor scale belongs to the 3Ω metaclass, and the octatonic scale appears in the 4+Ω metaclass.

As one might suspect, the 0Ω metaclass contains a large number of scale classes (21). On the other hand, the 3Ω scale metaclass has few representatives (8), as do the 2Ω (13) and 1Ω (13) metaclasses. Although the 4+Ω metaclass contains the most scale classes, its total number of classes (22) closely approximates the number of classes in the 0Ω metaclass (21).

Scales with vectors that do not match may also relate in other ways. For example, the scales [0,2,5,6,7,t] and [0,3,6,9] produce the quite different vectors of 222000 and 004000 respectively, not matching in class or metaclass. As Figure 4.4a shows, however, both of these scales are symmetrical, the first consisting of mirrored major second/minor third/minor second combinations, and the second outlining a diminished seventh chord. Symmetry binds otherwise quite differently constructed scales together in special ways. Even inversionally symmetrical scales as diverse as those shown in Figure 4.4b (of 222000 and 250000 vectors) deserve such recognition because they both belong to the same metaclass.

Scales consisting of one interval—even though that interval may be different—can also relate apparently quite diversely vectored scales. As example, major-third (000300) and minor-third (004000) scales share this notion; furthermore, both are symmetrical (see Figure 4.4c).

Patterned scales—scales consisting of a single two- or three-pitch pattern—also relate, as demonstrated in Figure 4.4d, where scales with 440000 and 020200 vectors share their consistent use of repeating patterns. Although the analyses that follow do not particularly dwell on these possibilities, because doing so might confuse the points being made, readers are nonetheless encouraged to discover further such relationships themselves.

Scale use in diverse music requires different analytical techniques. For example, in order that I not confuse the actual meanings of secondary functions and modulation in tonality with similar concepts in post-tonality, I will substitute the terms *transient chromaticism*, *transpositional chromaticism*, *rotational chromaticism*, and *transformational chromaticism*. *Transient chromaticism* means that the chromatic pitches are temporary and do not belong to the scale in current use. *Transpositional chromaticism*, in contrast, indicates that a transposition of a current scale has replaced the current scale in the music under analysis. In Figure 4.1, the F-sharp in m. 2 represents a form of transient chromaticism, and the B-flat in m. 5 and beyond is an example of transpositional chromaticism. Unlike tonal music, however, not only may post-tonal music modulate to a transposed version of a current scale, but

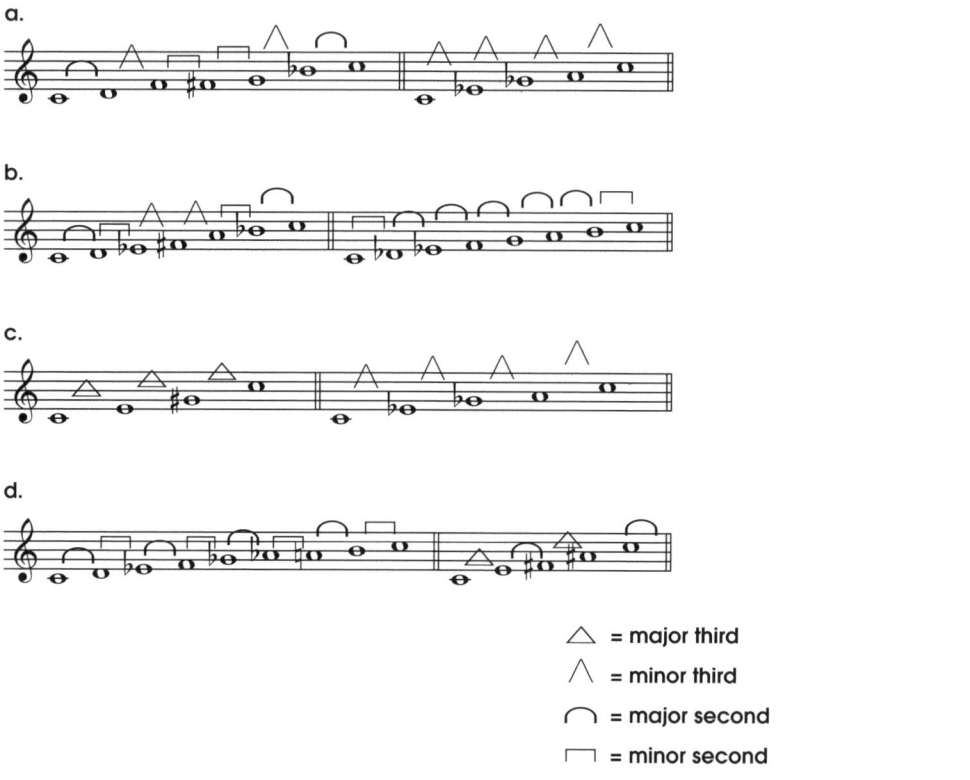

FIGURE 4.4 Four sets of scales related by symmetry (a, b, and c) and a repeating pattern (d).

may also modulate to a new scale entirely (similar in concept to major–to-minor key modulation in tonal music). If a different new scale in use belongs to the same vector class as the former scale, I use the term *rotational chromaticism*, because the various intervals in the scale in use have rotated to different positions. If a different new scale belongs to another vector class than the former scale, I use the term *transformational chromaticism*, meaning that the scale has actually transformed into combinations of new pitch classes and/or orders and types of intervals. Unlike tonal modulation between different modes (i.e., major to minor or vice versa), transformational chromaticism involves fundamental shifts between truly different scales, including scales containing different numbers of pitches.

The following more formal definitions of these terms should help clarify any remaining confusions over their meanings:

Transient chromaticism includes pitches foreign to a current scale that appear briefly, typically resolve to their associated scale degree, and/or appear in weak metric, rhythmic, and/or agogic circumstances;

Transpositional chromaticism includes pitches foreign to a current scale that repeat or otherwise become consistent over time, alter their native scale versions, and/or that appear in strong metric, rhythmic, and/or agogic circumstances, and which create a transposed version of the current scale in use;

Rotational chromaticism includes pitches foreign to a current scale that repeat or otherwise become consistent over time, alter their native scale versions, and/or that appear in strong metric, rhythmic, and/or agogic circumstances, and which create a different scale, but a scale of the same vector class;

Transformational chromaticism includes pitches foreign to a current scale that create—through repetition and in strong metric, rhythmic, and/or agogic circumstances—a demonstrably new scale of a different vector class.

Of course, defining what these terms mean and discovering their presence and placement in post-tonal music pose quite different problems. Also, having the above-described terms replace the terms *secondary* and *modulatory chromaticism* as it occurs in tonal music does not really provide much information on how to distinguish them in post-tonal music. Therefore, I will—after a brief discussion of implied pitches and the computational methods I use to detect scales—provide a series of brief analyses demonstrating scale analysis in post-tonal music.

As mentioned earlier, scales may appear even if certain scale members are absent. For example, Figure 4.5 shows an example of implied scale membership—eleven measures from Beethoven's Piano Sonata in E-flat, op. 7 (third movement). The 181 pitches here clearly define the E-flat minor scale. Notable about this set of pitches, however, is that the submediant scale degree of the key—C-flat—does not appear anywhere in these measures. In fact, the resulting scale might not even be analyzed as minor by a novice, but possibly as some form of a six-pitch scale. However, as evidenced by the tonal nature of this music, this passage is in the key of E-flat minor, with an implied C-flat, and with the D-flat and D-natural as subtonic and leading-tone pitches in the melodic minor version of this scale.

In order that readers not suspect that this music represents a rarity, I note that the initial C major statement of the theme of the Beethoven Piano Sonata no. 21, op. 53, in Figure 4.1, mm. 1–4, does not contain an F-natural, only an F-sharp (m. 2). Clearly, however, the first four measures of this sonata, by key signature and repetition of the tonic chord, define C major as the key. Even though implied memberships such as this F-natural and the previously mentioned C-flat can encourage creative analyses, they must be allowed in scales in both tonal and post-tonal music. Without these implied memberships, even tonal music would be reduced to scales of fewer than seven pitches, or non-tonal scales.

Implied pitches are therefore as important to tonal analysis as the inclusion of pitches foreign to a key. Any realistic analytical process applied to tonal music must take implied pitches into consideration or risk seriously misconstruing the diatonic nature of the music. I believe that the same considerations must also be afforded to post-tonal music and will endeavor to prove this as this chapter progresses.

Aside from counting pitch classes, the program Scale on the CD-ROM accompanying this book adds the durations in the third position of each note-event for all

FIGURE 4.5 Beethoven, Piano Sonata op. 7, mm. 97–105.

pitch classes in the indicated work, or some designated section of this work. These duration additions are then paired with their pitch classes, such as in "(2 15238)," where 2 indicates the pitch class, and 15238 represents the total duration in thousandths of a second of that pitch class. This list of pitch classes and their total durations, presented in order of longest duration to shortest, then acts as a model for creating parallel lists of possible scales, with each successive scale having one additional class—the one of the briefest overall duration—removed. Each scale possibility is presented in three ways: pitch classes transposed to begin on 0 in ascending order, as a linear interval vector, and by original pitch classes in ascending order. Figure 4.6 presents an example of this representation. From these lists users can select the pitch-class series that they feel—after listening to and otherwise analyzing the music under study—best represents the underlying scale in use. When an analyst chooses a scale with removed pitches, these removed pitches become transient chromaticism to an analyzed scale.

[0,1,2,3,4,5,6,7,8,9,t,e] w00000,[0,1,2,3,4,5,6,7,8,9,t,e]
[0,1,2,4,5,6,7,8,9,t,e] t10000,[0,1,2,4,5,6,7,8,9,t,e]
[0,1,4,5,6,7,8,9,t,e] 901000,[0,1,4,5,6,7,8,9,t,e]
[0,4,5,6,7,8,9,t,e] 800100,[0,4,5,6,7,8,9,t,e]
[0,1,2,3,4,5,6,7] 700010,[4,5,6,7,8,9,t,e]
[0,1,2,3,4,5,6] 600001,[5,6,7,8,9,t,e]
[0,1,2,3,4,6] 410001,[5,6,7,8,9,e]
[0,1,2,3,5] 310010,[6,7,8,9,e]
[0,1,3,5] 120010,[6,7,9,e]
[0,3,5] 011010,[6,9,e]
[0,3] 002000,[6,9]
[0] 000000,[6]

FIGURE 4.6 A series of possible scales, with each successive scale possibility lacking one of the previous scale's notes, the one with the shortest overall duration. Each line here represents the scale's transposed pitch-class set beginning on 0, its linear interval vector, and the original pitch-class set in ascending order.

These lists of scale possibilities can also be compared with other scale analyses representing phrases, sections, works, and so on, for their equivalent scale content or linear interval vector similarity. This comparison may then reveal scales that support even longer sections of music or that demonstrate other kinds of similarity (e.g., symmetry, as discussed previously). What would require hours of exhaustive processing by hand takes but a few seconds when using a computer to produce the results.

The Scale program lacks the ability to make best guesses for implied scale members. I have resisted adding code to the program to make these guesses algorithmically, because postulating such membership in a scale has provided my most interesting personal challenges. I rarely add more than one or two implied pitches—if any—and then only to scales that otherwise consist of five or six pitches or fewer. Implied pitches typically occur between awkward leaps in otherwise stepwise scales, where they produce relatively unnatural motions between pitch classes (e.g., an octatonic scale minus one member). A logical addition to Scale would be to have the program relate scale class sets to the full 2,048 possibilities, returning those sets with the greatest likelihood of possessing the missing members.

Although I could easily have figured dynamics, meter, and other considerations into the weighting process used by Scale, I have refrained from doing so for a variety of reasons. First, such considerations do not consistently map to all post-tonal music. In fact, when composing my own music—as I believe I can usefully argue—I avoid allowing these elements to take active roles in establishing scales. I use meter, for instance, to keep performers together, not to accent or otherwise influence pitch-class prominence. I also use softer dynamics as often as louder dynamics to articulate important pitches in a scale. Finding many of my own predilections in other post-tonal music, I have opted to avoid the apparent inconsistencies of weighting these factors by including pitch-class duration additions only (see Lerdahl 1989 for a somewhat different view of this).

Many composers, particularly polytonal composers, use more than one scale simultaneously. Although analyzing post-tonal music for two or more simultaneous scales is possible by grouping pitches by voice or other principle, I have not included such analysis processes in Scale to avoid confusing the basic principles discussed in this chapter. For example, non-scale and implied pitches become much less plausible in polyscalar environments. Likewise, the argument against scales serving as a basis for post-tonal music analysis on the basis of the difficulty of hearing such scales becomes even stronger if one asserts that more than one scale exists at the same time.

The choice of phrase lengths and placements in the following examples results from my own interpretations of the music shown. Obviously, many analyses of phrasing are possible; those given here represent just one set of decisions. Other choices for phrase length may produce other scales or may even more strongly support the case for the scales that I have chosen. To lessen bias in my approach to determining scales in this music, I made all decisions regarding phrasing prior to determining scale content.

VARÈSE'S *DENSITY 21.5*

Varèse's *Density 21.5* (1936) for solo flute, shown in its entirety in Figure 4.7, serves as a good work for scale determination, because the single line and post-tonal chromaticism lend themselves logically to scale analysis (Bernard 1977; Perle 1990). The fairly clear-cut phrase delineations provided by the composer also help to capture scale material in relatively unambiguous ways. Figure 4.8 presents a phrase-by-phrase computer analysis of Varèse's *Density* for reference during the following discussion.

The first easily differentiated grouping of pitches in *Density*, ending on the third beat of m. 3, provides a distinct five-pitch scale [1,4,5,6,7] with the resulting linear interval vector of 301001. Varèse has strengthened the sense of scale here by adding no new pitch classes in the following two-plus measures. The next three measures (from m. 6 up to and including the C-natural that ends m. 8), however, flesh out more details for a potential scale by creating a more complex [0,1,4,5,6,7,9,t] eight-pitch series, yielding a 521000 linear interval vector when combined with material from mm. 1–5. The music following m. 8 provides pitch classes 2, 3, and 8 in

FIGURE 4.7 Varèse, *Density 21.5* for solo flute.

FIGURE 4.7 continued

fairly quick order, with pitch class 11 not appearing until m. 18, thus completing the full chromatic scale in the music from the beginning of the work to this point. It would be easy here to analyze this opening passage as freely chromatic or, at the least, to reduce it to a twelve-pitch scale were it not for the fact that Varèse has so carefully defined important pitch classes by repetition and hyperextended duration, as well as by grouping notes as motives and variations of those motives throughout the first section of this piece.

Analyzing post-tonal music for nonharmonic tones is not a new concept (see particularly Solomon 2003 and 2005; Straus 2005). For example, George Perle (1990, 11–12) argues for a diminished seventh scale (i.e., C-sharp, E-natural, G-natural, B-flat) scale (004000) for the first nine measures of this work, even though these same pitches plus intervening pitches—D-sharp, F-sharp, A-natural, and C-natural, both actual and implied—could provide the basis for analyzing this music originating from a major octatonic scale (minus E-flat).

Section 1

mm. 1 - 8

[0,1,4,5,6,7,9,t] 521000 [0,1,4,5,6,7,9,t]
[0,1,4,6,7,9,t] 331000 [0,1,4,6,7,9,t]
[0,1,4,6,7,t] 222000 [0,1,4,6,7,t]
[0,3,5,6,9] 113000 [1,4,6,7,t]
[0,5,6,9] 102010 [1,6,7,t]
[0,1,4] 101100 [6,7,t]
[0,1] 200000 [6,7]
[0] 000000 [7]

mm. 9-14

[0,1,2,3,4,8,9,t] 610100 [0,1,2,3,4,8,9,t]
[0,1,2,3,4,9,t] 510010 [0,1,2,3,4,9,t]
[0,1,2,3,4,9] 401010 [0,1,2,3,4,9]
[0,1,2,3,4] 400100 [0,1,2,3,4]
[0,1,2,4] 210100 [0,1,2,4]
[0,1,3] 111000 [1,2,4]
[0,1] 200000 [1,2]
[0] 000000 [1]

mm. 15-23

[0,1,2,3,4,5,6,7,8,9,t,e] w00000 [0,1,2,3,4,5,6,7,8,9,t,e]
[0,2,3,4,5,6,7,8,9,t,e] t10000 [0,2,3,4,5,6,7,8,9,t,e]
[0,1,2,3,4,5,6,7,8,9] 901000 [2,3,4,5,6,7,8,9,t,e]
[0,1,2,3,4,5,7,8,9] 711000 [2,3,4,5,6,7,9,t,e]
[0,1,3,4,5,7,8,9] 521000 [2,3,5,6,7,9,t,e]
[0,3,4,5,7,8,9] 412000 [2,5,6,7,9,t,e]
[0,3,5,7,8,9] 222000 [2,5,7,9,t,e]
[0,3,5,8,9] 113000 [2,5,7,t,e]
[0,2,5,6] 111001 [5,7,t,e]
[0,2,6] 010101 [5,7,e]
[0,4] 000200 [7,e]
[0] 000000 [e]

Section 2

mm. 24-28

[0,1,2,3,7] 300110 [1,2,3,4,8]
[0,1,3,7] 110110 [1,2,4,8]
[0,1,3] 111000 [1,2,4]
[0,1] 200000 [1,2]
[0] 000000 [2]

mm. 29-beat 1 of m. 36

[0,1,2,3,4,5,6,7] 700010 [4,5,6,7,8,9,t,e]
[0,1,2,3,4,5,6] 600001 [5,6,7,8,9,t,e]
[0,1,2,3,4,6] 410001 [5,6,7,8,9,e]
[0,1,2,3,5] 310010 [6,7,8,9,e]
[0,1,3,5] 120010 [6,7,9,e]
[0,3,5] 011010 [6,9,e]
[0,3] 002000 [6,9]
[0] 000000 [6]

rest of m. 36-m. 40

[0,1,2,3,e] 400100 [0,1,2,3,e]
[0,1,2,3] 301000 [0,1,2,3]
[0,2,3] 111000 [0,2,3]
[0,3] 002000 [0,3]
[0] 000000 [3]

Section 3

mm. 41-first note of 50

[0,1,3,4,5,6,7,8,9,t] 820000 [1,2,4,5,6,7,8,9,t,e]
[0,1,4,5,6,7,8,9,t] 711000 [1,2,5,6,7,8,9,t,e]
[0,1,4,5,6,7,9,t] 521000 [1,2,5,6,7,8,t,e]
[0,1,4,5,6,7,t] 412000 [1,2,5,6,7,8,e]
[0,1,5,6,7,t] 311100 [1,2,6,7,8,e]
[0,1,6,7,t] 211010 [1,2,7,8,e]
[0,1,6,t] 110110 [1,2,7,e]
[0,5,9] 001110 [2,7,e]
[0,5] 000020 [2,7]
[0] 000000 [2]

rest of m. 50 to first beat of m. 53

[0,5,6,7,8,9] 401010 [0,5,6,7,8,9]
[0,5,6,7,8] 300110 [0,5,6,7,8]
[0,5,6,8] 110110 [0,5,6,8]
[0,1,3] 111000 [5,6,8]
[0,2] 020000 [6,8]
[0] 000000 [8]

last 3 beats of m. 53 to end of piece

[0,1,2,3,4,5,6,7,9,t,e] t10000 [0,1,2,3,4,5,6,7,9,t,e]
[0,1,2,4,5,6,7,9,t,e] 820000 [0,1,2,4,5,6,7,9,t,e]
[0,1,2,4,5,7,9,t,e] 630000 [0,1,2,4,5,7,9,t,e]
[0,1,2,4,5,7,t,e] 521000 [0,1,2,4,5,7,t,e]
[0,1,2,4,7,t,e] 412000 [0,1,2,4,7,t,e]
[0,1,3,6,9,t] 222000 [1,2,4,7,t,e]
[0,1,3,9,t] 220001 [1,2,4,t,e]
[0,1,3,t] 120010 [1,2,4,e]
[0,2,9] 11010 [2,4,e]
[0,2] 020000 [2,4]
[0] 000000 [4]

FIGURE 4.8 Computer scale analysis of the phrases of the three sections of Varèse, *Density 21.5* (see Figure 4.7), with author's determination of best scale possibility in boldface.

Post-tonal music also contains scalar patterns that can help delineate a scale in use. For example, in Varèse's *Density 21.5* in Figure 4.7, the second pitch of m. 6, G-natural, up to the D-natural beginning m. 11 reveal the possible scale of G, A, B-flat, C, D-flat, and D-natural.

Even though the music does not place these pitches one after another in typical scale order, the fact that the music in these measures contains *only* these pitches clearly suggests the quasi-tonal scale pattern. Without the D-flat (possibly a chromatic passing tone), this pattern could be construed as a G minor scale, even though the surrounding context might belie that analysis. Although such scale patterns do not appear as commonly in post-tonal music as in tonal music, they definitely require special observation when they do occur.

Developing a single scale from mm. 1–18, or, more likely, m. 23, the end of the first section of this piece, thus appears to have limitations. Furthermore, mm. 9–14 of *Density* constitute such a distinct possibility for a separate phrase that the likelihood of another scale in use should not be overlooked. This second phrase reduces to a scale of [0,1,2,3,4,8,9,t] having a linear interval vector of 610100. Although this vector differs from the vector of the first eight measures of this piece (521000), changing but one pitch class of the scale (4 to 5) produces a linear interval vector of 521000, which demonstrates this scale's close proximity to the scale analyzed in mm. 1–8. Also, the interval vector of 610100 for the unaltered scale of mm. 9–14 belongs to the same vector metaclass (4+Ω) as 521000, thus further emphasizing this passage's similarity to the scale of the first eight measures. Ultimately, deciding whether a section contains one or more separate scales is more a matter of individual preference than of applying a particular principle. In this book, I do not analyze regions separately from overall scales, so that the basic points of my arguments remain clear.

Measures 15–23 of *Density* contain all twelve pitches of the chromatic scale. However, viewing smaller and smaller numbers of scale pitch classes—discarding the ones with less overall durational value—produces the scale of [2,3,5,6,7,9] yielding the 521000 linear interval vector, the identical vector class that resulted from the analysis of mm. 1–8 of this work. Identifying this 521000 scale for mm. 15–23 requires the elimination of *four* pitch classes from the collection of twelve pitch classes that occur during the passage. As the computer analysis in Figure 4.8 shows, however, these four pitch classes (0, 1, 4, 8, or C-natural, C-sharp, E-natural, and G-sharp) all have less durational value than the eight included in this analysis, and thus make sense as transient chromaticism.

Looking at the entire first section of *Density* by phrase then generates the following three linear interval vectors: 521000 (mm. 1–8), 610100 (mm. 9–14), and 521000 (mm. 15–23). Only the third vector requires note deletion, with the first two phrases using all of their pitches to build their relevant scales (shown in boldface in Figure 4.8). I should note here that the alignment of scale boundaries with phrase and section boundaries requires assumptions that may not necessarily be valid. For example, in tonal music, many phrases contain modulations, and less often do new phrases suddenly begin in different keys. Even with this in mind, however, it makes more sense at this point to analyze by phrase and section rather than by some other technique, simply because in Western music phrases and sections often fall within single keys.

Note that my decision to suppress low-duration pitches here is based not on a fixed threshold or on any innate sense of these pitches as foreign to the music being analyzed, but on a desire to find identical or closely related scale structures in different phrases that I feel tend to unify the music. Clearly, then, my search for scale similarities as described here does not result from a neutral point of view, but rather from a focused desire to discover them.

The second section of *Density 21.5* contains three distinct phrases—mm. 24–28, m. 29 through the first pitch of m. 36, and the second pitch of m. 36 through m. 40, as indicated in Figure 4.8. Using the Scale program to analyze the note-events of these phrases produces the identical 310010 class in each case. In phrase 1, the chosen linear interval vector does not require any transient chromatic eliminations. Contrastingly, in the second phrase, three pitches must be removed to reveal this vector. The third phrase requires that only one pitch be omitted.

The third section of *Density* also consists of three phrases—m. 41 to the first note of m. 50, the rest of m. 50 to the first beat of m. 53, and the final three beats of m. 53 to the end of the piece, as shown in Figure 4.8. The first and last phrases here produce 521000 linear interval vector classes, with the second phrase of 401010 linear interval vector sandwiched in between. The phrase-by-phrase analysis of this section resembles the phrase-by-phrase analysis of section 1, both producing A–B–A scale structures at this micro-level, with the scales of 521000 linear interval vector acting as the A in both sections.

Analyzing the three sections of this piece as entire sections, rather than as separated phrases within these sections, produces a nine-pitch linear interval vector of 630000 in each case, as shown in Figure 4.9. In each section, the three weakest overall-duration pitches have been removed in order to create the scale vector. Given the twelve-pitch content of each of these sections, this nine-pitch vector provides a chromatic framework without the necessity of resorting to the full chromatic scale. Since there are three unique classes containing nine pitches—800100, 711000, and 630000—the appearance of the shared 630000 linear interval vector here does not seem coincidental. Interestingly, the only phrase analyzed in Figure 4.8 that by itself contains a 630000 linear interval vector as a possibility is the final phrase of the work (with two extracted transient chromatic pitches), supporting the case for the 630000 vector analysis of the entire piece.

Although the three scales shown in boldface in Figure 4.9 differ somewhat in exact pitch-class content (compare the right-hand boldface non-transposed scales), the underlying linear interval vector of 630000 unifies them. The 630000 scales of sections 1 and 2 are transpositionally related (five neighboring minor seconds, with the sixth minor second removed by one major second), while the scales of sections 2 and 3 have a permutational relationship (the scale for the last section having four

Section 1. mm 1-23

[0,1,2,3,4,5,6,7,8,9,10,e] w00000 [0,1,2,3,4,5,6,7,8,9,t,e]
[0,1,2,3,4,5,6,7,9,10,e] t10000 [0,1,2,3,4,5,6,7,9,t,e]
[0,1,2,4,5,6,7,9,10,e] 820000 [0,1,2,4,5,6,7,9,t,e]
[0,1,2,4,6,7,9,10,e] 630000 [0,1,2,4,6,7,9,10,e]
[0,1,3,5,6,8,9,10] 440000 [1,2,4,6,7,9,t,e]
[0,1,3,5,6,9,10] 331000 [1,2,4,6,7,t,e]
[0,3,5,6,9,10] 222000 [1,4,6,7,t,e] *
[0,3,6,9,10] 113000 [1,4,7,t,e]
[0,6,9,10] 111001 [1,7,t,e]
[0,3,4] 101100 [7,t,e]
[0,3] 002000 [7,t]
[0] 000000 [7]

Section 2. mm. 24-40

[0,1,2,3,4,5,6,7,8,9,t,e] w00000 [0,1,2,3,4,5,6,7,8,9,t,e]
[0,1,2,3,4,5,6,7,8,9,e] t10000 [0,1,2,3,4,5,6,7,8,9,e]
[0,1,2,3,4,6,7,8,9,e] 820000 [0,1,2,3,4,6,7,8,9,e]
[0,1,2,3,4,6,8,9,e] 630000 [0,1,2,3,4,6,8,9,e]
[0,1,2,3,6,8,9,e] 521000 [0,1,2,3,6,8,9,e] †
[0,1,2,3,6,9,e] 412000 [0,1,2,3,6,9,e]
[0,1,2,5,8,t] 222000 [1,2,3,6,9,e] *
[0,1,4,7,9] 113000 [2,3,6,9,e]
[0,3,6,8] 012100 [3,6,9,e]
[0,3,6] 002001 [3,6,9]
[0,3] 002000 [3,6]
[0] 000000 [6]

Section 3. mm. 41-61

[0,1,2,3,4,5,6,7,8,9,t,e] w00000 [0,1,2,3,4,5,6,7,8,9,t,e]
[0,1,2,4,5,6,7,8,9,t,e] t10000 [0,1,2,4,5,6,7,8,9,t,e]
[0,1,3,4,5,6,7,8,9,t] 820000 [1,2,4,5,6,7,8,9,t,e]
[0,1,3,4,5,6,7,9,t] 630000 [1,2,4,5,6,7,8,t,e]
[0,1,3,4,5,6,7,t] 521000 [1,2,4,5,6,7,8,e] †
[0,1,3,4,5,6,t] 420100 [1,2,4,5,6,7,e]
[0,1,3,5,6,t] 230100 [1,2,4,6,7,e]
[0,1,3,6,t] 121100 [1,2,4,7,e]
[0,1,6,t] 110110 [1,2,7,e]
[0,5,9] 001110 [2,7,e]
[0,9] 002000 [2,e]
[0] 000000 [2]

FIGURE 4.9 Computer analysis of Varèse, *Density 21.5*, by complete section with author's determination of best scale possibility in boldface and secondary possibilities marked by "*" and "†."

half steps grouped, with the other two half steps separated by single whole steps). The computer scale analysis of complete sections of *Density 21.5* in Figure 4.9 also provides alternative scale possibilities marked by "*" and "†." Note the 521000 linear interval vector presence in sections 2 and 3 in Figure 4.9, interesting because this linear interval vector played such a strong role in the phrase-by-phrase analysis shown in Figure 4.8.

Figure 4.10 presents musically notated versions of the ascending original pitch-class scales of the three sections of *Density* as defined in Figure 4.9. Connecting these pitch classes in Figure 4.10 to their section-dependent pitches—the right-hand group of pitch-class numbers in the boldface lists in Figure 4.8—and to their actual pitches in Figure 4.7 provides a sense of how the single overarching 630000-vectored scale materializes musically. Note how the whole steps here (easier to count than the half steps, because there are fewer of them) bunch into groups of two and one in the first and second sections (2–4, 4–6, and 7–9; 4–6, 6–8 and 9–e, as transpositionally related), while in section 3 the whole steps appear separately as 2–4, 8–t, and e–1, permutationally relating the first two sections.

Figure 4.11 shows the first section of *Density* with non-scale tones—according to the analysis in Figure 4.9—circled (again easier, because there are usually fewer of these tones than there are scale tones). Note that these non-scale tones often appear in collections, just as regions do for different keys in tonal music. Most of the non-scale collections found in *Density* represent transformational chromaticism in that the new scales formed in these regions diverge from the current linear interval vector. Somewhat atypically, mm. 11 and 12 in Figure 4.11 contain only two pitches

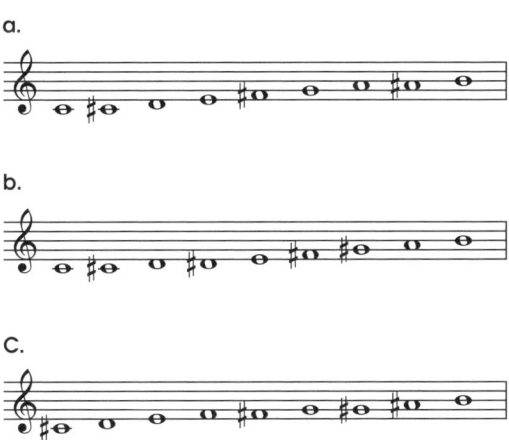

FIGURE 4.10 Unordered but nontransposed scale pitch classes for each section in Figure 4.7.

FIGURE 4.11 The first section of Varèse, *Density 21.5*, with non-scale tones circled.

belonging to the current scale (D-natural and A-natural). This short passage may be analyzed separately as a 200200 linear-interval-vectored scale, as in [2,3,8,9].

One particularly notable exception to the grouping of non-scale tones in Figure 4.11 appears in m. 1, on the first note of the piece. One might argue that beginning a work on a non-scale tone tends to discourage hearing a scale in use. I would argue that this note—which initiates both the first and second phrases—has a very brief duration and acts more as a propellant to initiate the motives here than as something that defines an important scale pitch. Ending a phrase or section on a non-scale tone, on the other hand, poses a significantly different problem, and I avoid eliminating such pitches from scale analysis whenever possible.

Without entering into a polemic more properly belonging to music perception and cognition (Avdeev and Ivanov 1993), note that I, at least, *hear* the three versions of the 630000-vectored scale in use in *Density*. My hearing these versions results from aurally determining the conglomerates of six half steps and three whole steps, rather than directly perceiving the scales themselves. In short, I hear the vectoral relationships, rather than the precise versions of the three 630000 scales. In many ways, this parallels the perception of scales in tonal music, where determination of actual keys, functions, and even scale degrees is often elusive, though not for experienced musicians. Discovering the presence of a certain scale informs me of one more fundamental structural element of post-tonal music and ultimately leads to a better understanding of this work. For me, the scales underpinning post-tonal music unify the music beyond the motives present, regardless of one's ability to clearly discern these scales.

The scale analysis presented here does not, of course, begin to reveal the other structural details of this work. However, such analyses are available elsewhere (see Cope 2000). And as I mentioned earlier in this chapter, scale determination should be used to enhance, rather than supplant, other types of analysis.

SCHOENBERG'S SIX LITTLE PIANO PIECES, OP. 19, NO. 1 (1911)

The first of Schoenberg's Six Little Piano Pieces, op. 19 (1911), shown in Figure 4.12, provides several opportunities to observe scalar transposition and transformation at work. Measures 1–4 of this seemingly straightforward nine-measure work establish—though pitch repetition and melody above harmony—a relatively clear scale of 521000 linear interval vector. All of the pitches of this passage fit into this scale with no transient or implied pitches, as seen in Figure 4.13. Measure 5 and the first half of m. 6 also produce a scale of 521000 linear interval vector, though this analysis requires excluding E-natural (F-flat) and B-flat appearing on beat 1 of m. 5. This 521000 linear interval vector scale represents a rotational variation of the scale in mm. 1–4, because the major seconds and minor third in the scale are in slightly different relationship to one another ([0,1,3,6,7,8,9,e] compared to [0,2,3,6,7,8,9,e]).

The ensuing measures of Schoenberg's music prove difficult to parse into phrases. As with *Density 21.5*, each different phrase determination can cause different scale interpretations and relationships. Here, for example, analyzing the music from beat 3 of m. 6 through m. 7 produces a 440000 linear interval vector. This phrase interpretation could, in turn, break into two distinct groups or scales, with the former as the held chord (320010) on the second half of m. 7, and the latter as the whole-tone transformational scale (060000, m. 7, without its first eighth note, and when including the first beat of m. 8 with an implied pitch class 1, which does occur on the second half of beat 3 of that measure). However, viewing chords alone and parts of

FIGURE 4.12 Schoenberg, Six Little Piano Pieces, op. 19, no. 1 (1911).

measures as complete phrases seems a bit myopic. Interestingly, the final measure of this work by itself analyzes to another 521000 linear interval vector scale, thus wrapping the entire piece—when analyzed as four phrases—in bookends, the resulting 521000–521000–440000–521000 creating a kind of A–A–B–A scale structure.

However, as Figure 4.13 shows, the analysis data from Scale when provided note-events from Schoenberg's op. 19, no. 1, demonstrate that the 521000 linear interval vector pervades this work when viewed in three phrases. I have highlighted the 521000 linear interval vectors and related scales. Note that the next levels upward—the nine-pitch scales—in both sections 2 and 3 analyze as 711000, contrasting the nine-pitch 630000 of Varèse's *Density 21.5*. Note here as well that the actual scales of the three 521000-vectored sections of Schoenberg's work represent rotational variations, with all three sections having different arrangements of the five half steps, two whole steps, and one minor third present in their scales.

Phrase 1; mm. 1-4

[0,2,3,6,7,8,9,t] 521000 [0,2,3,6,7,8,9,t]
[0,2,3,6,7,8,t] 412000 [0,2,3,6,7,8,t]
[0,2,3,7,8,t] 311100 [0,2,3,7,8,t]
[0,3,7,8,t] 202100 [0,3,7,8,t]
[0,3,7,t] 101200 [0,3,7,t]
[0,4,8] 000300 [3,7,t]
[0,4] 000200 [7,t]
[0] 000000 [t]

Phrase 2; mm. 5-6.5

[0,1,3,4,6,7,8,9,e,t] 820000 [0,1,3,4,6,7,8,9,e,t]
[0,1,3,6,7,8,9,e,t] 711000 [0,1,3,6,7,8,9,e,t]
[0,1,3,6,7,8,9,t] 521000 [0,1,3,6,7,8,9,t]
[0,1,3,7,8,9,t] 420100 [0,1,3,7,8,9,t]
[0,1,3,7,9,t] 230100 [0,1,3,7,9,t]
[0,1,3,7,t] 210200 [0,1,3,7,t]
[0,3,7,t] 101200 [0,3,7,t]
[0,7,t] 100110 [0,7,t]
[0,4] 000200 [7,t]
[0] 000000 [7]

Phrase 3; mm. 6.5-9

[0,1,2,3,4,5,6,7,9,e,t] t10000 [0,1,2,3,4,5,6,7,9,e,t]
[0,1,2,3,4,5,6,7,e,t] 901000 [0,1,2,3,4,5,6,7,e,t]
[0,1,2,3,5,6,7,e,t] 711000 [0,1,2,3,5,6,7,e,t]
[0,2,3,5,6,7,e,t] 521000 [0,2,3,5,6,7,e,t]
[0,2,3,5,6,7,t] 420100 [0,2,3,5,6,7,t]
[0,1,3,4,5,9] 311100 [2,3,5,6,7,t]
[0,1,4,5,9] 202100 [2,3,6,7,t]
[0,1,4,9] 102010 [2,3,6,t]
[0,1,9] 101100 [2,3,t]
[0,8] 000200 [3,t]
[0] 000000 [t]

FIGURE 4.13 Computer readouts from a three-phrase analysis of Schoenberg, Six Little Piano Pieces op. 19, no. 1.

Since most works—tonal as well as post-tonal—contain all twelve pitches, it is no surprise that Schoenberg's short work, when viewed as a whole, does as well. Figure 4.14 presents just such a single-scale analysis of op. 19, no. 1. Interestingly, the unordered scale here (left-hand scale of the highlighted line) duplicates the scale of phrase 3 of the phrase-by-phrase analysis shown in Figure 4.13. Also of interest, the nine-pitch scale vector appears as 630000 in Figure 4.14, the same vector that the scale analysis of Varèse's *Density 21.5* produced. Plotting the actual pitch names of the right-hand scales proceeding downward toward the 521000-vectored scale indicates the necessary transient chromatic pitch classes for this analysis.

OTHER MUSICAL EXAMPLES

As an example of implied scale pitches, I present a brief passage from one of my own works, where I can verify the accuracy of the analysis. The Concerto for Cello and Orchestra (1994) conforms to a post-tonal style while occasionally including triadic and otherwise quasi-tonal or modal passages. The cello and instrumental parts that appear in Figure 4.15 represent typical examples of this kind of synthesis. From my perspective, the music in this example connects related scales over time, with the phrases clearly delineated by extended-duration cadences. The analysis that follows reflects my tendency to include implied pitches when I feel it makes coherent musical sense.

The first phrase in Figure 4.15—m. 79 through the first two beats of m. 82—presents a straightforward eight-note scale of 610100 linear interval vector, as

[0,1,2,3,4,5,6,7,8,9,t,e] w00000 [0,1,2,3,4,5,6,7,8,9,t,e]
[0,1,2,3,5,6,7,8,9,t,e] t10000 [0,1,2,3,5,6,7,8,9,t,e]
[0,2,3,5,6,7,8,9,t,e] 820000 [0,2,3,5,6,7,8,9,t,e]
[0,2,3,5,6,7,9,t,e] 630000 [0,2,3,5,6,7,9,t,e]
[0,2,3,5,6,7,t,e] 521000 [0,2,3,5,6,7,t,e]
[0,2,3,5,6,7,e] 420100 [0,2,3,5,6,7,e]
[0,2,3,6,7,e] 311100 [0,2,3,6,7,e]
[0,3,6,7,e] 202100 [0,3,6,7,e]
[0,3,7,e] 101200 [0,3,7,e]
[0,4,8] 000300 [3,7,e]
[0,4] 000200 [7,e]
[0] 000000 [e]

FIGURE 4.14 Computer analysis of the entirety of Schoenberg, Six Little Piano Pieces op. 19, no. 1.

COMPUTER ANALYSIS OF SCALES IN POST-TONAL MUSIC 173

FIGURE 4.15 From the author's Concerto for Cello and Orchestra (1994).

FIGURE 4.15 continued

COMPUTER ANALYSIS OF SCALES IN POST-TONAL MUSIC 175

FIGURE 4.15 continued

176 HIDDEN STRUCTURE

FIGURE 4.15 continued

shown in Figure 4.16. The cluster of half steps bordered by F-sharp and B-natural (pitch classes 6–e) provides the distinguishing characteristic of this scale. Following this phrase—from the last beat of m. 82 through the first half of m. 85—the music transforms to a distinctly different scale of 311100 linear interval vector. However, the addition of pitch classes 0 and 3 to the topmost possibility for phrase 2's non-transposed pitch-class scale, as shown in boldface below the phrase analysis in Figure 4.16, produces a 610100 linear interval vector, just like that of the first phrase. The implied pitch class 3 (E-flat) occurs in both the previous and the following—mm. 86–88—phrase scales. Pitch class 0 (C-natural) appears as the result of a glissando in m. 35. I believe these neighboring and glissando appearances help solidify the analyzed scale and provide the music here with an overall logic, which was my reason for using these scales in the first place. The third phrase then reduces to a linear interval vector of 610100 without any eliminated chromatic-to-the-scale pitches or added implied pitches.

Measures 89–91 (phrase 4) in Figure 4.15 yield several possible scales. As shown in Figure 4.16, maintaining the eight-note configuration of the previous three phrases suggests 440000 as one possibility. The boldfaced 630000 linear interval vector also makes sense for this passage, with the scales of ten or more pitches approximating a chromatic scale too closely for consideration. Interestingly, the analysis of phrase 5, which does not list the linear interval vector of 610100 of the first three phrases as a possibility, does not show linear interval vectors of 440000 or 630000 either. However, adding pitch classes 2 and 5 as implied pitches to the analysis of phrase 5 produces a linear interval vector of 630000, a nine-pitch scale, a version of which also appears in phrase 4. Again, both the preceding and the subsequent phrases have these pitch classes present, which tends to substantiate these implications. Otherwise, the scales of phrases 4 and 5 are sufficiently different as to cause doubt that they relate.

The next two phrases—phrases 6 and 7—both return to the scale vector of the first three phrases, the 610100 linear interval vector, as shown in Figure 4.16. Phrase 8, however, contains only five pitches, not enough to generate the eight-pitch scales in five of the last seven phrases, nor does this phrase contain enough pitches to produce the 630000 linear interval vector of phrases 4 and 5. However—and this represents the biggest reach of the scale analyses thus far—by adding *three* pitch classes (3, 4, and t) to the analyzed scale of phrase 8, as shown in Figure 4.16 in boldface, the scale here resolves to a 610100 linear interval vector, creating an ABA three-section grouping of the eight phrases of this passage (610100–630000–610100 scale vector class types). Note that the three implied pitch classes in this phrase appear in the preceding phrase (7).

As mentioned previously, using implied pitches to complete scales may lead to rather creative analyses, where analysts can seem to arbitrarily fill out scales to make them compare favorably to whatever point about the music they wish to make. However, discreet inclusion of implied pitches, where logic and neighboring scales appear to enhance and encourage their presence, can make as much sense

Phrase 1. mm. 79-first half of 82
[0,1,3,4,5,6,7,8] 610100 [3,4,6,7,8,9,t,e]
[0,1,3,4,6,7,8] 420100 [3,4,6,7,9,t,e]
[0,1,3,4,6,7] 320010 [3,4,6,7,9,t]
[0,2,3,5,6] 220001 [4,6,7,9,t]
[0,1,3,4] 210100 [6,7,9,t]
[0,2,3] 111000 [7,9,t]
[0,3] 002000 [7,t]
[0] 000000 [7]

Phrase 2. last beat of m. 82-first half of 85
[0,1,3,4,8,9] 311100 [1,2,4,5,9,t]
[0,1,4,8,9] 202100 [1,2,5,9,t]
[0,4,8,9] 101200 [1,5,9,t]
[0,4,9] 001110 [1,5,t]
[0,9] 002000 [1,t]
[0] 000000 [1]

[0,1,2,3,4,5,9,t] 610100 [0,1,2,3,4,5,9,t]

Phrase 3. second half of m. 85-88
[0,1,3,4,5,6,7,8] 610100 [3,4,6,7,8,9,t,e]
[0,1,3,4,5,6,8] 420100 [3,4,6,7,8,9,e]
[0,2,3,4,5,7] 320010 [4,6,7,8,9,e]
[0,2,3,4,5] 310010 [4,6,7,8,9]
[0,2,3,5] 120010 [4,6,7,9]
[0,1,3] 111000 [6,7,9]
[0,2] 020000 [7,9]
[0] 000000 [7]

Phrase 4. mm. 89-91
[0,1,2,3,4,5,6,7,8,9,t,e] w00000 [0,1,2,3,4,5,6,7,8,9,t,e]
[0,1,2,3,4,5,6,7,8,9,t] t10000 [0,1,2,3,4,5,6,7,8,9,t]
[0,1,2,3,4,5,6,7,9,t] 820000 [0,1,2,3,4,5,6,7,9,t]
[0,1,2,3,4,5,7,9,t] 630000 [0,1,2,3,4,5,7,9,t]
[0,1,2,3,5,7,9,t] 440000 [0,1,2,3,5,7,9,t]
[0,1,2,4,6,8,9] 331000 [1,2,3,5,7,9,t]
[0,1,2,4,6,8] 230100 [1,2,3,5,7,9]
[0,1,2,4,8] 210200 [1,2,3,5,9]
[0,1,4,8] 101200 [1,2,5,9]
[0,1,4] 101100 [1,2,5]
[0,1] 200000 [1,2]
[0] 000000 [1]

Phrase 5. mm. 92-95
[0,3,6,8,9,t,e] 412000 [0,3,6,8,9,t,e]
[0,3,6,8,9,e] 222000 [0,3,6,8,9,e]
[0,3,6,9,e] 113000 [0,3,6,9,e]
[0,6,9,e] 111001 [0,6,9,e]
[0,9,e] 111000 [0,9,e]
[0,9] 002000 [0,9]
[0] 000000 [0]

[0,2,3,5,6,8,9,t,e] 630000 [0,2,3,5,6,8,9,t,e]

Phrase 6. mm. 96-first half of m. 99
[0,1,2,3,4,5,6,7,8,9] 901000 [1,2,3,4,5,6,7,8,9,t]
[0,1,2,3,4,5,6,7,8] 800100 [1,2,3,4,5,6,7,8,9]
[0,1,2,3,4,5,6,8] 610100 [1,2,3,4,5,6,7,9]
[0,1,2,3,4,6,8] 420100 [1,2,3,4,5,7,9]^
[0,1,3,4,6,8] 230100 [1,2,4,5,7,9]
[0,2,3,5,7] 130010 [2,4,5,7,9]
[0,2,3,5] 120010 [2,4,5,7]
[0,1,3] 111000 [4,5,7]
[0,1] 200000 [4,5]
[0] 000000 [4]

Phrase 7. mm. 101-106
[0,1,3,4,5,6,7,8] 610100 [3,4,6,7,8,9,t,e]
[0,3,4,5,6,7,8] 501100 [3,6,7,8,9,t,e]
[0,4,5,6,7,8] 400200 [3,7,8,9,t,e]
[0,4,5,6,8] 210200 [3,7,8,9,e]
[0,4,5,8] 101200 [3,7,8,e]
[0,1,4] 101100 [7,8,e]
[0,4] 000200 [7,e]
[0] 000000 [7]

Phrase 8. mm. 107-112
[0,1,2,5,9] 202100 [0,1,2,5,9]
[0,1,4,8] 101200 [1,2,5,9]
[0,1,4] 101100 [1,2,5]
[0,3] 002000 [2,5]
[0] 000000 [2]

[0,1,2,3,4,5,9,t] 610100 [0,1,2,3,4,5,9,t]

FIGURE 4.16 The author, Concerto for Cello and Orchestra (1994), computer analysis by phrase

in post-tonal music as it does in tonal music, where implied pitches must occur, or scales other than major and the three minors would necessarily prevail.

Figure 4.17 presents a computer analysis by section of the concerto excerpt in Figure 4.15. As shown by the highlighted scales, sections 1, 2, and 4 of this music have the 222000 linear interval vector in common. Since these sections contain all twelve pitches, each of these reductions requires the selective elimination of several transient chromatic pitches. Section 3 shares only one linear interval vector with the other sections (111000 in section 2). Of the scale possibilities in section 3, the 230100 linear interval vector seems most likely, having six pitch classes in its scale, as do the scale choices for the other three sections. Note that several other vectors—marked with the special symbols *, ‡, and ø—match in these sections. However, none of these matches accounts for more than two sections. Allowing ten pitches per scale produces an 820000 linear interval vector in both the first and last sections. Again, however, I tend to avoid scales with such large numbers of pitches because they so closely approximate the chromatic scale. For similar reasons, I have also ruled out the eleven-pitch scale with a linear interval vector of t10000, also possible in the first and last sections. Interestingly, the vector I have ultimately chosen for each section contains a different collection of transient pitches, ensuring that the actual pitch content of each scale prior to a transposition to 0 is unique.

Figure 4.18 shows a computer analysis of the entire concerto passage shown in Figure 4.15, taken as one section of music. Note that the 521000 and the 630000 linear interval vectors are the same as those used in Schoenberg's Six Little Piano Pieces op. 19, no. 1, and in Varèse's *Density 21.5*, respectively. The 820000 vector occurs here too, as it did in the analysis of sections 1 and 4 of this passage of the concerto. Of the three possible scales, I prefer the 630000-vectored scale, even though it appears only in the section 4 analysis (see Figure 4.17). Each of these perspectives—phrase, section, and entire passage—provide useful insights into my music, and I find it helpful to compare the similarities and differences between my intended scales and the scales that computer analysis provides. In this case, the sectional analysis most closely approximates my intent for this music.

Every scale has a complementary scale that contains all of those pitches that remain when that scale is compared with the full chromatic scale. Although this may seem obvious, it has some interesting benefits. For example, some scales (e.g., the whole-tone scale) have a transposed version of themselves as their complements. Other scales have different versions of themselves as complements (e.g., the octatonic scale, whose minor version is the complement to its major version). Still other scales have seemingly unrelated scales as their complements (e.g., the major scale). Complements do not mean much unless—as they occasionally do—the complements appear in the same movement or work together. For example, in my Concerto for Cello and Orchestra the scale used in the third movement has a related complement used much as the dominant key might be used in a tonal concerto. Figure 4.19 demonstrates this relationship.

Section 1: mm. 79-91
[0,1,2,3,4,5,6,7,8,9,t,e] w00000 [0,1,2,3,4,5,6,7,8,9,t,e]
[0,1,2,3,4,5,6,7,8,9,t] t10000 [1,2,3,4,5,6,7,8,9,t,e] ‡
[0,1,2,3,4,5,6,8,9,t] 820000 [1,2,3,4,5,6,7,9,t,e] ø
[0,1,2,3,4,5,6,8,9] 711000 [1,2,3,4,5,6,7,9,t]
[0,1,3,4,5,6,8,9] 521000 [1,2,4,5,6,7,9,t]
[0,3,4,5,6,8,9] 412000 [1,4,5,6,7,9,t] *
[0,3,5,6,8,9] 222000 [1,4,6,7,9,t]
[0,5,6,8,9] 211010 [1,6,7,9,t]
[0,6,8,9] 111001 [1,7,9,t]
[0,6,8] 010101 [1,7,9]
[0,6] 000002 [1,7]
[0] 000000 [1]

Section 2: mm. 92-95

[0,3,6,8,9,t,e] 412000 [0,3,6,8,9,t,e] *
[0,3,6,8,9,e] 222000 [0,3,6,8,9,e]
[0,3,6,9,e] 113000 [0,3,6,9,e]
[0,6,9,e] 111001 [0,6,9,e]
[0,9,e] 111000 [0,9,e]
[0,9] 002000 [0,9]
[0] 000000 [0]

Section 3: mm. 96-all but last sixteenth-note of 99

[0,1,2,3,4,5,6,7,8,9] 901000 [1,2,3,4,5,6,7,8,9,t]
[0,1,2,3,4,5,6,7,8] 800100 [1,2,3,4,5,6,7,8,9]
[0,1,2,3,4,5,6,8] 610100 [1,2,3,4,5,6,7,9]
[0,1,2,3,4,6,8] 420100 [1,2,3,4,5,7,9]
[0,1,3,4,6,8] 230100 [1,2,4,5,7,9]
[0,2,3,5,7] 130010 [2,4,5,7,9]
[0,2,3,5] 120010 [2,4,5,7]
[0,1,3] 111000 [4,5,7]
[0,1] 200000 [4,5]
[0] 000000 [4]

Section 4: mm. 101-112

[0,1,2,3,4,5,6,7,8,9,t,e] w00000 [0,1,2,3,4,5,6,7,8,9,t,e]
[0,1,2,3,5,6,7,8,9,t,e] t10000 [0,1,2,3,5,6,7,8,9,t,e] ‡
[0,1,2,3,5,7,8,9,t,e] 820000 [0,1,2,3,5,7,8,9,t,e] ø
[0,1,2,3,5,7,8,9,e] 630000 [0,1,2,3,5,7,8,9,e]
[0,1,2,4,6,7,8,t] 440000 [1,2,3,5,7,8,9,e]
[0,1,4,6,7,8,t] 331000 [1,2,5,7,8,9,e]
[0,3,5,6,7,9] 222000 [2,5,7,8,9,e] *
[0,5,6,7,9] 211010 [2,7,8,9,e]
[0,1,2,4] 210100 [7,8,9,e]
[0,2,4] 020100 [7,9,e]
[0,2] 020000 [7,9]
[0] 000000 [7]

FIGURE 4.17 Computer analysis of the excerpt from the author's concerto in Figure 4.15, by section.

[0,1,2,3,4,5,6,7,8,9,t,e] w00000 [0,1,2,3,4,5,6,7,8,9,t,e]
[0,1,2,3,4,5,7,8,9,t,e] t10000 [0,1,2,3,4,5,7,8,9,t,e]
[0,1,2,3,5,7,8,9,t,e] 820000 [0,1,2,3,5,7,8,9,t,e]
[0,1,2,3,5,7,8,9,e] 630000 [0,1,2,3,5,7,8,9,e]
[0,1,2,5,7,8,9,e] 521000 [0,1,2,5,7,8,9,e]
[0,1,4,6,7,8,t] 331000 [1,2,5,7,8,9,e]
[0,1,4,6,8,t] 141000 [1,2,5,7,9,e]
[0,4,6,8,t] 040100 [1,5,7,9,e]
[0,6,8,t] 030001 [1,7,9,e]
[0,6,8] 010101 [1,7,9]
[0,2] 020000 [7,9]
[0] 000000 [7]

FIGURE 4.18 Computer analysis of the entirety of the excerpt from the author's concerto shown in Figure 4.15.

FIGURE 4.19 Selected measures of the solo cello part of the author's concerto. The scale used in the third movement has a related complement used much as the dominant key might be used in a tonal concerto.

The beginning passage from the third movement of Stravinsky's Three Pieces for String Quartet (1914) contains all twelve tones. However, a scale analysis (see Figure 4.20) by the Scale program on the CD-ROM of this book indicates that a more likely explanation would be the major/minor set [0,2,3,4,5,7,8,9,t,e] with the linear interval vector of 820000. This set contains both versions of the mediant, submediant, and leading-tone/subtonic pitches, as one would expect of such a scale combination. Note that the output shown in Figure 4.20 uses Lisp syntax (parentheses, no commas, and so on) rather than the scale/set syntax described in previous examples. I have printed the output exactly so that program users will not be surprised by the differences. Conversion to scale/set syntax should be obvious upon comparing this example and, say, Figure 4.18.

((0 1 2 3 4 5 6 7 8 9 10 11) V1200000 (0 1 2 3 4 5 6 7 8 9 10 11))
((0 1 2 3 4 5 7 8 9 10 11) V1010000 (0 1 2 3 4 5 7 8 9 10 11))
((0 2 3 4 5 7 8 9 10 11) V820000 (0 2 3 4 5 7 8 9 10 11))
((0 2 3 4 5 8 9 10 11) V711000 (0 2 3 4 5 8 9 10 11))
((0 2 3 4 5 8 9 10) V521000 (0 2 3 4 5 8 9 10))
((0 2 3 4 5 8 9) V412000 (0 2 3 4 5 8 9))
((0 2 3 4 5 9) V311100 (0 2 3 4 5 9))
((0 2 3 5 9) V121100 (0 2 3 5 9))
((0 2 3 9) V111001 (0 2 3 9))
((0 2 9) V011010 (0 2 9))
((0 9) V002000 (0 9))
((0) V000000 (0))

FIGURE 4.20 A scale analysis of Stravinsky, Three Pieces for String Quartet (1914), 3rd movement (opening), as shown in Figure 1.19.

PROGRAM DESCRIPTION

The code used to derive linear interval vectors from scales expressed as pitch classes can be coded quite succinctly in Lisp. As shown below, the function count-intervals uses the Lisp primitive count to produce a straightforward listing of the intervals from 1 to 6 provided by its incrementally ascending optional argument. Note that the argument of count-intervals is a series of intervals between the pitch classes of the scale and not the scale itself (the function get-intervals-from-pitches defined in Chapter 2 will output the intervals necessary for count-intervals here).

```
(defun count-intervals (intervals &optional (size 1))
  "Counts the interval types present."
  (if (> size 6)()
      (cons (count size intervals)
            (count-intervals intervals (+ size 1)))))
```

The output of a run of count-intervals on an octatonic scale in pitch classes will provide a simple example of how the function works. As explained in previous chapters, combining simple functions such as this can provide powerful ways to analyze music. This is shown in the full program found on the CD-ROM accompanying this book.

The following example—as well as many of those yet to come in this book—represents a kind of Lisp pseudo-code, where the code follows all of the proper protocols but consists of yet-to-be-written functions. Hopefully, these functions have names that describe their actions well enough that readers who have followed the Lisp processes thus far described can create them themselves. Using pseudo-code such as this allows me to describe top-level functions of some sophistication without having to duplicate the entire code presented in the CD-ROM that accompanies this book.

```
(defun produce-scale (events)
  (order-from-zero
   (remove-all-duplicates
    (convert-to-pitch-classes
     (collect-pitches events)))))
```

This function produces a pitch-class scale given any set of note-events for a work or excerpt of a work of music once all four of the functions it calls for—`order-from-zero, remove-all-duplicates, convert-to-pitch-classes,` and `collect-pitches`—have been successfully coded. Since readability is extremely important in coding, programmers will often write code that duplicates existing primitives in Common Lisp to ensure that its name reflects exactly what it does. In the above function, `remove-all-duplicates` represents just such a function: its results are the same as those of `remove-duplicates`, but without the latter's sometimes confusing optional arguments.

The software program Scale (Macintosh and PC compatible) on the CD-ROM that accompanies this book offers readers the ability to access all 2,048 possible equal-tempered scale sets in a variety of ways—identifying, collecting, and/or perusing these scales by lists of pitch classes, linear interval vectors, or a combination of the two. Also, one may search the database in various ways. For example, the program allows searches for all scales having the initial pitch classes of 0, 1, or 2, or all scale sets with one or more minor seconds, or scale sets that contain one minor third, and so on. These processes hopefully provide useful advantages to both analysts and composers. The program also analyzes collected note-events in the manner previously described. I have also included all of the music in the figures in this chapter as note-events, both as examples for readers to follow and for verifying my findings. The manual that accompanies Scale provides detailed instructions for operating the program.

A number of functions in the Scale program, particularly `organize-by-duration` and `rotate-scale`, use a function called `mapcar`. This mapping function takes two arguments. The first argument must be a function preceded by the special indicator # and a single quotation mark. The second argument must be a list on each element of which the first argument will operate. For example, the code `(mapcar #'1+ '(1 2 3 4))` will map the function 1+ over the list provided to produce (2 3 4 5) as output. When programmers in Lisp wish to map a function they cannot imagine ever using again, they will often use `mapcar` to map what is termed a "no-name" function. No-name functions are indicated by using `lambda` which allows functions to be created on the fly. No-name functions do not clutter programming workspace with function names that have one use only. Another way to program the above code, then, is (mapcar #'(lambda (x)(+ x 1)) '(1 2 3 4)) where "x" is a local variable name.

As mentioned earlier in this chapter, scales represent special kinds of pitch-class sets. Like major and minor scales in tonal music, post-tonal scale sets represent entire passages or complete works and do not account for the appearance of every note. Scale sets are nonetheless pitch-class sets and, as such, suffer from the limitations described in Chapter 3—specifically, they lack information about register. Register can play an important role in scale determination, just as it does in expanded definition of pitch-class sets. For example, many composers use what are called pitch fields in their compositions. Pitch fields have register-rigid pitches that suggest scales of more than one octave to more clearly portray their sonic relationships. Figure 4.21 presents just such a pitch field. It covers a two-octave span and

FIGURE 4.21 A pitch field that covers a span of two-plus octaves and contains two exclusionary hexachord pitch-class sets.

contains two exclusionary pitch-class sets. Because all of the notes in this brief passage have inexact durations, a scale drawn from this music would, according to the principles thus far discussed, present a dodecachord—a panchromatic scale consisting of all twelve tones of the octave. Such a chromatic representation would reveal very little about the music they represent. A more logical scale for this passage appears in Figure 4.22, with its two-octave range.

Although pitch fields do not occur in all, or perhaps even much, music, pitches relegated to particular registers (see Chapter 3) for periods of time occur in significant numbers of musical works. Figure 4.23 presents just such an example, where the pitches C-sharp, G, and B appear only in the upper register and where the pitches E-flat, F, and A appear only in the lower register. Thus, this passage would lose true scale definition if we reduced all the pitches to pitch classes. Figure 4.24 demonstrates the scale differences between a one-octave representation and a two-octave representation.

FIGURE 4.21 continued

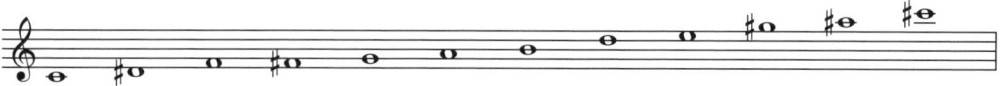

FIGURE 4.22 A scale with a range of two-plus octaves for the example shown in Figure 4.21.

FIGURE 4.23 An example where the notes C-sharp, G, and B appear only in the upper register and the notes E-flat, F, and A appear only in the lower register (Arnold Schoenberg, *Das Buch der hängenden Gärten*, II).

FIGURE 4.24 The scale differences between a one-octave representation and a two-octave representation of the music in Figure 4.23.

Determining whether a passage requires a multiple-octave or a single-octave analysis requires a simple program that counts pitches in various registers and informs users when more than a certain threshold of pitches unique to a given octave has been reached, suggesting that one or more further octaves be added to analyses to reveal the registral importance of these pitches. Given the somewhat unusual nature of two-octave scales, I have not provided a program here to analyze for them, leaving it to readers to determine whether and when music would require such extended scales.

Scales that vary in their upward and downward motion should also be considered an important contributor to some music. The melodic minor tonal scale is a good example of such a scale, with its raised sixth and seventh degrees in the ascent and natural—according to the operative key signature—forms of these scale degrees in the descent. To analyze for such scales, a computer program would require code to differentiate between pitches occurring in only rising or falling motion in music and catalog their presence in the resulting upward and downward scales. In effect, two scales will result from such analysis.

Scales need not be limited to pitch. After all, scales result from the cumulative membership of any given parameter in music—duration, articulation, dynamics, and so on. For example, durational scales can reveal interesting if not significant detail about a work or a passage. A durational scale that excludes or has relatively infrequent occurrence of certain durations can explain significant analytical aspects about the music it represents. Music that creates a durational scale of ♪, ♩, and 𝅝, for example, reveals a great deal about its source. Lacking dotted rhythms, quarter notes, triplets, and so on, this durational scale indicates the music's more or less squareness and probable jerky quality due to shifts between durations of quite differing values. Of course, without any reference to the quantity of each of these durations, we are left with the possibility that the passage consists almost entirely of eighth notes, with a half note and whole note providing rhythmic cadences. Therefore, adding proportions—providing a sense of "chromaticism" to the "diatonicism" of a durational scale—can indicate subtle nuances in it, as in

♪ ♪. ♪ ♪. ♩ ♩. ♩ 𝅝
22 / 29 / 48 / 1 / 6 / 14 / 12 / 1

which provides a great deal more information about the overall durational context of the music. The whole note represents but $1/133$ of the overall number of durations, while the eighth note holds a $48/133$ advantage. Both the whole note and the eighth note hold such marginal roles in this music that one could catalog them as nondiatonic to the durational scale in use, even though the whole note clearly has a substantial durational weight lasting eight times the duration of the eighth note and most likely occurring as the ultimate note of the music. Articulations, dynamics, timbre, and so on can be extracted from music in much the same way as durations. Aligning various parametrical scales could then indicate consonant or dissonant relationships, much as the dynamic algorithmic information theory graphs do as discussed in Chapter 2 of this book.

CONCLUSIONS

In the four or so centuries of its predominance in Western music theory, tonal analysis has presented two particularly important doctrines. The first is that tonal music relies on scales—typically major and minor scales—to provide continuity and consistency. The second is that these scales produce hierarchy in the sense of scale degree and musical function. If post-tonal music too can be analyzed according to scales, then it seems logical that post-tonal music also has hierarchy based on scale degree and function. In the next chapter I describe one of the possible methods for discovering such hierarchy in post-tonal music based on the scales revealed in the present chapter.

FIVE
Function and Structure in Post-Tonal Music

> The whole history of music, from, say, Berlioz to Boulez can be understood as one in which nonfunctional class membership becomes increasingly important, ending in serialism, set theory, and the compositions arising from them. Thus, in the analysis of much contemporary music, the pitch class of a tone is more important than its function.
>
> Leonard Meyer, *The Spheres of Music* (2000), 267

This chapter begins by introducing object-oriented programming in Common Lisp, an extension of the more traditional form of Lisp programming covered thus far in this book. This discussion is immediately followed by a proposal of the possibly provocative notion that post-tonal music has function just as tonal music does, and that these post-tonal functions can be analyzed and represented in logical ways. This concept of post-tonal function emerges from the scale analysis described in Chapter 4. Because the pitches contained in scales do not have the same importance, or the same implied destinations, defining their various roles directly relates to musical function. Although certainly not new, the idea of function in post-tonal music continues to cause controversy, and even among those who agree that function exists there is little consensus as to what form such functions take. In turn, post-tonal functions portend structural hierarchy, a subject that itself provokes a degree of controversy. The lack of agreement on these subjects presents complex problems for music analysts, problems that computational technology may be well suited to engage and resolve. This chapter, then, concerns Principle 3 as described in Chapter 1.

OBJECT-ORIENTED PROGRAMMING

Thus far in this book, I have described Common Lisp as a *functional* language. The word *functional* here relates to programming and does not carry the same meaning as it does in music. As we have seen since Chapter 2's initial presentation, functions in programming languages operate by command-line input—typing function names and their arguments into Listener windows, resulting in some sort of desired output. For example, the code

```
? (first '(1 2 3))
```

represents a functional operation, with the function `first` returning the first element of its argument. Functional programming such as this provides an excellent environment for prototyping and testing ideas. However, most applications we use today have a different look—they have menus, windows, buttons, scroll bars, and so on. We can enter and manipulate data by using real-world parallels such as mouse-controlled checkboxes, sliders, and pop-up menus, rather than typing on keyboards. Creating mouse-clickable visual interfaces requires a different type of programming called Object Oriented Programming (OOP). Common Lisp's version of OOP is called CLOS, for Common Lisp Object System. Most versions of Common Lisp include CLOS. Using a mouse rather than a keyboard is one very simple way to distinguish between object-oriented programming techniques and functional programming techniques.

Building interfaces that require integrated menus, windows, and so on falls well outside the scope of this book. However, knowing how OOP works in Common Lisp will prove valuable for the ensuing discussions of musical function, hierarchy, and other concepts presented later in this book that require a broader view of programming than that provided in Chapter 2. OOP offers a rich vocabulary of processes better matched to these more complex formal and structural musical ideas.

As an example, imagine that a user wishes to analyze the pitches of a group of note-events representing beat 129 of a long work containing, say, one thousand such note-events. Locating the note-events of beat 129 in the long list of note-events, collecting this beat's note-events from the longer list of note-events, extracting the pitches from these collected note-events, and so on would require the use of a series of functions each and every time this information was needed. However, if this beat and all other beats were initially collected by the series of functions just described and then stored in separate objects named by their beat number—such as beat-129—locating individual beats would be simple. OOP offers perfect ways to do this.

A study of object-oriented programming, even a brief study such as this, usually begins with an example of `defclass`, such as:

```
(defclass beat ()
   ((note-events :initarg :note-events
                 :initform nil
                 :accessor note-events)
    (pitches     :initarg :pitches
                 :initform nil
                 :accessor pitches)
```

```
            (beat-number    :initarg :beat-number
                            :initform 1
                            :accessor beat-number)))
```

Classes—such as this one called `beat`—are not functions, but rather abstract declarations of how this class's *instances* will behave. As we shall shortly see, classes and instances, although closely related, have different purposes. Classes describe how their instances will act. Instances represent individual objects that follow their class descriptions. Classes resemble recipes, while instances constitute the actual food produced from such recipes.

The above class named `beat` has three types of *slots* (also called arguments)—`note-events`, `pitches`, and `beat-number`. Each of these slots has several keywords that follow its declaration. Keywords allow arguments to be called in any number and any order as long as the actual argument is preceded by a keyword prefixed with a colon. In the case of note-events, for example, the slot has an initial argument (:initarg, itself described by the keyword `note-events`), an initial form (:initform with its default value of nil), and an accessor (:accessor with its default value of `note-events`), the last of which can be used just like a function to access the data in instances of the associated class without being defined further. I will describe these slots in more detail momentarily.

In order to place a musical work into OOP-class beats requires that each beat of that work be placed a separate instance of the beat class. To use the class beat, then, we have to create an instance of it containing the data for a particular beat. To access the data in each of the slots, we call their accessors as if they were functions. For example, the following succession of code represents the creation of one instance of the just-described `beat` class.

```
? (setq beat-129
        (make-instance 'beat :note-events
                             '((129000 50 1000 1 127))
                             :pitches '(60)
                             :beat-number 129))
#<BEAT #xF1C676>
? (note-events beat-129)
((129000 50 1000 1 127))
? (pitches beat-129)
(60)
?(beat-number beat-129)
129
```

Here, `make-instance` creates an instance of the class `beat` with all of its initial slots established. Note that the slots presented are each referenced by their colon-prefixed slot names. This type of slot calling allows for the arguments to appear in any order; slots that are not called revert to their default values, presented in the class definition itself. Note how the accessors look and act like functions, returning information here from the object beat-129.

Each new instance of an object of the class beat can have different information in its slots. The information stored in the slots of these instances can also be easily changed. To do this, programmers typically use setf, which takes two arguments —a location and the new data. The following code, for example, alters the information located in the beat-number slot of beat-129:

```
? (setf (beat-number beat-129) 128)
128
? (beat-number beat-129)
128
```

The first argument to setf here defines the location as the beat-number slot of beat-129. The second argument to setf provides its new value. This can be read as "set the beat number of beat-129 to 128." We now have a class of objects defined, instances of these objects each containing information in appropriate slots, and a process enabling us to alter any of this information whenever we wish. Because objects now exist as independent entities, we can find them simply by referencing their names, as in

```
? beat-129
#<BEAT #xF5432E>
```

where the returned information indicates that the object belongs to the beat class, and a reference number represents an internal symbol to distinguish objects from one another.

OOP also has class-related *methods* to differentiate them from standard Common Lisp functions. Methods are defined using defmethod. As seen below in pseudocode (i.e., play-events has not yet been defined), defmethod must reference the object class to which it belongs so that when called it can expect the proper slot accessor information.

```
(defmethod play ((beat-class beat))
  (play-events (note-events beat-class)))
```

The above method definition play takes a list of arguments, each of which consists of a class name (to the right—beat) and a nickname for that class name (to the left—beat-class) for use within the method definition. Classes may have as many methods as needed. The method play is then used much like a function or accessor, as in

```
(play beat-129)
```

with the note-events of beat-129 played as a result.

Methods, defined separately for each class, have many advantages over functions. For example, in functional programming a function has but one form, described by its definition. The function first, for example, returns the first element of its list argument in all circumstances. Provide this function with a non-listed number, for example, and it will return an error. OOP methods offer programmers the opportunity to use *polymorphic* processes. The word *polymorphic* here means that methods with the same names may have many different definitions, each definition associated with a particular object class. Although initially confusing, especially for functional programmers, polymorphism has many advantages. For example, two accessors both called play but bound to two different classes may take very different kinds of information as arguments, depending on the associated class definition. One method `play` could play note-events in a list as argument, while another method `play` could play individual note-events not in a list as argument. To users of such a system, the accessor `play` serves both needs transparently, as long as it is provided instances of the proper class. If we did not have OOP polymorphism, we would have to create several functions such as `play-events`, `play-event`, and so on, for such computations. These extra names complicate and clutter the programming environment.

Thus far, we have discussed objects only as representing instances of individual classes. OOP programming includes another feature, one that most closely resembles one of the subjects of this chapter: hierarchy. In OOP, classes may inherit from other classes, and these other classes may in turn inherit from still other classes, and so on. These variously related classes inherit the slots and values of the classes to which they belong. As example, the following definition of the `beat` class described earlier in this chapter

```
(defclass beat (measure)
   ((note-events   :initarg :note-events
                   :initform nil
                   :accessor note-events)
    (pitches       :initarg :pitches
                   :initform nil
                   :accessor pitches)
    (beat-number   :initarg :beat-number
                   :initform nil
                   :accessor beat-number)))
```

now includes the name of another class called `measure` in the list following its name. The definition of `measure` given below includes different slots than the class `beat`, but by definition, the class `beat` will inherit the slots of the class `measure`.

```
(defclass measure ()
   ((beats         :initarg :beats
                   :initform nil
                   :accessor beats)
    (meter         :initarg :meter
                   :initform 4
                   :accessor meter)
```

```
(number       :initarg :number
              :initform nil
              :accessor number)))
```

In this case, the class measure is called a *superclass*, and the class beat is called its *subclass*. Therefore, subclasses inherit the slots and their values from their superclasses. Thus, creating instances of measure and beat produces the following output:

```
? (setq measure-50 (make-instance 'measure))
#<MEASURE #xF4D02E>
? (setq beat-129
        (make-instance 'beat :note-events '((129000 50 1000 1
          127))
                             :pitches '(60)
                             :beat-number 129))
#<BEAT #xF4D236>
? (meter beat-129)
4
? (meter measure-50)
4
? (beat-number measure-50)
> Error: No applicable method for args
```

Note that the beat class, defined as a subclass of the measure object, inherits all of the slots and their values of the measure class, but that the reverse is not true. In other words, the hierarchy moves in one direction only.

The following code creates a phrase object that itself contains a list of beat objects for each beat in its phrase of music. The code presented below, although not self-contained, appears in full in the file called "Root Object Code" in the folder "Root" on the CD-ROM accompanying this book.

```
(defclass phrase ()
  ((beats :initarg :beats
          :initform ()
          :accessor beats)))

(defmethod initialize-instance ((object phrase) &rest initargs)
  (apply #'shared-initialize object t initargs)
  (setf b-number 0)
  (setf (beats object) ())
  (loop for beat in *beat-event-lists*
        do (setq *note-events* beat)
        do (setq beat-number (create-beat-number object))
```

```
              do (set beat-number (make-instance 'beat))
              do (setf (beats object)(push beat-number (beats
                object))))
    (setf (beats object)(reverse (beats object)))))
(defclass beat (phrase)
  ((note-events  :initarg :note-events
                 :initform ()
                 :accessor note-events)
    (pitches     :initarg :pitches
                 :initform ()
                 :accessor pitches)
    (root        :initarg :root
                 :initform ()
                 :accessor root)))
(defmethod initialize-instance ((object beat) &rest initargs)
  (apply #'shared-initialize object t initargs)
  (setf (note-events object) *note-events*)
  (setf (pitches object) (get-pitches object (events object)))
  (setf (root object) (get-root object (pitches object))))
(defmethod get-pitches ((object beat) note-events)
  (loop for note-event in note-events
        collect (second note-event)))
(defmethod create-beat-number ((object phrase))
  (incf b-number)
  (implode (list 'beat- b-number)))
(defmethod get-root ((object beat) ordered-pitches)
  (get-the-pitch (arrange ordered-pitches)
                 (find-root
                   (mapcar #'get-intervals (arrange ordered-
                   pitches)))))
```

The class called phrase here has but one slot, a list of beat objects initially set to the empty list (). These beat objects are created in the fifth through ninth lines of the method initialize-instance of the beat object, within the loop call (see Chapter 4 for a discussion of loop). The beat object has three slots, one for the note-events of a beat, one for the extracted pitches of those beat note-events, and one for the root pitch of the beat. The initialize-instance method for the beat object assigns the proper values for the beat object's slots. The code (apply #'shared-initialize object t initargs) in the two initialize-instance methods fills the slots of the class with its default values. The call to mapcar in the get-root method maps the function get-intervals across every sublist of its second argument. The function incf—the increment function—in the create-beat-number method incrementally increases the current value of b-number. The function incf is "destructive" in that it actually alters the state of its b-number argument. Note that all of the methods defined here are bound to their appropriate class.

To use this object-oriented version of the root identification program requires a single call to make-instance, such as

```
? (setq phrase-object (make-instance 'phrase))
#<PHRASE #x11997DE>
? (beats phrase-object)
(BEAT-1 BEAT-2 BEAT-3 BEAT-4 BEAT-5 BEAT-6)
? (root beat-4)
65
```

where creating the phrase object names these objects, invests all of the slots of the beat objects with appropriate data, and then lists the beat objects by name in numerical beat order in its beats slot. A call to any of the three accessors of any beat object returns the appropriate analysis of that particular beat. Looking at the file "Root Object Code" reveals a mix of OOP and functional code similar to that in the "Root" file. As an alternative, one could redefine these functions as methods to produce the same results, thus keeping the entire process within OOP style. Many programming languages (Java, for instance) pride themselves on being OOP exclusive, while others (C, for instance) do not include object procedures (C++ does, however). Common Lisp, on the other hand, allows for what many feel represents a healthy mix of functional programming and OOP techniques.

Storing musical works in hierarchies such as the one just described can be very useful. Interestingly, deciding whether the top level consists of phrase objects and the bottom level consists of beat objects, or vice versa, poses a challenge for music analysts. Clearly musical structure follows a pyramidal form, with notes at the bottom, followed—possibly—by beats, measures, phrases, sections, movements, and then works. However, one might not need to give beats access to information about the works to which they belong, whereas works may very well need to have access to the information that notes possess. Certainly, works require access to the notes that belong to them. For composers, especially those who improvise their music, notes may logically reside at the top level of the class structure. In Experiments in Musical Intelligence (see Cope 1996 and 2005), however, object hierarchy begins with a work superclass and ends with a beat sub-sub-subclass. This process results from the program's need for notes, beats, and so on, to always have access to their location in their associated work, which is accomplished only by an approach where inheritance follows a downward flow from the work to the note. Analysts must obviously decide such issues of hierarchy in class structure prior to analysis.

Interestingly, programming technique itself also tends to follow top-down or bottom-up paradigms. For example, professional programmers tend to work from the top down, creating top-level functions first and then fleshing out the details while always maintaining an overview of the program they have in mind. Unfortunately, when using top-down approaches one cannot actually test a program until all of its parts are coded. Therefore, novice programmers, who need to feel confident that lower level functions will work before they use them, tend to program using bottom-up processes. The problem with bottom-up programming is that although each successive function can be debugged until it actually works, one may lose sight of the ultimate goal or, worse yet, digress into solving irrelevant problems that have little to do with the overall program. Like analysts, programmers must decide which approach suits a particular project and never attempt to work from both directions at once in a vain hope that the two will somehow magically connect in the middle.

I typically choose top-down programming as a model. Therefore, as previously mentioned, readers should be aware that although the code on the CD-ROM accompanying this book works as described, the code shown in the latter part of this book will not operate as it stands. This code represents top-level functions and object classes that contain code not shown. Unfortunately, it may seem counterintuitive to some to analyze music from a top-down perspective. For example, analyzing form without knowing the actual musical ideas present does not bode well for success. Therefore, many analysts may prefer using a bottom-up approach, beginning with musical functions that inform concepts of phrase and ending with sections informing form.

My reasons for presenting OOP at this point in *Hidden Structure* have to do with the nature of the material about to be discussed: musical function and hierarchy. Deciding how to represent the analyses of function and hierarchy in post-tonal music will greatly affect the understanding of these two important facets of music. On a practical level, it seems highly advantageous to hide such elements as function names, hierarchical representations, and so on in objects rather than nesting them in lists along with note-events. Even more important, however, creating hierarchical object classes that inherit from one another allows storage of important structural information that allows access to every level. In fact, it *requires* that an analyst analyze structurally. As an example, Figure 5.1 presents one possible overview of the structure of a work of music that simultaneously represents visual and musical parallels *and* an OOP hierarchy. Seen in this way, OOP processes not only serve as analogies for musical structure, they actually serve as vehicles for explaining that musical structure. As we shall soon see, this approach has many computational advantages as well.

DEFINITIONS

Musical set theory—see Chapter 3 for more information—offers analysts opportunities to analyze post-tonal music by grouping it into sets and then reducing these

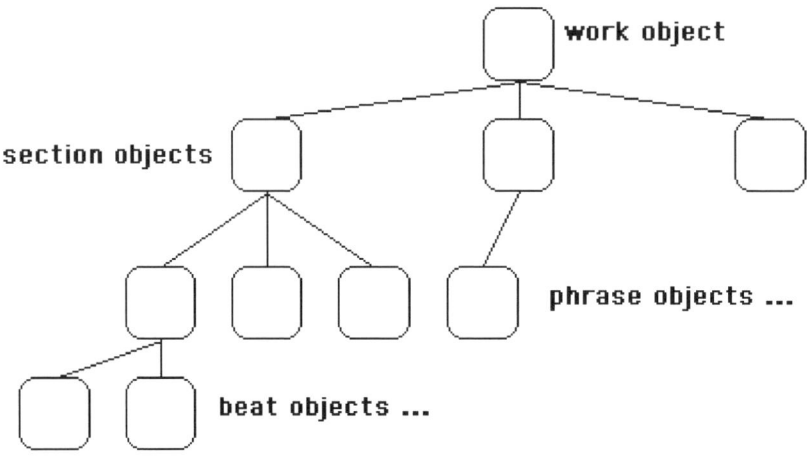

FIGURE 5.1 One possible overview of the structure of a work of music that is at one and the same time a visual/musical representation and an OOP representation.

sets into various categories. As important as this reduction-and-categorization process is, however, arguing that sets represent an alternative to tonal function for post-tonal music poses many difficulties. In fact, one could rationally posit that set theory does little beyond grouping post-tonal music into chord types similar to the various triadic form types of tonal music (e.g., major and minor triads).

I therefore do not agree with Leonard Meyer's implication, presented at the outset of this chapter, the implication that pitch-class membership can act as a substitute for function ("the pitch class of a tone is more important than its function"; Meyer 2000, 267). An equivalent view for tonal music would be that a major triad can substitute for a tonic function, something we know to be false because many different tonal functions consist of major triads. Interestingly, both tonal scales and functions represent pitch-class sets, but we do not typically use pitch-class sets to analyze tonal music, because doing so reveals little of the music other than its tertian origins.

Defining the word "function" as it applies to music here seems necessary, especially before attempting to use the term in reference to post-tonal music. Webster's Collegiate Dictionary (1991) defines the word *function* as "the purpose for which something is designed or exists." Because I find very little if anything without purpose, every note, certainly every chord and pitch-class set in music—tonal, post-tonal, or otherwise—has purpose and function, and attempting to discover these purposes is not only appropriate but paramount to the analysis of post-tonal music.

Therefore, for this book at least, the concept of musical function derives from the notion of hierarchy that itself derives from scale membership, and chord roots in cases where two or more pitches occur simultaneously. All pitches in music, any music, have "class membership," as Meyer terms it, which does not necessarily change simply because musical styles themselves change. That said, *function exists in post-tonal music*. The only question that remains is how to discern function and determine its purpose.

Musical function represents one of the most salient features of any kind or style of music. Musical function helps define syntax—expectation, fulfillment, deception, and so on—and semantics—tension, release, voice-leading constraints, and so forth. Discovering function in post-tonal music, however, presents enormously challenging difficulties. Using computers may make this discovery more feasible and hopefully more likely, and accomplished in less time than the millennium it roughly took to discover function in modal and tonal music.

As previously mentioned, each pitch in a scale, no matter how far removed from tonality that scale may be, suggests—possibly even demands—a unique relationship with the other members of that scale. Paul Hindemith comments that

> anyone to whom a tone is more than a note on paper or a key pressed down, anyone who has ever experienced the intervals in singing, especially with others, as manifestations of bodily tension, of the conquest of space, and of the consumption of energy, anyone who has ever tasted the delights of pure intonation by the continual displacement of the comma in string-quartet playing, must come to the conclusion that there can be no such thing as atonal music, in which the existence of tone-relationships is denied. (Hindemith 1942, 155)

Hindemith's unqualified statement here suggests that function can be found in all music, regardless of its complexity.

Defining function in post-tonal music obviously requires more specific criteria than has thus far been discussed. Certainly computer programs will need clear instructions on how to compute these functions. The following three categories represent my own views of post-tonal function:

1. *Root*, acoustically defined and referenced to a current scale

2. *Tension*, as defined by acoustical principles

3. *Context*, as defined by the proximity of the music under analysis

Certainly roots (category 1) of groupings play an important role in function, because these roots help define the various degrees of a scale in use. However, roots alone cannot determine the function of groupings, particularly in the case of post-tonal music, where a single phrase may consist of many different chord types. Tension (category 2) also contributes to function, because some groupings require resolution to more stable groupings. However, even roots and tension together cannot define function. As an example, Figure 5.2a presents a seven-group phrase, each group of which has the same root and thus represents the same scale degree. However, the interval content of these groupings differs in such ways that all the groups produce different tensions. In this example, the tensions increase steadily until the final grouping, which returns to a tension similar to the opening grouping. Clearly, the penultimate grouping here has a different function from the first grouping of the passage, even though it shares the same root and thus the same scale-degree representation. In fact, one could easily imagine the final two groupings representing a dominant-tonic authentic cadence were it not for their identical roots.

The same problems exist when using tensions to determine function in post-tonal music. As an example, Figure 5.2b presents a phrase containing groupings of similar tension, so that tensions alone seem unlikely to produce significant enough differences between groupings to assign them anything but the same function throughout. However, the chord roots, and thus the scale-degree representations, differ substantially. In this example, it would make more sense to give greater weight to roots than to tensions.

It would seem that both roots and tensions contribute in varying degrees to the determination of function in post-tonal music but cannot reveal function by themselves. Context provides the necessary conclusive element in defining musical function. Just like the relationship of chords to keys in tonal music, function in post-tonal music requires the context of the roots and tensions of neighboring groupings, as well as not-so-neighboring groupings that provide larger structural contexts.

Of course, one could further include dynamics, articulations, metric placements, and so on in determining function. Concentrating as I have in this book on pitch, however, suggests that although not all inclusive, pitch offers a good start to identifying function as a shared composite of many factors.

We shall now see how these three important fundamentals—root, tension, and context—triangulate to define function in post-tonal music.

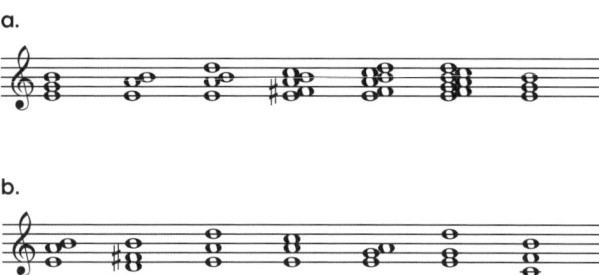

FIGURE 5.2 Examples where (a) roots remain the same but tensions change and (b) tensions remain fairly equal but roots change, demonstrating how neither process alone can determine function in post-tonal music.

THE ACOUSTIC THEORY OF CHORD ROOTS

The following abridged description of Paul Hindemith's acoustic root theory (Hindemith 1942) has been modified following both my own interpretation and information revealed since his initial presentation of the theory (Backus 1969; Benade 1976). Much of my interpretation derives from computational, mathematical, and empirical data (see Cope 2005).

Hindemith's acoustic root theory originates—as do many theories of music analysis—with the overtone series, an incomplete example of which appears in Figure 5.3. The overtone series occurs naturally in one way or another in all but pure sinusoidal waveforms and acts as the basis for timbre and many other important musical phenomena. The overtone series consists of a fundamental—usually the loudest-sounding pitch of the series and the lowest pitch C in Figure 5.3—and a theoretically infinite series of overtones figured as incremental multiples of the fundamental frequency. Because humans generally hear little above 20,000 cycles (20 kHz) per second, and because the amplitude of the overtones generally diminishes as they extend above the fundamental, the series here consists of only fifteen overtones above the fundamental. The overtone series is also numbered in partials, beginning with the fundamental as the first partial. Thus, sixteen partials appear in Figure 5.3. These two different numbering systems—overtones and partials—can produce confusion. However, because using one system or the other has its advantages depending on circumstance, I will reference both systems, clearly identifying which I am using at the time.

Determining a grouping's root begins by (1) identifying all of the separate intervals present in the grouping, (2) locating each interval's lowest occurrence in the overtone series, (3) determining each interval's root, and (4) finding the strongest root among the roots present. Steps 1 and 2 seem simple enough. Steps 3 and 4, however, require some explanation. To define a single interval's root involves locating the

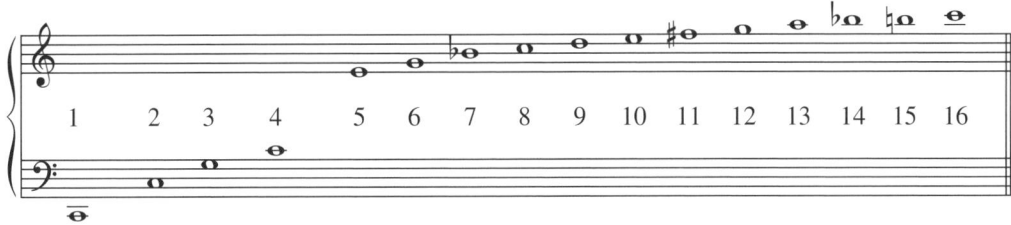

FIGURE 5.3 The overtone series from the fundamental C.

member of that lowest-appearing interval that represents an upward octave projection of the fundamental in any overtone series (Hindemith 1942). For instance, the perfect fifth's root is its lower pitch, because the lowest fifth appearing in the overtone series has as its lower pitch an octave projection of the fundamental (overtone 1 or partial 2). The interval of a fourth—the inversion of the fifth—has its upper pitch as the root, because this pitch falls two octaves above the fundamental (overtone 3 or partial 4). Without figuring each interval separately, the roots of all intervals smaller than an octave can be easily remembered as the lower pitches of all odd-numbered intervals (thirds, fifths, and sevenths), and as the upper pitches of all even-numbered intervals (second, fourths, and sixths). The tritone has an ambiguous root because it falls midway between octave projections of the fundamental. Differences between major and minor versions of seconds, thirds, sixths, and sevenths will not be distinguished here owing to their close approximations to one another. Roots of compound intervals will also match the roots of their corresponding intervals within the octave in this definition. For example, the root of a ninth is its upper pitch, because it reduces to a second, and the root of a second is its upper pitch.

Interval derivations based on the overtone series along with their root designations appear in Figure 5.4a, from the largest to the smallest interval within the octave. Lower-occurring and lower-rooted intervals produce the strongest roots, and upper-occurring and upper-rooted intervals produce weaker roots. From this list, then, seconds have the least root strength because they occur highest in the series (16/15) and have upper roots. Sevenths have slightly stronger roots because of their lower projections, but nonetheless occur very high in the series (15/8). Sixths have more root strength than sevenths because they occur lower in the series (5/3), but they have less root strength than thirds because thirds occur lower in the series (5/4 and 6/5) and have lower roots. As just mentioned, the tritone, even though it has low placement in the series (7/5), divides the octave in half, and therefore does not have a clear root. The perfect fifth has the strongest root of all intervals owing to its low placement (3/2) and lower root. The perfect octave—not shown—ultimately projects the strongest root but represents doubling, because both members belong to the same pitch class. The interval root strengths appear in Figure 5.4b in order of strength. The lowest strongest interval occurring more than once in a grouping produces the grouping's root.

Figure 5.5 provides six groupings as examples of the above-described root-identification process. In grouping (a), the fifth D–A represents the strongest interval present, with its lowest member the root of the grouping. Figure 5.5b poses more complex problems, but C–G-sharp (A-flat) is the strongest interval, with its upper pitch (G-sharp) as root. In Figure 5.5c, the root results from the perfect fifth D-flat–A-flat. The perfect fifth E–B in Figure 5.5d produces the root E. Figures 5.5e and Figure 5.5f have the same root, C, the result of the perfect fifth C–G. From these simple examples, one can see how this root-finding process poses few problems

a.				b.		
int	ratio	root		int	ratio	root
M7	(15/8)	lower		P5	(3/2)	lower
m7	(16/9)	lower		P4	(4/3)	upper
M6	(5/3)	upper		M3	(5/4)	lower
m6	(8/5)	upper		m3	(6/5)	lower
P5	(3/2)	lower		M6	(5/3)	upper
A4	(7/5)	unclear		m6	(8/5)	upper
P4	(4/3)	upper		M2	(9/8)	upper
M3	(5/4)	lower		m2	(16/15)	upper
m3	(6/5)	lower		m7	(16/9)	lower
M2	(9/8)	upper		M7	(15/8)	lower
m2	(16/15)	upper		A4	(7/5)	unclear

FIGURE 5.4 (a) Interval derivations from the overtone series along with their root designations, and (b) interval root strengths shown in order of strength.

FIGURE 5.5 Six groupings to serve as examples of the root-identification process.

compared to tonal harmony built in thirds, where unwinding thirds in inverted chords can require quite complicated operations.

Interestingly, one might imagine that the leftmost zero of prime-form pitch-class sets would be the root of the set. However, although this is true for some prime-form sets, many other sets have different roots. For example, the twelve prime-form trichords turn out as follows, with the prime-form pitch-class set presented to the left and the set's pitch-class root to the right.

0,1,2	2
0,1,3	0
0,1,4	0
0,1,5	5
0,1,6	1
0,2,4	0
0,2,5	5
0,2,6	2
0,2,7	0
0,3,6	0
0,3,7	0
0,4,8	0

With more complex chords (pentachords, and so on), the roots vary as well. For example, the first four pentachords in pitch-class-set order have 0, 5, 0, and 5 as roots, and the first four hexachords in pitch-class-set order have 5, 0, 5, and 5 as roots.

A simple example of pseudo-code appears below, where an object-oriented method assigns a root to instances of an object class called set.

```
(defmethod initialize-instance ((object set) &rest initargs)
   (declare (ignore initargs))
   (if (> (tension-range object)(root-range object))
       (put-functions-into object tensions)
       (put-functions-into object roots-and-scales)))
```

Here, the conditional if computes which of the ranges—tension or root—will determine the function. Although the functions tension-range, root-range, and put-functions-into do not actually exist in the files accompanying this book on CD-ROM, readers who have followed the discussion of Lisp functional and OOP processes should, with the assistance of one or more of the Lisp books listed in the bibliography (Graham 1995; Steele 1990; Touretzky 1990; Wilensky 1986), be able themselves to produce a working model based on this pseudo-code.

Whereas roots in tonal music tend to be the sole determining factor in deciding function, roots in post-tonal music can have much less influence on function. As has just been shown, roots of groupings can be strong, as determined by perfect fifths and fourths, or relatively weak, as determined by sixths and thirds. As we will soon see, a strongly defined root tends to support its determination of function, while a weak root does just the opposite.

Although all pitches contribute to a scale in use, chord roots especially tend to define scale membership. In order to clearly place roots into scales, we need a notation that is both simple and easy to understand. Therefore, the notation I will use in this book consists of movable-*do* pitch-class numbers. Members of scales in this post-tonal approach appear simply as pitch classes in the scale in which they belong.

Hence, a 7 indicates a perfect fifth above 0. All numbers not present in the scale have a small suffix "ø" to indicate their out-of-scale nature. Therefore, the [0 1 2 3 4

5 6 7 8 9 t e] set indicates a full chromatic scale in t-normal form. The major and octatonic scales are listed below as further examples of this notation:

Major Scale

   1ø   3ø   6ø   8ø   tø
0   2   4 5   7   9   e 0

Octatonic Major Scale

   1ø   4ø   7ø   tø
0   2 3   5 6   8 9   e 0

Obviously, any scale based in the twelve-tone temperament can be represented in this way.

This notation for representing scale membership of pitch class roots, although it has several drawbacks, has many virtues. The principal drawback involves the movable-*do* use of 0–e pitch classes. In other words, 0 no longer represents C but rather the first pitch of the analyzed scale. Of course, looking at this representation as a t-normal set resolves this problem. The main virtue of this representation is that it requires no memorization of new symbols aside from the ø, nor does it in any way contradict or cause confusion with the Roman numerals of tonal functional analysis.

As alluded to earlier, the notation just discussed indicates only a numbering notation for scales and roots within those scales. This notation does not necessarily indicate actual musical function. The pitch class 0 might represent a function such as tonic (home base, etc.) in tonal music but may not indicate the same for post-tonal music. As we will see, this concept of scale degrees and roots projecting possibly different functions is extremely important.

MUSICAL TENSION

Figure 5.6 presents a list of intervals from a perfect unison to a perfect twenty-ninth and my own views of their tensions. The SPEAC Analysis software—discussed in more detail later in this chapter—that accompanies this book on CD-ROM allows users to adjust these levels according to their own personal tastes. Although the list presented here involves some simple mathematics—especially when considering octave projections of intervals within the octave—I have not produced it using any overall mathematical formula. I prefer to gauge tension based on refinement of rough estimates derived from formulae (see Cope 2000).

Computations of groupings require the addition of the tensions of all of the intervals present. For example, to find the tension of a major triad in closed position would require the addition of the tensions of a major third, a perfect fifth, and a minor third, the three intervals present. Doublings, dynamics, and so on, all viable factors in the effective evaluation of grouping tension, have not been included here,

unison	0.0	minor sixteenth	.925
minor second	1.0	major sixteenth	.725
major second	.8	minor seventeenth	.175
minor third	.225	major seventeenth	.125
major third	.2	perfect eighteenth	.475
perfect fourth	.55	augmented eighteenth	.575
augmented fourth	.65	perfect nineteenth	.025
perfect fifth	.1	minor twentieth	.2
minor sixth	.275	major twentieth	.175
major sixth	.25	minor twenty-first	.625
minor seventh	.7	major twenty-first	.825
major seventh	.9	perfect twenty-second	0.0
perfect octave	0.0	minor twenty-third	.91
minor ninth	.95	major twenty-third	.71
major ninth	.74	minor twenty-fourth	.135
minor tenth	.175	major twenty-fourth	.11
major tenth	.15	perfect twenty-fifth	.46
perfect eleventh	.5	augmented twenty-fifth	.56
augmented eleventh	.6	perfect twenty-sixth	.01
perfect twelfth	.05	minor twenty-seventh	.185
minor thirteenth	.225	major twenty-seventh	.16
major thirteenth	.2	minor twenty-eighth	.61
minor fourteenth	.65	major twenty-eighth	.81
major fourteenth	.85	perfect twenty-ninth	0.0
perfect fifteenth	0.0		

FIGURE 5.6 A list of intervals weighted according to their tension levels.

because these computations are so particular to individual contexts that these calculations would require several hundred pages to describe.

Figure 5.7 provides simple examples of this process. The major and minor triads have three positions, each with increasing tension. The tensions described in the figure caption reasonably fit standard expectations, with the second-inversion triad having the most tension and the first-inversion triad having less tension than the second-inversion but more tension than the root-position triad. Figure 5.8 shows four other familiar triads for tension analysis. These triads show ever-increasing levels of tension, though these results may not exactly agree with some readers' interpretations.

From this point on in this book I will often use the terms *stable* and *unstable* interchangeably with tension levels. *Stable* infers less tension and less need to resolve that tension. *Unstable* infers more tension, suggesting the necessity of resolu-

FIGURE 5.7 Figuring interval weights from the bass note by using the chart in figure 5.6 produces 0.3 (M3 at 0.2 + P5 at 0.1), .5 (m3 at 0.225 + m6 at 0.275), and 0.8 (P4 at 0.55 + M6 at 0.25), respectively. The minor triad and its inversions produce 0.325 (m3 at 0.225 + P5 at 0.1), .45 (M3 at 0.2 + M6 at 0.25), and 0.825 (P4 at 0.55 + m6 at 0.275).

FIGURE 5.8 The augmented triad at 0.475 (M3 at 0.2 + m6 at 0.275), the diminished triad at 0.775 (m3 at 0.225 + A4 at 0.55), the dominant seventh chord at 1.0 (M3 at 0.2 + P5 at 0.1 + m7 at 0.7), and the diminished seventh chord at 1.125 (m3 at 0.225 + A4 at 0.65 + M6 at 0.25).

tion of that tension. Although these terms are vague, they serve a useful purpose when one compares two groupings with different tensions. As we shall see shortly, tension is relative: a chord that may seem unstable in the abstract may in fact be either stable or unstable, depending on its context.

Figure 5.9 shows four less common chord types, with their respective tensions presented in the figure caption. The low tension score of the third chord in this series—sometimes referred to as an added-sixth chord—may indicate why it often occurs in final cadences of popular music, its tension remaining relatively low even with four different chord members present. Interestingly, the strongest interval in this chord—a perfect fifth—suggests C as its root instead of A, the root when it is calculated as a submediant chord in standard tonal harmonic analysis.

Figure 5.10 shows four more chords based on projections of intervals other than thirds. These four chords show how instability can increase in more complex music. The results here—with the calculations presented in the figure caption—indicate the third chord as the most unstable and the first as the most stable. Again, however, I remind readers that later in this chapter we will see how stability and instability are relative, with chords like the first chord in Figure 5.10 becoming unstable in otherwise consonant circumstances and chords like the third chord becoming more stable when surrounded by chords containing several more minor seconds.

FIGURE 5.9 Four chords producing tensions of 1.2 (M3 at 0.2 + P5 at 0.1 + M7 at 0.9), 1.25 (m3 at 0.225 + P5 at 0.1 + m7 at 0.7), 0.55 (M3 at 0.2 + P5 at 0.1 + M6 at 0.25), and 2.0 (M3 at 0.2 + P5 at 0.1 + M7 at 0.9 + M2 at 0.8).

FIGURE 5.10 Chord tensions adding to 1.0 (M2 at 0.8 + M3 at 0.2), 1.225 (m2 at 1.0 + m3 at 0.225), 1.8 (m2 at 1.0 + M2 at 0.8), and 1.475 (P4 at 0.55 + m7 at 0.7 + m3 at 0.225).

Each of the examples shown thus far appears outside of any such context. I argue that context very much influences how we perceive stability. Metric placement and duration represent two of these contextual factors (I will discuss others in the next section). To calculate the metric placement of musical rhythm I employ the simple mathematical formula $p = (b \times 0.1)/m$, where p equals placement value, b refers to beat number, and m represents metric beat. This latter variable accounts for changes in tension from, for example, beat 1 to beat 2 in 4/4 meter, where beat 2 has more tension than beat 1, and so on. Concomitantly, this linear formula also gives beat 3 in 4/4 meter more tension than beat 2, thus contradicting the more commonly considered opposing point of view. Interestingly, my own conception of beat tensions more closely matches the formula's output than tradition suggests. Although this tension formula may seem surprisingly simple, I have experimented with a variety of different tension-calculating processes and always return to the formula presented here. However, no simple mathematics can compute the complex metric relationships of beats in all meters. Therefore, I use lookup tables for this purpose.

Figure 5.11 presents a simple lookup table of metric tensions for principal beats in twelve different meters. I have omitted offbeats in order to present a more readable example, and because offbeats can be computed using the same formula as presented above. This lookup table results from a strict application of the previously described formula. I then adjust these calculations to suit my personal concepts of stability and instability of beats and sub-beats in standard meters. These adjustments rarely exceed 0.05 in either direction and amount to fine-tuning rather than radical change.

	1	2	3	4	5	6	7	8	8	10	11	12
12	.008			.03			.06			.083		
9	.011			.044			.078			x	x	x
8	.0125		.038		.063		.088		x	x	x	x
7(3+2+2)	.014			.06		.09		x	x	x	x	x
7(2+3+2)	.014		.057			.09		x	x	x	x	x
7(2+2+3)	.014		.042		.07			x	x	x	x	x
6	.02			.67			x	x	x	x	x	x
5(3+2)	.02			.08		x	x	x	x	x	x	x
5(3+2)	.02		.06			x	x	x	x	x	x	x
4	.025			.05			.025			.075		
3	.033				.067				.1			
2	.025						.05					

FIGURE 5.11 A simple lookup table of metric tensions for principal beats in twelve different meters.

Notes of extended duration provide agogic weight. For example, a half note beginning on beat 2 of a 4/4 measure extends over the higher-tension third beat of the measure. Although this extension should not include the complete metric weight of this third beat, the half note should receive some kind of added durational tension. In my book *Computer Models of Musical Creativity* (2005) I describe some of the complicated processes required for calculating duration as stability and instability:

> Figuring durational weightings is complicated due to my belief that consonant groupings are made more consonant by extending duration, while dissonant groupings are made more dissonant. To account for this, I use a combination of percentages derived from adding a grouping's duration multiplied by .1 to the same grouping's tension multiplied by .1. Thus, a quarter note major triad, for example, receives an additional durational weight of .025 (1/4 × .1) added to .03 (.3 × .1) or .055, while an eighth note dominant-seventh chord receives a durational weight of .0125 (1/8 × .1) added to .1 (1.0 × .1) or .1125. (Cope 2005, 232–233)

and I will continue using this formula here.

In that book I also compute approach tension figured between the roots of two successive groupings. Because the interval tensions given previously can serve as a guidepost for horizontal root motions, I use them multiplied by 0.1 in calculating approach tensions (my latest variation in a long succession of variations of this particular factor). Thus, a grouping approached by the interval of a fifth from a preceding grouping receives an additional 0.01 weight, while this same grouping approached by a minor second from a preceding grouping receives an additional 0.09 weight. As an example, the tension of a strong dominant-tonic motion in a tonal cadence is little affected by the approach motion, while a weaker root motion of a third—as in a tonic-to-mediant progression—has more tension and achieves a greater additional weight as a result.

Figure 5.12a provides an example of tension computation based on combinations of interval content, metric placement, duration, and motion of approach to the root in tonal music. Some of the tensions shown in this example from Bach might appear counterintuitive. For example, the lowest-tension chord—the second chord of the passage—represents a subdominant rather than a tonic function. However, in terms of computation, based on the four previously mentioned factors, these tensions make sense. The first, fourth, and last chords, for example, though exactly the same in pitch, register, voicing, and duration, do not have exactly the same tensions because the chords occur on different metric beats and thus play different roles in the music. As well, the most dissonant—and hence unstable—chord of the phrase has the highest tension (the second-to-last chord).

Figure 5.12b presents the same type of analysis as Figure 5.12a but for a posttonal passage by Schoenberg. This music obviously has a greater range of tensions than does the Bach of Figure 5.12a. The Schoenberg also appears to have a roughly sinusoidal shape, peaking first at 9.47 and then again at 16.34. The tensions here are compounded by my figuring all pitches present rather than ignoring the decaying pitches of previously struck chords. I have also freely grouped the second half of m. 4 to avoid using each new entrance as a new grouping. Obviously, when groupings such as these have high tension levels, tensions based on metric placement, duration, and approach to the root play significantly smaller roles than in tonal music.

Thus, four factors contribute to the tension of a given grouping: interval content, metric placement, duration, and root-to-root approach interval. Of these contributors, only one involves context between groups—root-to-root approach interval. I mention this here because context will play an increasingly important role in interpreting tension and thus stability and instability when determining function as we proceed. This tension-calculating process, dependent as it is on intervals, meter, and duration, does not fully account for all of the factors involved with tension.

CONTEXT AND SPEAC

No two musical pitches or groups of pitches in a musical composition are equivalent, even if they appear to be so. This statement represents a simple truth, for no two objects can occupy the same time and space, and thus they vary from one another in at least these two aspects. Musical context varies pitches or groups of

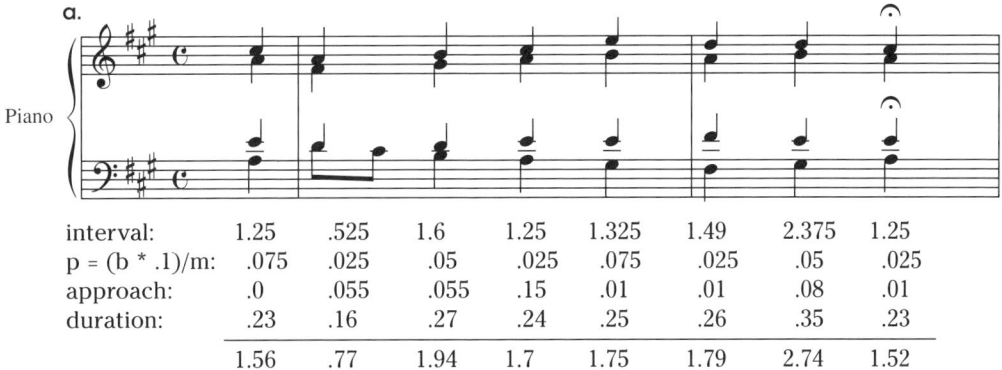

FIGURE 5.12 (a) J. S. Bach, Chorale no. 42, demonstrating the same chord in differing contexts; (b) Schoenberg, *Sechs kleine Klavierstücke* op. 19, no. 6, opening measures, demonstrating the same types of contextual differences.

pitches yet further. The notion of apparent equalities being unequal owing to discrepancies of time and space is an extremely important real as well as conceptual one.

In order to fully understand how the same music may have different functions, we need to look beyond roots and tensions of groupings toward a kind of musical semantics. This musical semantics can inform analysts about music's expectation and fulfillment or deception, predictability and unpredictability. In short, the fundamental motion of music—all music—results from its context. Furthermore, analyzing musical context reveals important relationships about music regardless of the style or type of music involved.

Language can provide a good analogy. In language, for example, we assume that context reveals a great deal about the meanings of words and phrases. The following sentence presents an instance of how words that are spelled and pronounced the same can have quite different functions and meanings, even when placed in close proximity to one another:

> I light the light with a light touch.

The word *light* appears three times in this sentence, with each appearance having a different meaning and making a different syntactic contribution. Only the context distinguishes each word's true function and meaning. We adjust to such subtle shifts in meaning by using contextual references, giving language another powerful way in which to express ideas.

"Verbing" represents another example of this kind of language context. Verbing involves treating a noun or other non-verb as a verb. In context, this typically makes immediate sense to anyone familiar with the language being spoken. Examples include "I was carded at the door" and "I will text him your answer." In both cases here, the word *verbed*—interestingly, itself an example of verbing—is a noun relying on syntax and context for understanding. Languages develop in this way, by providing a rich source of new words coupled with a true sense of context.

The same is true of music. In tonal music, leading tones represent one way in which context differentiates between apparently identical functional motions in music. The leading-tone pitch in C major, B, for example, strongly leans toward the tonic pitch when appearing alone or when found in dominant, dominant seventh, and leading-tone harmonies. However, when this pitch appears as the fifth of the mediant triad, it does not particularly lean toward the tonic pitch. In fact, the leading-tone pitch in the mediant chord often moves more naturally elsewhere—to the submediant pitch, for example. Thus, the same leading-tone pitch can be analyzed differently depending on its context.

Schoenberg took into account this notion of context overriding predisposed function when he stated that "every tone that is added to a beginning tone makes the meaning of that tone doubtful":

> If, for instance, G follows after C, the ear may not be sure whether this expresses C major or G major, or even F major or E minor; and the addition of other tones may or may not clarify this problem. In this manner there is produced a state of unrest, of imbalance which grows throughout most of the piece, and is enforced further by similar functions of the rhythm. The method by which balance is restored seems to me the real *idea* of the composition. (Schoenberg 1983, 123; italics in original)

As we have seen, the music in Figure 5.12 provides two examples of contextual differentiation in music. In Figure 5.12a, the chords that sound on the upbeat to full measure 1, the third beat of full measure 1, and the third beat of full measure 2 consist of exactly the same pitches. However, the upbeat chord to full measure 1 introduces the melody and key of the chorale. The third beat of full measure 1 substantiates that key as well as acting as the harmonic grounding for the leap that appears subsequently in the melody. The third-beat chord of full measure 2, on the other hand, verifies the key and acts as a cadential tonic function. These three chords, then, although they contain precisely the same pitches, play very different roles and, one could posit, have very different functions. I would argue that the same thing occurs in the post-tonal passage in Figure 5.12b, from op. 19, no. 6, by Schoenberg, where the three-pitch chord in the right hand repeats twice, as does a three-pitch chord in the left hand, though what the different functions are is not as clear in Figure 5.12b as it is in Figure 5.12a.

One might argue that traditional analyses indicates different functions for identical chords as well, particularly when such chords appear in different keys. For example, a C–E–G tonic chord in C major in one location in a work does not have the same function as a C–E–G subdominant chord in G major elsewhere in the same work. One could further argue that pivot chords in modulation provide even more complicated double meanings. However, these tonal examples clearly represent special cases. To offer the kind of differentiations referred to in the previous paragraphs requires that an analysis process delineate differences between C–E–G chords in exactly the same register *within* the same key. Therefore, the previously discussed processes might actually designate a C–E–G chord in C major in one location in a work and a C–E–G in G major elsewhere in the same work as equivalent in function. In each of these last two cases, the context determines the analysis, not the opposite.

For many years I have usefully employed a contextual analysis process called SPEAC (pronounced "speak"). SPEAC stands for S (*statement*) for stable, P (*preparation*) for weakly unstable, E (*extension*) for fairly stable, A (*antecedent*) for very unstable, and C (*consequent*) for strongly stable. SPEAC identifiers thus follow the order of stability of A–P–E–S–C, with the most unstable identifier on the left and the most stable identifier on the right. Basing analysis on a combination of root, musical tension, and context most clearly parallels my musical sensibilities and represents the core of the analysis component of my algorithmic composing programs (see Cope 1991 and 1996). SPEAC antecedents have more tension than statements, preparations, or extensions. Likewise, statements have more tension than either preparations or extensions. Following the work of Heinrich Schenker (1979), SPEAC provides useful insights into musical function, especially in the analysis of post-tonal music.

SPEAC analysis first requires segmenting music into groupings defined either by some arbitrary length or by each note onset and then calculating vertical tension separately for each grouping following the processes described earlier in this chapter. To determine a grouping's tension involves slicing the grouping vertically, according the slice with the least tension the overall tension of the grouping, because the program assumes that the higher-tension slices contain nonharmonic tones that resolve. In Figure 5.12a, for example, beat 1 of full measure 1 divides into two vertical slices (onbeat and offbeat); the onbeat slice is used for SPEAC analysis because it contains the least tension.

To assign SPEAC identifiers generally requires the setting of the highest tensions of a series of groupings to antecedents (A) and the lowest tensions to consequents (C), with statements (S) closest to consequents (C), preparations (P) closest to antecedents (A), and extensions (E) falling equidistant between Cs and As. Other factors must also play a role. For example, the first-heard chord or grouping will most likely receive a P or an S, depending on its tension level. These assignments result from a lack of context within which to judge the music.

As a result of these processes, no two groupings labeled A in SPEAC have precisely the same amount of "A-ness." Therefore, not only can SPEAC differentiate between two identical groupings, but it can also further differentiate between two groupings, both of which have the same SPEAC analysis. Suffixed subscripts allow SPEAC to represent such differentiations. Thus, a C_1 and a C_2 both represent consequences, but they have different degrees of consequence. The hierarchy of these subscripts flows from high value to low value in inverse proportion to the size of the number. Therefore, a C_1 has more C-ness than a C_2. For example, in the passage P_1 S_1 A_2 C_2 A_1 C_1 the final C_1 has deeper consequence than the earlier occurring C_2.

Figure 5.13 presents the same examples as does Figure 5.12. In Figure 5.13, however, the numerical tensions have been translated into SPEAC functional descriptors. In Figure 5.13a we see the duplicate chords that sound on the upbeat to full measure 1, the third beat of full measure 1, and the third beat of full measure 2 with different representations—P_1, C_2, and C_1. Bach's phrase, when viewed in terms of its most unstable and most stable elements provides, an S_1, A_1, C_1—or statement, anticipation, consequent—logic. Interestingly, the Schoenberg passage in Figure 5.13b has precisely the same functional progression.

SPEAC assignments are not definitive. Analysts have the right (even the obligation) to assign SPEAC symbols as appropriate to their personal interpretations. As an example, consider the extension (E_2) that I have assigned to beat 1 of m. 3 in Figure 5.13a. Following the anticipation of the final chord of the previous measure and the fact that this extension is a variant of the chord that appears on beat 1 of m. 2, it might more likely represent an S or C. Situations such as this require that the balance between root and tension, even between the various contributors to tension itself, contribute their weightings in different proportions to one another, as I mentioned earlier in this chapter. This strategy allows one to interpret numerical scores more liberally, a fact that may give some readers pause. However, more than likely, such personal interpretations should be viewed as refinements to the approach to function described here, rather than aberrations of it. Because computers do not as of yet have personal views of anything, programming these interpretations is possible only by using artificial intelligence techniques, many of which I discuss in Chapter 7 (association networks, fuzzy logic, etc.).

Obviously, many other factors play roles in the tensions we hear in music. Chromaticism, timbre, dynamics, register, and so on can affect and even override the

FIGURE 5.13 SPEAC analysis of the music in Figure 5.12a and b.

tension that SPEAC generates through its various pitch analyses. However, such factors are often mitigated by the small degree of effect that they impose on tension. Therefore, the approach described above provides enough substantive information to be useful in defining function.

FUNCTION

Allen Forte frequently writes about function in tonal music as well as post-tonal music, taking note of how analysts have difficulty applying systematic approaches:

> When the trained analyst examines a musical score, he associates certain signs with others to form units and makes a series of basic decisions about the temporal spans of such units and their internal structuring. In a metaphorical sense he places a template over the score to frame patterns and to show how they are interwoven to form local contexts. Although the decisions the analyst makes may rest upon years of practical experience, they are often unsystematic and are subject to many influences that are not easily identified. (Forte 1993, 56)

In contrast to what Forte describes here, the approach described below follows a more systematic application of the basic principles discussed thus far in this chapter. The functional notation I use, resulting as it does from a triangulation of root, tension, and context, appears as a combination of scale degree (defined by root), tension, and context:

0^{S_1}

Here 0 represents the scale degree of the root of the grouping being analyzed and the notation ^{S_1} indicates a first-level Statement, the combination of root, tension, and context. Any root notation can have any SPEAC tension and context identification. For those familiar with more static notation, such as I, IV, V, and so on in tonal music, the dynamic representation of post-tonal function can be initially confusing. The root-SPEAC identifications pose interesting resonances and contradictions, because 0—what one might presume as a kind of tonic—can appear as 0^S, 0^P, 0^E, 0^A, or 0^C, giving it a full range of stable and unstable characterizations.

If one further identifies each member of the movable-*do* 0–e notation as belonging to either T, D, or S (tonic, dominant, or subdominant) functions, as envisioned by Hugo Riemann (Harrison 1994; see Chapter 1 of this book for more information), the problems of comparing scale-degree-SPEAC function with tonal functions are yet further exacerbated. The following list provides possible T, D, and S equivalents:

0 = T
1 = D
2 = D
3 = T
4 = T
5 = S
6 = S
7 = D
8 = S
9 = S
t = D
e = D

In SPEAC terms, it would seem natural that T(onic) would resemble S and C, that D(ominant) would resemble A and possibly P, and that S(ubdominant) would resemble P and possibly E. Thus, potential contradictions increase significantly. Such contradictions, however, can provide fascinating analytical information. A work ending on, say, a 0^{A_1} would suggest that either one or more aspects of the analysis system I propose here are incorrect, or that the music under analysis terminates with something significantly not representing resolution or stability. Thus, even though I do not typically evoke the TDS approach in tandem with roots and SPEAC, I find more than occasional interest in following their connections (and lack thereof).

In summation, function in post-tonal music as I define it involves the analysis of scale, roots, tension, and context to derive a simple but inclusive representation such as 0^{C_1}. When SPEAC and root-scale assignments agree, the results support, but do not necessarily confirm, a strong functional definition. When SPEAC and root-scale assignments disagree, one of two possibilities exists: the music's function is confused, or the interpretation is wrong or misguided. In cases where the latter interpretation is suspected, I find that the earlier reference to personal interpretation can often resolve the problem. Of course, such solutions can prompt the question of whether one is simply massaging the solution to fit the problem. In general, however, tweaking tensions or SPEAC interpretation based on aurally perceived contradictions resembles, for example, how one determines modulation versus secondary regions in tonal music.

Fred Lerdahl describes a similar—but nonetheless fundamentally different—approach to post-tonal functional analysis (Lerdahl 2001; see particularly 347 ff.). Lerdahl's theory involves five classifications: RS (referential sonority—a kind of tonic replacement), Dep (departure—forward-branching), Ret (return—backward-branching), N (neighboring—subordinate within a strong progression), and P (passing—subordinate particularly to Dep or Ret). Lerdahl analyzes (in 2001, 353–368) Schoenberg's Three Piano Pieces, op. 11, no. 1 according to these principles and includes a hierarchical prolongational analysis as well. Lerdahl points out that

> without an ordered space and with the concomitant perceptual dependency on salience for organizing prolongational structure, there is a relatively weak correlation in most atonal music between elaboration and tension. Hence, it is preferable to refer not to atonal prolongational tension and relaxation but just to atonal departure and return. (Lerdahl 2001, 348)

Thus, Lerdahl distances his analytical approach to post-tonal functional music analysis from tonal functional music analysis. RSDepRetNP, then, like SPEAC, relies on contextual rather than static definitions. Nonetheless, music thus analyzed generates rich hierarchical functions that gather strength as they ascend toward the higher and more abstract structural levels.

FORM AND STRUCTURE

Musical form and structure represent very different aspects of music, though invoking these names often produces similar interpretations. For this book, *musical form* refers to aspects of the musical surface that state, contrast, and develop themes and motives. For example, terms such as *A* and *B*—representing contrasting areas of material—often catalog the formal aspects of a musical work. *Musical structure*, on the other hand, refers to the process of hierarchical differentiation of more significant elements from less significant elements. (I should note here that the word *structure* in this book's title refers to the generic notion of structure as order, not the notion of structure as hierarchy. Unfortunately, *Hidden Order* is the title of a well-known book by John Holland, one that I reference several times here, and thus was not available.)

Computationally discovering formal thematic areas, as well as their similarities and differences, requires pattern matching to indicate when themes return, vary, or contrast:

> One of the purposes of analyzing musical structure and form is to discover the patterns that are explicit or implicit in musical works. Pattern in music is generally described in ordinary language, supplemented by technical musical terms: for example, "the movement is in sonata form," "the opening section is in the key of C major[,] it is followed by a section in the dominant, then a return to the original key[,]" "the chord is a G seventh[,]" "the slow movement is written in 3/4 time." No complete formalism has existed for describing a musical pattern precisely, its exact nature can be communicated only by writing out the music *in extenso*—the actual notes in musical notation. Although some abbreviation is achieved by such notation as figured bass, all established notations set forth the notes essentially in the order of their temporal occurrence. (Simon and Sumner 1993)

The use of the word *pattern* in this passage reveals its importance when one is dealing with both form and structure in music. As we shall see, my analysis programs use pattern recognition to discover both form and structure in post-tonal music.

As opposed to signatures, which require the matching of patterns in at least two separate works for the identification of style (Cope 1991, 1996, 2000, and 2001), some patterns have local importance and relate to harmonic, thematic, and rhythmic elements of a theme or other distinctive musical idea. Discovering such patterns can be quite important for revealing musical form. I have named these patterns *unifications* (see Cope 2000, 171–74, for more information). Unifications are patterns found most frequently in a single section of a work that unify the section and distinguish it from other sections. Unifications maintain unity in music at the foreground, or formal, level.

I use three basic techniques to discover unifications in music. First, and most obviously, patterns are collected only from the music of a phrase or section of music. Second, my programs match patterns using intervals, not pitches. Lastly, my programs look for patterns that conform to certain prescribed limits *within* individual phrases rather than *between* phrases. In effect, only patterns integral to the basic continuity of the music appear.

My analysis programs also ascertain the number, location, and variance types of unifications. For example, knowing that a certain pattern is repeated during a passage is of little use if one does not also know whether this pattern repeats a few or many times, repeats only in certain circumstances, repeats only after predictable delays, repeats only with certain variations such as sequence, and so on. Unlike other types of patterns, unifications may be quite numerous and, rather than spreading their use over entire compositions, appear in close quarters, even in combination and contiguously.

In order to discover unifications, music must obviously be separated into phrases. The processes used to computationally accomplish this are complex and often redundant—to ensure that supposed phrases are phrases in fact. Rather than repeat the descriptions of the processes I use for detecting phrases in music here, particularly because these processes require significant space to describe, I refer readers to Cope 1996, 2000, and 2001, in particular. Once phrases are detected and separated out from their original work, unifications can be revealed computationally in several ways. The method described below provides the best way that I have found to accomplish this analysis.

Figure 5.14 presents an example of a unification (Figure 5.14a) as derived from Schoenberg's Three Piano Pieces, op. 11, no. 1 (Figure 5.14b). As seen here, the

FIGURE 5.14 An example of a unification as derived from Schoenberg, Three Piano Pieces op. 11, no. 1: (a) the unification, and (b) the first 8 measures of the work from which the unification was drawn. Note the other unifications present here as well.

chosen unification appears three times in various guises—the same pitches, but different metric placement. Pattern matchers have little problem with discovering unifications such as this. In fact, pattern matchers can typically discover unifications without much difficulty once phrases are delineated clearly. Thus, unifications reveal material and this material's variations for different sections in a work, and they help reveal that work's form.

In order to match patterns that resemble but do not duplicate one another, I use controllers, variables set to numbers representing thresholds defined by their names. For example, an *intervals-off* controller contains the number of allowable incorrect intervals before the pattern matcher considers two patterns unequal. Figure 5.15 presents an example of how this controller works with two patterns presented, a target pattern (a) and a potential matching pattern (b). If the *intervals-off* controller is set to 2, the two patterns will not match. However, if the *intervals-off* controller is set to 3, the two patterns will match. Many controllers can exist simultaneously in such situations, controllers such as *interval-amount-off*, a controller that defines how much an interval can differ in order not to cause even one incorrect interval to produce a failed match.

A good music pattern matcher typically contains as many as a dozen or more such controllers in order to allow, say, tonal variations to pass easily, rejecting variations that do not conform to typical tonal alterations. Given enough time and experimentation, most works, even very complex contrapuntal works, will reveal their formal designations in this way. In particularly problematic circumstances, I use several small programs (outlined in Cope 2000, chapter 5) in concert with those described here.

Obviously, discovering form represents a greater problem with some works than I have described here. The processes for discovering such forms, however, remain the same. The difficulties must be overcome by rephrasing the work under analysis, varying controller levels, or some combination of these two processes.

One of the ways to help discover structure in music, as opposed to form, involves *meta-patterns*, patterns whose members occur noncontiguously (see Cope

FIGURE 5.15 Two patterns, a target pattern and a potential matching pattern. If the *intervals-off* controller were set to 2, the two patterns would not match. However, if the *intervals-off* controller were set to 3, the two patterns would match.

1996). Meta-patterns are discovered by hierarchical pattern-matching processes that utilize unique pattern matchers. This hierarchical pattern matcher reduces the actual number of matchings necessary by first evaluating foreground material in terms of importance and using only those pitches and intervals that surpass certain thresholds.

The discussion of pattern matching in Chapter 2 of this book provides general insights into the usefulness of pattern matching for music analysis. However, for more intricate pattern-matching processes—such as those required of formal analysis and the discovery of meta-patterns—using object-oriented programming and controllers greatly refines the process. In the first section of this chapter, we learned how to store data in objects, name them according to how best to locate them, and, whenever needed, access them by referencing their names rather than storing them in long lists and then searching for them. This process works as well with locating a particular stored pattern as it does for groupings. By locating certain patterns and then storing them in well-named objects, they become available in exactly the same way.

The pattern-matching process that produces meta-patterns resembles what Experiments in Musical Intelligence uses to find patterns with interpolated pitches. Figure 3.7 of *Experiments in Musical Intelligence* (Cope 1996, 89) shows how Chopin buries repetitions of his themes in extremely ornamented variations. In such cases, two highly varied patterns can match owing to a high setting of the controller designated to allow interpolated notes. Although effective for matching patterns in music by composers who, like Chopin, use such ornamental techniques for variation, a high setting of the interpolation variable can also allow all manner of unwanted patterns—noise—to enter into the analysis of music of composers who do not use such techniques. Hierarchical analysis, on the other hand, does not depend on the approach composers use to vary their music, but rather pattern matches music and derives its inherent meta-pattern.

Unlike formal analysis, structural analysis does not rely on material repetition, variation, and/or contrast. Structural analysis attempts to reveal the architecture of the music, the harmonic and melodic superstructure. The hierarchical processes I use resemble those used in Schenkerian or layer analysis (Schenker 1979). Typically, however, Schenkerian analysis follows middleground patterns of descending scale degrees. My programs make no such assumptions about the music they analyze, but simply assign various tensions to pitch groupings and then apply filter thresholds. Such filter thresholds typically produce results that, on the one hand, have more pitches than those usually provided by Schenker-type middlegrounds, but on the other hand, fewer notes than the foreground or surface of the pattern being analyzed.

Figure 5.16 provides an example of this process. Figure 5.16a shows a simple phrase of music composed by Mozart (the theme of the first movement of the Piano Sonata in C Major, K. 545). Figure 5.16c presents the meta-pattern revealed by a hierarchical pattern matcher. This meta-pattern surfaces from the matching process by virtue of its agogic tensions, placement in the metrical structure, and relevance to the key or scale in use (not unlike the processes described earlier in this chapter for defining function). The various patterns in the music in Figure 5.16a have lines connecting them to their correlates in newly composed music (Figure 5.16b). The meta-pattern in Figure 5.16c then demonstrates how, through the composition process, the fragments reorganize while concomitantly retaining much of their original coherence. The meta-pattern serves as a guide for a simple composing program. Although only half the pitches fall in the same place in their respective measures in Figure 5.16b, the variation of the original succeeds because the meta-pattern occurs so prominently in both phrases. This obviously simplistic example nonetheless demonstrates the basic principles of deriving and successfully modeling meta-patterns.

Software filters can help to reveal structure in music by discarding pitches during analysis that for one reason or another do not survive certain tests—tension, duration, and so on. These tests in many ways resemble structural analysis in tonal music, where certain pitches do not survive middleground analysis (see Cope 1991). In structural analyses of tonal music, these tests include scale degree importance, implied or explicit function, register, phrase placement, and so on. The notion of filtering out less important pitches in order to highlight more important ones is the basic principle of structural analysis. Such filtering of post-tonal music can, I believe, produce equally rewarding structural maps. For example, filtering could easily include tests of varying degrees of severity such that a wide range of Schenker-like foregrounds, middlegrounds, and backgrounds could emerge.

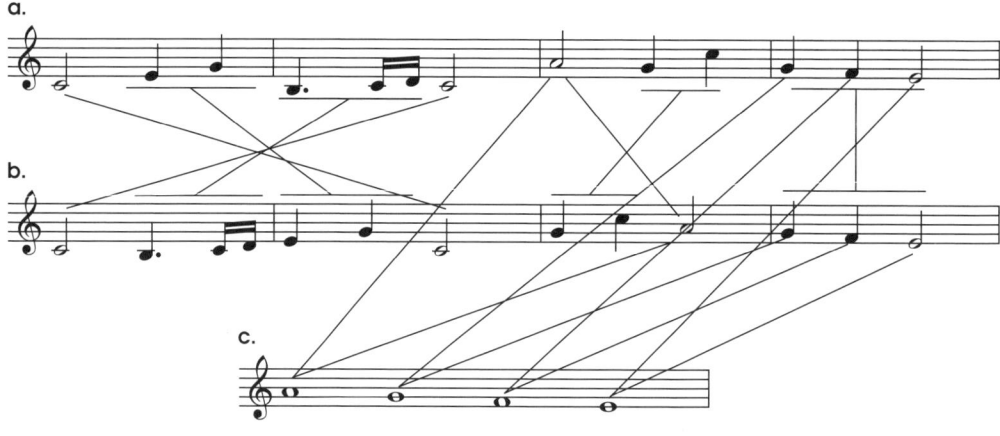

FIGURE 5.16 A phrase of music by Mozart (a); a machine-composed replication (b); and the meta-pattern that binds them together (c).

Applying five simple but useful filtering elements—duration, dynamic, register, metric placement, and scale membership—can provide useful and possibly meaningful gradient maps of post-tonal music, as presented in Figure 5.17. Figure 5.17a represents unanalyzed music and Figure 5.17d a background as realized by the filters imposed. The intervening maps show increasing note removal produced by filters imposing ever-harsher restrictions on the music of the previous maps. The structural mapping software available on the CD-ROM accompanying this book produced this map and requires only the use of the scale software from Chapter 3 in order to analyze music in the manner described here. The function call and note-event output that produced the musical notation in this figure appear at the bottom of the example.

SPEAC analysis at the structural level informs analysts that repeated material need not necessarily serve the same function as the material it repeats. For example, material initiating a work will most likely provide a statement (S). However, this same material recognizably returning at a later point in this same music may be an extension (E), preparation (P), anticipation (A), or even consequence (C), depending on its role in the structure. A SPEAC analysis at a structural level represents music that contains many smaller SPEAC functions.

Averaging lower SPEAC functions to derive an overall tension and then using this more inclusive formal SPEAC identity in competition with the required syntax of its own level produces the most effective analysis. Thus, a structural level (S) may actually represent music that at a lower level has a predominantly (A) identity. Although this may seem contradictory, various hierarchical levels in music can serve very different purposes, just as in language (see Cope 2000).

Many other approaches to form and structure have been attempted, often without the aid of computers. For example, Joseph Straus comments that Schoenberg's op. 33a reveals a form (and structure of a type) defined by the transpositions of its primary pitch-class set:

> The large-scale progression of the piece, then, is A_0–A_2–A_7–A_0. Obviously Schoenberg has in mind some kind of analogy to the tonal motion I–II–V–I. But there is more than an analogy at work here. Look again at the first three notes of the series—they form set class 3-9 (0,2,7). The set of areas A_0–A_2–A_7 thus reflects the initial set of pitch classes. The large-scale progression of the piece composes out its initial melodic idea. (2005, 259)

Straus's approach very much resembles a meta-pattern as described in this chapter.

Although my own discussions of form and structural analysis here barely scratch the surface of what can and will be accomplished with the aid of computers, the processes I have described represent strategies that have proven quite useful in my computer-composing programs such as Experiments in Musical Intelligence (see Cope 1996 and 2001, in particular) and Alice (see Cope 2000 and accompanying software). Therefore, although I am not claiming any degree of thoroughness for these techniques, I do believe that pattern matching in the ways

FIGURE 5.17 Various levels (gradient map) of music revealed by applying filters.

described here will prove valuable as prototypes for more complex and encompassing programs to come.

MUSICAL EXAMPLES

The structural graph (a result of using the Structure Map program described in more detail in the next section of this chapter) partially shown in Figure 5.18 of the opening of the third movement of Stravinsky's Three Pieces for String Quartet (1914) presents a dense and complicated set of connections that produces equally complicated connections between one node (pitch) and all other nodes (pitches). The information of the initial lowest pitch of this piece is displayed in a separate window, the result of clicking on the relevant node. The scroll bar to the right in this rectangle suggests that there is a great deal more information about the relationships between this node and all other nodes in this passage. Even with the small amount of information shown, this window within the graph presents nineteen separate tensions for closely associated pitches, with event-2 having the most tension (0.6) in relation to the initial low pitch. Looking back at the music of this passage, shown in Figure 1.19 we see that this low D-natural has the most tension relative to the following D-flat.

Interestingly, the opening passage of the third movement of Stravinsky's Three Pieces for String Quartet offers as much tension with its often chromatic voice-leading as that created by vertical groupings. This voice-leading tension creates a very difficult problem for harmonic analysis. However, applying the [0,2,3,4,5,7,8,9,t,e] C-based scale first described in Chapter 4 of this book produces

```
   1ø              6ø
0    2  3  4  5      7  8  9  t  e
```

which itself presents a very interesting root analysis, as shown in Figure 5.19. Note here that all of the roots occur within the principal scale, that pitch class 1 occurs often in the bass voice of the violoncello part, and that the single pitch class 6 occurs in m. 4 of the viola part.

A simple SPEAC analysis of this same opening passage from the third movement of Stravinsky's Three Pieces for String Quartet, shown in Figure 5.20, contains no statements or extensions, with a predominance of anticipations and consequences and with an occasional preparation, especially near the beginning of the passage. The tensions provided above each column confirm the analysis with tensions ranging from 1.4 to 3.3.

PROGRAM DESCRIPTION

The Root program on the CD-ROM that accompanies this book returns the root of any grouping of pitches provided as an argument. This simple five-function program

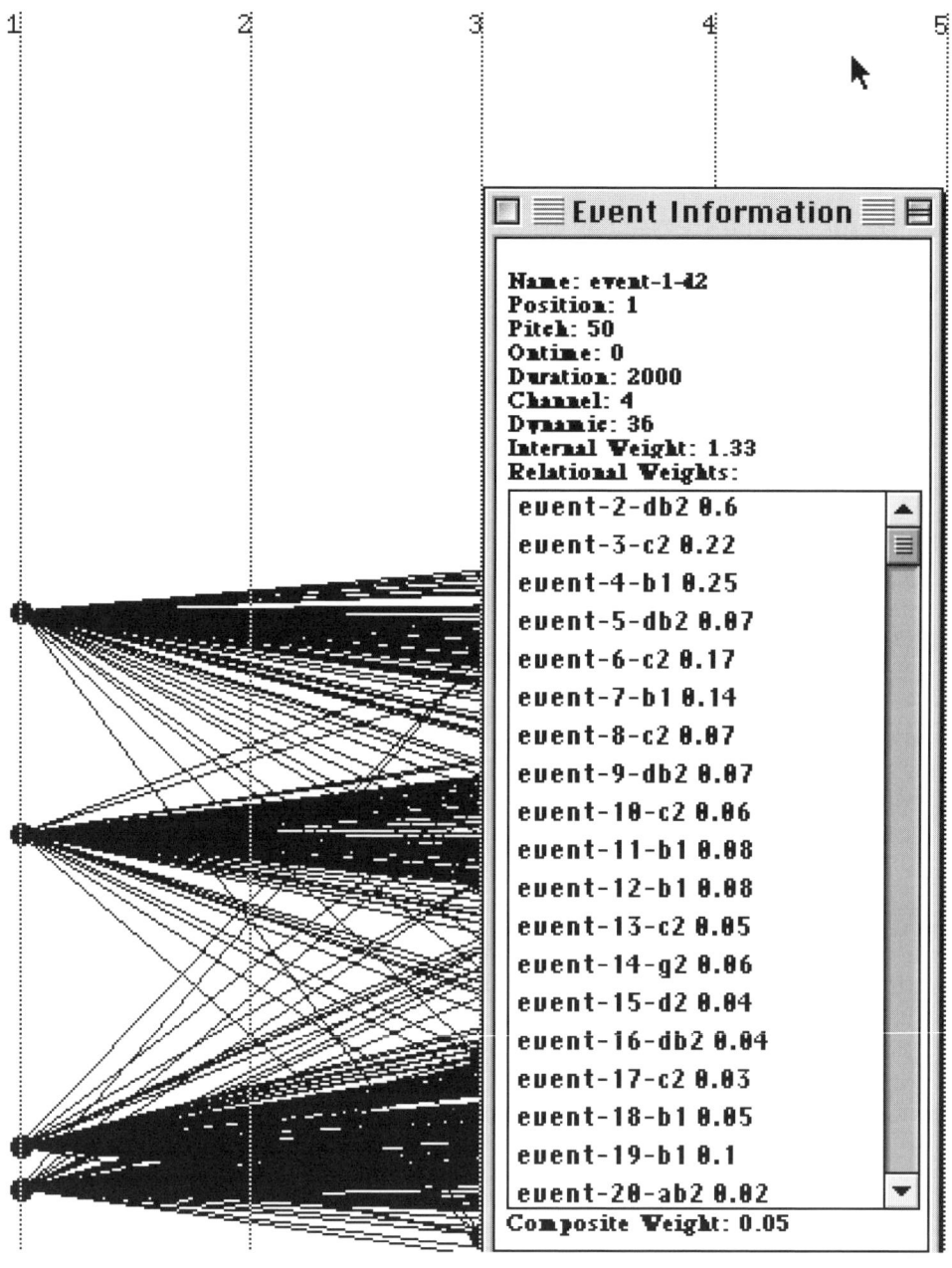

FIGURE 5.18 The opening few beats of a graphical analysis of Stravinsky, Three Pieces for String Quartet (1914), 3rd movement.

FIGURE 5.19 A root analysis of Stravinsky, Three Pieces for String Quartet (1914), 3rd movement.

first reduces pitches to intervals and then calculates their individual stengths based on a series of strengths found in the variable called `*interval-strengths*`. The Root program can be used with any software that requires roots for function determination.

The Structure Map program returns selected note-events that the program has determined represent the music analyzed on ever-higher structural levels. Users can determine for themselves how many levels they wish to view. Structure Map requires a separate program from Chapter 4 that returns the scale in use to help the

228 HIDDEN STRUCTURE

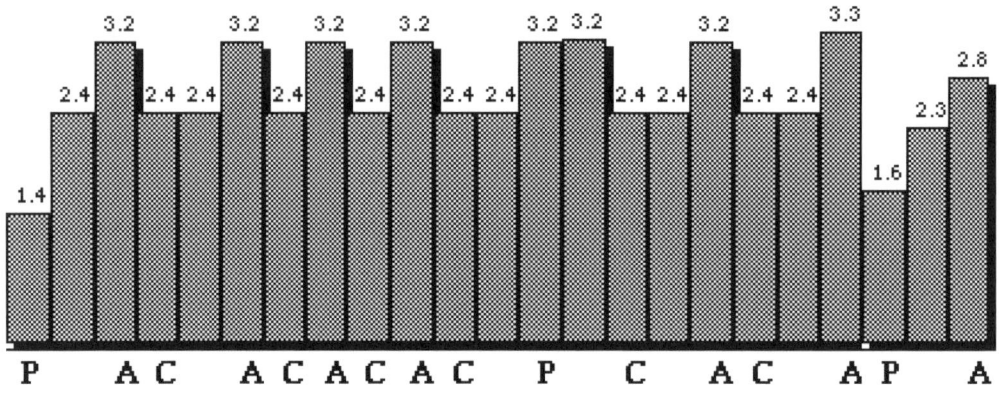

FIGURE 5.20 SPEAC analysis (by chord change) of Stravinsky, Three Pieces for String Quartet (1914), 3rd movement.

structural functions determine the various levels. Structure Graph creates structural graphs of segments of music, each node of which, when clicked, produces a window containing important information about the note which it represents. As an example, Figure 5.21 shows a structural graph of a section from the author's *Triplum* for flute and piano. All the pitches in this passage appear in this graph, with the circled notes representing pitches that the program has found structurally important. Although standard functional code produced the structural information here, the graphic output results are almost entirely from OOP.

The three pitches circled in the graph in Figure 5.21 result from precise cumulative tensions that, again, appears when one clicks upon the circled pitch. These circled pitches do not represent a tonal center, but rather the strength of the pitch based on the various parameters in the internal tension less the multiple of the constant of the average of the relational tensions, as discussed earlier in this chapter. Combined with the other parameters influencing the tension of pitches, these high-tension pitches arguably represent important structural pivots in the post-tonal music being analyzed. Computing the tensions of all of the pitches in even a simple one-line phrase poses such extraordinary obstacles that I would not attempt it—nor, perhaps, even have conceived of the process—without access to computer software such as Structure Map.

CONCLUSIONS

The functional and structural programs presented in this chapter, along with the basics of object-oriented programming, provide a frame for the chapter that follows—

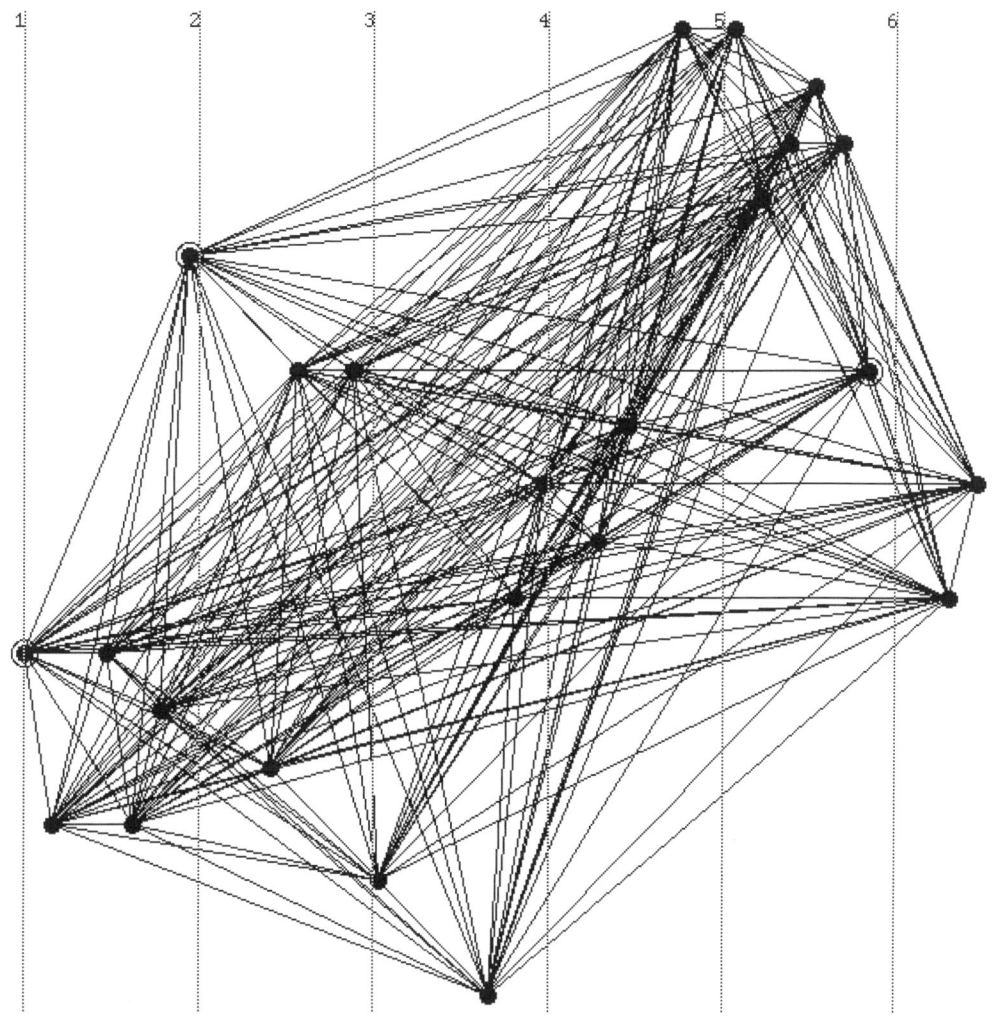

FIGURE 5.21 A structural graph of a section from the author's *Triplum* for flute and piano.

a chapter concerned with, first, building models of short segments of music as continuations of existing works, and, second, creating complete musical works in the style of music under analysis. Although the software described in the current chapter does not directly contribute to either of the modeling processes described in Chapter 6, this software serves an important role in comparing the simulations of Chapter 6 to the originals and thus helping to verify the success or failure of the modeling processes.

SIX
Generative Models of Music

> A computer is an ideal instrument by means of which analytical ideas can be tested, since the investigator starts with certain hypotheses from which he formulates operating principles; he supplies this information to the computer; the computer then generates music based upon these principles; and the investigator then analyzes the results to further his investigation. This, of course, is essentially nothing more than a standard example of experimental scientific method, but the unusual thing is that computers provide a practical experimental technique for carrying out such research in the musical field.
>
> Lejaren Hiller and Leonard Isaacson, *Experimental Music* (1959), 166

Music theories and even resultant analyses can appear logical and effective, but unless they can produce output similar to the music under analysis, they lack a certain validity. In this chapter, I will describe several methods for using probabilities—implicit and explicit—to analyze music and then, using that analysis, create complete compositions roughly equivalent—at least stylistically—to the analyzed music. I will also describe a program that can compose missing portions of the input music exactly. This process of regenerating music from its analysis—similar to the concepts of algorithmic information theory presented in Chapter 2 of this book—may indicate, at least to a degree, more than just the success or failure of a theory; it also may indicate many of the subconscious techniques that composers actually use in creating their music. Most of this chapter therefore deals with Principle 4 as discussed in Chapter 1 of this book.

MODELING

Throughout the common-practice period in Europe, young composers often learned their craft by modeling recognized works. Established masters typically assigned their apprentices the creation of new music following the classics of the past. Even when composers did not explicitly study their craft, their personal styles often revealed the music they used for models. For example, it would be hard to imagine a J. S. Bach without an Antonio Vivaldi, a Wolfgang Mozart without a Joseph Haydn, a

Ludwig van Beethoven without a Wolfgang Mozart, and so on. It seems no less logical to use these same modeling techniques as an approach to music analysis.

Modeling offers analysts the ability to view music during its composition and thus the opportunity to test a work in progress as well as when complete. Steven Wolfram (2002) and many others have postulated that such modeling, rather than reverse engineering, represents the better way to accurately understand how things work. Wolfram uses dynamic two-dimensional cellular automata to produce visual models to prove that extremely complex output can result from extremely simple rules (see Cope 2005, 68, figure 3.6 for examples). Wolfram comments that

> much of the emphasis over the past century or so has been on breaking systems down to find their underlying parts, then trying to analyze these parts in as much detail as possible . . . but just how these components act together to produce even some of the most obvious features of the overall behavior we see has in the past remained an almost complete mystery. (Wolfram 2002, 3)

and

> it has seemed that whenever one tries to get to another level of accuracy, one encounters more complex phenomena. And at least with traditional scientific intuition, this fact suggests that models of progressively greater complexity will be needed . . . could it even be that underneath all the complex phenomena we see in physics there lies some simple program which, if run for long enough, would reproduce our universe in every detail? (Wolfram 2002, 465)

Like a salmon swimming upstream against a current too strong for it, Wolfram suggests, we are currently waging a losing battle in attempting to understand the universe by taking it apart and analyzing its individual components. Science, according to Wolfram, should rather create computer models of the universe, choose the one that achieves the closest resemblance to reality, and study the principles of our modeling processes. I believe the same to be true of understanding music.

John Holland comments that "although model building is not usually considered critical in the construction of scientific theory, I would claim that it is" (Holland 1998, 4). Although Holland refers here primarily to the sciences, I believe that his words have as much use for music analysts. He adds that

> in the beginning were rule-bound sacrifices to the gods—we modeled the world in terms of personalities and ways of propitiating those personalities. Later, we discovered mechanisms (gates, pumps, and wheels) and ways of using them to control parts of the world, and we began to model the world with mechanisms instead of personalities. Eventually, we arrived at complex computer-controlled devices and models, and scientific models that employ abstract mechanisms. (Holland 1998, 10)

The Melody Predictor software found on the CD-ROM accompanying Cope 2000 represents a musical modeling program that extends simple tonal melodies. Melody Predictor has only three basic rules in its algorithm:

1. If the preceding three pitches represent a scale, continue the scale in the same direction.
2. If the preceding pitch represents a leap from its preceding pitch, either continue leaping in the same direction following triadic formation, or fall back a scale step in the opposite direction based on pitch motion previous to the leap.
3. If the preceding three pitches represent a pattern, continue the pattern including repeated pitches.

Melody Predictor uses the scale of a piece under analysis and does not predict chromatic pitches.

Figures 6.1a and 6.1c show two melodies given to the predictor, the initial themes of Mozart's Piano Sonatas K. 279 and K. 533. Figure 6.1b and d shows the results of the program's attempt to predict the pitches Mozart chose. Of its guesses, 64 and 71 percent correctly match. These percentages are quite high when compared to the percentages—between 0 and 12 percent—achieved by the program when attempting to match randomly created tonal melodies.

FIGURE 6.1 (a) Mozart, Piano Sonata K. 279, 1st movement, mm. 1–3; (b) results of the Melodic Predictor; (c) Mozart, Piano Sonata K. 533, 1st movement, mm. 1–4; (d) results of the Melodic Predictor.

Although approaching accuracy in the case of the Mozart examples, especially given the simplicity of the program, this accuracy does not prove either that Mozart was a predictable composer or that by extending the program it could compete with Mozart's melodic composing skills. The Melody Predictor's results do demonstrate, however, that Mozart used rather straightforward rules to compose his melodies and that his pitch choices were often based, at least in part, on the rules listed above. Although we might rather imagine that each pitch of Mozart's music was an inspired original, the fact remains that a great deal of his music, like that of most of his contemporaries in the classical period, follows algorithms, and that these algorithms produce relatively predictable results. The extraordinary nature of Mozart's musical genius, of course, arises from those occasions when he avoids the routine choices.

Many analysts believe that composers compose and analysts analyze. However, one of the most effective ways for analysts to understand the music they study is to use their theories to compose music and compare this music to the originals. When this comparison fails, theories lose much if not all of their validity. Over the past twenty-five years or so, I have attempted to verify my theories of music analysis by creating programs that produce demonstrable results. Experiments in Musical Intelligence represents such a program. The Extend program described later in this chapter represents another example of this kind of verification process.

RECOMBINANCY

The thousand or so compositions produced by Experiments in Musical Intelligence can be reverse engineered. These works have a kind of compositional provenance. In fact, *Virtual Music* (Cope 2001) provides a full description of the creation of a machine-composed sonata movement in the style of Mozart. The processes described in that book follow a principle known as *recombinancy*, a principle I will briefly describe here. I will also point readers to several more complete descriptions presented elsewhere (see Cope 1990, 1991, 1996, and 2005). Interestingly, the compositional processes used by Experiments in Musical Intelligence do not resemble any of the analytical processes presented thus far in this book. Although composition and subsequent analyses need not match one another precisely, analytical processes that have no relation to their associated compositional processes seem more contradictory than complementary.

When I began Experiments in Musical Intelligence in 1981, having an intermediary —myself—form abstract sets of rules for composition seemed artificial and unnecessarily premeditative. Also, having to code new rules for each new style or work proved daunting. I therefore set out early on to create new output derived from music stored in a database. The concept—of first deriving rules from a database of music and then using those rules to compose new music—seemed logical then and still does. As with Wolfram's approach to discovering the rules of the universe and then modeling those rules to prove their robustness, my programs have created musical compositions that hopefully stand as testimony to the validity of the processes used to create them.

I argue in my book *Experiments in Musical Intelligence* (1996) that recombinancy appears everywhere as a natural evolutionary and creative process. The recombination of atoms, for instance, produces new molecules. Complex chemicals derive from the recombination of more rudimentary particles. Humans evolve through genetic recombination and depend on recombination for communication, because language itself results from the recombining of letters, words, and sentences. Music is no different: most of the great works of Western art music result from recombinations of the twelve different pitches of the equal-tempered scale, as well as resultant groupings of those pitches. The secret of creativity lies not in the invention of new letters or words for language, or of pitches or groups of pitches in music, but in the subtlety and elegance of their recombination. Musical recombinancy can thus be defined as a method for producing new music based on the recombination of elements of extant music.

Simply breaking musical works into smaller parts and randomly combining them into a new order, however, will almost certainly produce nonsense. Effective recombination requires extensive musical analysis and very careful recombination to be effective. Therefore, my first attempts at recombinant analysis and composition began by using music with which I had familiarity—Bach chorales (Riemenschneider 1941). My initial programs grouped this music into beats and saved these beats as OOP objects. I had this program also store the name of the pitch to which each voice moved in the subsequent beat (the destination pitch). I further had the program collect these beats into groupings called lexicons, delineated by shared pitches and registers of their entering voices, as in C1–G1–C2–C3, with the arabic numerals referring to the octaves in which the pitches appear. To compose, then, the program simply chooses the first beat of any chorale in its database, examines this beat's destination pitches, and then selects one of the stored beats with those same first pitches, assuming enough chorales have been stored to make more than one choice possible. New choices then create the potential for different offbeat motions and different destination chords while maintaining the integrity of Bach's original voice-leading rules.

A simple pseudo-code example of the above processes might look like this:

```
(defun compose-recombinantly (many-works-in-note-events)
   (let* ((grouped-music (group-music many-works-in-note-
          events))
 (music-objects (objectify-the-music grouped-music))
 (lexicons (put-groupings-into-object-lexicons music-objects))
 (composition (compose lexicons)))
```

where `let*` acts as a kind of binding function wherein each of its listed arguments consist of a variable name (e.g., `grouped-music`) followed by functions and their arguments, defined elsewhere. The asterisk following the `let` here allows for previously bound variables to be used within the same call to `let` as in `grouped-music` used in the binding of `music-objects`. In short, `compose-recombinantly` groups the music, puts these groups into objects, places these objects into appropriate lexicons, and then uses these lexicon-stored grouped objects for recombinant composition.

Figure 6.2 demonstrates how this recombining process can lead to the completion of a new Bach-like chorale phrase. Each of the new grouping choices here is absolutely correct in terms of chord-to-chord voice-leading, but without the program having to initiate any user-supplied rules. The music, a product of very simple syntactic networking, inherits the voice-leading rules of the works upon which it bases its replications. In effect, the program extracts its data's algorithms and then uses these algorithms to create new instances of stylistically faithful music.

Although I do not think that Bach composed his chorales by recombinantly assembling them from parts of previously composed chorales, clearly his voice-leading rules led him to revisit certain voicings time and time again. One can certainly imagine him remembering previous solutions and either reiterating those solutions or deliberately attempting to avoid them to create more original-sounding music. Whatever his exact process, however, Bach's voice-leading recombinancy at least partially agrees with the one Experiments in Musical Intelligence uses for composing.

Most music does not consistently move as Bach chorales do, in four-voice textures with similar character and few rests. Experiments in Musical Intelligence, therefore, analyzes character in the original music before breaking this music into beat-size groupings. This character analysis ensures that changes of musical character take place at reasonable locations during recombinancy. The program then stores representations—typically rhythmic and textural values—of this musical character in each grouping object so that continuity can be maintained in output. Having information about an originating work's beat-to-beat character, for example, allows the program to produce works that have unifying elements. One can imagine that if the program were not able to access this kind of information, many beats of a resulting work would have different types of internal patterns, suddenly shifting from one musical context to another (see Figure 6.3). This lack of unity would most likely be uncharacteristic of either the style or the intent of the original music. Its stored character attribute allows the program to produce works having more logic and continuity than would otherwise be the case.

Even with the textural continuity just described, music composed in this way often wanders, with very unbalanced and uncharacteristic phrase lengths. No real musical logic exists beyond chord-to-chord syntax. Further, phrases are simply strung together randomly, without any large-scale form or structure, usually in a single key, and without any sense of the types of repetition and development necessary for intelligent music composition.

FIGURE 6.2 Recombination process leading to the completion of a new Bach-like chorale phrase.

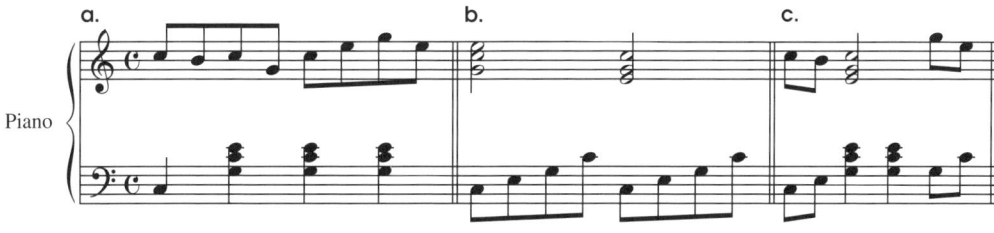

FIGURE 6.3 An example of differing types of internal patterns causing problems in recombination: (a) and (b) originals, (c) a recombination without regard to texture sensitivity.

In order to avoid such wandering, Experiments in Musical Intelligence also makes formal and structural aspects of the music inherent in its database. This involves separate analyses so that the program can store formal and structural information with each grouping along with destination pitches and character. For example, Experiments in Musical Intelligence analyzes the original distance to cadence, the position of the grouping in relation to meter, and other formally and structurally sensitive features. Each new substitution must now meet criteria in relation to destination pitches of each voice, cadence, and other phrase-dependent factors.

Having programs also compare the locations of cadences one to another helps to produce effective phrase and section endings over the course of an entire composition. Using a single work in the database as a model helps to produce more stylistically faithful recombinant multi-phrase music creations. Of course, retaining too much information with each grouping causes the program to simply reiterate one of the works in its database. Therefore, whenever possible, the program chooses new possibilities rather than old ones. Providing very large databases also helps guarantee that more than one possible correct grouping exists at each recombinant point of choice.

The process of discovering thematic areas, their similarities and differences, and ensuring that such relationships transfer in principle to output music requires several sub-programs. In summary, however, formal analysis relies on pattern matching models in a database to indicate when themes return, vary, or are contrasted with other themes (see the discussion of unifications and meta-patterns in Chapter 5). Once located, these themes are labeled and then classified in as many ways as possible—scales in use (see Chapter 4), length, tessitura, and so on. This composing program then attempts to emulate this formal analysis in new music (for more detail on these processes see Cope 1996, 2000, 2001, and 2005).

Many examples of Experiments in Musical Intelligence's output appears in my other books (e.g., Cope 2001), on the Internet, and in publication (e.g., spectrumpress.com). Figure 6..4 presents the beginning of the Rondo Capriccio for cello and orchestra arguably in the style of Mozart (Cope 2006). This work resulted from a database of various divertimentos, serenades, violin concertos, and so on, rather than works by Mozart for cello and orchestra, because Mozart did not compose any works for cello and orchestra. This example demonstrates the elements discussed above: consistency of texture (character), formal thematic statement, structural integrity, and so on. Though not an example of post-tonal recombinancy, Figure 6.4 nonetheless presents a good model of strict recombination as described here and elsewhere (Cope 1991 and 1996). Like the Experiments in Musical Intelligence Mozart sonata described in *Virtual Music* (Cope 2000), this work too could be analyzed for its constituent parts and each part traced to a particular passage in a particular work composed by Mozart. Of course, Mozart's works can be reverse engineered in much the same way as I describe in several books (see in particular Cope 2005, 149).

Reverse engineering the music of Experiments in Musical Intelligence can produce quite valuable results. At the least, such analysis would prove or disprove the numerous criticisms that this music either sounds too little or too much like the originals on which it is based. Discovering the differences between computer-generated music and human-composed music might help us to reevaluate our understanding and appreciation of the latter. To date, very little serious research exists on the relative merits of computer-composed replications. It would, for example, seem natural for anthologies of music designed for students of music theory and musicology to encounter some of this music in order to clearly demonstrate their knowledge of both style and theory of the music upon which these computer-created works are modeled.

Such reverse engineering is not simple, however. One must be aware of the complete possibilities for recombination and equally aware of where the particular recombinant bits may originate. Of course, computers can aid analysts in reconstructing

FIGURE 6.4 An example of Experiments in Musical Intelligence output: the beginning of the Rondo Capriccio for cello and orchestra arguably in the style of Mozart.

240 HIDDEN STRUCTURE

FIGURE 6.4 continued

FIGURE 6.4 continued

FIGURE 6.4 continued

FIGURE 6.4 continued

sources in this way, as evidenced by my work with my computer program called Sorcerer (see Cope 2005).

One of the problems encountered in creating stylistically correct new music based on existing pieces of music involves their allusions to other music. Such allusions can cause problems for recombinancy by breaking these allusions into unrecognizable smaller groupings. On page 175 of my book *Computer Models of Musical Creativity* (Cope 2005) I discuss the opening measures of the third movement of Beethoven's Piano Sonata in F Minor, op. 2, no. 1, and account for every note as an allusion to Bach, Mozart, or to Beethoven himself (figure 5.39 in that book). Each of the fragments accounted for in earlier pieces is documented by composer, work, movement, and measure number. Of course, such allusions represent only one part of analysis:

> Every work of music, unless it has been composed entirely by a formalism (and possibly even then), contains within it many pointers to the musical culture that helped to create it. These pointers, whether they be quotations, paraphrases, likenesses, frameworks, or commonalities, help us to relate to that work, even if we are hearing it for the first time. These pointers also point to other musical styles and works that themselves have pointers, providing us with a rich history of the cultural evolution of the work being heard. (Cope 2005, 175)

Considering allusions as compositional technique at one extreme (the music of Ives and certainly the music of Experiments in Musical Intelligence, for example) and pure formalism (isorhythmic motets and fugues, for example) at the other extreme places most music in a more or less centrist position—combinations of allusions and rules.

Discovering the sources of music, except in the most obvious cases, can prove extremely difficult for analysts. Composers using formalisms can inadvertently produce allusions. Likewise, composers using allusions from very esoteric sources that follow the rules of composition currently in play can make the discovery of these allusions nearly impossible. The resultant mix of allusions and rule-created music can produce incredible difficulties for those of us intent on using the proper techniques for modeling the music we wish to better understand.

However, analyzing music for its quotations, paraphrases, and allusions to other music would seem just as important to understanding music as attempting to define context-independent reductions by using, for example, roman numerals, pitch-class sets, and letter representations of formal sections. Computer programs with large databases of compositions have the potential to identify such quotes, paraphrases, and allusions, for which we would otherwise have to rely entirely on analysts' listening experiences. As mentioned earlier in this book, in *Computer Models of Music Creativity* (Cope 2005) I describe the computer program called Sorcerer, which returns a subset of possible references from a large database (e.g., see particularly Cope 2005, chap. 5).

However, Sorcerer represents just a beginning to this kind of study. Programs following a similar design but with significantly larger databases should help determine potential sources for hermeneutic, semiotic, referential, and other types of analysis that provide both semantic and syntactic information about the fundamental nature of musical compositions.

Figure 6.5 provides an example of allusion, part of a computer composition in Beethoven's style (a) followed by one of the originals upon which it was based (b). The entire second movement of a recombinant Beethoven symphony appears as an appendix in Cope 2005 and will give readers further opportunity to analyze the structure, form, SPEAC, and other subjects discussed in this chapter in more detail.

Obviously, music does not exist in a vacuum. Discovering a German augmented sixth chord in Bruckner does not carry the same weight as discovering a similar German augmented sixth chord in Bach. Context provides an extraordinary frame for even the simplest analytical discovery. Even the music we choose to analyze has survived at least in part because of its context—idiomatic performability, uniqueness in the repertoire, meaning of its title, life of the composer, and so on all play important roles. How we analyze this music should be determined at least in part by that context. For example, the German augmented sixth chord in Bach mentioned above will probably be analyzed as a series of nonharmonic tones, rather than an individual chord, while Bruckner's version will stand on its own as a German augmented sixth chord. Because analysts cannot invent individual systems for each work they analyze, they often depend on analytical processes that are fairly devoid of these important individual contexts. Theorists such as Robert Gjerdingen (1988) have attempted with some success to approach music analysis more from a contextual point of view. However, far too often—and particularly with post-tonal music—contextual relationships appear more often in program notes than in musical analyses.

Interestingly, it may be the context of the musical analysis—apart from the discovery of musical allusions—that most effectively defies the computer's ability to assist human analysts. Although one could imagine a computer connected to the Internet gathering mountains of potentially contextual information about a composer or work, deciphering that information and siphoning out the data of actual relevance to the music under analysis still requires human analysts. At the same time, understanding musical provenance—meaning here the ties of a work to past music—would seem as important to its understanding as discovering its functions or other features. Computers make such studies much more feasible than depending on human memories of past music (see Cope 2005).

Judging new compositions that approximate but do not exactly match that of the original music require some kind of criteria other than source identification. Logic alone cannot evaluate the effectiveness of such musical solutions. The use of the term *musical* here, a term with which most readers of this book are familiar, is difficult to define. Webster's Collegiate Dictionary (1991) defines *musical* as

246 HIDDEN STRUCTURE

FIGURE 6.5 An example of allusion in (a) an Experiments in Musical Intelligence replication, and (b) a Beethoven bagatelle Op. 119, no. 1 (1820) upon which it is partially based.

FIGURE 6.5 continued

"melodious" and the word *melodious* as "musical," offering little help. Attempting to avoid a polemic, I offer a more quantifiable definition of the term *musical*:

> The word *musical* means that, within the context of a particular piece of music, logical, intuitive, and physical interpretations agree. Being logical infers the following of explicit rules. Being intuitive infers the following of implicit rules. Being physical infers the following of natural physical laws (referring here to human performability). A musical passage is therefore one in which the user of the term finds all of the above criteria acceptable and in coincidence.

Not wanting to belabor this definition, all outputs of the program described here that precisely coincide with the original human work are musical, and that those do not match the original work should be taken as musical only as they individually fulfill the above criteria.

Interestingly, one of the tests that computer music analysis makes possible is what I call the *jigsaw test*. Like a jigsaw puzzle, a single piece of music is carved into thousands of multiple-note varying-size note-event groupings and shuffled so that they do not occur in any particular order. Ontimes of the note-events are reset so that they relate to one another in their respective groupings but no longer give any hint as to their original temporal location. Analysts then must put the pieces back into proper order again, using whatever rules they wish to employ. This Humpty Dumpty approach poses very difficult problems for even the simplest of tonal works, no less for complex post-tonal music. Familiarity with the jigsawed work can certainly give analysts an advantage. However, for most, the test poses severe problems—even for this *single* work process—as the example of a Bach chorale in

FIGURE 6.6 A Bach chorale as example of a jigsaw puzzle.

Figure 6.6 proves. The solution for this puzzle is discovering the source chorale number in Bach's 371 chorales as published in Riemenschneider (1941). Solving this puzzle will require all four principles described in Chapter 1 of this book and will further demonstrate the complexities involved in recombinancy and the need for using computers in analysis.

PROBABILITIES

As discussed in Chapter 1, probabilities played an important role in early attempts at computer music composition and analysis (Hiller and Isaacson 1959). The Monte Carlo method, stochastics, Markov chains, and so on that these individuals used in their early experiments all fall under the general rubric of probability theory, where a limited range of choices regarding the occurrence of certain events governs compositional and analytical processes. Probabilities can reveal both the predictable and the unpredictable and can even provide access to those special moments that sometimes indicate more about a musical composition than all of the more generic materials that surround them. Statistically small-probability passages often provide the key to a work's musical character. Using Markov chains (discussed later in this chapter in more detail) and similar processes first to analyze music and then to compose using the information thus gathered can provide invaluable information about the workings of music.

Probabilities contribute to the understanding of almost everything. The world is gray, not black and white, and where we find grayness, probabilities offer one of the best potentials for our comprehension. Probability theory helps to predict outcomes so that decisions made from among many choices will be informed, not random (Freund 1973).

Understanding probabilities requires the understanding of possibilities. For example, the probabilities of tossing a coin and producing heads after having already tossed a coin and producing heads fifty times in a row remains 50/50, or 0.5. *Every* toss of a coin—all other factors being equal—has a 0.5 probability of producing heads and a 0.5 probability of producing tails. Coins know nothing about previous tosses. Although most likely obvious, knowing the true outcome possibilities helps us to understand probability.

Many such possibilities, though, do not prove as simple, even if they initially appear simple. For instance, ask someone to select a single pitch from an imaginary piano keyboard and keep the choice secret. Now, try to figure out the probability of choosing which pitch they selected. The answer—the simple part of this question—is obviously 1 in 88, or 0.01136. However, discovering the probability of having two people independently choose the same pitch in their heads does not prove so simple. The correct response to this more difficult question depends on the number of composite possibilities involved. In this situation, the composite number rises significantly as one would expect, from 88 to 88^2, or 7744. However, the number of possible correct matches between the two participants increases as well. Each key on the imaginary keyboard can be correctly chosen by both participants once, producing a total of 88 possible correct matches. Thus, the probabilities of both individuals choosing the same key is 88 in 7744, surprisingly the precise same probability as one person choosing the same single pitch—0.01136.

Understanding probabilities of the *musikalisches Würfelspiele* discussed in Chapter 1 also requires carefully figuring of possibilities. These combinatorial musical dice games created by composers such as Kirnberger, C. P. E. Bach, Haydn, and Mozart involve the tossing of dice to make selections from matrices containing numbers keyed to measures of music. These measures of music are then joined together to create musical phrases and short musical compositions (see Figure 1.10). Computing the probabilities based on tosses of dice would seem as simple as computing the probabilities of coin tosses and the mental selection of pitches on a keyboard. However, dice tosses hold many surprises. As the examples in Figure 1.10 point out, the total number of different outcomes from tossing a pair of dice is eleven (rolling the number 1 is not possible). Furthermore, the possibilities of tossing additions of two dice totaling 2 through 12 are not equal. There is, for example, only one way for the combination of two dice to add up to either the number 2 (1 and 1) or the number 12 (6 and 6). However, there are several ways for two dice to add up to the number 6 (i.e., 3 and 3, 2 and 4, 1 and 5). In fact, the possible ways to toss numbers decreases toward the extremes (2 and 12) in ways that make the dice throws in *musikalisches Würfelspiele* probabilistically quite uneven. Thus, understanding the possibilities involved in games such as this will lead to better computations of probabilities. One would imagine the composers of these dice games knew this and created their music in ways that matched the increased likelihood of certain choices with their most interesting musical measures.

Studies of probability also include concepts of *probability functions*. Probability functions take variables as input and provide the probability of the variable's having a certain value as output. The set of probabilities that a function assigns to all of its variables is known as a *distribution*. Variables can be *independent*, as with the coin example given previously, or *dependent*, as with the example given previously of two individuals making keyboard pitch choices and with *Musikalisches Würfelspiele*. Dependent variables can also be *conditional*—that is, the probability of one variable may differ given the state of the other variable.

Probabilities can also change over time. In other words, new information may alter probabilities. The *Bayes rule* follows the relatively simple notion that adding new information to existing information impacts probabilities and their distributions. For example, consider a situation in which a bass drum strikes on the downbeat of the first measure of a work. The probabilities of this bass drum strike occurring on the downbeat of m. 2 of this same work are 50/50 or 50 percent—the bass drum strike can either occur or not occur with equal certainty. However, if the bass drum strike does occur on the downbeat of m. 2 of this same work, the probability for it occurring on the downbeat of m. 3 changes to 66.7 percent. A third occurrence increases the odds to .75 for a fourth occurrence, and so on.

The Bayes rule appears in Figure 6.7 in mathematical form. This mathematical form roughly translates into English as "The probability of A given B equals the probability of B given A times the probability of A, divided by the probability of B." The variable A represents the current state of data, while the variable B refers to new information that will most likely cause a change in the probabilities of A. There are many such rules that can affect probability—more than we can investigate here (for more information see particularly Temperley 2007, 7–19; Ghahramani 2005). The Markov chains (discussed later in this chapter) that underlie much of this chapter's approach to musical analysis rely on such probabilities.

Initially, probabilities might seem more important to composers than to music analysts. After all, many composers (most notably Xenakis, who used stochastic probabilities to compose much of his music) have explicitly used probabilistics in their compositional processes. However, understanding the probabilities of the choices that composers make in their compositions, whether they do so explicitly or not, represents a significant component of music analysis (Temperley 2007). Most composers make the same or similar choices more than once, with their choices dependent on other choices that then change over time. Knowing about such probabilities enables music analysts to develop methods for understanding and representing such choice making.

Using probabilities in computer programs requires the presence of as much relevant data as possible. Data-driven computer programs, the ones that I prefer, provide perfect environments for probability analyses of music. Interestingly, the manner in which data is stored in databases greatly influences both the effectiveness of computation and, even more important, the types of applications that programmers might want to develop. Methods of data representation can enhance or limit the imaginations of those who use them. For example, large amounts of data stored according to pitch numbers rather than ontime numbers will most likely support the counting of pitches in a work while concomitantly discouraging pitch pattern recognition. Unfortunately, such storage processes would also make performance, formal, and structural analyses less feasible, as well as posing problems for analysts intent on studying temporal analysis strategies. Therefore, data representation and storage should be as flexible as possible to allow as many approaches to analysis as conceivable.

$$P(A \backslash B) = \frac{P(B \backslash A)\, P(A)}{P(B)}$$

FIGURE 6.7 The Bayes rule.

RULES AND MARKOV CHAINS

As mentioned previously, generating new music from an analytic system and then comparing the results with the actual music used for generation represents one of the most straightforward forms of validation of the effectiveness of that analytical system. Completing a known work separated from its ending and then comparing a new ending with the real ending provides another example of such validation. Interestingly, it is much more difficult to add music to an incomplete version of an extant score than to compose stylistically credible music from scratch. For example, interrupted voice-leading requires a newly composed extension to initially meet goals that the rules may not adequately prepare the program to meet. Indeed, if an interrupted interval does not already exist in the database as a completed voice-leading (i.e., it represents its first appearance), then a work cannot be completed at all. Even if this interval exists once in the database, there may be no way the program can possibly complete the piece in the same or a similar manner to that used by the work's originator.

I have chosen music from Béla Bartók's *Mikrokosmos* to computationally analyze for its rules and produce viable new endings. All four of the examples used for analysis here appear in the third volume of the *Mikrokosmos*: 80, 81, 91, and 92. These works share a number of common features that make them attractive to use for research as described here. First, each work resembles a two-part invention, rarely exceeding two voices in texture. This textural consistency provides excellent clarity for discovering rules. Second, each of the four pieces exhibits extensive chromaticism appearing at roughly similar rates. Third, the two-part counterpoint in these selections exhibits the kind of tension and release typical of many other post-tonal works.

Deriving rules from music is a critically important process for computer analysis programs (Maxwell 1992; Schwanauer 1993; Widmer 1992). Markov chains can greatly help this analysis by classifying rules by their probability of occurrence. Markov chains are probabilistic processes often expressed in terms of *orders* (Ames 1989). A *zero-order* Markov chain, for example, makes random decisions, with no applicable rules. A *first-order* Markov chain, however, bases new decisions on immediately preceding choices. A *fifth-order* Markov chain bases its decisions on the previous five choices. Figure 6.8 shows a matrix (called a state transition matrix) for a first-order Markov chain involving all twelve pitches of the chromatic scale. The numbers in the matrix here represent probabilities that add to 1.0—or 100 percent—in each horizontal line. To interpret this matrix, a program would find a current pitch in the left-hand column, and then read the various probabilities of potential following pitches along the associated horizontal row. The probability of the pitch A being followed by another pitch A in the state transition matrix given here, for instance, is 10 percent (0.1); of the pitch A being followed by the pitch B-flat, 20 percent (0.2); and so on.

As a more musical example of this process, imagine that a melody-composing program chooses new pitches by virtue of their immediately preceding pitches

	a	bb	b	c	db	d	eb	e	f	gb	g	ab
a	.1	.2	.1	.2	.1	.1	.0	.1	.1	.0	.0	.0
bb	.2	.1	.1	.2	.1	.1	.0	.1	.0	.0	.1	.0
b	.1	.2	.1	.1	.1	.1	.0	.2	.1	.0	.0	.0
c	.2	.2	.1	.1	.1	.0	.0	.0	.1	.1	.0	.1
db	.0	.1	.0	.3	.1	.1	.0	.1	.1	.2	.0	.0
d	.1	.1	.1	.0	.2	.2	.0	.1	.1	.1	.0	.0
eb	.1	.2	.1	.2	.1	.1	.0	.0	.0	.0	.1	.1
e	.1	.1	.1	.1	.1	.1	.0	.2	.2	.0	.0	.0
f	.1	.2	.1	.0	.0	.1	.2	.2	.1	.0	.0	.0
gb	.1	.2	.1	.0	.1	.1	.1	.0	.1	.0	.0	.2
g	.0	.2	.1	.2	.1	.1	.0	.1	.1	.0	.0	.1
ab	.3	.2	.1	.1	.0	.2	.0	.1	.0	.0	.0	.0

FIGURE 6.8 A state-transition matrix for a first-order Markov chain involving all twelve notes of the chromatic scale.

(first-order Markov chain). If only a major or minor second in any direction is allowed between consecutive pitches, such a first-order Markov chain would produce simple meandering, stepwise melodies. A more elegant program might have new choices depend on two preceding pitches. For example, if the previous two pitch choices represented a leap upward, then new choices might be limited to pitches moving a second in contrary motion. Other rules would then need to exist for other pitch combinations. This second-order Markov chain would produce considerably more interesting music than a first-order Markov chain.

Second-order Markov chain state transition matrixes appear much like expanded first-order state transition matrixes. Figure 6.9 shows a portion of the upper left-hand corner of a twelve-pitch matrix such as that shown in Figure 6.8. Here, each row states the probability of pitches following two previously established pitches. Note that the probabilities in each horizontal rank must still total 1.0. Second-order Markov chains have far more constraints—conditional probabilities—than do first-order Markov chains, as do third-order Markov chains over second-order Markov chains, and so on.

Common Lisp provides useful ways of organizing data to represent state transition matrixes. Instead of describing explicit probabilities as in state transition matrixes, pitches appear in lists such that duplications increase the probabilities proportionately. For example, the following simple list

254 HIDDEN STRUCTURE

		a	bb	b	c	db	d	eb	e	f	gb	g	ab
a	a	.1	.2	.1	.2	.1	.1	.0	.1	.1	.0	.0	.0
a	bb	.2	.1	.1	.2	.1	.1	.0	.1	.0	.0	.1	.0
a	b	.1	.2	.1	.1	.1	.1	.0	.2	.1	.0	.0	.0
a	c	.2	.2	.1	.1	.1	.0	.0	.0	.1	.1	.0	.1
a	db	.0	.1	.0	.3	.1	.1	.0	.1	.1	.2	.0	.0
a	d	.1	.1	.1	.0	.2	.2	.0	.1	.1	.1	.0	.0
a	eb	.1	.2	.1	.2	.1	.1	.0					
a	e	.1	.1	.1	.1	.1	.1	.0					
a	f	.1	.2	.1	.0	.0	.1	.2					
a	gb	.1	.2	.1	.0	.1	.1	.1					
a	g	.0	.2	.1	.2	.1	.1	.0					
a	ab	.3	.2	.1	.1	.0	.2	.0					

FIGURE 6.9 The upper left-hand corner of a second-order Markov chain state transition matrix.

```
(60 (62 64 64 64 65 71 71 71 71 71))
```

indicates that the MIDI pitch 62 (D) follows the MIDI pitch 60 (C) with a 0.1 probability (1 of 10 possible following pitches), the MIDI pitch 64 follows the MIDI pitch 60 with a 0.3 probability, with the probability of MIDI pitch 65 at 0.1, and that of MIDI pitch 71 at 0.5. Duplicated pitches indicate the higher probability of their being chosen in a resulting composing process. Only existing probabilities appear in this matrix, with all other pitch possibilities understood to be 0. Although this notation may not be as readable as a more traditionally notated state transition matrix, it works especially well for computational purposes. The Markov program accompanying this book on CD-ROM collects the first-order probabilities of any succession of pitches in music in a database and places the resulting probabilities in lists representing a simplified state transition matrix. The resulting analysis is then used by this Markov program to produce new music in a style roughly comparable to that of the original upon which it is based.

Complete rules in the Markov program look like the following, stored as a Lisp-style list form state transition matrix here given the symbol name *stm*.

```
? *stm*
((60 (61))
 (61 (65 64))
 (64 (63 63))
 (63 (61 65))
 (65 (68 68))
 (68 (71 69))
 (69 (67 71))
 ((71 (72 72))
 ((72 (69))
 (67 (64)))
```

This form of rule storage represents just one of the many possible—arrays, tables, objects, and so on, being obvious alternatives—but follows the Lisp list vocabulary especially well. The asterisks surrounding the "stm" symbol here indicate that it represents a *global variable*. Global variables can be accessed anytime by users and code function, and their values typically have relevance to more than one process. For example, the global variable *tempo* would likely need to be available to many different functions. Global variables differ from local variables defined in function argument lists or in let statements. Such local variables can only be accessed from within their parenthetical function definitions, and calling them outside of these environments will cause errors.

A large enough amount of data must be used for a state transition matrix; otherwise, the program output can easily lapse into repetitive back-and-forth motions or other types of dead ends most likely atypical of the analyzed music. Figures 6.10 and 6.11 present both successful and unsuccessful examples of Markov output representing extensions of the melody from Bartók *Mikrokosmos* nos. 71 and 77. In Figure 6.10, the Markov program required just five runs to duplicate the actual pitches that Bartók composed.

The first argument to the function compose-new-music-based-on-markovian-probabilities, the top-level function of the Markov program on the CD-ROM accompanying this book, includes all but the final five pitches that the program then returns as its best attempt to duplicate the original music. The data used as the third argument to the function compose-new-music-based-on-markovian-probabilities requires that the final pitch entry occur at least one other time in the list, so that it is not followed by a nil pitch. Such nils do not cause errors, but create further nil pitches, which then continue indefinitely because nil pitches do not otherwise exist in the state transition matrix. The code below presents the calls to compose-new-music-based-on-markovian-probabilities that produced the music in Figure 6.10.

```
(defVar bartok-2
  '(67 65 64 65 67 65 67 64 65 67 67 65 64 67 65 64 62 64 65)
  "mikrokosmos 71.")
```

FIGURE 6.10 (a) Original, Bartók, *Mikrokosmos*, no. 71, transposed to begin on G; (b–f) five computer extensions beginning five notes from the end of the passage.

a.

b.

c.

d.

FIGURE 6.11 (a) Original, Bartók, *Mikrokosmos*, no. 77, transposed to begin on D; (b–d) three computer extensions beginning five notes from the end of the passage.

```
(compose-new-music-based-on-markovian-probabilities
  65
  5
  (67 65 64 65 67 65 67 64 65 67 67 65 64 67 65 64 62 64
  65))
  (67 65 64 65 64)
(compose-new-music-based-on-markovian-probabilities
  65
  5 (67 65 64 65 67 65 67 64 65 67 67 65 64 67 65 64 62 64
  65))
  (67 65 67 67 65)
```

258   HIDDEN STRUCTURE

```
(compose-new-music-based-on-markovian-probabilities
  65
  5
  (67 65 64 65 67 65 67 64 65 67 67 65 64 67 65 64 62 64
  65))
  (64 65 67 64 67)
(compose-new-music-based-on-markovian-probabilities
  65
  5
  (67 65
  64 65 67 65 67 64 65 67 67 65 64 67 65 64 62 64 65))
  (64 65 64 65 64)
(compose-new-music-based-on-markovian-probabilities 65 5
  (67 65 64 65 67 65 67 64 65 67 67 65 64 67 65 64 62 64
  65))
  (64 62 64 65 64)
```

The fifth run of compose-new-music-based-on-markovian-probabilities here produces the actual ending Bartók composed. Even the previous four unsuccessful attempts reveal logical orders of pitches that make musical sense, lacking only cadence and other patterns that higher-order Markov chains would catch. Viewing the state transition matrix for this example proves that the resulting correct solution exists in the data itself.

```
((67 (65 65 67 64 65 65))
 (65 (64 64 67 67 67 64))
 (64 (65 62 67 65 65))
 (62 (64)))
```

Figure 6.11 presents an unsuccessful example of first-order Markovian output. No matter how many runs the program makes, it never achieves the results that Bartók created. The reason, of course, lies in the state transition matrix, where the final pitch 62 does not follow pitch 67 in the original and thus will never appear in that order in the output.

```
((62 (65 65 65 65 65))
 (65 (69 62 62 69 62 62 67 69))
 (69 (67 67 71))
 (71 (69))
 (67 (65 65 65)))
```

Like all but the final example presented in Figure 6.10, these three unsuccessful outputs in Figure 6.11 retain much of the logic of Bartók's original music, even though they do not match Bartók's ultimate solution.

The Markov program on the CD-ROM accompanying this book cannot produce pitch orders or pitches themselves that have not already occurred in the data. This represents a significant problem, because composers commonly transpose pitches, motives, harmonies, and so on, creating new pitch orders and new pitches. For Markov to accomplish this requires the use of intervals instead of pitches in its rules. Using intervals enables the program to follow the intervallic template of the analyzed music, and, using that template, output music that more likely follows what a composer would create. Because the Markov program deals with numbers, translating pitches to intervals at the outset and then converting the intervals back to pitches at the output level will convert the program properly. The problem with using intervals, of course, is that these intervals will not necessarily conform to a scale in use. This shortcoming can cause numerous out-of-scale pitches to occur, pitches that might never appear in the original music. Including analyzed scales requires adapting code from Chapter 4 of this book, and thus more discussion of the Markov program than is deserved here. Therefore, rather than convert Markov to an interval base at this point, I will now describe a more elaborate program that attempts to extend Bartók's two-part contrapuntal music using a similar Markovian model, but one using intervals instead of pitches.

The Extend program presented on the CD-ROM accompanying this book gathers interval rules from its database music and then uses these rules to compose. Rules, particularly voice-leading rules as in the Extend program, may be considered separately from the pitch classes that define them and thus reveal other important aspects of the music being analyzed. Examining how the rules produce output identical to that of a human composer can lead analysts to important discoveries as to what constitutes proper and improper voice motions. As with the Markov program, even studying the rules of unsuccessful output can reveal significant insights into compositional process and thus produce a better understanding of a work under analysis.

As an example, Figure 6.12 presents a simple one-against-one two-voice counterpoint in which each voice moves stepwise. The pitches, the consonance or dissonance they produce when sounded together, and other aspects all contribute to the complete phrase in which they occur (not shown here). Each of these attributes also contributes to the functions implied here, with phrases beginning on tonic, ending on tonic, and having penultimate dominant functions that help provide final cadences. Clearly, the voice-leading of this simple counterpoint supports this simple analysis. The voice-leading contributes to a sense of functional continuity without which a phrase's implied harmonic direction would suffer.

Figure 6.13, in contrast to Figure 6.12, presents an example with various two-pitch groupings that lack clear traditional functions. Interestingly, this example consists of the same voice motions (without regard for vertical simultaneities) in different orders than the music of Figure 6.12. Therefore, one might argue that not all of the functions in Figure 6.12 have disappeared from the music in Figure 6.13.

Figure 6.14b and 6.14c present two computer extensions to the original Bartók first phrase presented in Figure 6.14a (mm. 5–7). Figure 6.14b uses a first-order Markov process, while Figure 6.14c uses a second-order Markov process. Figure 6.14b is substantially different from the original, with awkward leaps, unusual

260   HIDDEN STRUCTURE

FIGURE 6.12 A simple two-voice counterpoint in which each voice moves stepwise in various directions.

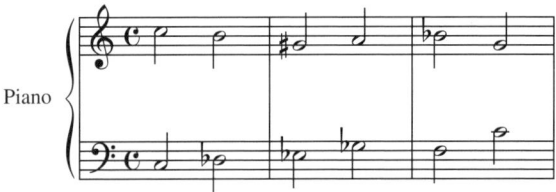

FIGURE 6.13 A post-tonal example, where the various two-note groupings do not have clear functionalism.

consecutive vertical intervals, and almost continually parallel motion. Figure 6.14c, however, matches the original exactly. Thus, second-order Markov extensions prove more robust than first-order, particularly when trying to match the original rather than varying it (as is the case with most style composing programs).

Evaluating different extensions such as that in Figure 6.14b also poses many problems—for example, determining whether completing one of, say, Bartók's works by anyone other than Bartók *can* be as good or better than Bartók's own completion. Anyone aware of my other books on algorithmic music (see bibliography) will probably predict my response to these problems: certainly such extensions can be as good as or better than the original, as well as worse than the original. Making such choices, however, requires that listeners shed their notions that the only music worth the definition must originate with human composers.

The extensions presented in this chapter do not include rhythm, meter, dynamics, articulation, phrasing, and so on, all critical ingredients in the full musical experience. In order to make these extensions fit reasonably with their appropriate works, I simply use the rhythm of the extended passage, tying pitches that repeat. Hence, the Extend program available on the CD-ROM accompanying this book

Hommage à R. Sch.

FIGURE 6.14 Two possible nonidentical computer extensions (b and c) to the original by Bartók (*Mikrokosmos*, no. 80) presented in (a).

b.

c.

FIGURE 6.14 continued

represents only a beginning to an approach to modeling. Like many of the programs presented in this book, the Extend program provides a useful beginning for musical investigation that will ultimately help theory become reality in order to verify hypothesis.

Other programs can complete extant works as does Extend. For example, in Cope 2004 and 2005 I describe a relatively simple computer program called Gradus that analyzes musical output for its rules and then creates new musical data following those rules (Principle 4). Gradus differs from the Extend program just described in that Gradus actually learns by decreasing the backtracking necessary when reaching dead ends until such backtracking is no longer necessary. Originally designed to produce two-voice one-against-one Fux-like vocal counterpoint, the same counterpoint often encountered in beginning theory courses at many American universities, the program can—by using different databases—compose music following any rules (including, say, twentieth-century counterpoint by Bartók). Unfortunately, although flexible in terms of the two-voice music in its database, the program only collects allowable vertical intervals and horizontal voice motions. Therefore, although Gradus has many interesting features—learning, style acquisition, and so on—it has little flexibility in regard to completely new situations, where neither allowable vertical intervals nor allowable horizontal voice motions play roles. For example, it would not make much sense to use Gradus to analyze serial music for, in the program's current state, none of the more salient features of serial music would translate to Gradus's output. Although such a program could be created and, indeed, could be extremely valuable, it should also be a separate program and not an expansion of Gradus.

Alice (the ALgorithmically Integrated Composing Environment) is a Macintosh interactive computer composing program (see Cope 2000) designed to provide an introduction to basic interactive music composition in the style of the composer using the program. Alice differs from Experiments in Musical Intelligence but resembles both Extend and Gradus in its use of inherited voice-leading rules rather than recombinancy. Alice presents a variety of analytical methods to aid composers in setting variables to produce music more to their liking. Figure 6.15 shows three different forms of analysis provided by Alice. In Figure 6.15a, a single window indicates percentages of pitch classes in a pie chart. A column chart provides identical information, but with a computational range of mode possibilities. These charts are then followed by a linear diagram of when pitch classes first enter, a texture analysis, a pitch/duration intersecting analysis scatter plot chart, and a channel-timbre-use column chart. Figure 6.15b presents a rules window with rules consisting of the current and the destination pitch classes, interval-class voice motion, and the channel in which motion takes place (discussed in detail shortly; also see Cope 2000). Figure 6.15c presents a structural analysis defined by straight lines and a formal analysis defined by curved lines.

Alice creates its rules by first grouping the music appropriately, converting the pitches of these groupings into pitch-class sets, and then deriving voice-leading rules from the results of these processes. A rule in Alice takes the form

```
(((3 3) 2 1) ((5 1) -2 2) ((0 0) 2 3) ((8 5) -1 4))
```

with each rule sublist (e.g., ((3 3) 2 1)) consisting of a head sublist followed by two numbers. The numbers in this head sublist represent the origin and destination pitch classes. The number immediately following the head sublist indicates the direction and amount of scale-degree motion between the two pitch classes in the rule sublist, with negative numbers indicating downward direction. The last number in the rule sublist represents the channel to which the rule part applies (each voice in Alice must be assigned to a different channel). Therefore, the rule sublist ((3 3) 2 1) indicates the motion of an upward major second between pitch class 3 in the chord of origin and pitch class 3 in the chord of destination in channel 1. Although origin and destination pitches appear as pitch classes, motion is measured in scale degrees according to the current scale. Hence, the 2 in rule part ((3 3) 2 1) indicates a major second upward only given that the scale here is measured in half steps. Using a scale defined in whole steps, this 2 would equate to a major third. Figure 6.16 shows the rule (((3 3) 2 1) ((5 1) -2 2) ((0 0) 2 3) ((8 5) -1 4)) as it would appear in music notation with scale degrees measured in half steps.

Voice motion in rule notation must be flexible enough to represent more than scale degrees. This notation must also be able to represent chromaticism when using scales other than the chromatic scale. In Alice, each half step above a scale degree that is not itself a scale degree receives a superscript caret, one per half step. Hence, the half step raising the second degree of the pentatonic scale of

264   HIDDEN STRUCTURE

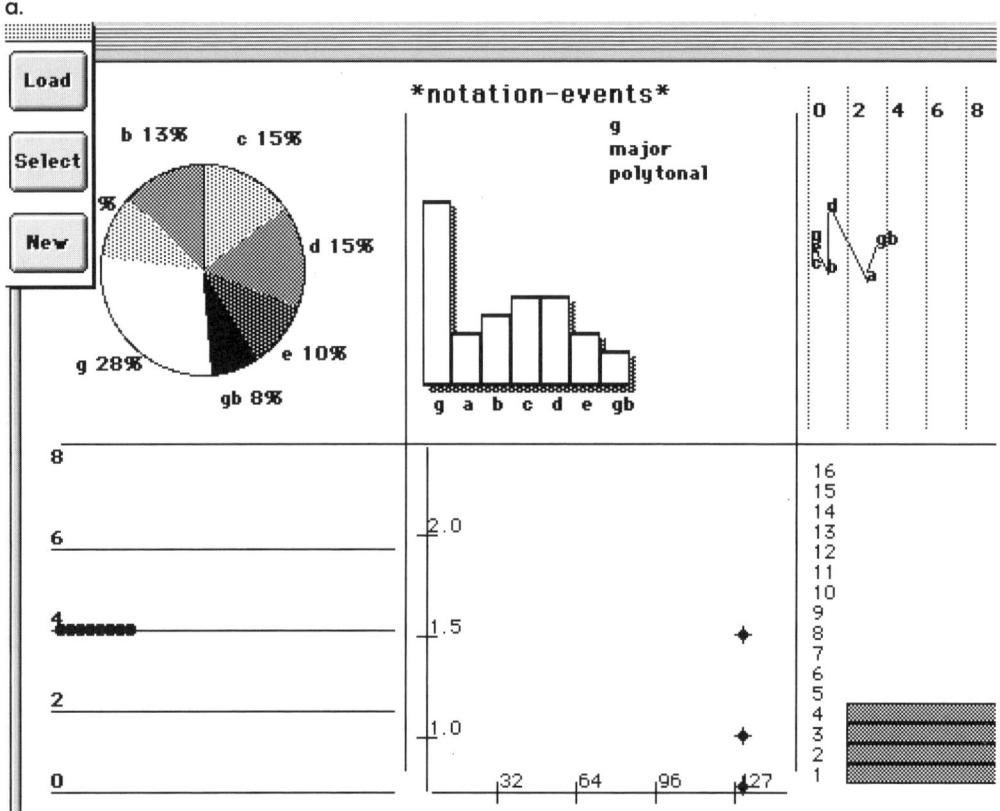

FIGURE 6.15 Three different forms of analysis provided by Alice.

GENERATIVE MODELS OF MUSIC

b.

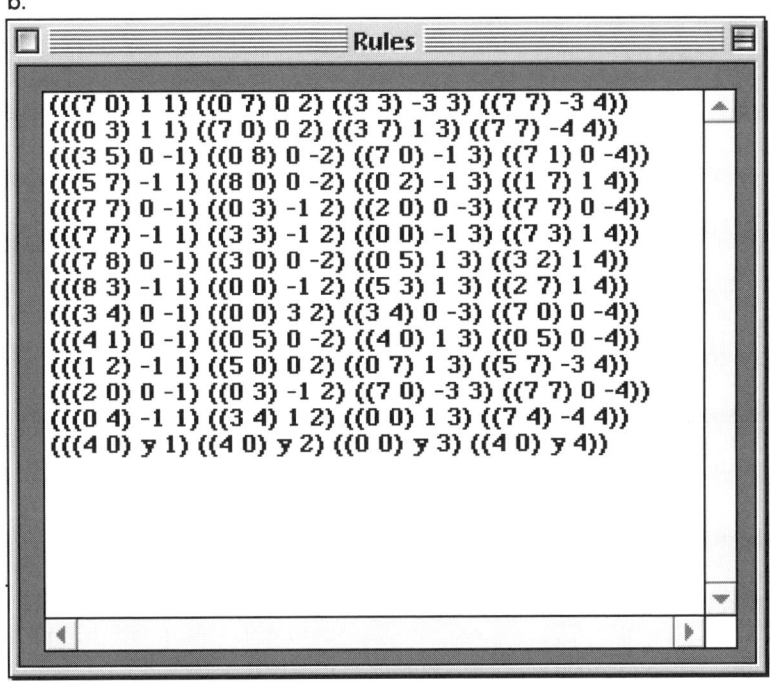

c.

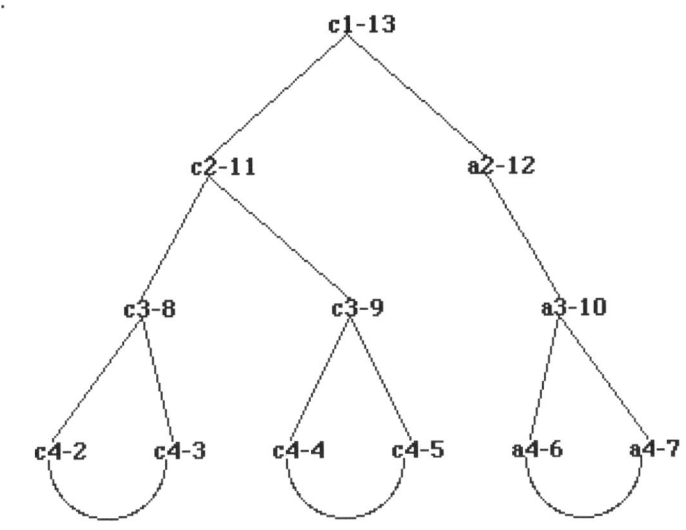

FIGURE 6.15 continued

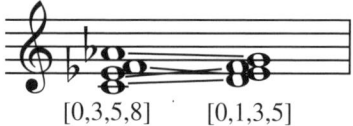

FIGURE 6.16 The rule (((3 3) 2 1) ((5 1) -2 2) ((0 0) 2 3) ((8 5) -1 4)) in music notation.

C–D–F–G–A would be 2^ for D-sharp, and the double raising of this second degree would be notated as a 2^^ for E-natural. All pitches chromatic to a given scale are figured as raised scale degrees in Alice. Hence, no lowered form of notation need exist. This chromatic notation allows for every possible motion between members and nonmembers of any scale. Such inclusivity greatly enhances Alice's ability to adapt to various styles of music.

To create new groupings using these rules, an appropriately analyzed and named set is matched to an OOP lexicon of such sets in a database. An alternate but identically named set is then substituted for the current set. This process of substituting similarly named sets can produce new orderings of the original set based on matching two sets with new voice motions, a new destination set, or some combination of these two possibilities to create new music. As an example, the initial pitches of a first set [0,2,4,7] are rearranged to match the newly found pitch-class set's [4,7,2,0] pitch-class order. This ensures that the new rule motion will be applied properly. The new rule then replaces the original rule.

The two distinct motions shown in Figures 6.17a–6.17c will make this process clearer. Figure 6.17a shows the original motion of two groupings in the database. Figure 6.17b shows the rule formed by this motion with the applicable scale in this case measured in half steps. Note that the order of the rule follows the sets from lowest to highest channel. Figure 6.17c shows a second motion whose first set reduces to the same set as in Figure 6.17a. This equivalent set, however, moves to a different destination set with this movement shown in the rule of Figure 6.17d. Alice then substitutes the first set of Figure 6.17a for the first set of Figure 6.17c and uses the voice-leading of Figure 6.17c to create a different—but correct—motion to the second set of Figure 6.17c. In order to link the elements of the first sets together logically, the program exchanges them so that their equivalent elements connect (i.e., so that the first set connects appropriately with the applicable rule). Hence, the first set of Figure 6.17c must be made to have the set-member order of the first set in Figure 6.17a. Once this is accomplished, however, the actual motion from the first set of Figure 6.17a using the rule of Figure 6.17c–d follows channels rather than set numbers. The results of this process appear in Figure 6.17e. The rule derived from Figure 6.17e, shown in Figure 6.17f, demonstrates how the elements of 6.17d have been rearranged with different channel settings.

I have recounted Alice's rule-based analysis and composing processes here because they relate directly to modeling and because, by creating extensions to

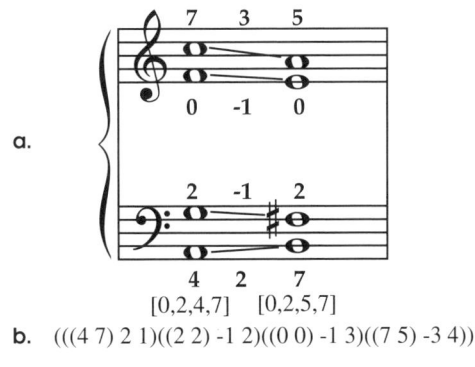

a.

b. (((4 7) 2 1)((2 2) -1 2)((0 0) -1 3)((7 5) -3 4))

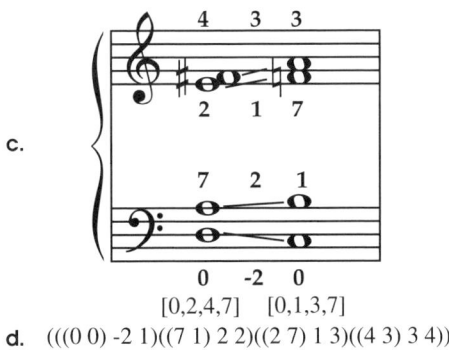

c.

d. (((0 0) -2 1)((7 1) 2 2)((2 7) 1 3)((4 3) 3 4))

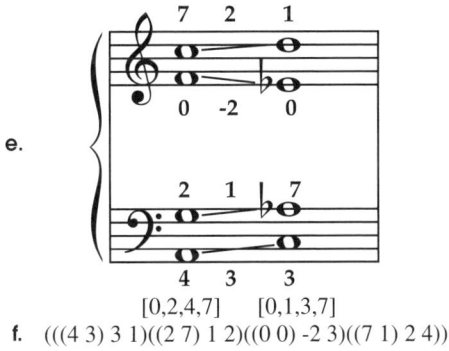

e.

f. (((4 3) 3 1)((2 7) 1 2)((0 0) -2 3)((7 1) 2 4))

FIGURE 6.17 Extending voice-leading rules.

existing music, Alice exemplifies the composing approach described previously in this chapter. I invite those readers who find Alice's processes difficult to follow or who remain curious about the program's potential for acting as an analytical tool to carefully review the chapters in Cope 2000 that relate directly to Alice's inferential rules-based analytical and composing tools.

Not all music analysts are as sanguine about modeling as a process for better understanding music. For example, in a reply to Stephen Smoliar's "Modelling Musical Perception: A Critical View" (Smoliar 1999), Peter Desain and Henkjan Honing state:

> Interestingly, even an algorithm that always produces a "correct" output is not good enough: it does not validate the algorithm as a model of the cognitive process itself. If we want to make statements about the architecture of human cognition, we have to relate the architecture of the program to that of the human subject. This is still one of major challenges of the computational modeling of music cognition. (Desain and Honing 1999, 114)

Obviously, I too believe that more than one way to create a particular composition exists, having proven here and elsewhere that both recombinancy and rules can produce precise replications of existing music. Believing in this multiplicity of approaches, however, does not negate the use of modeling as an analytical process for better understanding music. Indeed, I believe that composers compose using a hybrid of many approaches, rather than any single approach, and that identifying only one contributor could significantly diminish musical analysis.

Leonard Meyer comments on the possible differences between computer generations and human genius:

> Why, out of all the possible alternatives that the composer might have devised or considered for use in some work, was this particular one chosen rather than some other? To make the point forcefully and with only slight exaggeration, the difference between a crackpot and a genius is not primarily a matter of fecund invention; both readily devise novel, imaginative, even eccentric, possibilities. Rather the difference lies in the ability of the genius to choose with perspicacity. (Meyer 1989, 135)

The fact that given a set of rules captured from a database of previous compositions, a computer program can, among several outputs, generate the exact set of pitches that a human composer has created does not necessarily mean these outputs represent a credible or all-inclusive analysis of a work. However, such replicative extensions cannot be ignored either. Clearly, the rules discovered, and the choices between various correct possibilities made, bear close resemblance if not a strong overlap with those rules and choices that composers actually use and make. However, even if, as those who criticize the modeling process state, such extensions do not replicate those the composer actually used, they may still shed important light on what transpires in the music—a not inconsequential truth.

MUSICAL EXAMPLES

I occasionally assign advanced music students the completion of works of music just as Extend does. Figure 6.18b–d presents several such student-created extensions based on the Bartók work shown in Figure 6.18a. The students in this case ranged from college juniors and seniors in upper-division music theory courses to first-year graduate composition students. The results here do *not* follow the rules as closely as those produced by the Extend program. None of the student extensions remotely resemble the actual ending of the work. At the same time, most of these student extensions are interesting, certainly creative, and musical, though using such complimentary terms begs many questions.

Completing the opening section of Stravinsky's Three Pieces for String Quartet (1914) using even a program such as Extend that is limited to two rather than four voices is fairly easy given that the program not have to deal with rhythm, meter, dynamics, and so on, as does Alice's analyzing and composing processes. Stravinsky's style—often consisting of different-length cycles of chord repetitions—makes almost all output similar or the same. The final two measures of the movement, while resembling the opening material and mathematically generated from it, cannot, unfortunately, be predicted in the same way as continuing the first few measures can. Although the music later in the movement derives from rhythmic variations of the opening music, new sections contain related but impossible-to-predict material.

PROGRAM DESCRIPTION

The top level of the Extend program—the function `complete-the-composition`—requires three arguments: a list of symbol names representing the note-events for musical works, the Markov order number desired, and the last pitch of channel 1 of the music to be extended. A `scale-type` optional argument that defaults to the chromatic scale follows the required arguments. The function `complete-the-composition` accomplishes two things: it runs `get-rules`, which returns a full set of soon-to-be-described rules, and it runs the `completion` function, which returns one of the many possible extensions of the incomplete music indicated by the `channel-1-last-note` argument to `complete-the-composition`. This function appears below in pseudo-code.

```
(defun complete-the-composition
    (event-list-names markov-order channel-1-last-note
     &optional (scale-type 'chromatic))
  (get-rules event-list-names markov-order scale-type)
  (completion channel-1-last-note markov-order) *new-work*))
```

270 HIDDEN STRUCTURE

FIGURE 6.18 Several student-created extensions (b–d) based on Bartók (a), *Mikrokosmos*, no. 81.

GENERATIVE MODELS OF MUSIC 271

FIGURE 6.18 continued

Rules in the Extend program take the form

((((19 16) -3)) (((16 12) -4)) (((12 16) 4)) . . .

with each rule consisting of a list of the intervals between two consecutive vertical pitches, followed by the interval motion of the top voice. In detail, this means that the rule

(((19 16) -3))

signifies that the first sublisted set of two vertical intervals (assuming first-order Markov) of 19 and 16 (given a chromatic scale in use and indicating a perfect twelfth and a major tenth), and the top voice moves -3 (a minor third downward). Although this rule notation may seem initially awkward, in Lisp terms it characterizes all Extend requires in order to run the compositional modeling process. Figure 6.19 presents this rule in musical notation. In this case, the bottom voice remains stationary to account for the fact that the motion in the voice in channel 1

FIGURE 6.19 The rule (((19 16) -3)) in music notation.

creates the new interval shown. Including the motion of the lower voice would produce unnecessary redundancy.

The extension program that uses these rules, run by the Extend compose function, applies the rule with the channel-1-last-note argument to complete-the-composition described previously to create the next vertical interval. Depending on how much data is provided to the Extend program, many rule choices will exist for composition, as shown below when using the data in the bartok-79, bartok-80, bartok-81, bartok-91, and bartok-92 databases provided with the program:

```
'((((24 24) 1)) (((24 24) 5)) (((24 24) 1)) (((24 24) -7))
(((24 24) 1))
(((24 24) 5)) (((24 24) 1)) (((24 24) -1)) (((24 24) -5))
(((24 24) -1)) (((24 24) 5)) (((24 24) -1)) (((24 24) -1))
(((24 24) -1)) (((24 24) 2)) (((24 24) 1)) (((24 24) 1))
(((24 24) -5)) (((24 24) 6)) (((24 24) -4)) (((24 24) -3))
(((24 24) 2)) (((24 24) 2)) (((24 24) 1)) (((24 24) 1))
(((24 24) -5))
(((24 24) 2)) (((24 24) 1)) (((24 24) -1)) (((24 24) 2))
(((24 24) 1)) (((24 24) -3)) (((24 24) 1)) (((24 24) 3))
(((24 24) -3))
(((24 24) -1)) (((24 24) -3)) (((24 24) 5)) (((24 24) -1))
(((24 24) -1)) (((24 24) -2)) (((24 24) 1)) (((24 24) -1))
(((24 24) 1)) (((24 24) -1)) (((24 24) 1)) (((24 24) -1))
(((24 24) 4))
(((24 24) -3)) (((24 24) -1)) (((24 24) 5))
(((24 24) -5)) (((24 24) -1)))
```

Note the many duplicate rules that appear in this list. However, the program utilizes these duplicates to bias the program's output toward those rules that occur more often—the basis for the probabilities inherent in Markov state transition matrixes discussed earlier in this chapter.

Rules in Extend are stored in the *rules* global variable and can be examined by simply typing *rules* into the Listener window, followed by pressing the return key. Tracing functions when running the program can also be useful. To trace a function, simply use its name as an argument to `trace`, which allows for any number of such arguments. A trace typically looks like this

```
? (trace get-the-multiple-rules)
? (get-the-multiple-rules
            '(bartok-79 bartok-80 bartok-81 bartok-91 bartok-
            92)
            'chromatic)
Calling (get-the-multiple-rules
            (bartok-79 bartok-80 bartok-81 bartok-91 bartok-
            92)
            chromatic)
get-the-multiple-rules returned t
```

with the function and its arguments provided first and then whatever the function returns given last. Tracing lower-level functions while running higher-level functions provides the most effective use of `trace`. Typically, functions that recurse appear only once, to avoid filling listener windows with vast amounts of information and slowing programs significantly. Common Lisp provides ways to trace functions (see Steele 1990) with many or even all of their recursive calls, should this be necessary. Both forward and backward tracing provide useful techniques for debugging code.

Creating programs such as Gradus, Alice, and Extend also requires several approaches to functional computing that have not yet been discussed here. Although this may appear as a slight digression, I present them now so that readers can keep up with the more complicated kinds of code that such programs require. Since Chapter 2 we have used the Common Lisp function `cons` for recursion. However, recursive functions may use any similarly acting function to collect processed data from lists of arbitrary length. For example, the mathematical function + can be used in the following way:

```
(defun add-them-all (numbers-in-a-list)
  (if (null numbers-in-a-list) 0
      (+ (first numbers-in-a-list)
         (add-them-all (rest numbers-in-a-list)))))

? (add-them-all '(1 2 3 4 5 6 7))
```

Note that instead of using nil as a final argument for `if` in line 2 here, this function supplies the number 0, a final addition to the accumulating number.

Interestingly, there are other ways of computing the addition of all of the numbers in a list. For example, the code

```
? (apply #'+ '(1 2 3 4 5 6 7))
```

produces the same result of 28, as did the function `add-them-all`. Note that in this case, the function + appears as an argument to another function—`apply`—requiring the special prefix of #' to declare it so.

The function `apply` also has many other uses. For example, `apply` in the following example has a special effect:

```
? (apply #'append '((1)(2)(3)(4)()()()))
```

resulting in

```
(1 2 3 4)
```

thus reducing one level of sublists from a list of sublists including, in this case, the removal of a series of empty lists as well. So popular is this particular technique that it is often called the `apply-append` trick. However, one should take care not to use this trick too often, for it typically signals the correction of a mistake. After all, programmers should produce output in the right form in the first place, rather than correcting it after the fact. Common Lisp contains many interesting features, and interested readers should again review the sources listed in the bibliography to learn more (see especially Graham 1995; Steele 1990; Touretzky 1990; Wilensky 1986).

CONCLUSIONS

This chapter has explored the potentials of Principle 4—all patterns, scales, and functions in music (see Chapter 5) are best understood by modeling their processes—as discussed in detail in Chapter 1 of this book. With Chapters 2 and 3 concentrating on Principle 1 (all music consists of patterns), Chapter 4 dedicated to Principle 2 (all pitch patterns can be reduced to scales), and Chapter 5 concerned with Principle 3 (all elements of scales have different functions), all four of the principles of this book have been explored in some detail. Chapter 7, then, covers many of the future possibilities of computer music analysis and how they too might relate to these four principles. Unlike previous chapters, Chapter 7, though organized around several central themes, covers diverse ground—areas of mathematics and artificial intelligence, for example. I believe that each individual topic, however, will provide fertile subject matter for important future research in computer music analysis.

SEVEN
A Look to the Future

> The prevailing image of the present intellectual epoch, perhaps soon to be supplanted, is that of the machine, interpreted in its widest sense to subsume formalizations of any kind. The work of Frege, Russell, Gödel, Hilbert, Carnap, and so many others laid the foundations of the current *civitas mentis machinosae*, leading naturally through Church's Thesis and Turing.... To explicate something is, ultimately, to formalize it, that is, to make it into a machine at whose metaphorically whirring and clicking parts we are happy to stare, and be enlightened. As a child of my epoch, this is my belief.
>
> John Rahn, "On Some Computational Models of Music Theory" (1989), 663

In the preceding chapters, I have concentrated on one or two ideas shared between music and computer science, artificial intelligence, or mathematics. This chapter, by contrast, covers a wide range of diverse topics grouped according to general themes or categories. Many readers may thus find this chapter more postulatory than conclusory. However, this book attempts more than the persuasion of a particular view of music analysis; rather, it argues for a coalescence of music analysis with computers in ways that will hopefully unleash the full potentials of both. I offer no apologies for the smattering of approaches to analysis presented in this chapter. In some ways, this smattering may represent one of the more important presentations in this book, providing a diversity of ideas, one or more of which might encourage readers in pursuing their own particular version of the revolutionary new field of computer music analysis.

PRINCIPLES

I begin this chapter with what might seem to some a digression; however, my point will become clear as the chapter proceeds. In 1654 the noted mathematician Blaise Pascal discovered or formulated—depending on your point of view—the now-famous Pascal's triangle. Although earlier manuscripts from Asia present various versions of this mathematical construct, shown in Figure 7.1, Pascal was the first to truly begin to reveal its secrets. This simply stacked set of numbers offsets each

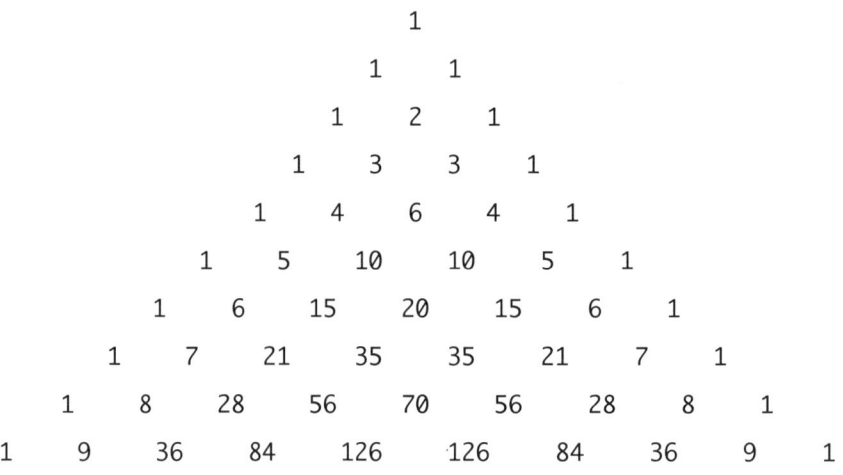

FIGURE 7.1 The top ten levels of Pascal's triangle.

successive line such that the addition of the two numbers to the upper left and upper right of any number add to produce the centered-between-them number below. One must imagine the numbers to the left or right of the outer 1s as virtual 0s. Thus, the second row (two 1s) results from the addition of 0 and 1 and 1 and 0 from the first row. The third row begins similarly, but the middle number is 2, the sum of the upper-left and upper-right 1s from row 2. Following each successive row will make this process evident. The simplicity of the resulting infinitely expanding triangle, however, is deceiving, for this assemblage of numbers hides an enormous concentration of significant mathematical information.

The following collection of observations represents but a small fraction of the various sequences and calculations the triangle contains:

1. The sum of each row results in increasing powers of 2 (i.e., 1, 2, 4, 8, 16, 32, and so on).

2. The 45° diagonals represent various number systems. For example, the first diagonal represents units (1, 1 . . .); the second diagonal, the natural numbers (1, 2, 3, 4 . . .); the third diagonal, the triangular numbers (1, 3, 6, 10 . . .); the fourth diagonal, the tetrahedral numbers (1, 4, 10, 20 . . .); and so on.

3. All row numbers—row numbers begin at 0—whose contents are divisible by that row number are successive prime numbers.

4. The count of odd numbers in any row always equates to a power of 2.

5. The numbers in the shallow diagonals (from 22.5° upper right to lower left) sum to produce the Fibonacci sequence (1, 1, 2, 3, 5, 8, 13 . . .), discussed in Chapter 4.

6. The powers of 11 beginning with 0 produce a compacted Pascal's triangle (e.g., $11^0 = 1$, $11^1 = 11$, $11^2 = 121$, $11^3 = 1331$, $11^4 = 14641$, and so on).

7. Compressing Pascal's triangle using modulo 2 (remainders after successive divisions of 2, leading to binary 0s and 1s) reveals the famous Sierpinski gasket, a fractal-like diagram made up of various-sized triangles, as shown in Figure 7.2, with the 0s (Figure 7.2a) and without the 0s (Figure 7.2b), the latter presented to make the graph clearer.

Therefore, while initial reactions to Pascal's triangle may suggest that it offers very little, when carefully considered, the triangle actually yields an immense amount of valuable information. I believe that many of the musical ideas and processes described in this chapter will prove similarly useful.

MATHEMATICS

Data in the form of numbers, no matter how those numbers are organized or what they might represent, offer potential for analysis using *any* mathematical process. Certainly, when such numbers represent music, they invite more traditional musical analyses. However, like Pascal's triangle, this data may also reveal valuable information when analyzed in ways that apparently have nothing whatsoever to do with music. I will here present several examples of such techniques that, although still experimental, have provided tangible results in my research.

Mathematical formulae represent a powerful way of manipulating numerical data to achieve results virtually impossible using any other method. For example, $c = \pi r^2$ helps us calculate the circumference of a circle by knowing the constant π or 3.14 . . . and the current radius of that circle. The formula $e = mc^2$ relates the square of the speed of light (c) to mass (m) and energy (e) and represents one of the more important mathematical abstractions of the twentieth century. Most formulae such as these derive from observations of data that then lead mathematicians to formulate symbolic representations and reductions of these observations. Music can often be described using similar formulae. For example, the circle of fifths can be represented mathematically by the formula $f_x = \mod_{(12)} (x + 7)$, an example of Principle 1, and all of the equal-tempered scales within a given octave can be derived from binary representations from 1 to 2^{11} (see Chapter 4 and Principle 2). Composers (e.g., see Morris 1987; Xenakis 1971) have generated music from mathematical sources that should in turn encourage analysts to analyze the music of these composers using these same processes. Analysts (e.g., Rahn 1980; Benson 2006) have also proposed mathematical procedures for analyzing post-tonal music. Guerino Mazzola (2002), in his book *The Topos of Music*, attempts to describe music purely in terms of mathematical, physical, and psychological terms.

When Milton Babbitt (1961), Allen Forte (1973), and others began using mathematical set theory (see Chapter 3) to analyze post-tonal music (Principle 1), many

a.
1
11
101
1111
10001
110011
1010101
11111111
100000001
1100000011
10100000101
111100001111
1000100010001
11001100110011
101010101010101
1111111111111111
10000000000000001
110000000000000011
1010000000000000101
11110000000000001111
100010000000000010001
1100110000000000110011
10101010000000001010101
111111110000000011111111
1000000010000000100000001
11000000110000001100000011
101000001010000010100000101
1111000011110000111100001111
10001000100010001000100010001
110011001100110011001100110011
1010101010101010101010101010101
11111111111111111111111111111111
100000000000000000000000000000001
1100000000000000000000000000000011
10100000000000000000000000000000101
111100000000000000000000000000001111
1000100000000000000000000000000010001
11001100000000000000000000000000110011
101010100000000000000000000000001010101
1111111100000000000000000000000011111111
10000000100000000000000000000000100000001
110000001100000000000000000000001100000011
1010000010100000000000000000000010100000101
11110000111100000000000000000000111100001111
100010001000100000000000000000001000100010001
1100110011001100000000000000000011001100110011
10101010101010100000000000000000101010101010101
111111111111111100000000000000001111111111111111
1000000000000000100000000000000010000000000000001
11000000000000001100000000000000110000000000000011
101000000000000010100000000000001010000000000000101
1111000000000000111100000000000011110000000000001111
10001000000000001000100000000000100010000000000010001
110011000000000011001100000000001100110000000000110011
1010101000000000101010100000000010101010000000001010101
11111111000000001111111100000000111111110000000011111111
100000001000000010000000100000001000000010000000100000001
1100000011000000110000001100000011000000110000001100000011
10100000101000001010000010100000101000001010000010100000101
111100001111000011110000111100001111000011110000111100001111

FIGURE 7.2 Pascal's triangle shown stacked to the left and modulo 2 with the zeros identifying the Sierpinski gasket (a), and zeros removed (b) to make the graphic more readable.

b.
```
1
11
1 1
1111
1   1
11  11
1 1 1 1
11111111
1       1
11      11
1 1     1 1
1111    1111
1  1    1  1
11 11   11 11
1 1 1 1 1 1 1 1
1111111111111111
1               1
11              11
1 1             1 1
1111            1111
1  1            1  1
11 11           11 11
1 1 1 1         1 1 1 1
11111111        11111111
1       1       1       1
11      11      11      11
1 1     1 1     1 1     1 1
1111    1111    1111    1111
1  1    1  1    1  1    1  1
11 11   11 11   11 11   11 11
1 1 1 1 1 1 1 1 1 1 1 1 1 1 1 1
11111111111111111111111111111111
1                               1
11                              11
1 1                             1 1
1111                            1111
1  1                            1  1
11 11                           11 11
1 1 1 1                         1 1 1 1
11111111                        11111111
1       1                       1       1
11      11                      11      11
1 1     1 1                     1 1     1 1
1111    1111                    1111    1111
1  1    1  1                    1  1    1  1
11 11   11 11                   11 11   11 11
1 1 1 1 1 1 1 1                 1 1 1 1 1 1 1 1
1111111111111111                1111111111111111
1               1               1               1
11              11              11              11
1 1             1 1             1 1             1 1
1111            1111            1111            1111
1  1            1  1            1  1            1  1
11 11           11 11           11 11           11 11
1 1 1 1         1 1 1 1         1 1 1 1         1 1 1 1
11111111        11111111        11111111        11111111
1       1       1       1       1       1       1       1
11      11      11      11      11      11      11      11
1 1     1 1     1 1     1 1     1 1     1 1     1 1     1 1
1111    1111    1111    1111    1111    1111    1111    1111
```

FIGURE 7.2 continued

analysts found their work controversial or even inappropriate. Today, however, almost every college music theory program in the United States uses set theory in the study of contemporary music. Most of today's analysts find set theory indispensable for deciphering the post-tonal music they study. Interestingly, set theory represents only one of the numerous subfields of discrete mathematics, many of which could be put to similar use in music. The following partial list of discrete mathematical categories seem particularly apt for analyzing music:

> *Cryptography*—the mathematical study of information transmission (Principle 1)
>
> *Complexity theory*—the study of input size as it relates to computer time and memory requirements (Principle 1)
>
> *Combinatorics*—the study of the possible orderings of finite collections of numbers (Principles 1 and 2)
>
> *Game theory*—a formal modeling approach to maximize results in game playing (Principle 4)
>
> *Graph theory*—the study of mathematical structures used to model relations between points in graphs (Principles 3 and 4)
>
> *Probability theory*—the study of probability (Principle 4)
>
> *Logic*—the study of formal systems relating to inference (Principle 4)
>
> *Number theory*—the study of numbers in general and integers in particular (Principles 1–4)

As mentioned earlier in this book, musical analysis itself represents a kind of cryptography. Complexity theory has already been discussed to a degree in this book (see Chapters 2 and 6). I have found that combinatorics (notably in relation to my work with recombinant music under the rubric of Experiments in Musical Intelligence) and graph theory particularly relevant to music. Combinatorics calculate the number of ways of logically combining sets of numbers or objects. At the smallest level, all composers use combinatorics by combining pitches in various ways; it is the fundamental principle behind all musical composition. However, the methods composers use to combine motives, phrases, sections, and so on also contribute to composition and, as such, deserve study in much the same way that musical sets do.

Game theory and music have a closer relationship than one might imagine. For example, highly formalistic music provides interesting correlations with board games, offering, as they both do, obedience to rules as well as a certain freedom of choice. Graph theory calculates the ways in which objects of any type relate or connect to one another. Such connections could certainly include the time-linear connections between adjacent musical ideas, the nonlinear connections when ideas are separated by significant time spans (the analysis of musical form), and so on. Although I have not gone very deeply into these last-mentioned subjects here, the various sub-disciplines of discrete mathematics offer many uses for the analysis of music in any style, with computers making these potentials more feasible.

Probability theory (see Hiller and Isaacson 1959) has already been discussed to some degree in this book in Chapter 6. Logic supports set theory and many other discrete mathematical processes by proving logical propositions given certain facts. Number theory represents a broad range of discrete properties of numbers and number patterns and thus possesses significant potential for music, as revealed later in this section.

Thus, music expressed as numbers represents an extraordinary opportunity for music analysts. Even with a small amount of data, one can produce almost endless discoveries. Many of these may seem more recreational than analytical, but they nonetheless can produce intriguing results. For example, the square root of the number 12,321 is 111; the square root of 1,234,321 is 1111; and so on. The center number of the palindrome represents the number of 1s in the square root. Another simple puzzle involves multiplying any number by 9 and then adding the single digits of the resulting number together until a single digit is reached. This process always produces 9, as in $9 \times 127 = 1143 = 9$, and so on.

Magic squares also belong in the arena of number theory. Magic squares consist of matrices in which each square contains a unique member of an incremental sequence beginning with 1 and ending with the number representing the number of squares in the matrix. Once completed correctly, each horizontal and vertical rank or column of a magic square adds to the same number. Figure 7.3 presents a simple five-by-five magic square in which all horizontal rows and vertical columns sum to 65 (even the diagonals in this particular magic square sum to 65). There are several ways to create magic squares. For example, beginning by placing the number 1 anywhere in the otherwise empty matrix and placing incrementally advancing numbers upward diagonally produces the desired result. When an occupied square is reached, choosing the square directly below the current square for the next number allows the numbers to continue. When moving off the matrix, treating the matrix as a torus by inserting the number in the square at the side opposite where it would normally go extends the process. The magic square in Figure 7.3 results from Chess-knight moves.

One way to use magic squares musically involves utilizing nonsymmetrical geometries while maintaining the principles so important to the magic square's definition. For example, in a two-by-six matrix such as

```
e 9 7 t 6 8
0 2 4 1 5 3
```

both rows add to 6 horizontally (the result of adding the digits of 51 and 15 together) and all six columns add to 11 vertically. Of course, the second horizontal row represents a mirror inversion of the top horizontal row, and such mirror inversions always produce equivalent additions such as this. Although not a magic square per se, this combination of numbers nonetheless fulfills many of the requirements of equivalent additions while having a semblance of musical meaning.

Anton Webern's Concerto for Nine Instruments (op. 24; see Figure 3.23) provides a more interesting example of a magic rectangle. Viewing the opening four trichords in terms of pitch range covered (left to right) and pitch class (top to bottom) produces interesting results.

```
B    B♭   D    =  13
E♭   G    F♯   =  13
G♯   E    F    =  13
C    C♯   A    =  13
e    t    2
3    7    6
8    4    5
0    1    9
─────────────
22   22   22
```

Webern follows this opening row statement using a similar process:

```
D    B♭   B    =  13
F♯   F    E♭   =  13
F    E    G♯   =  13
A    C♯   C    =  13
2    t    e
6    7    3
5    4    8
9    1    0
─────────────
22   22   22
```

This is the retrograde of the original. Ensuing trichords no longer follow this process. Granted that Webern's use of the original, inversion, retrograde, and retrograde inversion of these trichords tends to produce these kinds of relationships, the correlations between the two sets of matching additions presents a quite convincing case for Webern's conscious or subconscious application of such number-theory concepts to his musical thought processes. This work—and most others of Webern's mature style—also presents an example of music with very low information content (see Chapter 2).

One could argue, of course, that this example represents but one isolated instance of such a combinatorial magic-square occurrence. However, if we assume this as fact, a musical magic rectangle would be an even more important notion, clearly distinguishing this Webern work from the many others he composed using similar serial techniques.

11	24	7	20	3
17	5	13	21	9
23	6	19	2	15
4	12	25	8	16
10	18	1	14	22

FIGURE 7.3 A simple 5 × 5 magic square in which all horizontal ranks and vertical columns sum to 65.

Webern clearly favored particular formalisms that resemble magic squares. His favorite was:

```
S  A  T  O  R
A  R  E  P  O
T  E  N  E  T
O  P  E  R  A
R  O  T  A  S
```

The Latin here translates as "The sower Arepo holds the wheels with effort" (see Bailey 1991, 21) and indicates Webern's love for symmetry. This love is further demonstrated musically in his use of combinatorial twelve-tone rows and integral serialism of dynamics, rhythm, articulations, and tempos. However, whether or not composers used such techniques in their compositions, if such patterned structures exist in their music, analysts should attempt to find and evaluate them. Computers can make discovering these pattern contributions in music much easier.

There are many other ways to incorporate magic squares in music analysis. For example, Figure 7.4 presents a magic square containing intervals that sum to 5 in both top-to-bottom and left-to-right directions. Note that the numbers here represent intervals and not interval classes, hence the negative numbers indicating downward motion. I have used this particular magic square in several of my compositions, assigning the horizontal and vertical combinations to six-pitch motives. The resultant melodic line(s) obviously share the same tessitura—the perfect fourth—but because each motive retains its own distinct interval content, each

FIGURE 7.4 A magic square containing intervals that equate (when added together) to 5 in top-to-bottom and left-to-right directions, along with musical examples.

melodic line maintains its own separate identity. Interestingly, the number of rows and columns—including the diagonals—totals 12, and thus the entire collection can be used as a row offering the same prime, retrograde, inversion, and retrograde-inversion possibilities that any twelve-tone matrix normally would.

The music in Figure 7.5 from the second movement of my Concerto for Violoncello and Orchestra realizes the intervals appearing in the magic square shown in Figure 7.4 as top-down horizontal continuities. Readers can follow the perfect-fourth ambitus combined motion of each set, moving as they do every five intervals from C to F, from F to A-sharp (B-flat), from A-sharp to E-flat, from E-flat to A-flat, and finally from A-flat to C-sharp (D-flat). These combinations provide a level of cohesion to this passage that it might otherwise lack.

Figure 7.6 presents a magic cube with both incremental numbers and music intervals (with directions). Magic cubes require that the additions in each magic square and each vertical column of successive layers of magic squares match, so that straight lines in all three dimensions sum to the same single-digit number.

Entrepreneurs of magic squares have also created magic circles, spheres, and all manner of other symmetrical and asymmetrical matrices, producing some of the most beautiful and curious designs in the world of mathematics (Pickover 2002).

The Fibonacci sequence (0, 1, 1, 2, 3, 5, 8, 13 . . .) discussed in Chapter 4, in which each new number in the sequence results from the addition of the two previous numbers, has provided a model for many composers, most notably Debussy and Bartók (see Madden 2006). Dividing any number in the sequence by its predecessor converges on a special number called the golden mean or golden section (roughly 1.61803399 . . .), which has been used by painters, architects, and others as a benchmark for structure. A good example of the golden mean used in music appears in a formal analysis of the first eighty-nine measures of Bartók's *Music for Strings, Percussion and Celeste*. Here, the two primary divisions separate into groupings of fifty-five and thirty-four measures, respectively (Lendvai 1983, 74). The first fifty-five-measure grouping then contains two sub-sections of thirty-four and twenty-one measures, with the first of these subsections further dividing into two sections of twenty-one and thirteen measures. Even the second main section divides into two groups of thirteen and twenty-one measures, numbers that represent contiguous members of the Fibonacci sequence. Figure 7.7 presents all of these subdivisions.

I often use two variants of the Fibonacci sequence in my own compositions. These variants are formed by carrying Fibonacci's principle one step further by adding numbers further back in the sequence. For example, the sequence (0, 1, 2, 2, 3, 5, 7, 10, 15, 22, 32 . . . , seeded with 0, 1, 2) results from adding the second number previous to a current number and the current number to create a following number. This sequence converges approximately on the number 1.47—what I call the silver mean. The sequence (0, 1, 2, 3, 3, 4, 6, 9, 12, 16, 22, 31, 43, 59 . . . , seeded with 0, 1, 2, 3) results from adding the third number previous to a current number and the current number to create the following number and roughly converges on the number 1.38—what I call the bronze mean.

286 HIDDEN STRUCTURE

FIGURE 7.5 The author, Concerto for Cello and Orchestra, 2nd movement (excerpt).

1

-2	0	7	9	-9
11	-7	-5	2	4
-1	6	13	-10	-3
-8	-6	1	8	10
5	12	-11	-4	3

2

-8	-6	1	8	10
5	12	-11	-4	3
-2	0	7	9	-9
11	-7	-5	2	4
-1	6	13	-10	-3

3

11	-7	-5	2	4
-1	6	13	-10	-3
-8	-6	1	8	10
5	12	-11	-4	3
-2	0	7	9	-9

4

5	12	-11	-4	3
-2	0	7	9	-9
11	-7	-5	2	4
-1	6	13	-10	-3
-8	-6	1	8	10

5

-1	6	13	-10	-3
-8	-6	1	8	10
5	12	-11	-4	3
-2	0	7	9	-9
11	-7	-5	2	4

FIGURE 7.6 A magic cube with both incremental numbers and music intervals (with directions).

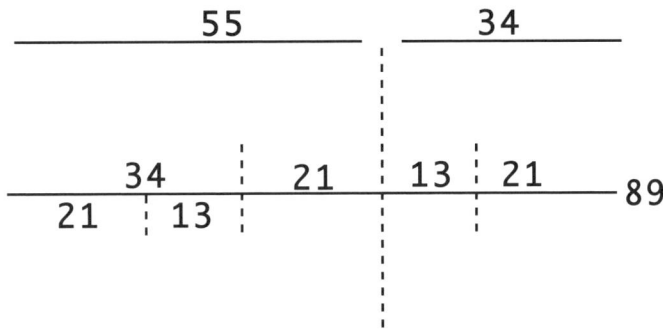

FIGURE 7.7 A formal analysis of the first 89 measures of Bartók, Music for Strings, Percussion and Celeste (Lendvai 1983, p. 74), based on the golden mean and the Fibonacci series.

Inverting the process of division (i.e., dividing the previous number by the following number) produces approximately 0.62 (Fibonacci), 0.68 (silver), and 0.73 (bronze), with these latter successively larger numbers often representing both phrase-length relationships and points of arrival in my music. I use particularly the silver mean to gauge tension relationships within phrases (i.e., the grouping having the most tension is placed at approximately 0.68 percent of the length of the phrase).

Another way to make such sequences musically viable is to apply modulo 12 (see Chapter 3) to each number in the sequence to create pitch classes. The resulting scales can then be compared with scales from actual music. As an example, the Fibonacci sequence limited to numbers below fifty produces the sequence [0,1,2,3,5,8,9,t]. Interestingly, when a modulo 12 scale is derived from a very large sequence, it often includes all pitch classes but pitch class 6. However, the silver variation, with very large sequences, produces the scale [0,1,2,3,4,5,6,7,9]. Interestingly, the measures shown in Figure 7.8, the first fourteen measures of Varèse's *Density 21.5*, produce the same prime-form pitch-class set as the silver variation, with but one non-scale tone present.

General systems theory assumes that a system—defined as any analytic method that operates on data in a continuous unfolding of syntactic relationships—represents a dynamic collection of cooperating and collaborating parts. Hiller and Levy note that

> an analytic method here will be thought of as a system which describes an operational process. That is, it will describe how something was operated on to produce something. In other words, analysis is itself a system which is used to describe some other system. (Hiller and Levy 1984, 297)

and

> because a musical system is a process with changes of state constantly taking place, it is also an aggregate of energy states resulting from the application of

FIGURE 7.8 The first 14 measures of Varèse, *Density 21.5*, with much the same pitch classes as the silver variation.

some given class of syntactic decisions to some given class of information in order to effect a change in another system—the listener. (Hiller and Levy 1984, 297)

In effect, general systems theory covers dynamically changing behavior that affects a current state of data. An advocate of general systems theory might argue that what currently passes for music analysis represents just another method of describing the superficial aspects of music and is little better than another type of music notation. This same individual then might argue that general systems theory attempts to discover the principles that make music itself a system. General systems theory would consider music not a static score, but an active process that unfolds over time, with its various parts acting and interacting in dynamic ways. Thus, what may be an accurate representation of musical analysis at one point during a musical composition can change as future events occur; a single point in time would then have many different interpretations depending on the unfolding of the musical events that surround it.

The completion concept presented in Chapter 6 of this book could provide a very simple verification process of a general systems theory analysis to a given point in a work. For example, if an extension of a phrase—an extension created by using rules based on the current analysis—proved close enough to the actual music the composer chose, it would help confirm the accuracy of the previous analysis. If such an extension proved off course, then a different approach would be required, one using different groupings, sets, scales, and so on. With each verification point and its previous analysis saved and subsequently reviewed, this process could provide a useful narrative of the way in which analyses of music change in the minds of audiences, analysts, theorists, and even composers during composition.

General systems theory would seem a perfect match for computer music analysis, though no one has yet successfully produced any significant analytical work using its processes. Aaron Copland remarks that "a composition is, after all, an organism. It is a living, not a static, thing. That is why it is capable of being seen in a different light and from different angles by various interpreters or even by the same interpreter at different times" (Copland 1957, 269).

Other mathematical processes such as fractals have proven relevant to certain types of musical analyses, particularly musical form (see particularly Madden 1999 and 2006). Fractals are self-imitating patterns occurring on different scales or dimensions. A work that begins, for example, with the pitches A–B–A and then uses that template for beginning each phrase of that work, each section of that work, and so on would present a good example of fractals used hierarchically. Several movements of Tom Johnson's *Formulas for String Quartet* (1994) are explicitly fractal in origin, and the composer writes eloquently of these origins in the program notes to this work.

Fuzzy logic offers analysts the ability to solve problems that have several variables. For example, chromatic note spelling, modulation, key identification, set relations, and so on all share the complexities created by numerous competing criteria. Discovering best groupings in post-tonal music poses incredibly difficult problems that fuzzy logic can often resolve. Fuzzy logic accepts such interactive variables and derives results compatible with each (see Cope 2005, chapter 3, for more information and examples).

One could continue the list of possible mathematical processes with subjects such as chaos theory, cellular automata, and genetic algorithms, the list being limited only by one's imagination. Any mathematical technique—whether designed for music analysis or not—can potentially produce useful and insightful results (again, see Cope 2001, chapter 3), and offer music analysts a rich arsenal of techniques with which to analyze music. Most of these processes were available previous to the advent of computers, but were seldom used owing to the exhaustive amount of time required to implement them. Computers now make the application of these techniques possible in a fraction of the time paper and pencil required. Thus, mathematics may now be used in as many ways as are conceivable, regardless of their apparent relevancy or irrelevancy to music.

ARTIFICIAL INTELLIGENCE

Like mathematics, artificial intelligence offers numerous processes that can potentially advantage those music analysts willing to take the risks necessary to study and use these processes. Neural networks, for example, offer music analysts a variety of ways in which to study music. The term *neural* in "neural network" derives from *neuron*, the primary functional unit of the central nervous system, including the brain. Neural networks receive input that triggers neuron substitutes called *hidden units*, hidden because their values do not reveal much about their contributions to the neural network's resultant output. Hidden units trigger initially random results. Neural networks then cycle through a series of forward feeds and/or back propagations (reversed-direction flow) that alter hidden unit values until the output matches or approximates the desired result. This training process involves presenting the network with a series of examples of problems and sample solutions for these problems. Figure 7.9 shows a simple model of a neural network. The number of forward feeds and/or back propagations necessary for neural networks to produce appropriate output values based on training varies depending on the complexity of the data involved and the type of network used. Many different types of neural networks exist. However, hundreds and often thousands of forward feeds and/or back propagations are typically required for successful output to be achieved.

Neural networks typically consist of many input and output nodes. As Dolson puts it,

> A neural network is basically an interconnected set of simple computational elements, each of which is typically functionally identical. Each element or unit receives inputs from other units and produces a single output, which is some simple function of its inputs. The similarity of this structure to that of a biological neuron has led some authors to prefer the terms "neuron" to that of "unit." (Dolson 1991, 4)

Each of these neurons or units then has

> a precise rule for determining the output of a unit: add together all of the weighted inputs and let the output be some nonlinear function of the resulting sum. To state the rule mathematically, we can let each of the N units in the network be identified with a unique number between 1 and N. The output x, of the ith unit in the network is given by
>
> $$x_i = f\left(\sum_{j=1}^{N} w_{ij} x_j\right)$$
>
> where
>
> $$w_{ij}$$
>
> is the weight from the jth unit to the ith, and f is some nonlinear function. (Dolson 1991, 4)

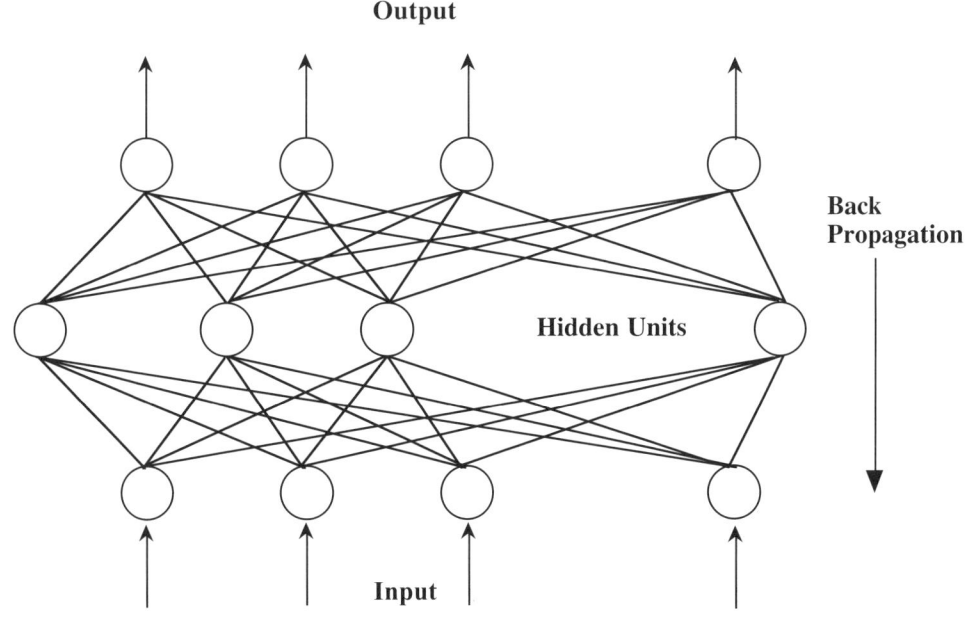

FIGURE 7.9 A simple model of a neural network.

Variable numbers of hidden units in a neural network have variable numbers of connections between inputs and outputs making the training process somewhat flexible in design, but usually inflexibly hardwired in both their hardware and software incarnations. Successful output relies on such neural network design. Once "taught," a neural network can efficiently solve new problems of the same general type on which the neural network was trained.

Robert Gjerdingen notes that neural networks

> offer elegant ways of dealing with multidimensional complexity of the type found in polyphonic, harmonically oriented music. One can, for example, define a musical event as an input pattern of activation that is then transformed by a network of interconnected processing units into an output pattern of activation representing an interpretation of the event. (Gjerdingen 1991, 138)

Many music analysts have used neural networks (Loy and Todd 1991) with varying degrees of success. Data representation and input can pose very difficult problems, especially for highly contrapuntal music. Nonetheless, neural networks continue to offer extraordinary potential for music analysis.

Association networks resemble neural networks in some respects (see Cope 2005, chapters 9–10). However, although neural networks compare output to input values through interconnected "hidden" units, association networks do not make such comparisons, nor do they have hidden units. The nodes in association networks can be accessed at any time, usefully revealing their weights for comparison to the weights of other nodes. Although neural networks generally have fixed numbers of nodes and connections, association networks can have virtually limitless numbers of interconnectable nodes, constrained only by their implementations. Although neural networks typically chain backward—back propagation—association networks chain omnidirectionally.

Association networks can *learn* through a process not dissimilar to the Gradus program (see Chapter 6; Cope 2005, chapter 5), though association networks use very different mechanisms. Where Gradus utilizes a straightforward analysis algorithm to create rules saved in variables that decrease mistakes, association networks invoke weighting shifts that slowly direct the program toward a particular goal. The effect, however, is roughly the same—learning. Association networks also offer opportunities for the integration of other important processes without the need to write new programs or append other software. The natural negation and reinforcement approaches allowed by association networks further develop meaningful links to inference and analogy (Cope 2005, chapter 5). Figure 7.10 presents a very simple example of an association network. The circular nodes in this figure may represent music or language, with output consisting of one or the other depending on the current input type.

Association networks offer many opportunities for music analysis. In fact, the creative processes by which association networks produce output *depends* on musical analysis. Because I discuss such analysis at great length in Cope 2005 (particularly chapters 10 and 11), I will not repeat myself here, but merely point readers toward this source. However, note that one of the features of data-driven programs is that they always require some kind of analysis in order to operate. Thus, Experiments in Musical Intelligence, Sara, Gradus, and Alice all have extensive analytic components capable of producing (hopefully) interesting new music.

Genetic algorithms (GAs) represent another type of artificial intelligence process with analytical capabilities. Genetic algorithms consist of virtual organisms that evolve by procreating, sharing parental attributes (called *crossover*) in offspring and responding to random mutations that affect the data and functions of these offspring. Genetic algorithms develop generationally in order to adapt over several generations to achieve particular goals, tested *en route* by certain fitness criteria described by the GA user. Genetic algorithms have proven very effective at pattern recognition and have been successfully used in various industrial systems to analyze problems and propose solutions to those problems. A number of composers have experimented with GAs to compose (see particularly Miranda 2001), but, unfortunately, very little as of yet has been accomplished using GAs for music analysis.

Cellular automata (CAs) represent a subcategory of genetic algorithms. However, CAs differ from genetic algorithms in that they do not have internal code. In one sense, CAs represent a kind of visual counterpart to genetic algorithms. John Conway's Game of Life (1970), for example, a very popular form of cellular automata

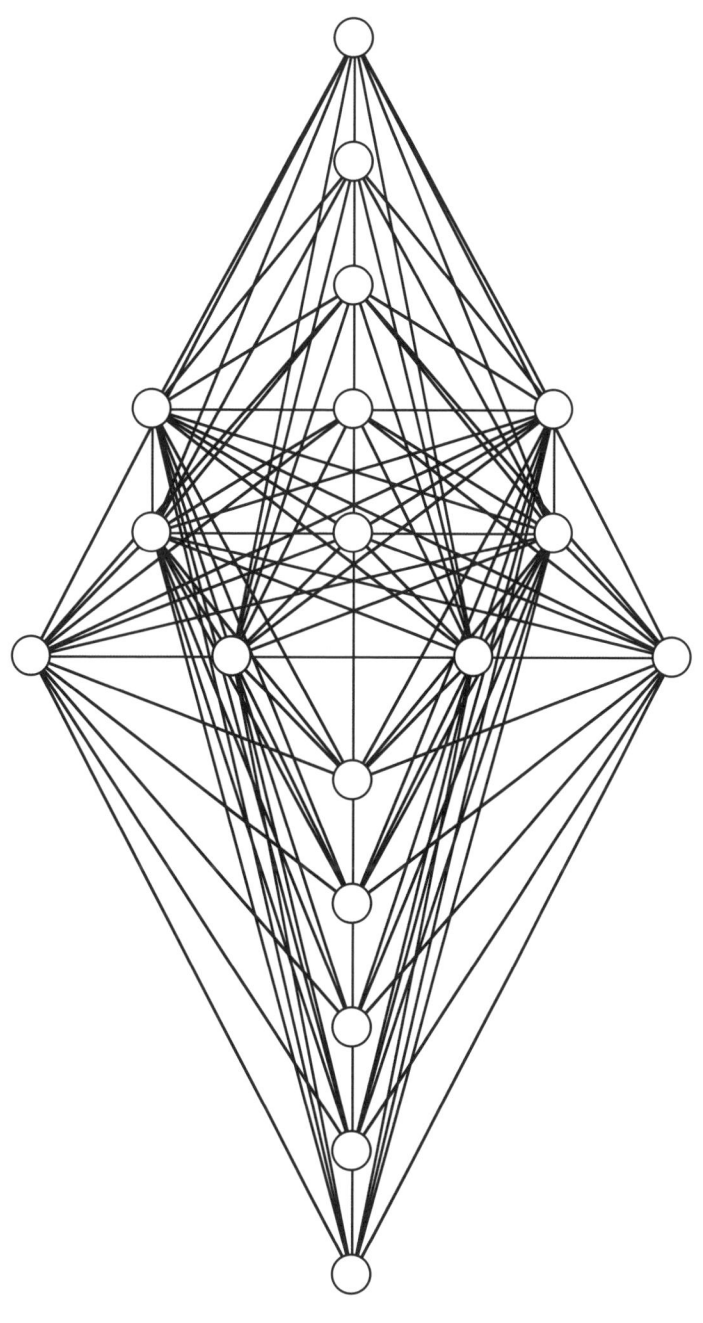

FIGURE 7.10 A simple example of an association network.

found at numerous Internet sites, has user-established initial states with cells controlled by the current states of adjacent cells. Pascal's triangle, presented in Figure 7.1, represents a kind of CA, with previous states added together to create new states.

Agents represent another category of artificial intelligence techniques that may prove useful for musical analysis. Agents are software objects (OOP; see Chapter 5) programmed to have internal structure—code in terms of both functions and data—that recognize and react to other agents as well as elements in their environment. Typically, agents do not procreate (like genetic algorithms) or share data or functions. Unlike cellular automata, which do not have internal functions or data, agents can adapt to their surroundings, collaborate, and even produce social structures. Agents and multi-agents—agents of different types coexisting in the same environment—have useful analytical abilities (Reis 1999). Depending on their internal structure, agents can locate patterns or processes that otherwise may go undetected. Composers and music analysts have just begun to explore the possibilities that agents and multi-agents offer (again, see Reis 1999).

John Holland uses agents in what he calls "complex adaptive systems" to describe a phenomenon known as *emergence*. Complex adaptive systems begin as agents that have the ability to adapt and achieve goals beyond the sum of their individual parts. As Holland describes it:

> The human immune system is a community made up of large numbers of highly mobile units called *antibodies* that continually repel or destroy an ever-changing cast of invaders called *antigens*. The invaders—primarily biochemicals, bacteria, and viruses—come in endless varieties, as different from one another as snowflakes. Because of this variety, and because new invaders are always appearing, the immune system cannot simply list all possible invaders. It must change or adapt its antibodies to new invaders as they appear, never settling to a fixed configuration. Despite its nature, the immune system maintains an impressive coherence. Indeed, your immune system is coherent enough to provide a satisfactory scientific definition of your *identity*. It is so good at distinguishing you from the rest of the world that it will reject cells from any other human. As a result, a skin graft even from a sibling requires extraordinary measures. (Holland 1995, 2)

No current complex adaptive system yet exists for musical analysis. However, one can imagine such a system developing extraordinary new ways to analyze music. Interestingly, the Emily Howell program (described in detail in Cope 2005) represents a complex adaptive system capable of generating what I feel is *creative* behavior; it has produced several works that demonstrate the emergent properties described by Holland. Emily Howell is an association network that accepts both words and music as input and analyzes both in order to produce new output. Unfortunately, aside from the complex community of weightings associated with all input and output, actual analysis in Emily Howell is relatively difficult to observe, so complex is the process necessary to actually produce new output. Developing more transparent methods to clarify these processes may help make both complex adaptive systems and association networks more adaptable to computer music analysis.

Studying emergence can further inform analysts about the origins of certain phenomena that may in turn reveal important information about their constitution.

> We are everywhere confronted with emergence in complex adaptive systems—ant colonies, networks of neurons, the immune system, the Internet, and the global economy, to name a few—where the behavior of the whole is much more complex than the behavior of the parts. (Holland 1998, 2)

Describing a kind of emergent phenomena, Douglas Hofstadter comments on how the human brain consists primarily of unintelligent neurons, and yet intelligence still emerges:

> Here we come back to the mysterious collective behavior of ant colonies, which can build huge and intricate nests, despite the fact that the roughly 100,000 neurons of an ant brain almost certainly do not carry any information about nest structure. How, then, does the nest get created? Where does the information reside? . . . Somehow, it must be spread about in the colony, in the caste distribution, the age distribution—and probably largely in the physical properties of the ant-body itself. That is, the interaction between ants is determined just as much by their six-leggedness and their size and so on, as by the information stored in their brain. (Hofstadter 1979, 359)

Complex adaptive systems and emergence should provide an enormously important resource for music analysis in the future. One might imagine that such processes might even explain music's ineffability and help us to actually describe the indescribable.

MUSE

The computer program Muse that accompanies this book on CD-ROM includes aspects of every program thus far described in this book, as well as several ideas presented thus far in this chapter. However, before detailing how Muse operates, I will present a short description of semiotics, alluded to but not mentioned explicitly to this point. Semiotics, particularly musical semiotics, offers several analytical principles that I find enormously useful when using computers to analyze post-tonal music.

Semiotics, a term coined by philosopher Charles Sanders Peirce, is the scientific study of signs and symbols, particularly with reference to the physical world or the world of ideas. Peirce began his study of semiotics in the 1860s, but it was not until the turn of the century and thereafter that he began to clearly separate the roles of the sign, its object, and its interpretant, the three dimensions that I will describe in more detail shortly. In music, semiotics has revealed that certain gestures in music, particularly of the classical period in Western music history, can be traced to previous sources and their composers (Agawu 1991; Gjerdingen 1988). Often such semiosis takes the form of quotation or allusion, as discussed in Chapter 5. These patterns, like musical signatures, typically integrate seamlessly into their immediate environment and take on both syntactic and semantic value (see Cope 1996). They often hold little interest in themselves, but great interest for what they tell us about what the music being studied might mean, or, at the least, where it originated.

Musical semiotics also poses many important criteria for the analysis and understanding of music (Camilleri 1987; Eco 1976; Karbusicky 1979; Tarasti 1994), not the least of which is its separation of music into three distinct categories:

Poietic dimension—reverse engineering a work, from the creator's point of view

Neutral dimension—systematic analysis from an explicitly stated, abstract point of view

Esthesic dimension—analysis from the perceiver's point of view.

It is the second of these dimensions that I find particularly important, at least for the Muse software, which I will describe shortly. The neutral dimension of musical semiotics suggests a ruthless analysis of music, achieved by breaking it into variously sized groupings and analyzing these groupings in as many ways as possible, regardless of their promise of success. Jean-Jacques Nattiez describes this neutral level:

> It should suffice to remember that a neutral level is a descriptive level containing the most exhaustive inventory possible of all types of configurations conceivably recognisable in a score. The level is neutral because its object is to show neither the processes of production by which the work unfolds (poietics) not the processes of perception (esthetics) to which it gives rise. In this sense it provisionally *neutralises* the poietic and esthesic dimensions of the piece. (Nattiez 1982, 244–245)

Dunsby (1982) adds that

> in his [Nattiez's] studies both of *Syrinx* and *Density 21.5* he developed relatively fleshless forms of enquiry, not only seeking to express the most neutral kinds of articulatory picture of a piece of music, but also investigating the uses of a descriptive, distributional account of musical information. In contrast to the ascetic in semiotic analysis, the "replete" is to be found everywhere, appropriately enough, and the more replete it is, the more it threatens the possibility of a methodological practice. (Dunsby 1982, 236)

Nattiez's article "Varése's 'Density 21.5' " (Nattiez 1982), referred to above, represents an excellent example of how one might segment a work into groupings by partitioning it into consistent but arbitrary-length segments and analyzing the music in however many ways possible, regardless of how appropriate the approach might seem to either music in general or the work under study. Nattiez's analysis demonstrates not only the validity of this approach, but also the obvious need for computational means to assist in maintaining an accurate and relatively unbiased approach. As Nattiez remarks, "What is appropriate to the neutral level is to make an inventory of all analytical possibilities" (Nattiez 1982, 364).

Tarasti (1994) adds that

> the structuralist method is characterized by study of the smallest significant units of a sign system. Especially during the first phase of musical semiotics, in the 1960s, semiotics was dominated by structuralism and the direct borrowing of linguistic methods. It was thought that in music also one might distinguish the units of the first articulation (meaningful items, musical "words") and the second articulation (musical "phonemes," meaningless items). Through a sort of *ars combinatoria*, musical semioticians tried to build units of signification from these small atoms. (Tarasti 1994, 5)

A computer program that can analyze musical data from as many arbitrary points of view as possible would be enormously valuable, even if it only confirmed what we already know. Such a program would, of course, be even more valuable if it could produce insights that its users had not even previously considered. I will now describe such a program, limited only by the data in its database.

The Muse program attempts to analyze post-tonal music as thoroughly as is conceivable. Understanding how Muse accomplishes this thoroughness requires a brief but important discussion of grouping processes. No matter how many different ways a program might analyze post-tonal music, these analyses will remain suspect if the manners in which musical groupings are collected have not been carefully sorted out.

Grouping music into logical collections of harmonic, melodic, and/or combinations of harmonic and melodic pitches poses one of the more difficult computational problems encountered thus far in this book. Although humans can visually and aurally separate seemingly appropriate collections of pitches into various-sized sets with little difficulty, computer programs—unless they are provided very strict constraints—cannot themselves determine a logical from an illogical grouping. To avoid such problems, the program I will soon describe here collects *all* combinations possible, leaving it to users to decide which analysis seem most logical. Interestingly, this brute-force approach has its advantages in that human analysts can for various reasons overlook groupings that may ultimately provide the best material for analysis. Therefore, regardless of the potential overkill in combinatorially collecting all possible groupings of pitches, the approach I present here is thorough, analyzing every group thus collected.

The Muse grouping process incorporates combinations of both harmonic and melodic collection. The grouping process follows a simple guideline: pitches must be contiguous. Figure 7.11 presents an example of this grouping process. Grouping for our purposes here is limited to trichords only to conserve space, and the music contains but two beats of three whole-note voices each. Note that each added beat will exponentially expand the number of possible groupings. The grouping process

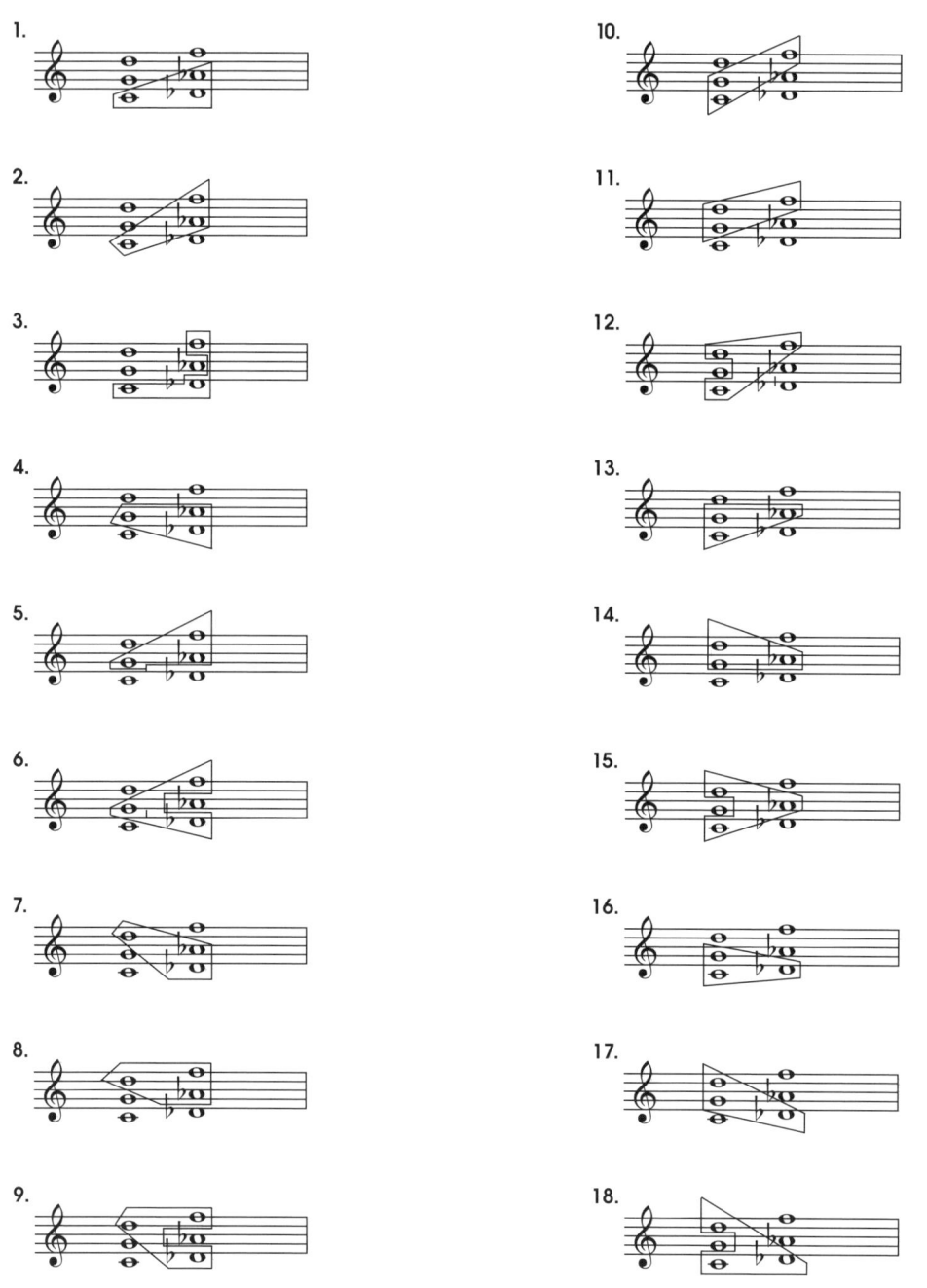

FIGURE 7.11 An example of Muse's grouping process.

here collects only those pitches that sound either simultaneously or immediately one after another.

In order to better understand the combinatorial possibilities described above, Figure 7.12 presents all of the possible trichordal permutations of a six-pitch list of non-repeating numbers, not including the original arrangement ([0,2,7] [1,5,8]) and its retrograde ([1,5,8] [0,2,7]). Note, however, that the second group of nine permutations here represent reversed, our-of-order duplicates of the first nine and thus can be removed, producing a total of nine discrete trichords. The principle here,

1. [8,0,1] [2,5,7]
2. [5,8,0] [1,2,7]
3. [0,1,5] [7,8,2]
4. [7,8,1] [0,2,5]
5. [5,7,8] [0,1,2]
6. [1,5,7] [8,0,2]
7. [8,1,2] [0,5,7]
8. [2,5,8] [0,1,7]
9. [1,2,5] [7,8,0]
10. [0,5,7] [8,1,2]
11. [2,5,7] [8,0,1]
12. [0,2,5] [7,8,1]
13. [7,8,0] [1,2,5]
14. [7,8,2] [0,1,5]
15. [8,0,2] [1,5,7]
16. [0,1,7] [2,5,8]
17. [1,2,7] [5,8,0]
18. [0,1,2] [5,7,8]

FIGURE 7.12 All of the possible permutations of a six-note list of nonrepeating numbers not including the original arrangement ([0,2,7] [1,5,8]) and its retrograde ([1,5,8] [0,2,7]).

that forward gathering will collect all possible unordered pitch-class groupings for trichordal sets from six pitches, applies to groupings of all sizes. Note that the number of permutations for a tetrachordal collection from an eight-pitch list is thirty-five. Considering the trichordal collections previously mentioned and the 126 pentachordal collections from a ten-length list, the relation to Pascal's triangle described at the beginning of this chapter becomes clear: this is the third through fifth numbers of the first vertical offset series to the left and right of center (10, 35, 126) in Figure 7.1.

The general thoroughness with which the Muse program gathers contiguous groupings ensures that every possible grouping will be analyzed and rated (a process to be described shortly). I remind readers here that Muse is only as useful as the accuracy and amount of data available allows. Like many data-driven programs, the code required for Muse's operation remains simple and quite small in comparison to the large database of music used for analysis.

Because collections of pitches will produce groupings larger than four or five pitches (i.e., ten, fifteen, even twenty pitches), I have limited the set-collecting program to first-order collections only. By "first-order" here, I mean that the initial set will combine only those pitch classes allowable by the established set size. Subsequent sets, however, will consist of sets following the order of the grouping itself less any pitch classes included in the initial set. As example, a trichordal grouping of nine pitch classes (1 2 3 4 5 6 7 8 9) might collect trichordal sets, such as (1 2 3)(4 5 6)(7 8 9), (1 2 4)(3 5 6)(7 8 9), (1 2 5)(3 4 6)(7 8 9), and so on, with initial trichords collecting combinatorially and the other trichords remaining mutually exclusive but ordered as closely as possible to the original grouping order. A first-order collection process indicates that only the first grouping has a specific ordering. An nth-order collection—one that figures the ordering of all sets—of a ten-length source would generate nearly four million (3,628,800 or 10!) different possibilities, and this number times four (or 14,515,200) for the collections of trichords, tetrachords, pentachords, and hexachords. However, a first-order collection of the same source produces only 792 collections. Although thoroughness suggests that an nth-order process creates more complete and potentially neutral collections, a first-order process produces a more practical number of set groupings, even using computational processes.

The task of analyzing even a very short passage of music with the very large number of possible groupings available in Muse's grouping approach makes finding best analyses very difficult. However, the number of groupings represents significantly less than half of the truly large number of groupings created by using several controllers (see Chapter 5 for definition) for pattern-matching purposes. Such controllers, with plausible ranges as wide as thirty or forty increments, increase the number of possible analyses significantly. In fact, these controllers can seriously impact the number of possible analyses, even with one incremental change of a single controller. The possible variable-grouping problem can thus grow to astronomical proportions. As I will now describe, however, the Muse program handles this difficulty by using only one setting of all controllers for each run through all of the possible analyses of the grouping combinations. This process reduces output from several billion trillion for a single run to several thousand or—depending on the size of the music analyzed—several million outputs.

The Muse program analyzes music by mapping an analysis program over all possible trichordal, tetrachordal, pentachordal, and hexachordal contiguous-pitch collections. Because this mapping process produces so many possible correct analyses, Muse presents the results separately for each output. In effect, each mapping produces one grouping analysis, consisting of a rating and an analysis in a readable print format for the passage being analyzed. Such analyses then appear every few seconds continuously for hours, days, and even weeks, in some cases, to allow users to read them as they appear. Because the Lisp Listener window keeps a record of its contents, users can scroll back and view any previous result or save and print the output or any portion thereof.

Figure 7.13 presents a view of the listener window after the completion of one analysis by Muse. The rating appears first here. Ratings result from the figuring of the optimal value of each analysis divided by the number of analyses. For example, the best-case scenario for set analysis, only one of the many analyses applied, would be that all analyzed sets equate to the same prime form. The worst-case scenario for set analysis would be that each set differs from the rest. There is, of course, a range of possibilities between these extremes, and that range of possibilities has a number—the number of sets—resulting in a value of the number of equal sets divided by the number of sets overall. Thus, a ten-set phrase with four equal sets results in a 40 percent rating for that portion of the analysis. This rating represents just one of the many shown that contribute to the optimal rating.

The manner in which the analyses align with one another is another factor in the optimal rating. I have included this alignment statistic because the coincidence of

---

The rating for this analysis is: 7.13
The analyzed sets are: ((91 74 63) (60 90 75) (64 59))((91 74 63) (60 90 75) (64 59))
The pitch information content for these sets is: (1.0 1.0 0.0 1.0 1.0 0.0)
The dynamics information content for these sets is: (0.33 0.33 0.5 0.33 0.33 0.5)
The durations information content for these sets is: (0.33 0.33 0.5 0.33 0.33 0.5)
The texture information content for these sets is: (1.0 1.0 1.0 1.0 1.0 1.0)
The scales for these sets is: ((3 4 6 11) (0 2 3 4 6 7 11))
The roots of the current sets are: ((91 75 64) (91 75 64))
The SPEAC for these sets are: ((A C C) (A C C))
The functions for these sets are: ((7 3 4) (7 3 4))

FIGURE 7.13 A view of the listener window after the completion of one analysis by Muse.

various points of analysis provides a very important measurement of analytic cohesion. For example, if changes in root, tension, set, scale, and other such aspects occur simultaneously, the coincidence of this simultaneity creates a deeper focus than that generated by any of the analyses registered separately.

Investigating the code that produces the output in Figure 7.13 produces a curious function call (see Figure 7.14). Buried in Muse is a function called `sleep`. This function does precisely what its name implies—it forces the program to pause a certain number of seconds. In Muse, `sleep` sleeps for four seconds before printing subsequent analyses to give users time to read each output before progressing to the next. Without the call to `sleep`, Muse would—even though it has fairly complicated routines to run for each analysis—print nearly continuously, making its output unreadable while it runs. Therefore, this curious bit of cosmetic code slows the program from its analysis rate of microseconds to produce more human-intelligible results.

Many of the processes that Muse uses to analyze music rely on basic pattern-matching techniques. Creating an *unbiased* pattern matcher for Muse requires that this matcher be as flexible as possible. Ensuring that such a matcher can function effectively also requires that the data in the database it matches be stored as simply as possible. Neither the program nor the data should be organized in ways that reflect a programmer's or a user's sense of what would be musically viable or logical. In fact, if this matcher is to provide undiscovered insights into music, it should be designed as generically as possible in order to discover all of the matches in the numerical data under analysis.

Muse pattern matches musical data on several levels: pitch, interval, rhythm and meter, dynamic, channel, and combinations of these parameters. The Muse pattern matcher uses only two controllers (see Chapter 5), which give it flexibility in terms of (1) pitch variances that follow scale-degree matches rather than pitch-class matches and (2) ignored intervening pitches, such as embellishments between members of a pattern. Muse's pattern matcher further collects and attempts to separately match data grouped according to channel, duration, beat relation, and so on.

All of these groupings are then cross-referenced in order to discover as many different patterns as possible, no matter how unlikely one might be to hear, see, or otherwise perceive the pattern. The thoroughness with which Muse collects patterns is in many ways as important as its pattern-matching processes.

One program or concept from every previous chapter in this book contributes to the output report of Muse. From Chapter 1 Muse gains its sets perspective. From Chapter 2 Muse includes an AIT report (Principle 1). The registral emphasis from Chapter 3 also appears here, along with scale analysis (Principle 2) from Chapter 4. Functions (Principle 3) are analyzed according to the principles laid out in Chapter 5, and, although extensions (Principle 4) of the music provided for analysis do not explicitly occur, the rules-collection process described in Chapter 6 influences the overall rating provided by Muse. Thus, the program interlocks the various approaches to analysis that each chapter provides, all of them contributing to the final output in a meaningful way.

```
(defun COLLATE-SETS-AND-PRINT (set-1 set-2 &optional (set-2-save set-2))
  "The function that delivers the printouts of the various analytical information."
  (let* ((first-set (mapcar #'(lambda (x)(mapcar #'second x))(first set-1)))
         (second-set (mapcar #'(lambda (x)(mapcar #'second x))(first set-2)))
         (test (append (mapcar #'analyze-and-graph (mapcar #'set-to-zero (first set-1)))
                       (mapcar #'analyze-and-graph (mapcar #'set-to-zero (first set-2)))))
         (pitch-info (mapcar #'very-first test))
         (dynamic-info (mapcar #'very-second test))
         (duration-info (mapcar #'very-third test))
         (texture-info (mapcar #'very-fourth test))
         (scales (list (very-first (create-scale-listings (apply #'append (first set-1))))
                       (very-first (create-scale-listings (apply #'append (first set-2))))))
         (roots (list
                  (mapcar #'(lambda (x)(get-root x))
                    (mapcar #'(lambda (y) (mapcar #'second y)) (first set-1))))
          (mapcar #'(lambda (x)(get-root x))
                    (mapcar #'(lambda (y) (mapcar #'second y)) (first set-2)))))
         (speac (mapcar #'(lambda (z)(get-speac z))
                  (mapcar #'(lambda (x)(mapcar #'(lambda (y)(mod y 12)) x)) roots)))
         (functions (mapcar #'(lambda (z)(get-functions (apply #'append scales) z))
                     (mapcar #'(lambda (x)(mapcar #'(lambda (y)(mod y 12)) x)) roots)))
         (rating (my-round (overall-rating pitch-info dynamic-info duration-info texture-info
                    (mapccar #'(lambda (n)(* .1 n))
              (remove-duplicates (apply #'append
                 (mapcar #'(lambda (x)(mapcar #'(lambda (y)(mod y 12)) x)) roots))))
                    (mapcar #'(lambda (n)(* .1 n))
              (remove-duplicates (apply #'append
                 (mapcar #'(lambda (x)(mapcar #'(lambda (y)(mod y 12)) x)) roots))))
                    (mapcar #'(lambda (n)(* .1 n))
              (remove-duplicates (apply #'append functions)))))))
    (cond ((null set-2)
           (collate-sets-and-print (rest set-1) set-2-save set-2-save))
          ((null set-1) t)
          (t (progn (format t "~A~A~&" "The rating for this analysis is: " rating)
             (format t "~A~A~A~&" "The analyzed sets are: " first-set second-set)
             (format t "~A~A~&" "The pitch information content for these sets is: " pitch-info)
      (format t "~A~A~&"
             "The dynamics information content for these sets is: " dynamic-info)
             (format t "~A~A~&"
             "The durations information content for these sets is: " duration-info)
             (format t "~A~A~&" "The texture information content for these sets is: " texture-info)
             (format t "~A~A~&" "The scales for these sets is: " scales)
             (format t "~A~A~&" "The roots of the current sets are: " roots)
             (forrmat t "~A~A~&" "The SPEAC for these sets are: " speac)
             (format t "~A~A~&" "The functions for these sets are: " functions)
             (format t "~A~&" " ")
             (format t "~A~&" " ")
             (format t "~A~&" " ")
             (format t "~A~&" " ")
                 (sleep 4)
                 (collate-sets-and-print set-1 (rest set-2) set-2-save))))))
```

FIGURE 7.14 Muse's program includes a function called `sleep`.

Although I have just made a case for integration of the ideas presented in this book, I maintain that these ideas do not constitute a distinct analytical theory. Nor does this integration suggest that this particular collection of analytic approaches represents a unified whole. To the contrary, the analyses that I have presented in this book identify only a few of the many possible methods of analyzing post-tonal music. However, the types of analysis presented in this book have significant use, and their overall alignment posits a valuable way to understand post-tonal music.

Muse's approach to analysis—based as it is on the neutral dimension, a systematic analysis from an explicitly stated, relatively objective point of view—does not completely remove bias. Neutrality, however admirable as a goal, is very difficult to achieve. John Cage reminded me often of his desire to rid his music of his biases and of his resultant failure to achieve this goal. Coding a program that analyzes music from as many points of view as possible, using techniques that may or may not have relevance to the music under analysis, and ruthlessly applying these strategies to every conceivable grouping of the music regardless of the logic that such strategies or groupings may imply, does not, unfortunately, negate the fact that this program—despite my attempts to minimize them—contains biases.

Cage points out the contradictions that occur when attempting to analyze music using unbiased approaches:

> I always want to start from zero and make, if I can, a discovery ... it's very difficult, because we have a memory. There's no doubt of it. And we're not stupid. We would be stupid if we didn't have a memory. And yet it's that memory that one has to become free of, at the same time that you take advantage of it. So it's very paradoxical. (Cage 1980, 6)

One might argue that the paradoxes Cage refers to here can produce interesting as well as problematic results. For example, acquired musical skills should enhance the user's potential of computer programs to succeed. Truly unique discoveries, however, can be achieved only by following paths as yet not taken. Using previously defined skills, however admirable those skills may be, increases, rather than decreases, the chance of producing biased results. Rather than discovering the unexpected—the immensely valuable insights that result from thoroughness and tireless devotion to neutrality—one often simply verifies the biased assumptions with which one began.

Some analysts have taken to using off-the-shelf applications (e.g., Microsoft Excel) to achieve the neutral results they desire. Using such programs means that music analysis need not require programming expertise, specialized equipment, or even much knowledge of computer operation to be of use. Anthony Pople comments that his

> program is implemented in the form of an extensive Visual Basic "plug-in" for Microsoft Excel, with the simplified score representation taking the form of a spreadsheet: pitch data are supplemented by indications of metrical stress ... and by a "vertical" segmentation into harmonic areas. (Pople 2004, 150)

Interestingly, using such programs merely replaces one set of biases with another. Although the apparent irrelevancy of using such programs might itself produce interesting results—results that might otherwise have gone unnoticed—more likely these different programs will simply produce another set of biased outputs—Cage's paradox perpetuated. Although nonetheless not without biases, the Muse program described here will hopefully, by applying relevant but thorough analytical processes to the music in its database, reveal previously undetected and useful results.

MUSICAL EXAMPLES

As discussed in Chapter 6, analyzing complete works composed by computer programs offers interesting challenges and important opportunities for music analysts. Discovering what might be lacking in a stylistic replication can reveal significant aspects of the original music upon which the computer bases its composition. Likewise, verifying the presence of certain techniques in computer-composed music can confirm their contributions in defining the style of the original human-composed music. This is particularly valuable in analyzing post-tonal music, where stylistic traits are not necessarily shared among the works of a composer's oeuvre, but rather are particular to a work or group of works of that composer.

As an example, the *Eine Kleine Stück* arguably in the style of Arnold Schoenberg by Experiments in Musical Intelligence shown in Figure 7.15 demonstrates many attributes of Schoenberg's post-tonal compositional processes. For example, the overall style of this brief work resembles the opening of Schoenberg's op. 11, no. 1, shown in part in Figure 7.16. However, unlike op. 11, no. 1, the music in this computer-composed example does not evolve or develop in any serious way, but rather simply states ideas in various forms and then abruptly ends.

Eine Kleine Stück has serial elements but does not contain pitch or duration rows in any formal way. The recombinancy algorithm in Experiments in Musical Intelligence cannot recreate forms such as canons, fugues, or serialism. For these latter forms and processes, I use special algorithms described in my books (see Cope 1996 and 2005 in particular). Such algorithms did not contribute to the creation of *Eine Kleine Stück*, and thus the initial and subsequent quasi-twelve-tone rows appearing in this work surprised me as much as it might surprise readers. These coincidences occur occasionally with recombinancy producing them. That is, post-tonal music, containing as it does the seeds for serialism, generates music of like-minded formalisms that occasionally arrange themselves into formations that seem premeditated rather than serendipitous.

The final repeating C major chord over an E-flat dominant seventh–sounding chord seems more polytonal—more Stravinsky-like—than serial. Yet this computer-composed work holds together in surprising ways, with similar three-pitch motives

FIGURE 7.15 The *Eine Kleine Stück* arguably in the style of Arnold Schoenberg by Experiments in Musical Intelligence.

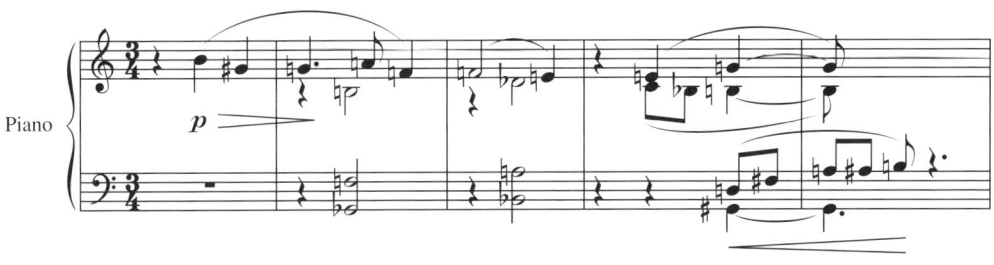

FIGURE 7.16 Schoenberg, Three Piano Pieces, op. 11, no. 1 (opening).

abounding and consistently dissonant harmonies. Certain pitches evade appearance: for example, pitch class 0 is missing from mm. 3 and 4, and pitch class 4 is missing from mm. 7 and 8. Repeated tones appear at apparent cadence points. Pitch-class set repetitions occur at times. For example, the pitch-class set [0,1,3] begins in the right hand, followed by pitch-class set [0,1,3] in a left-hand chord. These sets then move to pitch-class sets [0,1,4] and [0,2,5] before returning to pitch-class set [0,1,3] in the chord near the middle of m. 2 in the left hand.

The description just provided represents a brief paper analysis of *Eine Kleine Stück*. Using the various computer programs accompanying this book verifies many of these findings. In fact, using Muse to analyze the *two* works presented here—the Experiments in Musical Intelligence's work and Schoenberg's op. 11, no. 1—produces very similar results. Unfortunately, the printouts of even just the more likely successful attempts would require several dozen pages of this book to demonstrate. I therefore invite readers to carry out such comparative analyses themselves. Interestingly, the Experiments in Musical Intelligence *Eine Kleine Stück* uses several small pieces by Schoenberg as a database, but not the music to which the computer-generated work is compared here.

Analyzing computer-composed style replications for authenticity can prove extremely valuable. Even music theory students can make such analyses useful as testimony to their understanding of this music. As computer composition in historical styles becomes increasingly sophisticated, both analysts and laypersons alike will hopefully begin to better differentiate computer-composed style replications from the originals on which they are based. Interestingly, however, these replications, controversial as they may be, are also originals.

Existing works revised by computer programs should also prove intriguing for music analysts. A different version of, say, Beethoven's Symphony no. 5 would provide meaningful information about both Beethoven's Symphony no. 5 and its computer revision. The difference between these revisions and the music that Experiments in Musical Intelligence otherwise composes is, of course, that the latter contains direct quotes from only one work and develops that music in different ways from the original. Figure 7.17 presents the first page of the score to a work created by Experiments in Musical Intelligence in just the manner described here. Analyzing such variations can be very helpful in more thoroughly understanding the original music (see also the jigsaw test discussed in Chapter 6). Someday, computer-composed variations may prove more interesting and musically satisfying than the human-composed original, if one keeps an open mind to such possibilities.

Another example of post-tonal analysis continues the discussion of the third movement of Stravinsky's Three Pieces for String Quartet (1914) begun in Chapter 1 and continued in every chapter since. Pattern matching this work using Muse reveals that its opening section contains all pitch classes except pitch class 8. Bach's name (in the notes B-flat, A, C, and B-natural, which in German nomenclature spell B–A–C–H) appears in the second violin's first two notes and the violoncello's third and fourth notes and repeats several times thereafter. The principally stepwise melodic material in each voice derives from variations of the Dies irae, a medieval Latin sequence and the first words of the Requiem Mass (shown in Figure 7.18). Like the Dies irae, Stravinsky's music consists of mostly downward motion with stepwise voice-leading. In their parallel motion, the top two voices also resemble fourteenth-century organum.

Interestingly, thirteen measures before the interruption of the Mystic Circle of the Young Girls in Stravinsky's *Rite of Spring*, the music lapses into what later became a signature chorale technique of Stravinsky's: repeating fragments set against polytonal harmonies with severely limited ranges (see Figure 7.19). This *Rite of Spring* passage resembles the Cantique movement of the Three Pieces, with its limited leaps, repetitions, and falling chromatic motions. Were it not for the D-natural in the third measure as part of a descending chromatic line in voice 2 here, this orchestral passage would also contain only eleven notes, and it would suggest F-sharp major and B major as possible contributing keys.

Another passage in Stravinsky's Cantique resembles the Symphonies of Wind Instruments, as shown in Figure 7.20. The three polychordal statements followed by a more dissonant cluster resolving outward to the initial statement occur in both examples here—six years apart in composition, yet very close in concept.

My initial reaction to Stravinsky's Three Pieces when I first heard them in my teens—to label it the ugliest music I had ever heard—was matched by my even more powerful attraction to the music's dissonance and apparent lack of structure. I listened to this music over and over again, hoping to reconcile the polar opposites that confused me. I soon found that Stravinsky's work and style had influenced my own youthful compositional work and style, as shown in Figure 7.21, where the polytonality and fragmentary repetitions resemble Stravinsky's own, at least in certain superficial ways. Using the analytical approaches discussed thus far in this book has helped me to isolate the various contributors and better understand the combinations of the apparently disjunct materials in my own music.

A LOOK TO THE FUTURE 309

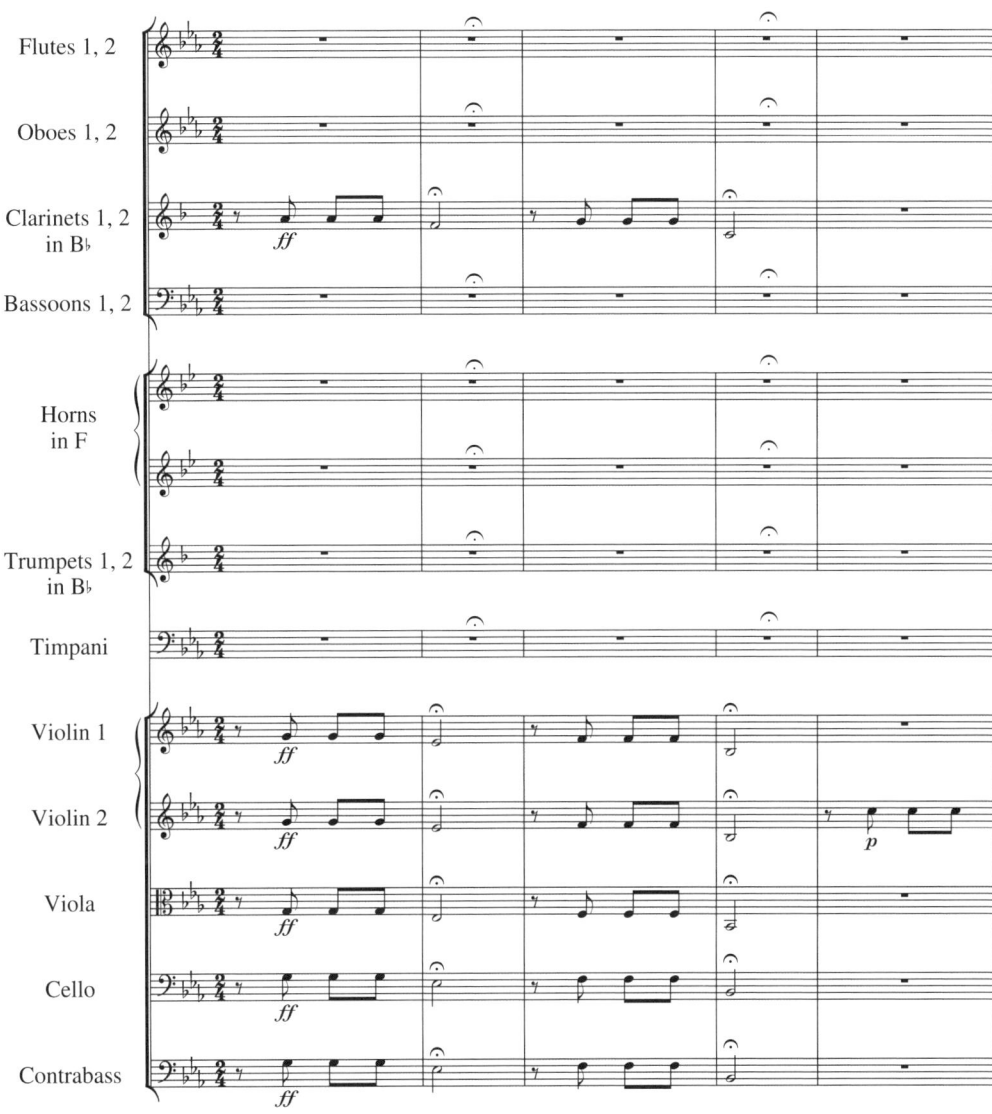

FIGURE 7.17 The first page of the score to Beethoven, Symphony no. 5, revision.

FIGURE 7.17 continued

FIGURE 7.18 Dies irae, a medieval Latin sequence and the first words of the Requiem Mass.

THE FUTURE

That computers will play ever-increasing roles in the analysis of music is, I believe, undeniable. The burning question that remains, however, is exactly what these roles will be. This book would not be complete without exploring those roles—aside from the various analytical techniques described in Chapters 2 through 6 of this book, and the preceding sections of this chapter—that I feel will most likely develop over the next few decades.

Surely one of the most basic and immediate future developments in computer music analysis will be improvements in existing music notation programs. For example, having capabilities comparable to those of word processors would be an important enhancement. Although most computer notation programs can locate and count measures, none of the most popular programs can return individual counts of pitch classes, a feature that almost all word processors possess, typically revealing letter, word, line, and paragraph counts.

Music notation programs also capable of searching for particular patterns would prove of immense value to composers, copyists, musicologists, and analysts alike. Discovering pitch patterns—in transposition—both vertically and horizontally would greatly enhance the ability of analysts and composers to find motives, otherwise nearly impossible to discover by eye given the single-page-size screens of most computers and our inability to see multiple pages in easily readable format. Although our ears can often locate these patterns, carefully listening and counting recognizable patterns can pose serious problems. Presenting discovered word patterns in text processing programs has traditionally been considered a prerequisite for a program, not an enhancement to one. The same ability to find musical patterns should also be true for music notation programs.

Although most computer music notation programs offer some sort of algorithmic attempt to spell notes correctly, few offer the ability to locate questionable pitch spellings and provide users an opportunity to make necessary changes. Again, word processors not only find potentially misspelled words, but offer numerous alternative spellings as well. Neither pitch spelling nor any of the other suggestions above would require major overhauls of software on the part of commercial music notation programs.

FIGURE 7.19 (a) A passage from the Mystic Circle of the Young Girls in Stravinsky, *The Rite of Spring*; (b) a passage from Stravinsky, Three Pieces for String Quartet.

Cantique

FIGURE 7.20 (a) A passage from the 3rd movement of Stravinsky, Three Pieces for String Quartet; (b) a similar passage in the Symphonies of Wind Instruments.

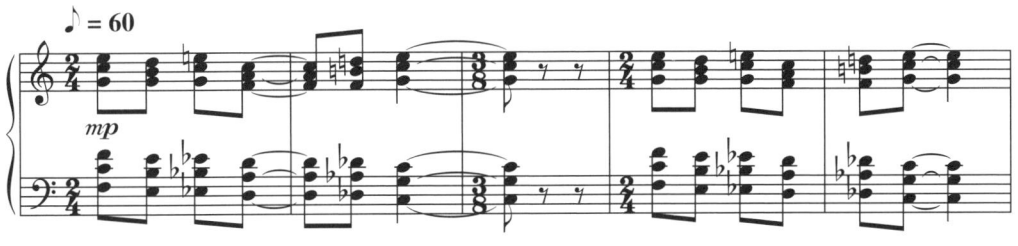

FIGURE 7.21 A post-tonal work by the author resembling Stravinsky's style.

In short, computer notation programs should model their engines on common word processing program design. In broadening the scope of these tools, music notation programs could produce, for example, counters that count particular chords, finders that find particular chords, and spellers that appropriately spell particular chords. Indeed, it would seem natural that such programs serve as a centerpiece for musicians of all specialties, but certainly for music analysts.

On another front, most music analytical processes consist of three broadly defined steps: reduction, representation, and functionalization. Reduction involves reducing important notes from doublings, disparate registers, and so on. Representation provides a way to signify the ordered content of these reductions (e.g., the $^6_5$ arabic representations of intervals above the bass note in baroque figured bass). These representations then qualify for certain musical functions defined according to a local context such as key, mode, and so on (e.g., I or tonic). Formal and structural analyses typically follow these initial three steps, and understandably so, because these processes only make sense when we are attempting to relate musical works to a model or to one another. Most of the analytical methods espoused in this book follow similar techniques.

Unfortunately, reductional, representational, and functional analyses fail on several counts that may be crucial for truly understanding music. For one thing, they fail to identify the unique qualities of individual works of music. This should not surprise us: reducing, representing, and functionalizing seek to discover commonalities between works of music so that we might understand not only one work, but a continuum of works. Although reductive, representational, and functional analyses occasionally do reveal unique chords, forms, and structures in music, such processes, by definition, eliminate much foreground material from analysis and point their processes directly away from the unique. Searching for what makes particular works special requires approaches that reducing, representing, and functionalizing typically fail to provide.

Discovering the differences between works of music often requires more dedication than finding the similarities between works, especially when such differences occur subtly in orchestration, form, tempo, dynamics, and so on. Making such discoveries possible while retaining current models should be one priority for future computer music analysis. However, even for computer programs the problems of detecting uniqueness remain complex. For example, to determine that a fragment of music is unique requires that that fragment be compared with an enormous number of other fragments to ensure that it has not occurred before. Otherwise, an element that may initially appear unique—a turn of phrase, a sudden dynamic shift, a particular rhythm, novel texture, or harmony—can trick us into believing it is original, whereas in fact it has been used previously.

Despite the difficulties involved with analyzing the unique attributes of works of music, the benefits of actually proving novel first instances in music far outweigh the problems incurred. No longer will conjecture and assumption be required to determine that certain chords (Tristan, Prometheus, etc.), scales (octatonic, whole tone, etc.), and even styles (those of Gesualdo, Berlioz, et al.) are unique. More important, the status of certain works that have become renowned for their individuality (Debussy's *Prélude à L'après-midi d'un faune*, Stravinsky's *Le sacre du printemps*, etc.) can be verified.

Computers can also make possible what I term *complementary* analysis. Complementary analysis consists of discovering the musical ideas that a work does *not* possess. Initially such analyses may seem frivolous. However, explicitly knowing what a work does not contain can reveal as much of importance about that work as discovering what it does contain. Imagine, for example, discovering that a classical-period keyboard work of substantial duration does not contain the popular Viennese simultaneous tonic/dominant cadence. And the importance of discovering a late work by Bartók that lacks any references whatsoever to some known Hungarian folk song could almost rival the significance of the discovery of all those works of his that do contain such references.

At present, the only way to determine such omissions, even when using computers, requires locating every conceivable pattern in a work and then analyzing these data for expected patterns. Heretofore, such processes have relied too heavily on an analyst's personal knowledge of musical patterns. Armed with appropriate data and software capable of capturing all possible patterns from a large database of music, a computer program should be able to fully analyze a work for the patterns it does not include, possibly even the patterns it does not include but that one would expect it to include.

One of the most important future goals for computer music analysts should also be the creation of a universal database, one consisting of a standard data type and interface. Like both Common Lisp and MIDI, such a universal database should be the work of a committee charged with making the data as complete as possible, as adaptable to as many existing and future programs as possible, and freely available to all interested in using that data. As mentioned in Chapter 1 of this book, the Digital Alternative Representation of Music Scores (DARMS), developed in 1963 by Stefan Bauer-Mengelberg (see Bauer-Mengelberg 1970), continues today as an important computer representation program. DARMS code is extremely accurate and currently appears in several dialects (Schüler 2000; Selfridge-Field 1997a). The International Society for Music Information Retrieval (ISMIR) currently offers enormous potential for the establishment of a common protocol for music storage and retrieval for future computer music analysis.

A universal database should also have a universal pattern matcher. The Humdrum Toolkit developed by David Huron (1995 and 1999), a powerful Unix-based music information retrieval computer program, searches for particular motives, compares voice-leadings in various repertories, defines and catalogues harmonic progressions, analyzes dissonance in relation to metric position, among other functions. Expanding this toolkit to include searches that do not require an input pattern (i.e., so that it can compare data with itself and return the patterns found in common) would make this pattern matcher more effective.

A universal computer analysis program might seem oxymoronic in that its goal of adaptability would necessarily make it more a computer language than an analysis program. Nonetheless, creating an easy-to-use program/language to access both the universal database and a pattern matcher would represent an extraordinary advance for the field of music analysis. To this point, however, too many well-meaning individuals are still creating independent databases and programs whose life expectancy is often very short.

Another difficult but fairly achievable goal for the future would be the musical—not waveform—analysis of sound files. The ability to analyze recordings for the types of musical information discussed in this book using print-represented notes would present an extraordinary opportunity for musical analysts to study patterns, scales, function, and so on in the raw world of sound. Such processes could produce more accurate analyses of electronic and computer music, music of oral/aural traditions, and other kinds of music not typically found in notated forms. Furthermore, the study of musical performance—a topic I have not treated in this book because of its obvious difficulty and complexity—would greatly benefit from such possibilities.

Several other computer music analysis techniques seem natural for future exploration. Space does not permit a complete explanation of these approaches, yet I present them in brief here in hopes that others may pursue them further:

1. An analytical process for discovering the role of *spectralism* (compositional decisions based on timbral structure) in music, a conscious or subconscious process used in post-tonal composition.

2. *Gestalt* analysis—analysis that treats all musical parameters as interleaved rather than as separate entities—likely paralleling the manner in which we perceive music and thus providing a more natural approach to computer music analysis.

3. *Transformational* analysis of invariants—the computational study of how musical transforms retain certain ideas while developing others over time.

4. *Hermeneutic* analysis—the computational study of the roles that nonmusical ideas such as language, physical representations, cultural artifacts, personal idiosyncrasies, and so on play in music.

5. Computer analysis of the roles that *symmetry* plays, particularly in post-tonal music.

6. A computational search for formal *commonalities* in diverse works including beginnings, endings, points, of arrival, and so on.

7. Creation of a musical first-order logic system (*predicate calculus*) contained in certain music or music as a whole made possible by computational processes and a universal database.

8. *Geometries* of music, where structures acquire balance or imbalance according to geometrical patterns.

9. Computational discovery of *narrativity* versus *stasis* in particular post-tonal works and styles.
10. *Interactive* analysis using computers in which analysts can test alternate strategies for any parameter of music on the fly to observe new implications and, possibly, why composers chose the solutions they did.

Each of these approaches to analysis, as imposing as some of them may seem, offers potential as an extraordinary tool for the future understanding of music.

CONCLUSIONS

> Day by day, the machines are gaining ground upon us. Day by day we are becoming more subservient to them; more men are daily bound down as slaves to tend them; more men are daily devoting the energies of their whole lives to the development of mechanical life. The upshot is simply a question of time, but the time will come when the machines will hold the real supremacy over the world and its inhabitants is what no person of a truly philosophic mind can for a moment question.
> Samuel Butler, as quoted in Heinrich Schwarz, *Art and Photography* (1985), 97

Butler was not referring to the chess-playing computer program Deep Blue, Experiments in Musical Intelligence, or even computers. He made this observation in 1863 about the invention of the *camera*. Phobias about using mechanical tools would appear to predate computers by several decades, if not centuries, if one were to freely interpret ravings from the distant past.

Interestingly, computer music analysis and photography share many of the same characteristics. For example, the squeezing of a camera shutter easily parallels the tap on the mouse or the key on the keyboard that many feel represents the only human activity associated with computationally analyzing music. Clearly, however, both photography and computer music analysis represent legitimate human endeavors whose time has come.

Computers can relieve analysts of the drudgery of detail and allow them to make more meaningful decisions about the musical universe in which they live. Every new step in computational technology represents a potential new step for understanding music. Using computers to analyze music offers an incredible opportunity for more deeply understanding how music moves us so profoundly and thus allows us to more deeply appreciate its subtleties.

Throughout this book I have referred to the four principles first presented in Chapter 1. I list them again here to allow readers to gauge whether or not the relevant text and figures in the intervening chapters have adequately demonstrated their veracity:

1. All music consists of patterns.
2. All pitch patterns can be reduced to scales.
3. All elements of scales have different functions.
4. All patterns, scales, and functions in music are best understood by modeling their processes.

Obviously readers can and will decide the validity of these principles for analyzing post-tonal music for themselves. However, regardless of the decisions they reach, these four principles will at least have provoked new considerations of musical analysis and the music these analyses represent.

It took roughly half a millennium—from the invention of polyphony to Rameau—for analysts to discover what they considered a more or less complete analytical approach to tonal music. It then took approximately another two hundred years for analysts to delve deeper into that so-called complete theory—from Rameau to Schenker—to create another complete theory. However, we may have just begun to understand tonal music, as indicated by recent discoveries in such areas as music cognition and empirical musicology (Clarke and Cook 2004; Deutsch 1999; Krumhansl 1990; McAdams and Bigand 1993). Tonal music will hopefully continue to be one of the foci of future analyses and theories.

As for post-tonal music, most analysts would agree that we have yet to seriously scratch its surface. Computers do not themselves offer a better understanding of post-tonal music; only humans can accomplish this. However, we can learn to better analyze and appreciate this music from our attempts with this extraordinary tool.

In this book I have presented a number of ways computers offer to enhance the analysis of music. Many of these types of analysis would require so much time by hand as to make them virtually impossible. With the increase of computer memory size, computational speed, and accuracy, however, we can apply techniques to music that hitherto might have seemed irrational or irrelevant in order to discover more of its secrets. Every work of music deserves as complete an analysis as possible, for even the simplest music contains a wealth of important information that we should not ignore.

I have always felt that at least part of the music we experience will never succumb to analysis, simply because of its personal, unique, and illusory qualities. Yet, I also feel that we must continue to attempt to understand as much as we can about music. Furthermore, we must truly value making the trip as much as we do achieving the goal. After all, even incomplete knowledge enhances our appreciation of music. In fact, this paradox of striving but never fully achieving makes music, at least for me, the most engaging of all the arts.

A few months ago, I received the following e-mail message from a young man, probably one still in high school:

> I am a young Catholic and science enthusiast, and recently I have heard a lot of discussion in the media saying that science and religion are irreconcilable. Since you are a famous scientist, I wanted to ask you a question. My physics teacher told me that lots of scientists have been Catholic, like Pasteur, Mendel, von Neumann, etc, and that they saw no apparent contradiction. Is it okay for me to be Catholic and a scientist too, or do I need to renounce my faith to continue to work in science? Thank you for your time.

I decided not to argue with his description of me as a "famous scientist," because I believe music to be a science as well as an art. I reply to most e-mail, so I responded:

> Thank you for your note. Science is great for answering all of those questions that can be answered. Religion is great for all of those questions that cannot be answered by science. And there will always be both kinds of questions. I do not view science and religion as contradictory, but as complementary.

This young man was probably disappointed by my response in that I did not directly deal with his apparent crises—what to do when science and religion both provide answers, but those answers are contradictory. However, my response reflects my belief that for some questions, no answers actually exist. I do not attribute this to human shortcomings, complexity, or any other simple explanation, but to the universe itself.

To a certain degree, we all analyze music as we listen, even if our analysis consists only of remembering and recognizing ideas as they vary and return in a work. If we did not perform this kind of analysis, music would simply contribute one more ambient sound to our sonic environment that we might then ignore. Taking advantage of the resources that computers provide extends our abilities to comprehend and ultimately better appreciate the music that fills our lives in so many important ways. I believe that music analysts stand on a threshold for which new computational tools will provide revelations not previously thought possible. We should eagerly welcome any such tool that allows new insights into why music finds such deep resonance within the human spirit.

Bibliography

Agawu, V. Kofi. 1991. *Playing with Signs*. Princeton, NJ: Princeton University Press.

Agmon, E. 1989. "A Mathematical Model of the Diatonic System." *Journal of Music Theory* 33/1: 1–25.

———. 1990. "Statistics and Compositional Balance." *Perspectives of New Music* 28/1: 80–111.

———. 1992. "Quantifying Musical Merit." *Interface* 21/1: 53–93.

Alphonce, Bo. 1980. "Music Analysis by Computer: A Field for Theory Formation." *Computer Music Journal* 4/2: 26–35.

Ames, Charles. 1989. "The Markov Process as a Compositional Model: A Survey and Tutorial." *Leonardo* 22/2: 175–87.

Aristoxenus. 1902. *The Harmonics of Aristoxenus*, translated by Henry S. Macran. New York: Oxford University Press.

Avdeev, L. V., and P. B. Ivanov. 1993. "A Mathematical Model of Scale Perception." *Journal of Moscow Physical Society* 3: 331–53.

Babbage, Charles. 1864. *Passages from the Life of a Philosopher*. London: Longman, Green, Longman, Roberts and Green.

Babbitt, Milton. 1955. "Some Aspects of Twelve-tone Composition." *The Score* and *I.M.A. Magazine* 12: 53–61.

———. 1960. "Twelve-Tone Invariants as Compositional Determinants." *Musical Quarterly* 46/2: 108–21.

———. 1961. "Set Structure as a Compositional Determinant." *Journal of Music Theory* 5/1: 129–47.

———. 1965. "The Use of Computers in Musicological Research." *Perspectives of New Music* 3/2: 74–83.

Backus, J. 1969. *The Acoustical Foundations of Music*. New York: Norton.

Bailey, Kathryn. 1991. *The Twelve-tone Music of Anton Webern*. Cambridge: Cambridge University Press.

Balaban, Mira. 1992. "Music Structures: Interleaving the Temporal and Hierarchical Aspects in Music." In *Understanding Music with AI: Perspectives on Music Cognition*, edited by Mira Balaban, Kemal Ebcioglu, and Otto Laske. Cambridge, MA: MIT Press: 110–38.

Bauer-Mengelberg, Stefan. 1970. "The Ford-Columbia Input Language." In *Musicology and the Computer: Three Symposia*, edited by Barry Brook. New York: City University of New York Press: 48–52.

Bailey, Kathryn. 1991. *The Twelve-Tone Music of Anton Webern*. Cambridge: Cambridge University Press.

Benade, A. H. 1976. *Foundations of Musical Acoustics*. London: Oxford University Press.

Benson, David J. 2006. *Music: A Mathematical Offering*. Cambridge: Cambridge University Press.

Bent, Ian. 2002. "Steps to Parnassus: Contrapuntal Theory in 1725." In *The Cambridge History of Western Music Theory*, edited by Thomas Christensen. Cambridge: Cambridge University Press: 554–602.

Berger, Anna Maria Busse. 2002. "The Evolution of Rhythmic Notation." In *The Cambridge History of Western Music Theory*, edited by Thomas Christensen. Cambridge: Cambridge University Press: 628–56.

Bernard, Jonathan W. 1977. *A Theory of Pitch and Register for the Music of Edgard Varèse*. New Haven, CT: Yale University Press.

Bharucha, Jamshed. 1993. "MUSACT: A Connectionist Model of Musical Harmony." In *Machine Models of Music*, edited by Stephan Schwanauer and David Levitt. Cambridge, MA: MIT Press: 498–510.

Blombach, Ann. 1981. "An Introductory Course in Computer-Assisted Analysis: The Computer and the Bach Chorales." *Journal of Computer-Based Instruction* 7: 70–77.

———. 1982. "Harmony vs. Counterpoint in the Bach Chorales." In *Computing in the Humanities*, edited by Richard Bailey. Amsterdam: North-Holland: 79–88.

Boethius, A. M. T. S. 1967. *De institutione musica*. Introduction and translation by Calvin Bower. Ann Arbor: University Microfilms.

Bower, Calvin. 2002. "The Transmission of Ancient Music Theory into the Middle Ages." In *The Cambridge History of Western Music Theory*, edited by Thomas Christensen. Cambridge: Cambridge University Press: 136–67.

Böker-Heil, N. 1972. "Musikalische Stilanalyse und Computer: einige grundsätzliche Erwägungen." *IMSCR* 1972: 45–50.

Brook, Barry. 1965. "The Simplified 'Plaine and Easy Code System.'" *Fontes Artis Musicae* 12: 156–60.

Brooks, Frederick, A. Hopkins, P. Newmann, and W. Wright. 1957. "An Experiment in Musical Composition." *IRE Transactions on Electronic Computers* 6: 175–82.

Browne, R. 1981. "Tonal Implications of the Diatonic Set." *In Theory Only* 5/1–2: 3–21.

Bruner, Cheryl. 1984. "The Perception of Contemporary Pitch Structures." *Music Perception* 2/1: 25–39.

Byrd, Donald. 1970. "Music Notation by Computer." *Computers and the Humanities* 5/2: 111.

Cage, John. 1980. "An Interview with John Cage." *Composer* 10/11: 6–22.

Camilleri, Lelio. 1987. "Towards a Computational Theory of Music." In *The Semiotic Web, 1986: A Yearbook of Semiotics*, edited by Thomas A. Sebeok and Jean Umiker-Sebeok. Berlin: Mouton.

Caplin, William. 2002. "Theories of Musical Rhythm in the Eighteenth and Nineteenth Centuries." In *The Cambridge History of Western Music Theory*, edited by Thomas Christensen. Cambridge: Cambridge University Press: 657–94.

Carey, N., and K. Clampitt. 1989. "Aspects of Well-Formed Scales." *Music Theory Spectrum* 11/2: 187–206.

Castine, Peter, Alexander Brinkman, and Craig Harris. 1990. "Contemporary Music Analysis Package (CMAP) for Macintosh." In *Proceedings of the International Computer Music Conference, Glasgow, 1990*. San Francisco, CA: Computer Music Association: 150–52.

Cazden, Norman. 1958. "Pythagoras and Aristoxenus Reconciled." *Journal of the American Musicological Society* 11/2–3: 97–105.

Chaitin, Gregory. 2001. *Exploring Randomness*. London: Springer-Verlag.

———. 2005. *Meta Math! The Quest for Omega*. New York: Vintage Books.

Clark, Eric, and Nicholas Cook, eds. 2004. *Empirical Musicology: Aims, Methods, Prospects*. Oxford: Oxford University Press.

Clough, John. 1980. "Diatonic Interval Sets and Transformational Structures." *Perspectives of New Music* 18: 461–82.

Cohen, David. 2002. "Notes, Scales, and Modes in the Earlier Middle Ages." In *The Cambridge History of Western Music Theory*, edited by Thomas Christensen. Cambridge: Cambridge University Press: 307–363.

Cook, Nicholas. 1987. *A Guide to Musical Analysis*. London: J. M. Dent and Sons.

———. 2004. "Computational and Comparative Musicology." In *Empirical Musicology*, edited by Eric Clarke and Nicholas Cook. Oxford: Oxford University Press: 103–26.

Cooper, Grosvenor, and Leonard Meyer. 1960. *The Rhythmic Structure of Music*. Chicago: University of Chicago Press.

Cope, David. 1990. "Pattern Matching as an Engine for the Simulation of Musical Style." In *Proceedings of the International Computer Music Conference*. San Francisco: Computer Music Association.

———. 1991. *Computers and Musical Style*. Madison, WI: A-R Editions.

———. 1996. *Experiments in Musical Intelligence*. Madison, WI: A-R Editions.

———. 2000. *The Algorithmic Composer*. Madison, WI: A-R Editions.

———. 2001. *Virtual Music*. Cambridge, MA: MIT Press.

———. 2004. "A Musical Learning Algorithm." *Computer Music Journal* 28/3:12–27.

———. 2005. *Computer Models of Musical Creativity*. Cambridge, MA: MIT Press.

———. 2006. "Capriccio for Cello and Orchestra. On *Mozartballs*, DVD, directed by Larry Weinstein and performed by Steven Isserlis. New York: Decca 074 3153.

Copland, Aaron. 1957. *What to Listen For in Music*. New York: McGraw-Hill.

Crocker, Richard. 1958. "Musica Rhythmica and Musica Metrica in Antique and Medieval Theory." *Journal of Music Theory* 2: 12–15.

———. 1962. "Discant, Counterpoint, and Harmony." *Journal of the American Musicological Society* 15/1: 1–21.

Desain, P., and H. Honing. 1999. "A Reply to S. W. Smoliar's 'Modelling Musical Perception: A Critical View.'" In *Parallel Distributed Perception: Musical Networks and Performance*, edited by N. Griffith and P. Todd. Cambridge, MA: MIT Press: 111–16.

Deutsch, Diana, ed. 1999. *The Psychology of Music*. 2nd ed. San Diego: Academic Press.

Devlin, K. 1993. *The Joy of Sets: Fundamentals of Contemporary Set Theory.* 2nd ed. New York: Springer.

Dolson, Mark. 1991. "Machine Tongues XII: Neural Networks." In *Music and Connectionism*, edited by Peter Todd and Gareth Loy. Cambridge, MA: MIT Press.

Dunsby, Jonathan. 1982. "A Hitch Hiker's Guide to Semiotic Music Analysis." *Music Analysis* 1/3: 235–41.

Ebcioglu, Kemal. 1992. "An Expert System for Harmonizing Chorales in the Style of J. S. Bach." In *Understanding Music with AI: Perspectives on Music Cognition*, edited by Mira Balaban, Kemal Ebcioglu, and Otto Laske. Cambridge, MA: The AAAI Press/MIT Press: 295–333.

Eco, Umberto. 1976. *A Theory of Semiotics.* Bloomington: Indiana University Press.

Erickson, Raymond. 1968. "Music Analysis and the Computer." *Journal of Music Theory* 12: 240–63.

———. 1969. "A General-Purpose System for Computer Aided Musical Studies." *Journal of Music Theory* 13: 276–94.

Ferreirós, J. 1999. *Labyrinth of Thought: A History of Set Theory and Its Role in Modern Mathematics.* Basel: Birkhäuser.

Forte, Allen. 1973. *The Structure of Atonal Music.* New Haven: Yale University Press.

———. 1989. "Banquet Address: SMT, Rochester 1987." *Music Theory Spectrum* 11/1: 95–99.

———. 1993. "A Program for the Analytic Reading of Scores." In *Machine Models of Music*, edited by Stephan Schwanauer and David Levitt. Cambridge, MA: MIT Press: 55–81.

Freund, John. 1973. *Introduction to Probability.* New York: Dover.

Gamer, C. 1967. "Some Combinational Resources of Equal-Tempered Systems." *Journal of Music Theory* 11: 32–59.

Gibson, Don. 1986. "The Aural Perception of Non-traditional Chords in Selected Theoretical Relationships: A Computer Generated Experiment." *Journal of Research in Music Education* 34/1: 5–23.

———. 1988. "The Aural Perception of Similarity in Non-traditional Chords Related by Octave Equivalence." *Journal of Research in Music Education* 36/1: 5–17.

Ghahramani, Saeed. 2005. *Fundamentals of Probability.* 3rd ed. Upper Saddle River, NJ: Pearson Prentice-Hall.

Gjerdingen, Robert. 1988. *A Classic Turn of Phrase: Music and the Psychology of Convention.* Philadelphia, PA: University of Pennsylvania Press: 138–49.

———. 1991. "Using Connectionist Models to Explore Complex Musical Patterns." In *Music and Connectionism*, edited by Peter Todd and Gareth Loy. Cambridge, MA: MIT Press.

Gould, Murray, and George Logemann. 1970. "ALMA: Alphanumeric Language for Music Analysis." In *Musicology and the Computer: Three Symposia*, edited by Barry Brook. New York: City University of New York Press: 57–90.

Graebner, Eric. 1974. "An Analysis of Schoenberg's Klavierstück, Op. 33A." *Perspectives of New Music* 12 1/2: 128–40.

Graham, Paul. 1995. *ANSI Common Lisp.* Upper Saddle River, NJ: Prentice-Hall.

Gross, Dorothy. 1975. "A Set of Computer Programs to Aid in Music Analysis." Ph.D. diss., Indiana University.

———. 1980. "A Project in Computer-assisted Harmonic Analysis." In *Proceedings of the International Computer Music Conference*, edited by Hubert S. Howe. San Francisco: Computer Music Association: 525–33.

———. 1984. "Computer Applications to Music Theory: A Retrospective." *Computer Music Journal* 8/4: 35–42.

Halmos, P. R. 1974. *Naive Set Theory*. New York: Springer-Verlag.

Harris, Craig, and Alexander Brinkman. 1989. "An Integrated Software System for Set-Theoretic and Serial Analysis of Contemporary Music." *Journal of Computer-Based Instruction* 16/2: 59–70.

Harrison, Daniel. 1994. *Harmonic Function in Chromatic Music*. Chicago: University of Chicago Press.

Herik, H. J. van den. 2000. "From Cognition to Perception." *ICGA Journal* 23/4: 201.

Hiller, Lejaren. 1964. "Informationstheorie und Computermusik." Special issue, *Darmstädter Beiträge zur Neuen Musik* 8.

Hiller, Lejaren, and Leonard Isaacson. 1959. *Experimental Music: Composition with an Electronic Computer*. New York: McGraw-Hill.

Hiller, Lejaren, and Burt Levy. 1984. "General System Theory as Applied to Music Analysis—Part I." In *Musical Grammars and Computer Analysis*, edited by Mario Baroni and Lelio Callegari. Firenze, Italy: Musicologia A Cura Della Società Italiana de Musicologia: 295–316.

Hindemith, Paul. 1942. *The Craft of Musical Composition. Book I: Theoretical Part*. Translated by Arthur Mendel. New York: Associated Music.

Hofstadter, Douglas. 1979. *Gödel, Escher, Bach: An Eternal Golden Braid*. New York: Basic Books.

———. 2001. "Staring Emmy Straight in the Eye—And Doing My Best Not to Flinch." In David Cope, *Virtual Music*. Cambridge, MA: MIT Press: 33–81.

Hofstetter, Fred. 1973. "Computer Applications to Music at OSU." *Computational Musicology Newsletter* 1/1: 2.

———. 1979. "The Nationalistic Fingerprint in Nineteenth-century Romantic Chamber Music." *Computers and the Humanities* 13 (1979): 105–19.

Holland, John. 1995. *Hidden Order: How Adaption Builds Complexity*. New York: Helix Books.

———. 1998. *Emergence*. Cambridge, MA: Perseus Books.

Honing, Henkjan. 1990. "POCO: An Environment for Analysing, Modifying, and Generating Expression in Music." *Proceedings of the 1990 International Computer Music Conference*. San Francisco: Computer Music Association: 364–68.

Howe, Hubert. 1965. "Some Combinational Properties of Pitch Structures." *Perspectives of New Music* 4/1: 45–61.

Huron, David. 1995. *The Humdrum Toolkit: Reference Manual*. Menlo Park, CA: Center for Computer Assisted Research in the Humanities.

———. 1999. *Music Research Using Humdrum: A User's Guide*. Stanford, CA: Center for Computer Assisted Research in the Humanities.

Isaacson, Eric J. 1996. "Issues in the Study of Similarity in Atonal Music." *Music Theory Online* 2/7.

Johnson, Tom. 1994. *Formulas for String Quartet*. Paris: Editions 75.

Karbusicky, Vladimir. 1979. *Systematische Musikwissenschaft*. Munich: Wilhelm Fink.

Klumpenhouwer, Henry. 2002. "Dualist Tonal Space and Transformation in Nineteenth-century Musical Thought." In *The Cambridge History of Western Music Theory*, edited by Thomas Christensen. Cambridge: Cambridge University Press: 456–76.

Kostka, Stephan. 1969. "The Hindemith String Quartets: A Computer-assisted Study of Selected Aspects of Style." Ph.D. diss., University of Wisconsin.

———. 1971. "Recent Developments in Computer-assisted Musical Scholarship." *Computers and the Humanities* 6/1: 15–21.

Krumhansl, Carol. 1990. *Cognitive Foundations of Musical Pitch*. Oxford: Oxford University

Kuusi, Tuiro. 2003. "The Role of Set-class Identity in the Estimation of Chords." *Music Theory Online* 9/3.

LaRue, Jan. 1970. "New Directions for Style Analysis." In *Musicology and the Computer: Three Symposia*, edited by Barry S. Brook. New York: City University of New York Press: 194–97.

Laske, Otto. 1972. "On Musical Strategies With a View to a Generative Grammar for Music." *Interface* 1/2: 111–25.

———. 1973. "On the Methodology and Implementation of a Procedural Theory of Music." *Computational Musicology Newsletter* 1/1: 15–16.

———. 1974. "In Search of a Generative Grammar for Music." *Perspectives of New Music* 8: 351–78.

———. 1992. "Artificial Intelligence and Music: A Cornerstone of Cognitive Musicology." In *Understanding Music with AI: Perspectives on Music Cognition*, edited by Mira Balaban, Kemal Ebcioglu, and Otto Laske. Cambridge, MA: The AAAI Press/MIT Press: 3–28.

———. 1993. "In Search of a Generative Grammar for Music." In *Machine Models of Music*, edited by Stephan Schwanauer and David Levitt. Cambridge, MA: MIT Press: 215–40.

Lawson, Colin, and Robin Stowell, 1999. *The Historical Performance of Music: An Introduction*. Cambridge: Cambridge University Press.

Lawvere, F. William, and Robert Rosebrugh. 2002. *Sets for Mathematics*. Cambridge: Cambridge University Press.

Lefkoff, Gerald. 1970. "Automated Discovery of Similar Segments in the Forty-eight Permutations of a Twelve-tone Row." In *The Computer and Music*, edited by Harry B. Lincoln. Ithaca, NY: Cornell University Press: 147–53.

Lendvai, Ernő. 1983. *The Workshop of Bartók and Kodály*. Budapest: Editio Musica.

Lerdahl, Fred. 1989. "Atonal Prolongational Structure." *Contemporary Music Review* 4: 65–87.

———. 2001. *Tonal Pitch Space*. New York: Oxford University Press.

Lerdahl, Fred, and Ray Jackendoff. 1983. *A Generative Theory of Tonal Music*. Cambridge, MA: MIT Press.

———. 1993. "An Overview of Hierarchical Structure in Music.' In *Machine Models of Music*, edited by Stephan Schwanauer and David Levitt. Cambridge, MA: MIT Press: 290–312.

Levy, Azriel. 1979. *Basic Set Theory*. New York: Dover.

Lewin, David. 1987. *Generalized Musical Intervals and Transformations*. New Haven, CT: Yale University Press.

Lieberman, Fredric. 1970. "Computer-aided Analysis of Javanese Music." In *The Computer and Music*, edited by Harry B. Lincoln. Ithaca, NY: Cornell University Press: 181–92.

Lincoln, Harry, ed. 1970. *The Computer and Music*. Ithaca, NY: Cornell University Press.

Lindley, Mark, and Ronald Turner-Smith. 1993. *Mathematical Models of Musical Scales*. Bonn: Verlag für systematische Musikwissenschaft GmbH.

Lofstedt, John, and Ian Morton. 1970. "FORTRAN Music Programs Involving Numerically Related Tones." In *The Computer and Music*, edited by Harry B. Lincoln. Ithaca, NY: Cornell University Press: 154–62.

Lovelace, Ada. 1843. "Notes." In *Scientific Memoirs, Selected from the Transactions of Foreign Academies and Learned Societies and from Foreign Journals*, edited by Richard Taylor. Vol. 3. London: art. 29, 666–731.

Loy, Gareth, and Peter Todd, eds. 1991. *Music and Connectionism*. Cambridge, MA: MIT Press.

Madden, Charles. 1999. *Fractals in Music: Introductory Mathematics for Musical Analysis*. Salt Lake City, UT: High Art Press.

———. 2006. *Fib and Phi in Music: The Golden Proportion in Musical Form*. Salt Lake City, UT: High Art Press.

Mathews, Max, Joan Miller, F. R. Moore, J. R. Pierce, and J. C. Risset. 1969. *The Technology of Computer Music*. Cambridge, MA: MIT Press.

Maxwell, John. 1992. "An Expert System for Harmonizing Analysis of Tonal Music." In *Understanding Music with AI: Perspectives on Music Cognition*, edited by Mira Balaban, Kemal Ebcioglu, and Otto Laske. Cambridge, MA: The AAAI Press/MIT Press: 335–53.

Mazzola, Guerino. 2002. *The Topos of Music*. Berlin: Birkhäuser Verlag.

McAdams, Stephen, and Emmanuel Bigand, eds. 1993. *Thinking in Sound: The Cognitive Psychology of Human Audition*. Oxford: Oxford University Press.

McCreless, Patrick. 2002. "Music and Rhetoric." In *The Cambridge History of Western Music Theory*, edited by Thomas Christensen. Cambridge: Cambridge University Press: 847–879.

McHose, Allen. 1947. *Basic Principles of the Technique of 18th- and 19th-century Composition*. Englewood Cliffs, NJ: Prentice Hall.

———. 1951. *The Contrapuntal Harmonic Technique of the 18th Century*. Englewood Cliffs, NJ: Prentice Hall.

Meyer, Leonard. 1956. *Emotion and Meaning in Music*. Chicago, IL: University of Chicago Press.

———. 1989. *Style and Music: Theory, History, and Ideology*. Chicago, IL: University of Chicago Press.

———. 2000. *The Spheres of Music: A Gathering of Essays*. Chicago, IL: University of Chicago Press.

Miranda, Eduardo Reck. 2001. *Composing Music with Computers*. Oxford: Focal Press.

Morris, Robert. 1987. *Composition with Pitch Classes*. New Haven, CN: Yale University Press.

Nattiez, Jean-Jacques. 1982. "Varèse's 'Density 21.5': A Study in Semiological Analysis." Translated by Anna Barry. *Music Analysis* 1/3: 243–340.

Newman, William. 1961. "Kirnberger's Method for Tossing Off Sonatas." *Musical Quarterly* 23: 460–80.

Palisca, Claude. 1980. "Theory, Theorists." In *The New Grove Dictionary of Music*, edited by Stanley Sadie. 20 vols. London and New York: Macmillan: 18:741–62.

Pascal, Blaise. 1963. *Traité du triangle arithmétique*. In *Oeuvres complètes*, edited by L. Lafuma. Paris: Éditions du Seuil.

Patch, Howard. 1935. *The Tradition of Boethius; A Study of His Importance in Medieval Culture*. New York: Oxford University Press.

Perle, George. 1990. *The Listening Composer*. Berkeley: University of California Press.

———. 1991. *Serial Composition and Atonality*. 6th ed. Berkeley: University of California Press.

———. 1996. *Twelve-tone Tonality*. 2nd ed. Berkeley: University of California Press.

Pickover, Clifford. 2002. *The Zen of Magic Squares, Circles, and Stars*. Princeton, NJ: Princeton University Press.

Pierce, John. 1980. *An Introduction to Information Theory: Symbols, Signals, and Noise*. [A revised version of *Pierce's Symbols, Signals, and Noise: The Nature and Process of Communication* (Harper & Brothers, 1961).] New York: Dover.

Pople, Anthony. 2004. "Modeling Musical Structure." In *Empirical Musicology*, edited by Eric Clarke and Nicholas Cook. Oxford: Oxford University Press: 127–56.

Rahn, Jay. 1987. "Some Recurrent Features of Scales." *In Theory Only* 2/11–12: 43–52.

Rahn, John. 1980. *Basic Atonal Theory*. New York: Longman.

———. 1989. "On Some Computational Models of Music Theory." In *The Music Machine*, edited by Curtis Roads. Cambridge, MA: MIT Press: 663–69.

Rameau, Jean-Philippe. 1971. *Treatise on Harmony*. Translated by Philip Gossett. New York: Dover.

Ratner, Leonard. 1970. "Ars Combinatoria Chance and Choice in Eighteenth-century Music." In *Studies in Eighteenth-Century Music: Essays Presented to Karl Geiringer on the Occasion of His 70th Birthday*, edited by H. C. Robbins Landon. New York: Oxford University Press.

Regener, Eric. 1967. "A Multiple-pass Transcription and a System for Music Analysis by Computer." In *Elektronische Datenverarbeitung in der Musikwissenschaft*, edited by Harald Heckmann. Regensburg: Gustav Bosse: 89–102.

———. 1974. "On Allen Forte's Theory of Chords." *Perspectives of New Music* 13/1: 191–212.

Reis, Ben. 1999. "Simulating Music Learning with Autonomous Listening Agents: Entropy, Ambiguity and Context." Ph.D. diss. Cambridge: University of Cambridge.

Riemenschneider, Albert, collector and ed. 1941. *371 Harmonized Chorales and 69 Chorale Melodies with figured Bass by J. S. Bach*. New York: G. Schirmer.

Rink, John, ed. 1995. *The Practice of Performance: Studies in Musical Interpretation*. Cambridge: Cambridge University Press.

Robison, Tobias. 1967. "IML-MIR: A Data-Processing System for the Analysis of Music." In *Elektronische Datenverarbeitung in der Musikwissenschaft*, edited by Harald Heckmann. Regensburg: Gustav Bosse: 103–35.

Ruggiero, Charles, and James Colman. 1984. *CASAP User's Guide* [software manual]. Okemos, MI: Okemos Music Software.

Salzer, Felix. 1962. *Structural Hearing: Tonal Coherence in Music*. New York: Dover.

Schaffer, John. 1994. "Threader: A Computer Interface for the Graphic Entry, Encoding, and Analysis of Musical Material." *Computer Music Journal* 18/1: 21–29.

Schenker, Heinrich. 1979. *Free Composition*. Translated and edited by Ernst Oster. Originally published as *Der freie Satz* (Vienna: Universal Edition, 1935). New York: Longman.

Schillinger, Joseph. 1946. *The Schillinger System of Musical Composition*. New York: Carl Fischer.

Schoenberg, Arnold. 1983. *Theory of Harmony*. Translated by Roy Carter. Berkeley: University of California Press. Originally published as *Harmonielehre*, 3rd ed. (1922).

Schüler, Nico. 2000. "Methods of Computer-assisted Music Analysis: History, Classification, and Evaluation." Ph.D. diss., University of Michigan.

Schüler, Nico, and Dirk Uhrlandt. 1994. *MUSANA 1.0 / 1.1: Ein Musikanalyseprogramm, Programmdokumentation*. Peenemünde: Dietrich.

Schwanauer, Stephan. 1993. "A Learning Model for Tonal Composition." In *Machine Models of Music*, edited by Stephan Schwanauer and David Levitt. Cambridge, MA: MIT Press: 512–532.

Schwarz, Heinrich. 1985. *Art and Photography: Forerunners and Influences*. Layton, UT: Peregrine Smith Books.

Seife, Charles. 2006. *Decoding the Universe*. New York: Penguin Books.

Selfridge-Field, Eleanor. 1997a. "Humdrum and Kern: Selective Feature Encoding." In *Beyond MIDI: The Handbook of Musical Codes*, edited by Eleanor Selfridge-Field. Cambridge, MA: MIT Press: 375–401.

———. 1997b. *Beyond MIDI: The Handbook of Musical Codes*. Cambridge, MA: MIT Press.

Shannon, Claude, and W. Weaver. 1949. *The Mathematical Theory of Communication*. Urbana: University of Illinois Press.

Shirlaw, Matthew. 1955. "Claudius Ptolemy as Musical Theorist." *Music Review*: 181–90.

Simon, Herbert and Richard Sumner. 1993. "Pattern in Music." In *Machine Models of Music*, edited by Stephan Schwanauer and David Levitt. Cambridge, MA: MIT Press: 83–110.

Simoni, Mary, ed. 2006. *Analytical Methods of Electroacoustic Music*. New York: Routledge.

Simonton, Dean. 1980. "Thematic Fame and Melodic Originality: A Multivariate Computer-content Analysis." *Journal of Personality* 48: 206–19.

Slonimsky, Nicolas. 1947. *Thesaurus of Scales and Melodic Patterns*. New York: Coleman-Ross.

Smoliar, Stephen. 1980. "A Computer Aid for Schenkerian Analysis." *Computer Music Journal* 4/2: 41–59.

———. 1993. "Process Structuring and Music Theory." In *Machine Models of Music*, edited by Stephan Schwanauer and David Levitt. Cambridge, MA: MIT Press: 190–212.

———. 1999. "Modelling Music Perception: A Critical View." In *Parallel Distributed Perception: Musical Networks and Performance*, edited by N. Griffith and P. Todd. Cambridge, MA: MIT Press: 97–110.

Solomon, Larry. 2003. Theory of Nonharmonic Tones. http://solomonsmusic.net/Nonharm.htm (accessed 31 December 2007).

———. 2005. Interval String Table for the Identification of Chords, Modes, Scales, and Melodies. http://solomonsmusic.net/intstring.htm (accessed 31 December 2007).

Standage, Tom. 2002. *The Turk*. New York: Berkley.

Steele, Guy. 1990. *Common Lisp: The Language*. 2nd ed. Bedford, MA: Digital Press.

Steinbeck, Wolfram. 1976. "The Use of the Computer in the Analysis of German Folk Songs." *Computers and the Humanities* 10: 287–96.

Straus, Joseph N. 2005. *Introduction to Post-Tonal Theory*. 2nd ed. Upper Saddle River, NJ: Prentice Hall.

Suchoff, Benjamin. 1968. "Bartók, Ethnomusicology, and the Computer." *Institute for Computer Research in the Humanities Newsletter* 4: 3–6.

Tarasti, Eero. 1994. *A Theory of Musical Semiotics*. Bloomington: Indiana University Press.

Temperley, David. 2001. *The Cognition of Basic Music Structures*. Cambridge, MA: MIT Press.

———. 2007. *Music and Probability*. Cambridge, MA: MIT Press.

Temperley, David, and Daniel Sleator. 1999. "Modeling Meter and Harmony: A Preference-rule Approach." *Computer Music Journal* 23/1: 10–27.

Touretzky, David. 1990. *Common LISP: A Gentle Introduction to Symbolic Computation*. Redwood City, CA: Benjamin/Cummings.

Wason, Robert. 2002. "Musica Practica: Music Theory as Pedagogy." In *The Cambridge History of Western Music Theory*, edited by Thomas Christensen. Cambridge: Cambridge University Press: 46–77.

Weakland, Rembert. 1956. "Hucbald as Musician and Theorist." *Musical Quarterly* 42: 66–84.

Werner, Eric. 1956. "The Mathematical Foundation of Philippe de Vitry's Ars Nova." *Journal of the American Musicological Society* 9/2: 128–32.

Widmer, Gerhard. 1992. "The Importance of Basic Musical Knowledge for Effective Learning." In *Understanding Music with AI: Perspectives on Music Cognition*, edited by Mira Balaban, Kemal Ebcioglu, and Otto Laske. Cambridge, MA: AAAI Press/MIT Press: 491–507.

Wilensky, Robert. 1986. *Common LISPcraft*. New York: W. W. Norton.

Williams, J. Kent. 1997. *Theories and Analyses of Twentieth-Century Music*. New York: Harcourt Brace.

Winnington-Ingram, Reginald Pepys. 1929. "Ancient Greek Music: A Survey." *Music and Letters* 10: 326–345.

———. 1932. "Aristoxenus and the Intervals of Greek Music." *Classical Quarterly* 26: 195–208.

Wolfram, Stephen. 2002. *A New Kind of Science*. Champaign, IL: Wolfram Media.

Wright, Ernest. 1939. *Gadsby*. New York: Wetzel.

Xenakis, Iannis. 1971. *Formalized Music*. Bloomington: Indiana University Press.

Youngblood, Joseph. 1958. "Style as Information." *Journal of Music Theory* 2: 24–35.

———. 1970. "Root Progressions and Composer Identification." In *The Computer and Music*, edited by Harry B. Lincoln. Ithaca, NY: Cornell University Press: 172–78.

Glossary

Acoustic root theory—*See* root theory.

Agogic accent—An accent that results from duration.

AIT—Acronym for algorithmic information theory, a branch of information theory that concentrates less on the communication accuracy of information and more on the precise amount of noncompressible information contained in a message.

Algorithm—A finite step-by-step process for solving a problem.

Algorithmic information theory—*See* AIT.

Ambitus—The distance between the highest and lowest pitch of a passage (range).

Argument—The value(s) passed to a computer language function as in (+ 1 2) in Lisp where both 1 and 2 are arguments to "+."

Artificial intelligence (AI)—The branch of computer science that attempts to digitally duplicate or approximate human intelligence.

Association networks—Networks with virtually limitless numbers of universally interconnectable nodes, constrained only by their implementation, and standing in contrast to neural networks, which generally have fixed numbers of nodes and connections.

Atonal—*See* post-tonal.

Back propagation—A method for training a neural network in which the initial system output is compared to the desired output and the system is adjusted until the difference between the two is minimized.

Bayes rule—Follows the relatively simple notion that adding new information to existing information impacts probabilities and their distributions. It can be expressed mathematically as the probability of A given B equals the probability of B given A times the probability of A, divided by the probability of B.

Cellular automata—Collection of cells on a grid that evolve in some way through discrete steps according to rules based on the states of neighboring cells.

Chromaticism—In conventional musical use, the pitches outside of a particular scale in use.

Class—A means of describing the rules by which object instances behave.

CLOS—Acronym for Common Lisp Object System.

Combinatorics—The study of the possible orderings of finite collections of numbers.

Complexity theory—Related to the study of input size as relating to computer time and memory requirements.

Cryptography—The mathematical study of information transmission.

DARMS—Acronym for digital alternative representation of music scores, developed by Stefan Bauer-Mengelberg in 1963.

Diatonicism (diatonic)—Pitches within a particular scale in use.

DMAIT—*See* dynamic musical AIT.

Duodecimal—The base-12 numbering system.

Dynamic musical AIT—Systematically refigures musical AIT for several musical parameters simultaneously.

Emergence—The process by which complex systems and patterns arise out of a multiplicity of relatively simple interactions.

Entropy—Related to information; measures the amount of improbability or unpredictability in data.

Fibonacci sequence—A numerical pattern in which each new number is the sum of the two preceding numbers.

Functional—In computer programming, command-based outcomes; e.g., typing function names and arguments achieves the output. In music, a hierarchic structure of pitch or chord progressions, as found in the tonic-dominant relationships of the Common Practice era. Musical function helps define syntax (expectation, fulfillment, deception, etc.) and semantics (tension, release, voice-leading constraints, etc.) as a means to describe style.

Fuzzy logic—A type of logic in which propositions can be represented with degrees of truthfulness and falsehood.

Game theory—A formal modeling approach to maximize results in game playing.

General systems theory—A system theory described by the nonlinearity of the system's interactions of its various components typically producing output that is more than the sum of its parts.

Genetic algorithm—A virtual population that produces a number of trial solutions to a problem, each of which is evaluated (fitness test) and a new generation created from the better of them. The process continues through many generations until an acceptable solution is achieved.

Generative theory of music—Follows the relationships between the syntactic structure of music and its semantic representation.

Global variable—A symbolic representation of a quantity or expression that does not depend on current circumstances for its value.

Graph theory—The study of mathematical structures used to model relations between points in graphs.

Guidonian hand—A visualization for locating the semitones in the central part of the medieval gamut (see Fig. 1.5). It serves as a kind of algorithm in itself, a simple organization of rules for memorization.

Hexachord—A six-note collection of pitches.

Hidden unit—Intermediate layers in a neural network that receive entire input patterns modified by the passage through weighted connections; provides the internal representation of neural pathways.

Information—In information theory, the non-redundant portion of any string of numbers.

Information theory—A branch of communications theory that deals with the amount and accuracy of information when transmitted from a source through a medium to a destination.

Interval—The number of half steps or scale degrees between two pitches.

IRCAM—Institut de Recherche et Coordination Acoustique/Musique; a long-standing part of the musical community in Paris associated with modern music.

ISMIR—International Society for Music Information Retrieval; an organization that currently offers enormous potential for the establishment of a common protocol for music storage and retrieval for future computer music analysis.

Local variable—A value only within a current closed environment.

Logic—The study of formal systems relating to inference.

Magic square—A matrix of n rows and columns. The first n^2 integers are arranged in the cells of the matrix in such a way that the sum of any row or column (optionally diagonal) is the same.

MAIT—*See* musical AIT.

Markov chain—Probabilistic processes often expressed in terms of *orders*. A zero-order Markov chain, for example, makes random decisions, with no applicable rules. A first-order Markov chain, however, bases new decisions on immediately preceding choices, while a fifth-order Markov chain bases its decisions on the previous five choices.

Mathematical sequence—An ordered list of objects, typically numbers, of finite or infinite length.

Method—In CLOS, a class-defined function.

MIDI—Musical Instrument Digital Interface; code to create a common interface between various electronic music instruments, as well as links between electronic performance and digital storage.

MIR—Musical Information Retrieval.

Modeling—The building of accurate replicas of objects or phenomena in order to better understand their structure.

Music analysis—A term used to identify specific instances when the principles encountered in music theory apply to the evaluation of a specific work or body of works.

Music theory—The basic tenets that govern all music. *See also* music analysis.

Musical—A term meaning that within the context of a particular piece of music, logical, intuitive, and physical interpretations agree. Being logical infers the following of explicit rules. Being intuitive infers the following of implicit rules. Being physical infers the following of natural physical laws (referring here to human performability). A musical passage is therefore one in which the user of the term finds all of the above criteria acceptable and in coincidence.

Musical AIT—One of two general types of information. The first contains data that occur repeatedly in various forms throughout the remainder of the work being analyzed. The second contains data unique to their first appearance in a work.

Musical set theory—*See* set theory.

Neural network—Like the human brain, an entity made up of interconnected neuron units that respond in parallel to a set of input signals. Consists of four main parts: (1) processing units, (2) weighted interconnections between processing units, (3) an activation rule, and (4) a learning rule that specifies how to adjust the weights for a given input/output pair.

Number theory—The study of dicrete numbers in general and integers in particular.

OOP—Object-Oriented Programming.

Ordered PC set—A pitch-class set whose order follows the order of the music it represents.

Pascal's triangle—A triangle of numbers generated by affixing a 1 to either end of a new row and then generating all numbers between those 1s by adding together the two numbers to the left and right above each number of the new row.

Polymorphism—The concept that methods of the same name may have different effects depending on the class with which they are associated.

Post-tonal—Music without a conventional tonal structure, including polytonal, octatonal, and serial styles.

Predicate calculus—A system of symbolic logic.

Probability theory—The study of probability.

Recombinancy—In music, a method for producing new music based on the recombination of elements of extant music.

Recursion—The act of a function calling itself during operation.

Register—The octaves in which pitches are used in musical compositions.

Root theory—Derived from the work of the composer Paul Hindemith and involving (1) identifying all of the separate intervals present in the grouping, (2) locating each interval's lowest occurrence in the overtone series, (3) determining each interval's root, and (4) finding the strongest root among the roots present.

Rotational chromaticism—Includes pitches foreign to the current scale that repeat or otherwise become consistent over time, alter their native scale versions, and/or appear in strong metric, rhythmic, and/or agogic circumstances, and that create a different scale but one of the same vector class.

SAM—System for Analysis of Music; designed by Eric Regener in the 1960s; includes an elaborate assembly-language program for the then state-of-the-art IBM 7090 computer.

Semiotics—The study of signs and symbols, what they mean, and how they are used, particularly in relationships established through cultural convention.

Set theory—An approach to analysis that involves the use of pitch classes in describing musical structures, especially those that involve post-tonal works. When applied to music, offers analysts opportunities to analyze post-tonal music by grouping it into sets and then reducing these sets into various categories.

SPEAC—S (*statement*) for stable, P (*preparation*) for weakly unstable, E (*extension*) for fairly stable, A (*antecedent*) for very unstable, and C (*consequent*) for strongly stable; pronounced "speak." SPEAC identifiers thus follow an A–P–E–S–C stability order, with the most unstable identifier on the left and the most stable identifier on the right.

State transition matrix (STM)—A matrix of probabilities for moving from one state to the next state in a Markov chain.

Structural analysis—An analytical method that, unlike formal analysis. which relies on material repetition, variation, and/or contrast, attempts to reveal the architecture (harmonic and melodic superstructure) of music.

Tessitura—The idiomatic range of a set of pitches, as opposed to the potentially wider range used.

Tetrachord—A four-note collection of pitches.

Transformational chromaticism—Includes pitches foreign to the current scale that create—through repetition and in strong metric, rhythmic, and/or agogic circumstances—a demonstrably new scale of a different vector class.

Transient chromaticism—Pitches foreign to the current scale that appear briefly, typically resolve to their associated pitch, and/or appear in weak metric, rhythmic, and/or agogic circumstances.

Transpositional chromaticism—Pitches foreign to the current scale that repeat or otherwise become consistent over time, alter their native scale versions, and/or appear in strong metric, rhythmic, and/or agogic circumstances, and that create a transposed version of the scale currently in use.

Trichord—A three-note collection of pitches.

Unordered PC set—A pitch-class set whose order does not matter.

Index

A
agents, 294
agogic, 156–57, 209, 222
AI. *See* artificial intelligence
AIT. *See* algorithmic information theory
algebra, 99
algorithm, 1, 3–7, 10, 12, 14, 16–18, 21, 22, 25, 32, 37, 40, 43, 57–58, 145, 148, 159, 213, 232, 234, 236, 260, 268, 305
algorithmic information theory (AIT), 43, 45–97, 99, 231
 See also information theory
Algorithmic Interactive Composing Environment (Alice), 37, 223, 263–64, 266, 268–69, 273, 292
Alice. *See* Algorithmic Interactive Composing Environment
allusion, 244–46, 296
Alphonce, Bo, 31
antecedent (A), 213–14
 See also SPEAC Program
L'antica musica ridotta alla moderna prattica, 14
Aristotle, 7–8
Aristoxenus, 7–9
artificial intelligence (AI), 3, 25, 46, 97, 214, 274, 275, 290, 292, 294
association network, 214, 291–95
atonality, 2
augmented sixth chord, 245

B
Babbage, Charles, 22–25
Babbitt, Milton, 22, 29, 99, 102, 106, 277

Bach, C. P. E., 17, 250
Bach, J. S., 4, 21, 23–24, 31, 32, 35, 36, 65–66, 68, 95, 114, 210–11, 214, 231, 235–37, 244, 245, 247–49, 308
 Chorale no. 2, 38
 Chorale no. 42, 211
 Suite no. 1 in G Major for Violoncello Solo, 66
 Wenn wir in höchsten Noten sein, 23
back propagation, 291
 See also neural networks
background, 32, 222, 223
 See also Hintergrund
Balaban, Mira, 35
Bartók, Béla, 2, 35, 252, 258–62, 315
 Mikrokosmos, no. 71, 255, 256
 Mikrokosmos, no. 77, 255, 257
 Mikrokosmos, no. 80, 261
 Mikrokosmos, no. 81, 69, 74, 75, 269–70
 Music for Strings, Percussion and Celeste, 285, 287
Bauer-Mengelberg, Stefan, 26
Bayes rule, 250–51
 See also probabilities
Beethoven, Ludwig van, 16, 17, 29, 35, 95, 244, 245
 Bagatelle, op. 119, no. 1, 246
 Piano Sonata in C Major, op. 53, 149–51, 157
 Piano Sonata, op. 7, 157, 158
 Piano Sonata, op. 2, no. 1, 244
 Symphony no. 5, 66, 68, 307, 309
Berg, Alban, 29

Bharucha, Jamshed, 35
binary numbers, 53, 60, 83, 88, 151, 152, 277
Blombach, Ann, 31–32
Boethius, Anicius, 8, 10–11
Böker-Heil, Norbert, 56
Boolean processes, 91
bottom-up programming, 196–97
Boulez, Pierre, 123, 125, 126, 131–32, 134, 189
   Structures, 123, 125, 126
   Second Sonata for Piano, 131–32, 134
Brahms, Johannes, 16, 66, 68, 72, 73, 95
   Symphony no. 1, 67
Brinkman, Alexander, 32
bronze mean, 285, 287
Brooks, Frederick, 27

C

Cage, John, 4, 304–5
calculus, 99
Campion, Thomas, 14
CASAP. *See* Computer-Assisted Set Analysis Program
CCRMA. *See* Center for Research in Music and Acoustics
cellular automata, 58, 60, 61, 232, 289, 292, 294
Center for Research in Music and Acoustics (CCRMA), 37
Chaitin, Gregory, 57, 60
   See also Algorithmic Information Theory
chaos theory, 289
chaos, 45, 54
Chopin, Frederic, 31, 75–77, 83, 84, 86, 89, 221
CHORAL Program, 35
chromatic scale, 72, 74, 114, 135, 146, 149, 151–53, 162, 164, 177, 179, 205, 252, 253, 263, 269, 271
class (object), 190–97
CLOS. *See* Common Lisp Object System
CM. *See* Common Music
CMAP. *See* Contemporary Music Analysis Package
Colman, James, 32
combinatorics, 17, 19, 151, 250, 280, 282–83, 297, 299, 300
Common Lisp, 41, 43, 46–49, 60, 91, 93, 183, 189, 190, 192, 196, 253, 273, 274, 315
   See also Lisp
Common Lisp Object System (CLOS), 190
Common Music (CM), 37
Comparison Program, 62
complementary analysis, 315
complexity theory, 280
compression, 51–52, 57–58, 60, 62, 65–66, 68, 71, 91, 93–95
   See also Algorithmic Information Theory
Computer-Assisted Set Analysis Program (CASAP), 32
conditional variable, 250
conditionals, 48, 204
consequent (C), 213–14
   See also SPEAC Program
Contemporary Music Analysis Package (CMAP), 32
Cook, Nicholas, 2, 31, 318
Cooper, Grosvenor, 36
Cope, David, 66, 95
   Concerto for Cello and Orchestra, 285, 286, 308
   Horizons for Orchestra, 27
   Three Pieces for Solo Clarinet, 67
   Triplum for flute and piano, 133, 135–38, 140, 228, 229
Copernicus, Nicolaus, 6
Corelli, Archangelo, 35
The Craft of Musical Composition, 21, 30
Cryptography, 2–3, 52, 57, 280

D

Dallapiccola, Luigi, 31
DARMS. *See* Digital Alternative Representation of Music Scores
de Garlandia, Johannes, 12

De harmonica institutione, 8, 10
De institutione musica, 8, 10
de Liège, Jacques, 12
De mensurabili, 12
de Vitry, Philippe12, 14
Debussy, Claude, 35, 113, 285, 315
   La cathédrale engloutie, 113
Deep Blue, 317
Desain, Peter, 35, 268
diatonicism, 14, 21, 114, 157, 187
Dies irae, 308, 311
Digital Alternative Representation of Music Scores (DARMS), 26, 315
discrete mathematics, 43, 99, 280–81
distribution, 250
DMAIT. *See* dynamic music algorithmic information theory
Dodecachordon, 14
dodecaphonic, 114
duodecimal numbers, 99, 113–20, 127, 133, 137, 139, 141–42, 144, 146
dyads, 114, 123–24, 127
dynamic music algorithmic information theory (DMAIT), 45, 71, 72, 74, 75, 83, 84, 91, 96

E
Ebcioglu, Kemal, 35
Elody, 37
emergence, 294–95
entropy, 28, 32, 45, 51, 57
esthesic dimension, 296
Experiments in Musical Intelligence, 21, 75, 76, 83, 196, 221, 234–39, 244, 246, 263, 292, 305, 307, 317
   Eine Kleine Stück, 305–7
   Rondo Capriccio for cello and orchestra, 238–43
   Symphony no. 5 (revision), 307–10
   See also recombinancy
Extend Program, 234, 259, 260, 262, 269, 271, 272
extension (E), 213–14, 223, 225
   See also SPEAC Program

F
Fibonacci sequence, 146, 276, 285, 287
foreground, 21, 32, 218, 221–22, 314
   See also Vordergrund
Forte, Allen, 22, 29, 32, 43, 99, 102, 106, 112, 215–16, 277
forward feed, 290
   See also neural networks
fractals, 277, 289
function,
   in music, 1, 3, 4, 7, 16, 21, 23, 24, 36, 37, 41, 105, 108–10, 144, 149, 155, 169, 188–229, 245, 260, 290, 314, 316, 318
   in probability, 250
   in programming, 46–49, 54, 62, 65, 90–95, 109, 141, 147–48, 182–84, 236, 255–59, 269, 272–74, 290, 294, 301–3
fundamental bass, 16
Fux, Joseph Johann, 14, 16–17
fuzzy logic, 289

G
Gadsby, 54–55
Galilei, Galileo, 6
game theory, 280
general systems theory, 287–89
generative theory of music, 31, 36
genetic algorithms, 289, 292, 294
gestalt analysis, 316
Gjerdingen, Robert, 245
Glarean, Henricus, 14
global variable, 255, 272
golden mean, 146, 285, 287
Gould, Murray, 26
Gradus Program, 16, 262–63, 273, 292
Gradus ad Parnassum, 14, 17
Grame, 37
graph theory, 280
Greek modes, 8
Gregorian Chant, 10–11
Gross, Dorothy, 31
Guido of Arezzo, 11–12
Guidonian hand, 12–13

H

Harris, Craig, 32
Hauptmann, Moritz, 19, 21
Haydn, Franz Joseph, 17, 19, 20, 31, 231, 250
hermeneutic analysis, 316
hexachord, 11–12, 110, 184, 204, 300, 301
hidden units, 290–92
hierarchy,
    in music, 188, 189, 197–98, 214, 217
    in programming, 190, 193–94, 197–98
Hiller, Lejaren, 28–29, 45, 231, 249, 281, 287, 288
Hindemith, Paul, 21–22, 29–30, 148, 199, 201–2
Hintergrund, 21
    See also background
Hofstadter, Douglas, 295
Hofstetter, Fred, 31
Holland, John, 294–95
Honing, Henkjan, 35
Howell, Emily, 294
Hucbald, 8, 10–11
Humdrum Toolkit, 35, 37, 315
Huron, David, 35, 315

I

Illiac Suite, 28–29
IML. *See* Intermediary Musical Language
information theory, 45–97, 99, 187, 231
inheritance, 196
instance, 191–96, 202, 204, 212
Institut de Recherche et Coordination Acoustique/ Musique (IRCAM), 37
Intermediary Musical Language (IML), 26
International Society for Music Information Retrieval (ISMIR), 26, 315
intersection, 100–1
interval summations, 113, 119–21, 126, 127, 130–33, 135, 139, 141
interval maps, 113, 119, 120, 126, 127, 130–35, 139

interval vector, 32, 109, 113, 119–21, 123, 126, 139, 141
inversion, 4, 16–19, 23, 36, 37, 41, 63–64, 90–93, 103–9, 114, 202, 206–7, 281–82, 285
inversional symmetry, 155
IRCAM. *See* Institut de Recherche et Coordination Acoustique/ Musique
Isaacson, Leonard, 28–29, 45, 231, 249, 281
ISMIR. *See* International Society for Music Information Retrieval
Le istitutioni harmoniche (Zarlino), 14

J

jigsaw test, 247–48, 308
Johnson, Tom, 289

K

KEITH Program, 31
Kepler, Johannes, 6
Kirnberger, Johann Philip, 17–18, 250
Kostka, Stephan, 30
Krenek, Ernst, 66–67, 95
    Suite for Violoncello, 66–67

L

LaRue, Jan, 30
Laske, Otto, 31
layer analysis, 221
Lefkoff, Gerald, 30
Lerdahl, Fred, 22, 31, 36, 217
lexicons, 51, 60, 110, 235–36, 266
Liber de arte contrapuncti, 14
Lieberman, Fredric, 30
Lincoln, Harry, 30
linear interval vectors, 113, 119–23, 126–27, 131, 139, 141, 148, 152–54, 158–60, 64–65, 167–72, 177, 179, 181–83
Lisp, 41, 43, 49–97, 108, 109, 112, 147–48, 182–83, 189–90, 192, 196, 204, 253–55, 271, 273, 274, 301, 315
    See also Common Lisp

local variable, 184, 255
logic, 19, 35, 99, 101, 280, 281, 316
Lovelace, Ada, 23

M

magic cubes, 285
magic squares, 281–85
MAIT. *See* musical algorithmic information theory
Marenzio, Luca, 56
Markov chains, 249, 251–54, 258
Markov Program, 254, 255, 258, 259
Mathews, Max, 26
matrix, 63–64, 252–55, 258, 281, 285
Mazzola, Guerino, 36
McCarthy, John, 46
McHose, Allen, 23–24
Melisma Music Analyzer, 36
Mendelssohn, Felix, 28
metaclass, 153–55, 164
meta-patterns, 220–23, 238
methods, 192–96, 204, 219
Meyer, Leonard, 22, 36, 189, 198–99, 268
Micrologus, 11–12
middleground, 21, 32, 221–22
    See also Mittlegrund
MIDI, xxiv, xxvii, 26, 36, 37, 62, 76, 90, 116, 254, 315
minimalism, 67–68
MIR. *See* Musical Information Retrieval
Mittlegrund, 21
    See also middleground
modulation, 72, 149, 156, 164, 213, 217, 289
modulatory chromaticism, 157
modulo, 102, 108, 111, 148, 277, 278, 287
Monte Carlo method, 28
Morley, Thomas, 14
Morris, Robert, 106, 142, 149, 277
Morse code, 53–54
Morse, Samuel, 53
Morton, Ian, 30

Mozart, Wolfgang Amadeus, 17, 19, 29, 35, 66, 95, 231, 232, 238–39, 244, 250
    Piano Sonata K. 279, 233–34
    Piano Sonata K. 533, 233–34
    Piano Sonata K. 545, 221–22
    Symphony no. 40 in G Minor, K. 550, 66, 95
MTW. *See* Music Theory Workbench
Multigraph Program, 62, 74, 76, 90, 96, 97
multiple-octave scale, 186
MUSANA, 32–33, 35
Muse Program, 295–305, 307, 308
music cognition, 5, 31, 57, 71, 169, 268, 318
MUSIC i–v, 26
music perception, 5, 169, 268
Music Theory Workbench (MTW), 36, 38
Musica enchiriadis, 10
musical algorithmic information theory (MAIT), 45, 65, 67–68, 71, 88
musical geometries, 281, 316
Musical Information Retrieval (MIR), 26, 35, 315
Musikalisches Würfelspiele, 17–19, 250
MUSTRAN, 26

N

Nattiez, Jean-Jacques, 296–97
neural networks, 35, 290–92
neutral dimension, 296–97, 300, 304
A New Way of Making Fowre Parts in Counter-point, 14
nonharmonic tones, 36, 37, 149, 162, 213, 245
normal form, 37, 103–12, 117–19, 137, 141
number theory, 99, 280–81

O

object-oriented programming (OOP), 189–90, 196, 204, 221, 228
octachord, 110

octatonal, 2, 147, 149, 151, 153, 155, 159, 162, 182, 205, 314
octatonic scale, 147, 149, 151, 153, 155, 159, 162, 182, 205, 314
OM. *See* OpenMusic
omega (Ω), 60, 153
   music and, 153–54
   mathematics and, 60
OOP. *See* object-oriented programming
OpenMusic (OM), 37, 39
ordered set, 99, 102–8, 117–20, 127, 130, 133, 135, 139, 195, 300, 314
orders, 52–53, 252
   Markov, 252
   Shannon, 52–53
organum, 10–12
overtone series, 16, 19, 21, 201–3

P

Palestrina, Giovanni Pierluigi da, 56
palindrome, 281
Pascal, Blaise, 275–78, 294, 300
Pascal's triangle, 275–78, 294, 300
pattern matching, 1, 7–8, 28–30, 32, 35, 37, 45–94, 99, 110, 122, 126, 155, 156, 164, 215, 218–23, 233, 236–38, 251, 258, 274, 281, 183, 289–302, 308, 311, 315–18
Peirce, Charles Sanders, 295
pentachord, 110, 135, 204, 300, 301
pentatonic scale, 153, 263
pi (π), 50–51, 58
Pierce, John, 28, 52, 90
pitch class, 63, 102–8, 111–20, 135, 137, 139, 141, 145, 151–53, 156–64, 167, 169, 172, 177, 179, 182–83, 185, 189, 198, 202, 204–5, 223, 225, 259, 263, 282, 287, 288, 300, 307–8, 311
A Plaine and Easie Introduction to Praticall Musick, 14
The Plaine and Easy Code, 26
Plato, 7–8
poietic dimension, 296

The Politics, 7
polymorphism, 193
polynomial formula, 147–48
polytonality, 2, 40, 41, 131, 160, 305, 308
Pople, Anthony, 2, 36, 304
Praetorius, Michael, 14
predicate, 48
predicate calculus, 35, 99, 316
preparation (P), 213, 214, 223, 225
   See also SPEAC Program
prime form, 31, 32, 63, 65, 91, 92, 105–12, 117–21, 135, 141, 142, 203, 285, 287, 301
prime numbers, 99, 147, 276
probabilities, 28, 51–54, 231, 249–58, 272
probability theory, 249, 280, 281
Proportionale musices, 14
pseudo-code, 182–83, 192, 204, 235, 269
Ptolemy, Claudius, 8
Pythagoras, 7, 43

Q

Quintilianus, Aristides, 8

R

Rahn, John, 102, 106, 142, 149, 275, 277
Rameau, Jean-Philippe, 16–19
recombinancy, 83, 234–38, 244, 245, 249, 268, 280, 305
recursion, 48–49, 109, 273
Regener, Eric, 29, 30
register, 25, 63, 72, 99–144, 184–86, 210, 213, 214, 222, 223, 235, 302, 314
The Republic (Plato), 7
Réti, Rudolph, 22
retrograde, 63–65, 90–93, 282, 285, 299
retrograde-inversion, 63–65, 91–93, 282, 285
Riemann, Hugo, 21, 216
Riepel, Joseph, 18–19
root, 21, 30, 36, 37, 102–4, 194–96, 198–207, 209–14, 216–17, 225, 227, 301–3
Root Program, 225, 227

rotational chromaticism, 155–57, 169, 170
RUBATO, 36
Ruggiero, Charles, 32
Ruwet, Nicholas, 22

S
Saint Augustine, v, 45
scale classes, 151–55
Schaffer, John, 35
Schenker, Heinrich, 21–23, 32, 68, 91, 213, 221–22, 318
Schillinger System of Musical Composition, 22
Schillinger, Joseph, 22
Schoenberg, Arnold, 2, 63, 126, 142, 148, 223, 224, 305
  Das Buch der hängenden Gärten, 186
  Sechs kleine Klavierstücke, op. 19, 111, 169, 170, 171, 172, 179, 210, 212, 214
  Suite for Piano, op. 25, 121–22
  Three Piano Pieces, op. 11, 217, 219, 305, 307
Schubert, Franz, 28
Schüler, Nico, xxiv, 26, 28–30, 32
Schumann, Robert, 28
secondary chromaticism, 72
secondary harmonies, 72, 149, 151, 155, 157
Selfridge-Field, Eleanor, 26
semiotics, 295–96
semiotics (musical), 245, 295–97
septachord, 110
serial music, 2, 4, 31, 63, 114, 122, 145, 189, 262, 282, 283, 305
Set Database Program, 110
Set Multiples Program, 141
set theory
  mathematics and, 99–102, 104, 105, 277, 280, 281
  music and, 4, 29, 32, 43, 97, 102, 106, 109–12, 148, 189, 197
SetMath Program, 114, 141

Shannon, Claude, 28, 52–55
silver mean, 285, 287–78
Simonton, Dean, 32
Sleator, Daniel, 36
Smoliar, Stephen, 32
SPEAC Program
statement (S), 213–14, 216, 223, 225
  See also SPEAC Program
statistics, 5, 23, 28, 30, 32, 35, 36, 52, 249, 301
Straus, Joseph, 2, 107, 112, 122, 127, 145, 149, 162, 223
Stravinsky, Igor, 2, 39, 305, 308
  Le sacre du printemps, 308, 312, 315
  Symphonies of Wind Instruments, 313
  Three Pieces for String Quartet, 39–41, 74–76, 142, 181–82, 225–28, 269, 308, 312–13
structural analysis, 32, 68, 70, 91, 142, 169, 189–90, 200, 217, 222, 223, 225, 227–29, 237, 238, 251, 263, 297
Structure Graph Program, 228
Structure Map Program, 225, 227, 228
subclass, 194, 196
subset, 31, 100–1, 244
superclass, 194, 196
Symbolic Composer, 37
Symmetry, 155, 156, 159, 281, 283, 285, 316
Syntagma musicum, 14

T
Taube, Heinrich, 36, 38
TDS, 21, 216
Temperley, David, 36, 251
tessitura, 25, 238, 283
tetrachord, 8, 110, 121–23, 126, 131–33, 142, 276, 300, 301
Tinctoris, Johannes, 14–15
T_n form, 106
T_nI form, 106
t-normal form, 108, 110–12, 117, 119, 141, 205

top-down programming, 196–97
transformational analysis, 316
transformational chromaticism, 155–57, 167, 169
transient chromaticism, 155–56, 158, 164–65, 169, 172, 179
transpositional chromaticism, 151, 155, 157, 165, 167
trichord, 110–11, 121, 123–24, 127, 130–31, 133, 135, 139, 142, 203, 282, 297, 299–301
Turing, Alan, 3, 25, 275
twelve-tone music, 2, 30, 114, 122, 145, 151, 205, 283, 285, 305
See also serial music

U

Uhrlandt, Dirk, 32
unification, 218–20
union, 100
unordered set, 99, 102–4, 106, 111, 117, 119, 167, 172, 300
Urlinie, 21

V

Varèse, Edgard, 2
  Density 21.5, 160–72, 179, 287, 288
Venn diagram, 101, 104
Venn, John, 101

verbing, 212
Vicentino, Nicola, 14
Visualize Program, 41
Vivaldi, Antonio, 231
Vordergrund, 21
  See also foreground

W

Webern, Anton von, 2, 65–66, 68, 95, 126
  Concerto for 9 Instruments, op. 24, 127–32, 282–83
  Symphony, op. 21, 29
  Variations for Piano, op. 27, 67, 122–24
whole-tone scale, 149, 153, 155, 169, 179, 263
Wolfram, Stephen, 2, 59, 232, 235
Wright, Ernest, 54–55

X

Xenakis, Iannis, 1, 26, 251, 277

Y

Youngblood, Joseph, 28, 30

Z

Zahorka, Oliver, 36
Zarlino, Gioseffo, 14–16
Z-relations, 43

UNIVERSITY OF ST. THOMAS LIBRARIES

DATE DUE